Assassination

ASSASSINATION

THE POLITICS OF MURDER

BY

LINDA LAUCELLA

LOWELL HOUSE

LOS ANGELES

CONTEMPORARY BOOKS

CHICAGO

Library of Congress Cataloging-in-Publication Data

Laucella, Linda.
    Assassination : the politics of murder / by Linda Laucella.
       p.   cm.
    Includes bibliographical references and index.
    ISBN 1-56565-628-8
     1. Assassination—History—Chronology.   I. Title.
HV6278.L36   1998
364.15'24'09—dc21   97-48721
                                            CIP

Requests for such permissions should be addressed to:
Lowell House
2020 Avenue of the Stars, Suite 300
Los Angeles, CA 90067

Lowell House books can be purchased at special discounts when ordered in
bulk for premiums and special sales.

Publisher: Jack Artenstein
Associate Publisher, Lowell House Adult: Bud Sperry
Managing Editor: Maria Magallanes
Text design: Laurie Young

Manufactured in the United States of America
10 9 8 7 6 5 4 3 2 1

"To die at the height of a man's career, the highest moment of his effort here in this world, universally honored and admired, to die while great issues are still commanding the whole of his interest, to be taken from us at a moment when he could already see ultimate success in view—is not the most unenviable of fates."

—*Sir Winston Churchill*

WEAPON OF CHOICE

ATTEMPT UNSUCCESSFUL

Contents

Preface

Assassination is defined as murder, usually of a political, royal, or public person. The term is derived from the order of the Assassins, a Muslim sect of the eleventh and twelfth centuries, whose members furthered their own political interests by murdering high officials. The origin of the word is *assassiyun,* Arabic for fundamentalists, from the word *assass,* foundation.

A suicide squad called the Assassins, a militant offshoot of the mystic Islamic Isma'ili sect, was founded by Hassan Sabah and operated from the Alamut clifftop fortress in the Elburz Mountains of northwestern Iran (then called Persia). In this fortress, built on a six-thousand-foot-high peak, Hassan, a scholar, also had one of the largest libraries of his time.

The Assassins were called *hashishiyun,* "smokers of hashish," by their enemies, because legend was that hashish gave them the vision to carry out their violent acts. In accounts of his travels, Marco Polo wrote about the impregnable fortress in the mountains of Persia where an evil old man lived. When the old man wanted to kill a religious or political enemy, he would ask for volunteers among his followers. Those selected would be given wine laced with hashish. While sleeping after drinking the wine, they would be transported to a lush green valley where fruit, drugs, and sexual treats were at their disposal. This eternal paradise they experienced was promised to them in exchange for their total loyalty to the old man. According to Marco Polo, the old man would sometimes order one of his drugged followers to jump to his death from a high window of his fortress in order to impress foreign guests and exhibit his absolute power over life and death. After carrying out a murder at the old man's instructions, the assassins would remain at the scene of the crime because they believed they would be martyred for their actions.

Introduction

This book captures the most fascinating assassination plots throughout history. It begins with an intriguing series of assassinations and reprisals revolving around Judea's powerful King David during 900 B.C., then chronicles compelling historic events that resulted in political assassinations, concluding with the assassination of Israeli prime minister Yitzhak Rabin in 1995.

Some philosophers might claim this record of violence indicates the decline of humanity, and some historians might say it shows that history repeats itself. This book does not attempt to justify either perspective. It simply recounts these historic events, including what inspired the would-be assassins and how their actions affected the world.

Still, a unique perspective of world history develops, offering some insight into how civilization got to be the way it is today. From 1760 B.C., when Babylon's sixth king, Hammurabi, imposed a code of law that stipulated, "If a man put out the eye of another man, his eye shall be put out," killing in order to gain power has seemed to result in more killing. Justifications and cover-ups for assassinations have become almost an art form, but in the end the perpetrators are usually held accountable for their actions.

The facts show that most assassination attempts take planning and nerve, and most are motivated by political, religious, or philosophical differences so extreme that they engender a detached lack of respect for human life. While some men and women set out to assassinate powerful and famous people in order to become powerful or famous themselves, other assassinations were bought and paid for by the target's enemies, and a surprising number resulted from a conspiracy.

Reading these accounts may resurface old feelings of disbelief and horror in those of us who lived through media coverage of the assassination of someone we admired. Researching and writing this book was at times an emotional experience as the harsh reality of our world history was fleshed out. The people in this book were not bloodless characters developed in the creative minds of novelists. These people, whether good or bad, were living, breathing human beings. Some have become heroes because they died trying to make the world a better place; all are now famous or infamous.

History can be a powerful teacher, but the sad truth is that it encourages those who attempt to repress others as much as it inspires those who seek freedom for all. As much as I would like to have slanted the outcome of these events to show that the peacemakers have always been safe and supported in their efforts, the facts show otherwise. What each of us learns from these events can affect our actions in everyday life and our efforts to create a better world for the generations to come. Our actions today are an example for the children who will become the adults of tomorrow.

B.C.

990 B.C.

AMNON (?–900 B.C.)
ELDEST SON OF JUDEA'S KING DAVID

ASSASSIN: Amnon's half brother, Absalom.

HISTORY: As told in the Bible, King David had many wives and many children with different mothers. Prince Absalom, David's third and favorite son, had a sister named Tamar, and they had a half brother named Amnon. As Tamar grew into a beautiful young woman, Amnon fell desperately in love with her. But because young men at that time were kept strictly apart from the girls, there was no way for Amnon to tell Tamar of his feelings. His love for her tormented him until he became ill from it.

One day Jonadab, Amnon's friend and cousin (the son of King David's brother Shime-ah), noticed that Amnon had been looking unwell, and he asked Amnon why the son of a king could possibly look so bad. When Amnon said that his love for Tamar was the reason, Jonadab, being a very clever fellow, suggested a scheme that would allow Amnon access to Tamar in order to tell her of his affection. "Go to bed and pretend you are very sick," Jonadab suggested. "When your father comes to see you, ask him to allow Tamar to come and prepare some food for you. Tell him you will feel better if she feeds you."

Amnon did as Jonadab suggested. Soon Tamar appeared in Amnon's quarters, prepared him some food and set the serving tray before him. But Amnon refused to eat. He instructed all the servants to leave them alone, then Amnon told Tamar he must go to bed and that he wanted her to feed him there. Doing as he said, Tamar followed Amnon to his bed and stood before him to feed him. But she was surprised when suddenly Amnon grabbed her and demanded that she come into the bed with him.

Tamar begged Amnon not to act so foolishly because it was a serious crime in Israel for them to do such a thing. She pleaded with him, "Please talk to the king and surely he will allow us to marry. Then neither of us will have to live in shame." Amnon, overcome by his desire, would not listen. He grabbed Tamar and forced her to lie with him. Afterward, to Amnon's surprise, his love for her suddenly turned to hate, and he screamed at her to leave him.

Tamar cried and begged Amnon not to reject her, saying it would be a worse crime than the one he had just committed. Amnon refused to listen. He shouted for his valet to come throw Tamar out of the room and lock the door behind her.

Outside, Tamar, who was wearing the long robe with sleeves that was customary attire for virgins of kings in that day, tore the robe and put ashes on her head. She went away crying. Her brother Absalom saw her acting in such a way and asked her what had happened. When she told him that Amnon had raped her, a great hatred grew in Absalom's heart toward Amnon. Still, Absalom said nothing to Amnon and invited Tamar to live with him in his quarters, where she could hide her shame. Upon learning what had happened, King David was very angry, but still nothing was said to Amnon.

And so it was for two years, until 990 B.C. As Absalom prepared to shear his sheep at Baal-hazor in Ephraim, he invited his father, King David, and all his brothers to come for a feast to celebrate the occasion. King David sent word that he very much appreciated the invitation, but it would be too great a burden for Absalom to entertain the entire family, and so he declined his son's offer. Absalom insisted on making this a family celebration and although his father still would not come, finally it was agreed that all of Absalom's brothers would attend, including Amnon.

EVENT: When the day came, Absalom had it all planned. He told his men to wait until Amnon was drunk; then he would give the signal for them to kill Amnon. Absalom's men were uncertain if they should do it and a little afraid that King David would disapprove of such an assassination. Absalom assured them not to be afraid, saying he was the one giving the orders and this was his command.

They ate, they drank, Absalom gave the signal, and his men murdered his half brother Amnon.

Seeing what was happening, and thinking they might also be in danger, the other sons of King David jumped on their mules and fled. Before they could reach Jerusalem, reports reached the king that Absalom had killed all of his other sons and not one was left alive. King David jumped up, tore at his robe and fell to the floor in grief. Just then Jonadab arrived and told the king that only Amnon had been killed and that Absalom had plotted to assassinate Amnon ever since Amnon raped Tamar.

AFTERMATH: Absalom escaped, taking refuge with King Talmai of Geshur, where he was safe from retribution. He stayed there for three years. As those years passed, King David accepted the death of Amnon and longed for the fellowship of Absalom.

General Joab, realizing how much the king longed to see Absalom, sent for a woman of Tekoa who had a reputation for great wisdom. He asked her to request an appointment with King David, and instructed her in what to say.

Tekoa, wearing mourning clothes and disheveled hair, pretended that she was in deep sorrow for a long time. When the king asked why she was mourning, she said her two sons had fought in a field and with no one there to separate them, one of them was killed. Although her family demanded that the surviving son be executed for murdering his brother, she did not agree with their wishes. Tekoa asked King David to intervene with her family on her behalf and to make sure her living son was spared.

At first, King David believed Tekoa's story and vowed to speak with her family. Then he became suspicious and asked if Joab had sent her. Tekoa admitted that Joab had sent her with instructions that she tell him this story so that David could see his own problem from another's point of view. King David understood and immediately sent for Joab. He told Joab that Absalom could return to Jerusalem but must stay in his own quarters. King David never wanted to lay eyes on his son again.

Upon returning to Jerusalem, Absalom asked Joab to intercede on his behalf and convince his father to see him. King David would not. This made Absalom very angry. He set out to avenge his father's rejection by winning the affection of all the people of Jerusalem away from his father.

Absalom was well regarded and had long been considered one of the most handsome men in Israel. He possessed a beautiful head of hair that he cut only once a year, and then only because it weighed three pounds and was too much of a burden for him to carry around. In time, Absalom's campaign to win the people's love succeeded. His father was forced to retreat for his own safety, taking with him his remaining loyal followers. But as David left Jerusalem, he instructed one of his trusted advisers, Ahithophel, to return to Jerusalem and pretend to pledge his loyalty to Absalom so he would be in a position to undermine Absalom's power.

Ahithophel easily convinced Absalom that he had chosen his side over his father's, and soon joined Absalom in scheming to humiliate King David. "Go to the house of your father," Ahithophel advised, "where all his wives have stayed behind, and sleep with each of them. This will humiliate King David before the people of Jerusalem." Absalom did as Ahithophel suggested.

Next, Ahithophel tried to convince Absalom that the only way he could truly prove that he was stronger than his father would be to set out with an army of men to find his father and kill only his father. Uncertain, Absalom turned to Hushai, another adviser, for council. Hushai said he didn't think this was a good idea, and Absalom agreed. Publicly humiliated, Ahithophel promptly hanged himself in shame.

Hushai suggested another plan, which Absalom enacted. He assembled a great army and set out to find his father and kill him, as well as all of his great warriors, who were being led by Joab. But David learned that Absalom and his men were on their way. In front of his entire army, the king directed Joab to be gentle with Absalom and save his life.

When Absalom and his troops confronted David and Joab's men in the Ephraim forest, a tremendous battle took place. Twenty thousand men were slaughtered. During the battle, Absalom, riding a donkey, saw that some of David's men were trying to escape into the forest. He rode toward them, and as he passed beneath a great oak tree his hair got caught in the branches. The donkey continued forward, leaving Absalom dangling from the tree. One of David's men saw this happen and rushed to tell Joab, who chastised him for not killing Absalom on the spot. The man explained that David had told them not to harm Absalom.

Joab took the matter into his own hands. He went to the tree where Absalom was still dangling. He plunged three daggers into Absalom's heart, then stepped back to allow ten of his men to finish the job. They threw Absalom's body in a deep pit and placed a huge pile of stones on top of it.

Word reached David that Absalom had been killed and the king lost control, weeping, mourning, and crying out for his dead son. After recovering sufficiently, King David and his men triumphantly returned to Jerusalem.

CHRONICLE: King David died in 961 B.C., and was succeeded by Solomon, his son by his second wife, Bathsheba (David had murdered Bathsheba's first husband so that he could marry her himself). One of Solomon's first official acts as king was to execute Joab, as revenge for the killing of Absalom in violation of King David's orders.

Solomon ruled from 974 B.C. to 937 B.C. as a fabulously wealthy king who enjoyed a fantastic and polygamous lifestyle, with seven hundred wives and three hundred concubines. Although these were glorious years of accomplishment for Solomon, the excesses enjoyed by the ruling class left the common people poorer than ever, resulting in a class war among the people of Jerusalem.

When King Solomon died, his son Rehoboam became an even harsher ruler. A revolt by the people against the House of David caused Palestine to split into two hostile kingdoms—the ten tribes of Israel, led by Jeroboam, and the two tribes of Judah, led by Rehoboam—which would fight each other for the next two hundred years. Around 722 B.C., the kingdom of Israel was destroyed. Some speculate that this eventually led to thousands of Jews being exported, disappearing from the pages of known history. These Jews are said to compose the ten tribes of Israel that have been the focus of search and speculation ever since but have never been absolutely identified.

 336 B.C.

PHILIP II (382–336 B.C.)
KING OF MACEDONIA

Although Philip II, known as the warrior king of Macedonia, was a great conqueror, history has accorded him less fame than his son, Alexander the Great. Philip was very aware of his country's image as a backward mountain province to the north of Greece, and tried to raise his country's cultural status to equal that of his neighbors to the south. He hoped by the end of his reign that his son and successor, Alexander, would be admired by the Greeks because of his culture, as well as his leadership. But Philip's ambitions resulted in Alexander and his mother, Queen Olympias, feeling threatened enough to take drastic steps to protect their own interests.

ASSASSIN: Pausanias, a young noble who is said to have had a bitter grievance against the queen's uncle, Attalus, and against Philip for failing to give him justice.

HISTORY: As the son of a former king, Philip was taken to Thebes as a hostage at age fifteen in an effort to control the behavior of his brother, King Alexander. While in captivity, Philip was exposed to the knowledge and culture of the Greeks and studied their literature, philosophy, and military theories, making him more tolerant of Greek society than anyone in his family. Back home in the violent kingdom of Macedonia, Philip's brother King Alexander was assassinated and his brother Perdikkas took the throne, only to be murdered as well.

Philip, by then twenty-three years old, returned from Thebes to Macedonia and fought with brutal efficiency to secure the throne for himself. As ruler of his country, Philip attempted to turn Macedonia into another Greece. After converting the army into a fighting machine superior to the Thebans' and, some say, equal to that of the Spartans, Philip conquered local hill tribes and set out to acquire everything from the Danube to the Hellespont, including Thebes and several other cities. As a political maneuver, he left Athens untouched, hoping to form an alliance with the city, which possessed a powerful fleet that could assist him in a war against Persia. During this time, Philip's son Alexander had proved to be one of his most effective generals.

In 336 B.C., Philip was ready to launch a major campaign against Persia, but before doing so, he returned to Macedonia's ancient capital, Aegae, to attend the wedding of his daughter. The happy occasion was marred by rumors that Philip planned to take another wife, one who could give him a better heir than Alexander, who, even after studying with Aristotle for three years, did not seem to share his father's respect for the Greek culture. Philip's queen, Olympias, the mother of Alexander, was deeply affected by the rumors of her husband's plan to replace her son in the line of succession simply because of his intense desire to be admired by the Greeks. Philip tried to make peace with his wife and son, assuring them that although he did plan to take another wife, it would be only for political purposes and not to interrupt the line of succession.

EVENT: Thinking himself invulnerable and wanting to demonstrate to the people he ruled that he had confidence in their devotion to him, Philip strutted around at his daughter's wedding without regard for where his bodyguards were positioned in order to protect him. Quickly it happened. Without an opportunity for anyone to stop him, Pausanias ran up to Philip and shoved a dagger into his side, killing him instantly. Pausanias himself was then killed without delay, having no chance to make a confession or explain his motives for such an extreme act.

AFTERMATH: An official explanation was soon issued: Apparently Pausanias assassinated Philip because he had bitter feelings toward the queen's uncle, Attalus, and Philip did not satisfactorily resolve his complaint. This vague and weak explanation of the young man's actions, combined with the prompt demise of the assassin, reinforced the assumption that Pausanias had been paid by Olympias to kill her husband so that her twenty-year-old son, later known as Alexander the Great, would be assured of inheriting the throne to become ruler of Macedonia.

 336 B.C.

BAGOAS (?–336 B.C.)
ADVISER TO THE KING OF PERSIA

The eunuch Bagoas was a powerful force in the Persian empire, who gained complete political control, as well as personal wealth, by installing kings of his own choosing and assassinating those who would not honor his wishes. Bagoas was commander in chief of the Achaemenid forces in

343 B.C. when they conquered Egypt. He used the opportunity to accumulate great wealth, in part by instructing his troops to raid Egyptian temples and seize valuables, including sacred writings, which he then sold back to Egyptian priests at outrageous prices.

ASSASSIN: Darius III, king of Persia.

HISTORY: Although King Artaxerxes III of Persia earned a reputation as a cruel monarch, it was while he was under the control of Bagoas, who dictated the king's every move. The king even put to death nearly all of his own relatives, as Bagoas instructed. By 340 B.C., Philip of Macedonia had attacked the cities of Perinthus and Byzantium and was threatening to push farther into Persian territory. Deciding how to handle this assault caused intense friction between King Artaxerxes III and his eunuch adviser. Finally, in 338 B.C., Bagoas became so impatient with King Artaxerxes that he assassinated the king and all his remaining sons except the youngest and weakest, Arses.

Bagoas then appointed Arses king, believing he would be a willing puppet, but during the next two years it became apparent to the eunuch that Arses was not easily manipulated. Arses opposed many actions of Bagoas, decided he must be eliminated, and devised a scheme to poison the eunuch. But word of the king's plans to poison him reached Bagoas, and he acted first. He had Arses and all his children killed, leaving no direct family member alive to serve as monarch.

Needing to find a suitable heir to the throne, Bagoas decided upon a collateral family member, a satrap of Armenia, and had him enthroned as Darius III, king of Persia. Bagoas soon realized that Darius was even less likely to be manipulated than Arses and Artaxerxes had been. Once again Bagoas found it necessary to plan a royal poisoning.

EVENT: If Bagoas had one failing, besides choosing kings who would not do as he said, it was to overestimate the loyalty of his men. Unaware that spies among his ranks were reporting the eunuch's assassination plans back to King Darius III, Bagoas set out with complete confidence on the evening the king was to die. He planned to dine with the king in his own quarters and delighted at being in a position to watch as Darius drank from a glass containing poison. But the evening didn't go as Bagoas had planned. Sitting at the same table with Darius, Bagoas watched as the glass containing the poison was placed before the king. Darius had a plan of his own. He pushed the glass in front of Bagoas and signaled to his guards, who stood near the eunuch, forcing him to drink the poison himself. This was the end of Bagoas.

AFTERMATH: With Bagoas eliminated, during the next five years Darius was left on his own to handle attacks on Persia from Alexander the Great of Macedonia. By the end of September 331 B.C., Alexander had captured the western third of the Persian Empire and marched 47,000 veteran troops into Mesopotamia (modern Iraq) to continue his quest. Darius stood ready to protect his territory, feeling confident with 250,000 soldiers strategically encamped on a battlefield near the village of Arbela, where he would have the ultimate advantage. Upon surveying the enemy battalion, Alexander realized his own disadvantage and decided to delay his assault. He ordered his troops to eat, sleep well, and prepare themselves to attack the next morning.

By morning, the situation was no more appealing, but Alexander, a brave and clever leader, angled his attack so that his vastly outnumbered Macedonian troops managed to divide the Persian throng. In an error of judgment, a unit of Darius's Persian cavalry did not wait for orders and galloped to assist their comrades, leaving a hole in the battle line. Alexander took the advantage and led his elite personal cavalry, the Companions, into the gap to divide and weaken the Persian army by half.

Darius stood in his chariot, watching Alexander's Companions race toward him and kill his driver with a javelin. In a panic, Darius jumped atop the nearest horse and galloped toward safety, deserting his troops on the battlefield. The Persian army, faced with Alexander's assault while watching their king ride away, also turned and ran. While Alexander's troops suffered no more than five hundred casualties, the Persian count may have been as many as ninety thousand men.

After leaving his army to be slaughtered, Darius escaped safely to Bactria (modern Afghanistan). There he was assassinated by Bessus, one of his own governors, who decided his loyalties were better placed with Alexander.

The Persian Empire, as well as the Persian army, was destroyed by the battle at Arbela. Alexander the Great would continue his conquest for eight more years. Although he went on to invade India, the battle of Arbela is considered his most decisive victory.

 48 B.C.

POMPEY THE GREAT (106–48 B.C.)
ROMAN GENERAL AND STATESMAN

Although some called Gnaeus Pompeius Magnus an egotistical general, his military and political career is one of the most impressive in Roman history. He gained acclaim while fighting for Sulla, assumed most of the credit for crushing the slave revolt of Spartacus, exterminated the pirate infestation of the Mediterranean, and completely subdued Mithriadates VI of Pontus in 65 B.C. Pompey joined with Crassus and Caesar in 60 B.C. to form the first Triumvirate, taking control of Rome and effectively eliminating democracy.

ASSASSINS: Servants of Ptolemy, eunuch vizier to King Ptolemy of Alexandria.

HISTORY: Pompey's alliance with Caesar was broken in 54 B.C. when Julia, Pompey's wife and Caesar's daughter, died. In 53 B.C. Crassus died, and the power struggle between Pompey and Caesar intensified. Each of the rivals believed he should be dictator of Rome. Caesar, however, was becoming increasingly popular among the people because of his personal charm and charisma, while Pompey's brilliance was dulled by his awkwardness and lack of consideration for others. But many members of the Roman Senate were apprehensive of Caesar's popularity, so Pompey used this to his advantage, joining forces with the Senate against Caesar.

A shift in their balance of power came in 49 B.C. when civil war erupted: Pompey and the Senate versus Caesar, winner take all. Caesar collected his troops and marched them across the Rubicon from Gaul. Although Pompey had more soldiers and political allies than Caesar, Caesar was famous for his bravery and blind ambition. He led his small armed forces to victory time after time against Pompey's impressive numbers.

The final confrontation came on August 9, 48 B.C., at Pharsalus. Pompey commanded 48,000 infantrymen with 7,000 horses. Caesar had only 22,000 men and 1,000 horses. Knowing that brother was fighting against brother in this civil war, Caesar ordered his men to spare the life of any Roman who would surrender. He especially instructed that Marcus Brutus, a young statesman he had groomed for high office, should be allowed to escape if possible. Otherwise, he should be taken uninjured. Caesar's troops fought an inspired battle, obliterating Pompey's impressive army, killing or wounding 15,000 men and causing 20,000 to surrender. The remainder of Pompey's soldiers escaped, as did Pompey himself, ripping the commander's insignia from his uniform in disgust.

Pompey boarded a ship and sailed toward Egypt, planning to collect his troops waiting there and hoping to enlist the assistance of Egyptian soldiers to return and fight Caesar. When Pompey reached Mytilene, he was met by Cornelia, his wife, who joined with others there, begging him not to leave. Pompey would hear none of it. He was determined to fight to the end. Yet, as he set sail for Alexandria with his small squadron, Pompey told the people at Mytilene that when Caesar arrived they should surrender to him without fear, assuring them, "Caesar is a man of great goodness and clemency."

EVENT: In Alexandria, word arrived that Pompey was on his way. The young king Ptolemy XII went to the sea, prepared to welcome Pompey the Great, but Ptolemy's advisers were concerned that they should not offend Caesar, as he was clearly winning the civil war. When Pompey's ship came near, a small boat was sent to ferry him ashore. There, as Pompey took a step to exit the boat, Pothinus, a eunuch vizier to King Ptolemy, ordered nearby servants to finish the work of Caesar. They pounced upon Pompey and stabbed him to death.

AFTERMATH: When Caesar arrived in Alexandria, Pothinus and his servants proudly displayed to him the severed head of Pompey. Caesar was deeply impressed by their actions: He turned away, weeping.

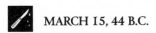 MARCH 15, 44 B.C.

JULIUS CAESAR (100–44 B.C.)
COMMANDER IN CHIEF AND
DICTATOR OF THE ROMAN EMPIRE

A tall and fair-skinned man, with keen dark eyes, Gaius Julius Caesar possessed courteous manners and great personal charm, insight, and daring. He was a writer and orator, known as one of the greatest of Rome. During his time, it was common for a man of ambition to spend his own fortune (and in Caesar's case, his wife's fortune, as well as some of Cleopatra's, his lover's) while seeking a public position of power. After gaining high office, he could live a lavish lifestyle and reestablish his own wealth at the expense of the public.

Caesar's first public appointment was as one of the guardians of the Appian Way (the great road that led southward from Rome and was the route for travelers to Greece and the East). He went on to exhibit gladiators (armed slaves extensively trained to fight in the public games). In one such expensive show, Caesar exhibited wild beasts in a theater with the spectators seated among furniture made entirely of solid silver. His popularity soared, not only among Roman noblemen but among the people as well. He became a legendary and ruthless military leader, conquering vast lands in the name of Rome.

Courageous and ambitious from a young age, Caesar was always confident of his future greatness. He could be ruthless in pursuit of power and money, and he made many enemies during his rise to the top. Yet he was also known for being a generous, forgiving and sympathetic human being. In the end, this powerful combination of fearless courage and personal compassion would lead to Caesar's demise.

ASSASSINS: A conspiracy that resulted in the assassination of Julius Caesar involved as many as sixty men; at least twenty-two of them were nominated by Caesar for public office, four had been generals during Caesar's Gallic campaigns, and seven others had fought for Caesar against Pompey. However, only twenty of the conspirators have been identified.

One of the conspirators, Cassius, fought with Pompey against Caesar in the civil war and had been passed over by Caesar for a command in an earlier war against Persia. Another conspirator, Marcus Brutus, was a remote ancestor of a man who abolished the Roman monarchy, also named Brutus. This familial connection seemed to inspire Marcus Brutus's idealism and intellectual attitude toward Rome. He also held a personal grudge against Caesar from earlier years. Caesar had had an affair with Servilia, the mother of Marcus Brutus, while she was another man's wife, resulting in speculation that Marcus Brutus was actually Caesar's unacknowledged illegitimate son. Also, during the civil war, it was rumored that Servilia offered Caesar the sexual favors of her daughter Tertia, Brutus's half sister, in exchange for financial opportunities. When the conspiracy to assassinate Caesar was enacted, Tertia was married to Cassius.

HISTORY: During the four years following the civil war, Caesar, as the victor, set out to mend fences and unite the Roman Senate. Still, some of Pompey's supporters refused to shift their allegiance to Caesar's side, believing a democratic Rome was better for the people than the dictatorship Caesar had established.

Many of the people of Rome were also suspicious of Caesar because a prophecy quoted from the books of Sibyl was circulating. It said Rome might conquer the Parthians if she put herself under the command of a king; otherwise she must fail. The last king of Rome, Tarquin the Proud, had been forced out of his position nearly seven centuries before, but the harsh legend of Tarquin lived on, and the populace of Rome was leery of being ruled by another king.

Still, others among the citizens of Rome and the Senate favored empowering the prophecy and began a campaign to transform Caesar from dictator to king. One day, as Caesar returned from Alba to the Capitol, some people among a crowd gathered to greet him were incited to call out to Caesar, "The king!" Others became indignant at this declaration, and it did not appear to be to Caesar's liking, either, when he responded, "I am no king, only Caesar." When next attending the Senate, Caesar did not rise to accept the compliment when hailed as king by many of the senators. Some were enemies of Caesar, hoping to feed his ego and cause his downfall. Others were sincere in their superstitious belief that the prophecy must be fulfilled. During the festival of the Lupercalia, Caesar sat in his official position on a gilded chair, wearing a triumphal robe while watching the sporting events. At one point, Antony placed a crown wreathed with bay leaves on Caesar's head, and a portion of the onlooking crowd began to applaud. The applause did not come from an overwhelming majority, however, and Caesar swiftly removed the crown from his head. The crowd then exploded with a shout of approval, but Antony again placed the crown upon Caesar's head. Once more Caesar rejected it, and the people let out a hearty cheer of approval.

Soon the statues of Caesar around Rome began to have crowns placed upon their heads, but Caesar would order them promptly removed; in time he also ordered that those men responsible for placing the crowns be imprisoned for their crime. The public disagreements incited by such events spurred on those conspiring to ruin Caesar, and they continued their campaign. Warnings began to arrive, telling Caesar that not only was his reputation in danger, but so was his life. Some speculate that many of the warnings came from the conspirators themselves in order to frighten Caesar, and eventually the tactic began to work. Caesar became so overwrought by the constant assault that he resolved not to leave his house on the day he was warned would be his last.

CONSPIRACY: Caesar had announced to the Senate that he would leave Rome on March 18 to conduct a war against Persia. At the time, Cleopatra was also living in Rome, but rumors were circulating that Caesar planned to rule the Roman Empire with Cleopatra from Alexandria. Caesar scheduled a meeting of the Senate for March 15, to take care of routine business before leaving for Persia. One month earlier, he dismissed his private Spanish veteran bodyguard and the conspiracy to assassinate him began to take shape. Cassius persuaded his brother-in-law Marcus Brutus that on March 15 Caesar intended to declare himself king before the entire senate. Marcus Brutus, a senator who believed in a more traditional Roman government (he was also head of the most important Roman judgeship) agreed with Cassius that the only way to save Rome was to assassinate Caesar.

Because he was widely respected, Marcus Brutus was easily able to enlist as many as sixty other people in the conspiracy, including twenty senators who were willing to commit the actual killing. Decimus Brutus, a distant relative of Marcus Brutus, was a former officer of Caesar's army and a longtime friend of Caesar who had free access to his home. He was also recruited by the conspirators. It was decided that March 15 was the perfect opportunity to assassinate Caesar and transfer power immediately to the Senate. Further, in order that no one person could be held individually responsible for Caesar's killing, it was agreed among the conspirators that each assassin would carry a dagger under his robe and take his turn stabbing Caesar that day.

EVENT: Caesar slept restlessly the night of March 14, 44 B.C. The wind blew open the windows and doors of his bedroom. He heard his wife, Calpurnia, groaning in her sleep. On the morning of March 15, Calpurnia begged Caesar not to go to the Senate, telling him of a dream she had had the night before in which she saw him lying dead in her arms. All the threats and predictions of doom made Caesar feel sick.

The group of conspirators met at the home of Cassius, using the excuse that his son was coming of age and the ceremonial party could be held that day. As Marcus Brutus executed his judgeship duties elsewhere, the conspirators escorted Cassius's son to the Forum and then to the meeting hall in a ceremonious manner. There, with the statue of Pompey looking on, the conspirators proceeded with their diversion, and Marcus Brutus arrived just before Caesar was scheduled to make his appearance.

When Caesar did not arrive at the appointed time, the conspirators became concerned and sent Decimus Brutus to Caesar's home. Caesar explained to Decimus Brutus that he was not well and asked him to tell the Senate he was canceling his meeting with them that day. Decimus Brutus convinced Caesar that the senators would be offended if he were the messenger of such news, and that Caesar must go to tell them himself. Reluctantly, Caesar agreed.

On the way to the meeting hall, Artemidorus of Cnidus, a teacher of Greek, passed a note to Caesar warning him of the conspirators' plans to assassinate him that day. Even though Artemidorus told Caesar to read the note immediately, he did not, giving the note instead to one of his slaves. Seeing this, Artemidorus moved close to Caesar, imploring him to read the note because it contained matters of great concern to him. Finally, Caesar took back the note, but he was suddenly distracted by a group of citizens waiting to honor him as he passed by. Antony, a man of great strength, who had been walking by Caesar's side to protect him, was diverted by Decimus Brutus. Caesar entered the meeting house carrying the note, still unread, in his hand.

It was just after 11 A.M. when Caesar took his seat before the Senate. The senators stood to greet him and moved to surround his chair. Tullius Cimber, a senator and governor-elect, began to address Caesar on behalf of his brother who had been banished. Caesar waved him away, rejecting his plea, and Casca, a tribune of the people, who had agreed with the other conspirators that he would strike the first blow against Caesar, moved around behind him. Tillius grabbed Caesar's robe near the neck and tore it, giving the other conspirators the signal to attack.

Casca pulled a dagger from beneath his robe and struck Caesar in the neck. It was not a fatal wound, or even a serious one, because Casca was so overwrought at the idea of committing such an act. Caesar spun around and grabbed Casca's dagger, holding it tight, saying in Latin, "Casca, thou villain, what art thou about?"

Casca called out to his brother in Greek, "Brother, help!"

Those senators who were unaware of the conspiracy were so horrified by what was happening that they did not speak or assist their leader. The conspirators surrounding Caesar each drew a dagger. Caesar turned to look at each man, from one to the other, and seeing only daggers ready to strike him, he began to struggle with all his will against this fate. Casca aimed and struck at Caesar's throat but missed, grazing his chest. Caesar grabbed his arm, turned him around enough to look him in the face, and gave him a hard shove, throwing him off balance. Turning and half rising as he did this, Caesar exposed his right side, allowing another attacker, possibly Casca's brother, to strike a more serious blow. Trying to turn and recover from this blow, Caesar was hit by Cassius with his dagger, this time in the face. At that, the other conspirators seemed to grow courage, each taking his turn, causing Caesar to stagger under the onslaught. Although blood dripped into his eyes, half-blinding him, Caesar continued to try to defend himself as each conspirator took a turn lunging at him, by now all crying out as they did so.

Although it is believed that Marcus Brutus had already stabbed Caesar once, he now approached Caesar again. This time he was recognized by Caesar, who allowed the will of the conspirators to take away his resistance. He covered his head with his robe and collapsed at the base of Pompey's statue. Brutus's dagger struck Caesar in the groin and the other assassins collected around his helpless body, stabbing at it one more time each—some striking each other in the confusion.

Finally, the deed done, Brutus moved to the center of the room to make a speech, but the horrified senators who had just witnessed the violent attack on Caesar all left the meeting hall. Outside, Caesar's trusty consul Antony, who had been detained by the conspirators, learned of what had happened and disguised himself as a slave in order to get home safely. The conspirators gathered at the Forum where Brutus, at last, had an opportunity to speak, but the crowd became angry with his announcement of Caesar's demise. Brutus and the other conspirators, who now feared for their own lives, were forced to flee to the Capitol, where they barricaded themselves inside for safety.

AFTERMATH: At the foot of Pompey's statue, Caesar's unattended body lay waiting for some slaves to arrive and take him home on a litter. The warning note that was given to Caesar by Artemidorus, containing an accurate account of the conspiracy, was found unopened, near the body. Later, an autopsy revealed twenty-three wounds, yet only one chest wound was fatal. No one knows which conspirator committed the fatal blow.

Caesar's funeral proved that the conspirators' efforts to discredit him did not affect his popularity. There was erected in the Field of Mars a grand pyre on which his body was to be burned. A gilded model of the temple of Mother Venus was installed in the Forum—Caesar was believed to have descended from Venus through Aeneas. The temple contained an ivory couch with covers of gold and purple and a trophy at its head with the robe Caesar was wearing when he was assassinated. In a ceremonial procession, high officials of Rome past and present carried the couch into the Forum. Some had the idea to burn it in the chapel of Jupiter in the Capitol, some in Pompey's Hall, where Caesar was killed. Suddenly, two men wearing swords at their sides, and each carrying two javelins, came forward and set fire to the temple with torches they held in their hands. The crowd of onlookers quickly fed the flames with dry brushwood, benches, and anything they had brought as a present for their dead leader. Flute players and actors took off the triumphal robes they wore and threw them into the flames; veteran soldiers threw in the decorations they had won in war; and mothers threw in ornaments made by their children.

The doors of the building where Caesar was assassinated were blocked so they could never be entered again. The day of March 15 was declared to be cursed, and no public business was ever to be done on that day again.

 DECEMBER 7, 43 B.C.

MARCUS TULLIUS CICERO (106–43 B.C.)
ROMAN ORATOR, STATESMAN, AND PHILOSOPHER

Cicero has been characterized by some historians as egotistical and indecisive, but his tendency to alter his position on political issues was probably more a sign of flexibility. While his alliances shifted as the political atmosphere changed, his belief in constitutional government and in the importance of abiding by the letter of the law never wavered. Although Cicero was not involved in the conspiracy to assassinate Caesar, it was clear by his oratories after the fact that he approved. He appeared not to notice that his famous oratories, many targeted against Marc Antony, put his political future and his life in danger.

ASSASSINS: Mark Antony's soldiers.

HISTORY: Cicero's fearless oratories, often venomously attacking Roman leaders, developed over the years. His series of speeches in 63 B.C. exposed Cataline's conspiracy. In 60 B.C., he was invited to join Crassus, Pompey, and Caesar as rulers of Rome, but he refused the offer, saying their acts were unconstitutional. He was banished by Clodius in 59 B.C. but recalled by Pompey in 45 B.C. Driven by his allegiance to Pompey, he attempted to undermine the relationship between Pompey and Caesar, and when the two leaders did turn against each other, Cicero bravely opposed Caesar in support of Pompey. After Caesar's assassination, few were surprised when Cicero encouraged the Senate to impose a general amnesty, relieving the conspirators of murder charges.

This enraged Antony as well as Octavian, Caesar's adopted son, but Cicero thought them powerless against him. Then it was reported back to Antony and Octavian that Cicero had told others in confidence that they should be given distinctions and then be disposed of. Cicero soon learned that the two men were discussing forms of vengeance they could enact against him, and he decided it was wise for him to leave Rome.

EVENT: Cicero fled on December 6, 43 B.C., traveling from Rome by boat on rough waters. Soon he became seasick and ordered his craft to land so that he could stay in his home at Formiae that night. The next morning, when faced with boarding the boat and suffering seasickness again on the choppy water, Cicero decided to wait at home for the assassins to come for him. But his devoted slaves would not allow it, and they loaded him upon a litter and carried him toward the boat. Suddenly Antony's assassins appeared. Cicero's servants wanted to fight to protect him, but he ordered them not to resist. By this time, Cicero was a pitiful sight. His hair and beard were not trimmed, his face was lined with worry, and he was covered with dust. Perhaps he believed death would be a relief, for he raised his head, making his neck an easy target for Antony's assassins, who chopped off his head.

AFTERMATH: Quickly the assassins returned to Rome to present Cicero's head and hands to Antony and his wife, Fulvia. Taking her own revenge on Cicero for speaking out so strongly against her husband, Fulvia cut out the tongue of Cicero's head. His tongueless head and hands were then placed on the speaker's platform at the Forum for all to see, the outspoken orator silenced at last.

A.D. 1 – 1900

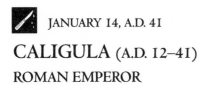

CALIGULA (A.D. 12–41)
ROMAN EMPEROR

During his four-year reign as Roman emperor, Gaius Caesar Germanicus, a.k.a. Caligula, was distinguished by his cruelty, insanity, and greed. His extravagant spending depleted the entire Roman treasury. When funds got low, Caligula decreed that a tax be collected on all food and wages, even the earnings of prostitutes. When those taxes did not replenish the dwindling treasury, Caligula accused wealthy men of treason, had them executed, and confiscated their fortunes.

Caligula suffered from epilepsy and insomnia, sleeping only three hours a night. If he wasn't occupied with sexual exploits, he would wander through the palace during the night commanding the sun to rise. His god complex and sexual desires compelled him to violate even the lowest moral ethics. Calling himself a god, he had sex with anyone he chose, male or female. He committed incest with all his sisters, including Drucilla, whom he forced to divorce her husband and marry him, so that she could be heir to the throne. His first three marriages ended in quick divorces, with one ex-wife ordered never to have sex with a man again. Any woman Caligula wanted, he got. If she was married, he would send her a letter of divorce on behalf of her husband, then order her to his bed. It is said that sometimes while embracing a wife or mistress,

Caligula would taunt her, saying, "Off comes this beautiful head whenever I give the word."

Caligula's cruelty touched every level of Roman life. He murdered at will when someone upset him, often personally giving poison to his victim. His father-in-law, Marcus Silanus, was ordered by Caligula to slit his own throat with a razor when he was suspected of plotting against the ruler. On a whim, he would close the granaries of Rome and watch gleefully as the people starved. During the exhibit of gladiators, Caligula would order that the canopies protecting the spectators from the blazing midday sun be removed so that he could watch them suffer from the heat. When Caligula was told the cost of feeding raw meat to the wild circus animals had increased, he declared that criminals would be a good thing for the animals to feed on instead. He considered Rome, "the city of necks waiting for me to chop them." During extravagant banquets, he found great fun in telling the guests that he could have them killed at any moment as they sat with him to eat.

ASSASSINS: Chaerea and Sabinus, both colonels in Caligula's guard.

HISTORY: Although Cicero's predecessor, Tiberius, had built up the Roman treasury during his twenty-three-year reign, by A.D. 37 the Praetorian (palace) Guard believed it was time to replace their feeble and ailing ruler. Macro, the prefect of the Praetorians, assassinated Tiberius, clearing the way for Caligula to become emperor. At first, Caligula considered Macro a trusted adviser, but soon he grew tired of Macro and had him executed. Knowing the power of the Praetorians to protect or destroy him, Caligula tried to buy their loyalty with gifts and money. These, however, were not enough to keep the ruler alive when his cruelty and abusiveness turned the Praetorians against him.

EVENT: On January 24, A.D. 41, Chaerea and Sabinus, two colonels of the Praetorian Guard whom Caligula had constantly ridiculed, had had enough. As the twenty-nine-year-old emperor walked from the palace through a secret passageway to the palatine games, Chaerea and Sabinus jumped him, stabbing him repeatedly. Seeing what was happening, other guards rushed forward, but instead of stopping their comrades, they happily helped, making sure their own swords were marked with the blood of the fallen lunatic leader. Believing the deed was done, the guards stopped for a moment to look upon the corpse. Suddenly, like a monster, Caligula seemed to come back to life, squirming on the marble floor, shouting, "I am still alive!" This time the Praetorians did a more thorough job, stabbing Caligula until he was truly, definitely dead.

AFTERMATH: News of Caligula's assassination began to circulate through Rome, but many citizens, believing it was one of Caligula's cruel tricks, were hesitant to celebrate his demise. Members of the Praetorian Guard who had not been at the palace rushed there to see if the rumors were true. Upon finding out that Caligula truly was dead, the Praetorians also killed Caligula's wife and smashed his young daughter against the wall, splitting open her head so that her brains spilled out. On their rampage through the palace, the guards found Claudius, Caligula's fifty-year-old uncle, cowering in terror. Claudius was considered an idiot because he walked with a limp and stammered when he talked, and the Praetorians decided he was the perfect choice to be the next emperor because they could easily control him. Claudius was declared emperor and presented before the Senate for confirmation. Besides being intimidated by the Praetorians' power, most senators also believed Claudius was a clever choice and looked forward with relief to dealing with a harmless idiot rather than the raving lunatic Caligula.

☠ OCTOBER 13, A.D. 54

CLAUDIUS (10 B.C.–A.D. 54)
ROMAN EMPEROR

Soon after being named Roman emperor by the Praetorian Guard, who believed he was harmless, Claudius revealed to the Senate that he wasn't really an idiot at all. He had only pretended to be in order to survive in the household of Caligula. Indeed, throughout his life he had used his physical disabilities—limping, partial paralysis, and stammering—to his advantage. The former emperors Augustus and Tiberius had kept Claudius around the palace, although out of public view, using him as a sort of court jester, but Caligula, realizing Claudius had a good mind, had allowed him to become consul in A.D. 37. During this time, Claudius studied many subjects and became an expert in linguistics, history, biography, and gambling, even writing books in these fields.

Still, after becoming emperor himself, Claudius began to exhibit some of the irrational traits of Caligula. Annoyed when mechanical devices in the arena failed to work properly, he would overreact, ordering the carpenters he considered inept to fight the lions. Worse, Claudius took a sadistic interest in executions by torture, watching them with great pleasure.

Claudius did return much of the money and property confiscated by Caligula, and he reduced the excessive taxes imposed by the former emperor. He publicly thanked the Praetorian Guard for showing their faith in him by naming him emperor, but believing it was not wise to condone the murder of an emperor, he also ordered the execution of those soldiers responsible for Caligula's assassination.

ASSASSINS: Empress Agrippina, Claudius's wife, with the help of the physician Stertinius Xenophon and Locusta, one of the most prolific and efficient poisoners of ancient Rome. Locusta, who personally poisoned hundreds of people, was often called upon by the imperial court to dispose of its enemies.

HISTORY: Although Claudius was a surprise to many, he proved to be weak-willed and easily controlled by his advisers and by his wives. The sexual exploits of his first wife, Messalina, were well known in Rome. She is said to have entered into a contest with a local prostitute to see which could satisfy the most lovers in one night. Messalina was always seeking new lovers, and if a man she desired was resistant to her advances, she would have Claudius intimidate the man into fulfilling her needs. In return, she would select attractive housemaids and present them to Claudius in his bed. When Messalina overstepped the bounds of public decency by "marrying" Caius Silius, in a traditionally showy manner, Claudius became suspicious of her. Quickly he learned that Messalina was conspiring with her handsome young "husband" to assassinate Claudius in order that Silius could become emperor himself. Claudius took strong action, ordering the execution of Messalina, Silius, and anyone else with whom his wife had slept, including hundreds who had joined in the empress's orgies.

Messalina's execution left the door open for the ambitious Agrippina the Younger, Claudius's niece and Caligula's sister. In A.D. 48, Agrippina took the opportunity to seduce her uncle in order to secure power for her son, Lucius Domitius Ahenobarbus, later renamed Nero. The cunning Agrippina persuaded Claudius to appear before the Senate and persuade the senators to change the laws of incest and allow him to marry his niece because it would be good for Rome. After their marriage, Agrippina convinced Claudius to adopt Nero as his son and began a campaign to see that Britannicus, Claudius's natural son, was displaced, putting Nero ahead of him in order of succession to the throne. Agrippina's first maneuver was to convince Nero to marry Octavia, Claudius's daughter, making Nero's position even stronger because he was the emperor's son-in-law and stepson. Britannicus was being forced away from the center of influence and power.

Meanwhile, Agrippina became the empress of terror, executing any woman who tried to seduce Claudius and any man who tried to win Claudius's favor. Agrippina had free reign over the Roman Empire for years. But when the sixty-four-year-old emperor became weak from too much work, sex, and ill health and believed he did not have long to live, Claudius acted swiftly to take back his power, naming his natural son Britannicus as his heir. Agrippina was furious and determined to do anything to secure the throne for Nero.

EVENT: Agrippina ordered a large portion of poisonous mushrooms from Locusta and had them served to Claudius in his stew. The emperor began gasping and sputtering and leaned over the table in intense pain. Helped to his bed, Claudius tossed and turned, delirious.

There are two different stories about the subsequent events of that night. One version says that Claudius's condition suddenly improved, but Agrippina did not panic. She had Locusta call upon Agrippina's friend, the physician Xenophon, to come to their assistance. Xenophon offered to induce Claudius to vomit by tickling his throat with a feather. The emperor did not suspect that the feather had been dipped in poison by Locusta.

The other story says Claudius vomited the poisoned stew during the night, but again, Agrippina did not panic. Soothingly, she told him she had something that would settle his stomach: the juice of a colocynth, a wild gourd from Palestine. Agrippina had Claudius drink the juice, and she also administered it to him in an enema.

Whichever version is true, the ending is the same: Claudius suffered twelve hours longer, unable to speak, and then died from one of the remedies by daybreak.

AFTERMATH: Although the senators were not sorry about Claudius's death, they were obliged to deify him because he was very popular with the people. Nero became the next emperor.

A.D. 59

AGRIPPINA THE YOUNGER (A.D. 16–59)
MOTHER OF NERO

As the mother of the Roman ruler Nero, Agrippina the Younger held a powerful position in the Roman Empire, often acting on Nero's behalf as well as behind the scenes to influence his decisions. She was also believed to be an accomplished assassin, poisoning her second husband, Caius Crispus, and her third, the emperor Claudius. Although many attribute her deadly acts to her motherly ambition for her son, Nero, the benefits of being the mother of the emperor were truly enjoyed by Agrippina.

ASSASSIN: Lucius Annaeus Seneca, one of Nero's councillors, who convinced Nero to have his mother assassinated.

HISTORY: Agrippina the Younger had been raised by her grandmother and was said to have had an incestuous affair with her brother Caligula, resulting in the birth of her son Lucius Domitius Ahenobarbus, later renamed Nero. After marrying Caius Crispus and then having him assassinated, Agrippina enticed her uncle, Emperor Claudius I, to marry her and to adopt her son, Nero. Claudius placed Nero next in line to become emperor, displacing his own son, Britannicus, and when Nero was sixteen years old, Agrippina had Claudius poisoned. Once he was proclaimed emperor, Nero allowed his mother to conduct many of the affairs of state, even though he was the official ruler. She even had her own image placed on gold coins, facing that of her son.

Problems developed between mother and son while Nero was being tutored by Seneca, the great philosopher and dramatist. Realizing that Agrippina's influence over Nero was not in his own best interest, Seneca devised ways to cause friction between Nero and his mother. Agrippina became incensed, and the battle lines were drawn, with members of the administration choosing to align themselves either with Nero or with

Agrippina. Seeing that she could not win against Nero's supporters, Agrippina declared that, indeed, her stepson Britannicus was the true heir to rule the Roman Empire and she would support him instead of her own son. But by threatening to throw her support to Britannicus, Agrippina incited Nero to eliminate the competition, and he commissioned Locusta to assassinate Britannicus in A.D. 55.

From then on, Agrippina's influence diminished. Although Nero was married to the virtuous Octavia, he became infatuated with Poppaea, the beautiful wife of his friend Salvius Otho. Poppaea, also enamored of Nero, refused to become his mistress, offering instead to marry him if he divorced Octavia. Agrippina, having Octavia as an ally, vehemently opposed the divorce. This turned Nero against his mother even more, and he decided she must be assassinated. In devising a plan for her demise, poison was eliminated as an option because Agrippina was very knowledgeable on the subject and regularly took antidotes as a precaution.

EVENT: Knowing that Agrippina planned to take a cruise to Baiae in the Bay of Naples, Nero had her transport ship reconstructed with a roof that would collapse, causing the entire ship to fall apart. On the night they sailed, Agrippina and a friend, Acerronia, were reclining on settees, and Crepereius Gallus, another friend, was standing in the cabin when, as planned, the timbers of the cabin fell. Although no further damage was done to the ship, Crepereius Gallus was killed. Seeing that the ship was still holding together, the oarsmen involved in the plot threw their weight to one side of the craft, trying to capsize it. Realizing this was an assassination attempt, Acerronia tried to save Agrippina by yelling, "Help! I'm the emperor's mother!" Believing in the darkness that she was Agrippina, the crewmen beat Acerronia to death with their oars. Agrippina escaped the ship and swam to safety.

Upon reaching Baiae, Agrippina sent a messenger to tell Nero that there had been a terrible accident and she barely had escaped alive. Certain that Agrippina would now send someone to kill him, Nero acted quickly, sending assassins to Baiae. Surprised by them in her bedchamber, Agrippina knew her fate was sealed. She opened her nightclothes, presenting her belly to the assassins. Her final command as mother of the emperor was to tell her assassins to stab her in the womb that had borne Nero. They did as she said, slashing her repeatedly.

AFTERMATH: By A.D. 68, Nero's popularity was at its lowest, and as his enemies increased in strength, his supporters left him. Nero had Octavia murdered so that he could marry Poppaea Sabina. The Praetorian Guard refused to serve Nero and applied pressure to the Senate to have him removed from office. Soon Nero was sentenced to death, and the Senate named Servius Sulpicius Galba, age sixty-five, emperor of Rome. Galba would serve fewer than six months before being challenged.

On June 9, A.D. 68, the anniversary of Octavia's death, thirty-year-old Nero stabbed himself in the throat, killing himself with the help of his scribe, Epaphroditus. Nero's death marked the end of the Julio-Claudian line of Caesars that had ruled Rome for 128 years.

 SEPTEMBER 18, A.D. 96

DOMITIAN (A.D. 52–96)
ROMAN EMPEROR

During his fifteen years as Roman emperor, although stern and competent, Domitian was also cruel, egocentric, and morbid, enacting a reign of terror on the Senate that is unmatched in the Roman Empire's bloody history.

ASSASSINS: The Empress Domitia and officers of her husband's court.

HISTORY: Domitian became emperor in A.D. 81 when his brother, the emperor Titus, died. Although there is speculation that Domitian was involved in his brother's death, this theory is based less on credible evidence than on Domitian's reputation as a tyrannical ruler. He demanded to be treated as a god, encouraged visitors to embrace his knees as he sat on the throne, and bestowed divinity upon his father, brother, wife, and sisters. Domitian's outrageous expectations resulted in a revolt led by one of his provincial governors, the senator Lucius Antonius Saturinus, in A.D. 88. In retaliation, Domitian purged the Senate of anyone appearing disloyal to him. In A.D. 89, all philosophers were banished from Italy because they supported the Senate against Domitian. He had many Christians executed, including his nephew Falvius Clemens, when they would not offer sacrifices to his image. (The Capitol was filled with statues of Domitian.)

As the Senators and others in power reacted to his tyrannical dictates, Domitian became insanely paranoid that everyone was against him. Even those who pledged their complete loyalty to him were not trusted. He lined the walls of the porticoes with shining stones so that he could see in the mirrored walls whatever was going on behind him as he walked through.

In time, Domitian's paranoid accusations drove even his household staff to fear him. He ordered the death of his secretary Epaphroditus, in A.D. 96, because twenty-seven years earlier he had aided Nero in killing himself. Soon servants of Domitian began to plot his assassination, aided by members of the Senate, his successor, Nerva, and even the emperor's own wife, Domitia.

No doubt Domitian remembered the astrological predictions that warned he would be murdered in the fifth hour of September 18, A.D. 96. As the day came closer, he had many of his close attendants executed, thinking this would keep him safe.

EVENT: Just before midnight on the night of September 17, Domitian became so afraid that he jumped out of bed to defend himself against an imaginary attacker. A few hours later, still frightened, he asked his wife's servants about the time. Involved in the conspiracy and instructed by the Empress Domitia to do so, they told the emperor that it was the sixth hour, even though it was not. Believing that the dangerous hour had passed, Domitian decided to take a bath. Afterward, he was told his niece's steward, Stephanus, was waiting in the bedroom to give him important news. There Stephanus handed Domitian a list of conspirators and lunged at the emperor, stabbing him in the groin. Although he put up a good fight, Domitian was overtaken by four other conspirators and died as predicted. It was the fifth hour of September 18, A.D. 96.

AFTERMATH: When the news of Domitian's assassination reached the Senate, its members were ecstatic and set out to destroy every image of the emperor that could be found in the chamber. It was decreed that all statues of Domitian in the entire country be destroyed and any inscription bearing his name be rubbed out.

When Marcus Cocceius Nerva, the former Roman consul, was appointed to succeed Domitian, one of his first official acts was to recall every citizen who had been exiled and to return any property that had been confiscated during Domitian's reign. The widow Domitia lived a long, distinguished life.

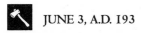 JUNE 3, A.D. 193

DIDIUS JULIANUS (A.D. 132–193)
ROMAN EMPEROR

Didius Julianus, the wealthiest Roman senator, called a vain old man by some, became Roman emperor by buying the position at auction.

ASSASSINS: Septimius Severus, a cruel and shrewd former lawyer and general, along with his soldiers.

HISTORY: Roman Emperor Pertinax, an honest and earthy disciplinarian, had been having difficulty controlling the Praetorian Guard, who were supposed to protect and serve him. In an effort to keep them in line, he began enforcing strict disciplinary rules within the palace, but this did not sit well with the self-willed Praetorians.

On March 28, A.D. 193, three hundred of the Praetorians entered the palace on a mission. They located the emperor, who approached them unafraid, stopping them in their tracks. Suddenly, one guard lunged forward and shoved his sword through Pertinax. The others then joined in, decapitating the emperor.

Now the Praetorian Guard was left with no emperor to protect and no ruler in house. They offered the position to several senators, but none would accept such an important position. The emperor ruled all of Italy and 150 million other citizens, from the Rhine eastward to the Euphrates and westward to the Thames—in essence, most of the civilized world at the time. Besides, Pertinax had been a popular ruler with the people of Rome, as well as with the senators, and it was suspected that the populace would not look kindly upon the man who succeeded him under these conditions.

On a whim, one of the guards suggested the position might go to the Roman citizen who would pay the highest price for it at auction, with the proceeds being divided equally among the Praetorians. This seemed like a good idea to the other Praetorians, and it was quickly announced throughout the city, "The empire is for auction! The empire is for auction!"

The auction proceeded until only two contenders remained: sixty-one-year-old Didius Julianus against Sulpicianus, father-in-law of the murdered emperor Pertinax. Sulpicianus bid 240 million sesterces (equivalent to almost a thousand dollars in modern currency for each of the 12,000 Praetorian soldiers). Didius Julianus offered 300 million sesterces, and the empire was sold.

After the auction, Didius Julianus went immediately to the Senate chamber, sat in the emperor's chair, and addressed the senators, asking that they confirm his appointment. Because the Praetorians stood nearby, intimidating them, the senators did not resist. Didius Julianus was then escorted to his new home, the royal palace, where he indulged in a magnificent feast and entertainment late into the night. Once the celebration ended, he was left alone in the darkness to reflect on the events of the night before. Had he acted in error while being caught up in the excitement?

Already, groups of irate citizens were gathering around the empire as news of the outrageous auction spread from Britain to Syria, Pannonia to Dalmatia. Powerful Roman generals were receiving the disturbing details. Septimius Severus, a handsome yet cruel former lawyer raised in Africa, gathered troops around him in his Pannonian camp. Soldiers were offered an equivalent of a $2,000 reward if they would leave their posts on the Danube, near the present site of Vienna, and go to Rome immediately. News bulletins of the movement of Septimius Severus and his troops were relayed to Didius Julianus daily. They were crossing the Alps and would soon reach Rome.

Didius Julianus, quickly losing interest in the affairs of state, appointed his son-in-law governor of Rome. He refused to allow a gold statue of himself to be erected, choosing one made of brass instead. Fearful for his safety and threatened by a lack of support from the Senate, he ordered the senators be massacred, then changed his mind. Upon learning that other Roman cities had not resisted the approach of Severus, Didius Julianus urgently installed stronger fortifications to protect himself and drilled the Praetorian soldiers so they would be ready to protect him when Severus arrived. He even tried to train elephants to attack, but they had only been used for parades and were too flabby and not aggressive enough to fight; besides, there were not enough skilled riders to handle the beasts.

As Severus came closer, Didius Julianus dispatched private assassins to stop him, but they failed because Severus traveled with six hundred personal bodyguards. Didius Julianus sent a messenger to offer Severus half the empire, with instructions that if he refused the messenger was to kill him. Severus refused, saying he preferred to have Didius Julianus as an enemy, not a colleague, and he killed the messenger. Didius Julianus then sent a group of priests to reason with Severus, and vestal virgins to entice him. Neither could stop Severus. Finally, Didius Julianus tried magical rites and sacrifices.

EVENT: Severus was determined to save the Roman Empire from the likes of Didius Julianus, or any man who believed the empire could be bought or sold. He marched eight hundred miles with his troops, striding in front of the men, wearing full armor and rarely stopping to eat, drink, or rest. They traveled twenty miles a day on foot.

On June 2, A.D. 193, their fortieth day, they reached Rome. Severus commanded his troops to enter the city, in violation of tradition, in full battle dress, while only he changed into civilian clothes to fit tradition. Upon learning of their arrival, the Praetorian Guard deserted their fearful leader, leaving him trembling and alone in the palace.

A dozen ordinary soldiers led Didius Julianus to the baths of the royal palace as he implored, "What harm have I done? Have I put anybody to death?" This made the soldiers laugh as they threw him down and cut off his head.

Didius Julianus had spent a fortune to become emperor and had reigned for only sixty-six tormented days.

AFTERMATH: Septimius Severus became the next emperor of Rome.

 DECEMBER 29, 1170

THOMAS BECKET (CA. 1118–1170)
ARCHBISHOP OF CANTERBURY
FROM 1162 UNTIL HIS ASSASSINATION

Thomas Becket was raised in a household of genial freedom and Norman refinement. His father, a London official, frequently invited barons and clerks to their home. His devout mother weighed Thomas every year on his birthday against money, clothes, and provisions, which she would then donate to the poor. As a young man, Thomas attended the University of Paris, then returned to London, where he fully enjoyed life with other youthful nobles. He was tall, handsome, bright-eyed, ready of wit and speech, and his firmness of temper was exhibited during various sporting activities. When his father lost his wealth, Thomas went to work in the court of Archbishop Theobald and soon became his confidant. At that time, Henry II, upon the death of his father, had become ruler of Normandy and Anjou, as well as Aquitaine, acquired by his marriage to Eleanor of Poitou. As Archbishop Theobald's agent, Thomas Becket played an integral role in the affairs of the church and became closely acquainted with Henry II.

By the time Henry, at age twenty-one, became King of England, a great friendship had developed between Thomas Becket and Henry. As Archbishop Theobald described it, the two men had "but one heart and mind." Henry would joke around with Becket in the chancellor's hall and would tear the cloak from his shoulders in horseplay as they rode through the streets. Although Henry trusted Becket, there is no evidence that Becket influenced Henry's decisions about reorganization of the government. When Henry was forced to go to battle to protect his lands, Becket served as head of seven hundred knights and fought bravely for his friend the king. In time, Becket was named chancellor, and when Archbishop Theobald died, it seemed natural to the king for Becket to become archbishop of Canterbury.

King Henry's decision was not made on friendship alone, but in the belief that he would have an advantage with the church because Becket would favor his desires.

When Henry first proposed to his friend that he become archbishop of Canterbury, Becket laughed at the suggestion. He pointed out that the king was asking him to surrender his luxurious attire to wear a monk's robe. Henry insisted it was best for the country. Becket responded, "You will soon hate me as much as you love me now, for you assume an authority in the affairs of the church to which I shall never assent." Still, Henry went ahead and forced the monks of Canterbury to elect Thomas Becket their archbishop in June 1162.

ASSASSINS: Four knights by the names of Reginald Fitzurse, Hugh de Morville, William Tracy, and Richard Vriton.

HISTORY: Thomas Becket changed overnight, taking seriously his duties as archbishop of Canterbury. Although he disliked the constitution Henry wished to implement because it would give the king power over the church's court matters, at first Becket agreed to it. But soon Becket found it necessary to excommunicate dissolute nobles, particularly a tenant-in-chief who encroached on Canterbury lands, and he protected a church clerk charged with assaulting a royal officer. It became clear to Becket that the new constitution was not in the best interest of the church, and he renounced his support of the king's plan.

With this act, the friendship between Becket and Henry was broken, and a battle of wills began between the two men. The king was furious and tried to bring charges against the archbishop. Becket fought back vehemently, further inciting the king's fury against him. Word came to Becket that his life was in danger, and he was urged to submit to the king's wishes. Becket's newfound belief in the church inspired his courage. Holding out his cross in front of the royal court, Becket declared that the noblemen had no power to condemn him and the pope would support him in his resistance. As Becket left the royal chamber, shouts of

"Traitor! traitor!" could be heard. He stopped and turned, fiercely responding, "Were I a knight, my sword should answer that foul taunt!" That night he left for France, knowing his life was truly in danger.

Becket lived in exile in France for six years, but the feud between the archbishop and the king continued. In 1170, King Henry II, fearing excommunication, planned the coronation of his son, Richard Coeur de Lion. With the archbishop of Canterbury still in exile, he asked the archbishop of York to conduct the ceremony. By this time, Pope Alexander III had established a more powerful position in Italy, had heard enough of this feud between Archbishop Becket and King Henry II, and declared to the king that he must submit to a peace between the two men. Becket and Henry were reconciled by the pope and the archbishop was allowed to return to England.

The people flocked around Becket upon his return to Canterbury, welcoming him home. His clerks, who had been with him in France for six years, declared happily, "This is England." But Becket knew well the character of his former friend King Henry and replied, "You will wish yourself elsewhere before fifty days are gone."

Even though Archbishop Becket had been warned that the king would have him killed, he was as aggressive as ever, opposing Henry II on one matter after another. Finally, the king exploded in rage, "What cowards have I about me, that no one will rid me of this lowborn priest?"

EVENT: Becket was right. Already orders had been issued in the name of the king's son for Becket's arrest. Four knights who became outraged during one of the king's tirades about the archbishop went to Canterbury to confront Becket. They forced their way into his chamber and engaged him in an argument. When Becket rebuffed them, the knights left to get their weapons. Becket's clerks persuaded him to hide in the cathedral, but as he reached the steps leading to the choir loft, the knights burst in from the cloisters.

"Where," cried Reginald Fitzurse in the dusk of the dimly lit cathedral, "where is the traitor, Thomas Becket?" Becket stopped and turned to them, "Here am I, no traitor, but a priest of God." He descended the steps and stood with his back against a pillar to confront the knights. "You are our prisoner," shouted Fitzurse, and the four knights grabbed him to drag him from the church. "Do not touch me, Reginald," shouted Becket, roughly shaking off the knight's grasp. "Strike, strike," yelled Fitzurse, slashing the archbishop with his sword. Blow after blow by the four knights' swords forced Becket to the floor. "Let us be off," Fitzurse shouted triumphantly. "This traitor will never rise again."

AFTERMATH: The brutal murder of Archbishop Thomas Becket caused a dramatic reaction among the religious. Miracles were said to have occurred at the martyr's tomb, and he was canonized by the church as Saint Thomas Becket in 1173. He became the most popular saint in English history.

CHRONICLE: Still fearing excommunication four years later, in 1174, Henry II did penance at Canterbury for the assassination of Thomas Becket—even though he continued to deny any responsibility for the murder, insisting he had not called for Becket's death but simply had asked a rhetorical question, which his knights misinterpreted. Under the pope's orders, Henry walked barefoot in a pilgrim's gown and hair shirt through the streets of Canterbury to Becket's tomb in the cathedral. There, after confessing and asking for a pardon, King Henry II bared his back, allowing all the monks at Canterbury to lash him seven times each, giving him hundreds of welts.

Even 350 years after his death, the resentment toward Becket by the English throne was still so strong that Henry VIII attempted to malign him once and for all. He ordered that Saint Thomas Becket's skeleton be brought before England's Star Chamber, where Becket was accused of usurping papal authority. After a formal trial and defense at public expense, Becket was convicted of treason. His bones were then publicly burned "to admonish the living of their duty to the crown."

 JULY 10, 1584

WILLIAM OF NASSAU (1533–1584)
PRINCE OF ORANGE

William, prince of Orange, was a brilliant but cautious man, called "the Silent" because of his discretion and careful thought before speaking about anything. William the Silent proved to be a resourceful general, as well as an able diplomat. While he earned the love of the Dutch people with his wholehearted patriotism, he became an enemy of Philip II, king of Spain, who offered a reward for William's assassination.

ASSASSIN: Balthazar Gerard.

HISTORY: One of the wealthiest men in the Netherlands, William the Silent possessed lands in southern France and in the British Empire, as well as in the Netherlands. Although a German, he had been governor of the provinces of Holland and Zeeland and somewhat a leader in a growing Calvinist (Protestant) religious movement, which opposed Catholic Spanish rule. The Netherlands at the time was a country divided by religious beliefs, with United Netherlands to the north and Spanish Netherlands to the south. In 1566, the Calvinist underground movement erupted in riots that destroyed monasteries, statues, stained-glass windows, and other symbols of Catholicism. The magnificent cathedral at Antwerp was virtually gutted. Although the riots were bringing political change, William wanted nothing to do with this violence. He surrendered his land to Spain, even leaving his own estates to be confiscated by the Spanish governor, and retired to Germany.

In an effort to take control of the chaos, Spain's King Philip II sent his emissary, the duke of Alva, to form a tribunal, which became known as the Council of Blood. Almost anyone suspected of being opposed to Spanish rule was charged with treason and executed. It is estimated that as many as 8,000 persons were executed, 30,000 were relieved of their property, and 100,000 left the country. An enormous tax of 10 percent was levied on all merchandise sold. Some goods, such as cloth, were taxed at every level of production; taxes sometimes added up to as much as 70 percent by the time of final sale. Many Flemish manufacturers were put out of business.

When word of the Spanish tyranny reached William in Germany, it became clear that the Netherlands needed him. He returned to lead a popular movement against the Spanish, vowing to protect Dutch citizens accused of heresy and marked for extermination by the Spanish Inquisition.

William's twelve-year battle against the Spanish began in 1569. He proved to be a formidable opponent, not easily defeated on the battle-field, at sea, or diplomatically. The support of the people of the Netherlands for William steadily increased, and King Philip decided he must take drastic measures. In 1581, Philip published a ban against William, declaring him to be a traitor and an outlaw, and offered a reward of 25,000 crowns (the equivalent of one million dollars) to any-one who would take the prince's life.

William the Silent replied with an "apology" to the charges against him, but at the same time he persuaded the representatives of the north-ern provinces of the Netherlands, assembled at the Hague, to officially renounce any allegiance to the king of Spain, break the royal seal of Philip II, and declare that Philip was deprived of all authority over them. This landmark document was, in essence, the Dutch declaration of inde-pendence, saying that any ruler who destroys the liberty of his subjects and treats them as slaves is not legitimate and can lawfully be deposed.

William miraculously survived numerous assassination attempts, but the generous reward offered by Philip inspired many would-be assas-sins. Shortly after he announced the Act of Abjuration, the assassination attempts began to hit their target.

ATTEMPT OF MARCH 1582: Jean Jaureguy armed himself with a pistol, prayed for God's assistance, pledging to donate a portion of the reward for God's work, went to Antwerp and shot William in the head. Jaureguy was promptly killed by William's aides. Although William survived, it was only after hovering on the brink of death for weeks. William's wife, Charlotte, was his devoted nurse during a slow recovery, but the strain of the ordeal took its toll on her. She suffered from exhaustion and fever, and died before William had made a full recovery.

ATTEMPT OF JULY 1582: A plot was devised by two conspirators to poison William and his ally the duke of Anjou. Before it could be set in motion, the plan was uncovered, and the conspirators were both arrested. One killed himself in his jail cell; the other stood trial and was convicted, then drawn and quartered.

ATTEMPT OF MARCH 1583: An ambush attempt was made on William, and although it failed, he felt unsafe in Antwerp and immediately moved his headquarters to Delft.

ATTEMPT OF APRIL 1584: Assassins who had followed William to Delft tried to kill him with explosives. Their attempt failed, and they were executed.

EVENT: Balthazar Gerard, a twenty-year-old religious zealot from Bergundy, went to see Spain's governor of the Netherlands, Alexander Farnese, duke of Parma. Gerard offered to kill William the Silent but said he needed a small amount of money to pay the expenses for his venture. Farnese did not believe the young man could complete the task and said no to the advance, but promised that if Gerard was successful the entire reward would be paid to him.

On July 10, 1584, Gerard went to William's court in Delft. According to one version of the story, Gerard claimed to be an impoverished supporter of William, and the prince gave him alms of twelve crowns. Another version says that Gerard went to William's court requesting a passport. Either way, after making his appearance in William's court,

Gerard pretended to leave, but instead, he hid in a small room in the palace. When William entered the room, Gerard shot him. The prince's guards ran toward him as William said, "My God, have pity on my soul! My God, have pity on these poor people!"

William of Orange was fifty-one years old when he was silenced forever.

PUNISHMENT: Gerard tried to escape but was captured and quickly taken from the palace to prison. There he was tortured: his joints were dislocated on a rack, and his body was "seamed and scarred with flames." Later, the assassin was further tortured during his execution but showed no emotion.

While being taken to the scaffold, Gerard seemed not to be concerned that it was the tradition of the time to first destroy the hand that had committed the regicide. A huge crowd watched as the assassin's right hand was burned off with a red-hot iron. Not even a groan escaped his lips, even though the pain must have been excruciating. His flesh was then torn in six different places with red-hot pincers. Next, his abdomen was cut open so that his bowels could be torn out. His legs and arms were chopped off as closely as possible to the trunk of his body. As the story is told, still Gerard was alive. He stopped breathing only after his heart was cut out and thrown in his face. The final act of the executioners was to sever the assassin's head from his body.

AFTERMATH: The full reward was paid to Gerard's parents. Dutch Catholics celebrated the assassination of William the Silent, the man who had led the twelve-year battle against their people, during which priests had died and churches had been desecrated. The assassin's head was secured and sent to Cologne as a precious relic, and for the next fifty years Dutch Catholics tried unsuccessfully to have Gerard declared a saint.

 JULY 1762

PETER III (1728–1762)
CZAR OF RUSSIA FOR SIX MONTHS DURING 1762

Peter III was actually the son of Peter I's eldest daughter, Anne, but he was adopted in 1741 by his aunt Elizabeth, empress of Russia, who had no children of her own. Elizabeth wanted Peter to have children, and knowing that he was a weak-willed young man who would someday take her place as ruler, she probably wanted him married to a strong woman. When Peter was sixteen years old, his marriage to his seventeen-year-old cousin, Sophia-Augusta (who changed her name to Catherine), was arranged by Elizabeth and Frederick the Great, King of Prussia (who wanted to minimize Austria's influence at Petrograd). But Elizabeth underestimated Peter's childishness, as well as Catherine's desire for power. As it turned out, the marriage that was to ensure Peter a successful reign led to his demise.

ASSASSIN: Alexei Orlov, the brother of Catherine's lover, Grigori, who acted at her instigation.

HISTORY: When Peter and Catherine were married, although she was not Russian, but a German princess from the small principality of Anhalt-Zerbst, she immediately set out to win the favor of the Russian people. She learned the Russian language, obviously conformed to the Russian Orthodox Church, and exhibited lofty patriotism. It had been made clear to Catherine by Elizabeth that she was expected to produce children, but Peter III did not, or could not, cooperate. At first, Catherine supposedly contemplated suicide, then she decided to occupy her time with reading and horseback riding, but eventually she began to take lovers. By some accounts, Peter III was impotent and sterile, his impotence supposedly due to a malformed penis and remedied, as the story goes, when his friends got him drunk and persuaded him to have corrective surgery. In any event, after ten years of marriage and two miscarriages, Catherine finally gave birth to a son, although her lover, Sergei Saltykov, a young Russian nobleman, is believed to have been the father. Peter was reported to have said, "I don't know how it is that my wife becomes pregnant."

By the time Elizabeth died and Peter III took the throne in 1762, he was believed to be half insane, and Catherine was looked to as the real ruler of Russia. Although Peter III was the grandson of Peter the Great, he had no special affection for the Russian people and quickly alienated most of Russian society, including the aristocracy, the Russian Orthodox Church, and the imperial guards, through his ineptitude, inflexibility, and self-involvement. During his six-month reign, he exhibited the mental traits of a seventeen-year-old even though he was thirty-four, and spent his time playing with toy soldiers and flaunting his liaisons with whores and mistresses, perhaps in retaliation for his wife's sexual exploits.

After Peter took the throne, Catherine was convinced that her husband was going to divorce her and send her into exile in Siberia. Further, although she had by then become very popular with the Russian people, Peter's insanity seemed to threaten her chances of ever becoming their actual ruler. Catherine decided she must take control of the situation and planned a coup d'etat, with the help of her lover, Count Grigori Orlov, and his two brothers, all officers in the horse guard.

In June 1762, Peter traveled from the capital of Saint Petersburg to his palatial lodgings in Oranienbaum, accompanied by his favorite whore, Lizanka. Believing her time was running out, Catherine took this opportunity to make her move. She dressed in a lieutenant's uniform, rode into the capital leading a detachment of the imperial horse guard, and declared that she was empress and ruler. Approval was quickly given by the Senate, the church, and, of course, the palace guard, who proceeded to Oranienbaum to arrest Peter and inform him that he had been ousted. Although he formally abdicated his throne to his wife, he was shattered by this loss of power and sent groveling letters to Catherine from Ropsha, where he was confined, begging for his pet monkey, his violin, and his mistress, Lizanka. Catherine sent the monkey and the violin to Peter, but she sent Lizanka to a Siberian prison.

EVENT: In July of 1762, Catherine the Great, now empress of Russia, decided it was time to permanently dispose of the embarrassment she called a husband. Alexei Orlov, the brother of her lover, Grigori, was sent to complete the task. He traveled to Ropsha, entered the quarters of the deposed ruler, now called Peter the Mad, and visited with the immature Peter. They drank a while, and when Peter was good and drunk, Alexei strangled him.

AFTERMATH: Catherine gave huge cash endowments to Alexei and Grigori as a reward for their loyalty and for the assassination. Although Grigori Orlov remained Catherine's lover for many years, and they had three children together, she refused to marry him because she did not want to end the Romanov dynasty. Grigori retaliated by making a harem of Catherine's ladies of the court. Finally, he went too far, seducing Catherine's thirteen-year-old cousin, and he was subsequently refused access to the empress. Grigori went slowly mad, haunted by the ghost of Peter III, and died completely insane.

Catherine became famous throughout Europe for her sexual exploits and her ambition for her country. Indeed, during her reign, Russian territory was expanded by more than 200,000 square miles (although it was at the expense of the farmers who inhabited the lands), and the work of Peter the Great was consummated as Russia became a truly great power. An administrative system was enacted that divided the country into districts with a governor in each and who reported to a central government. Church property was divided among the various religious organizations, breaking up the power of the clergy. Catherine made a concerted effort to make Russia appear cultured in the eyes of Europe. She established schools and academies and encouraged the speaking of French in polite society. Criminals were no longer tortured but were exiled to Siberia as capital punishment. She took a personal interest in literature and science, corresponded with scholars and philosophers throughout Europe, and invited them to her court. She pensioned Diderot, the author of the great encyclopedia, and pretended to promote education for the masses, though it was the upper class that benefited, rather than the common people. Still, at the time of her death in 1796, Catherine had transformed Russia into a great power.

 JULY 13, 1793

JEAN PAUL MARAT (1743–1793)
FRENCH REVOLUTIONARY LEADER AND JOURNALIST

Jean Paul Marat was a hero to the revolutionary crowds of Paris. As editor of the journal *L'Ami du peuple (Friend of the People)*, he advocated extreme violence and was considered the most merciless of the three primary leaders of the French Revolution, which resulted in hundreds of so-called traitors of the revolution being sent to their deaths.

Before becoming interested in politics, Marat was a scientist and a man of letters. A physician by profession, he was well respected in the field of medicine as well as for making contributions to the science of physics. While living in Great Britain for several years, he became aware of the political inequity of the ruling class's pretending to represent the masses while promoting narrow class interests. He became convinced that reform was necessary so that all the people could benefit from ruling-class decisions, and that change would come only by direct popular action. Returning to France, he became editor of the revolutionary newspaper *L'Ami du peuple* and used its pages to launch a campaign against the court, the clergy, the nobles, and even the bourgeois members of the French governing body, the Assembly. He was totally focused on the cause of revolution, sacrificing everything for the good of the downtrodden, even suffering personal poverty, misery, and persecution. At one time, he was forced to hide out in cellars and sewers, where he contracted a loathsome skin disease that would plague him for the remainder of his life. Still he persisted, and by 1792 he was revered by the common people of Paris and hated by the authorities.

ASSASSIN: Charlotte Corday (Marie Anne Charlotte Corday D'Armnot), an attractive twenty-five-year-old Girondin patriot from Saint Saturnin, France, who became incensed by the slaughter of innocent victims of the revolutionary movement by the Jacobins.

HISTORY: In 1787, France's working class was suffering the effects of an economic crisis. Typical workdays were fourteen to sixteen hours, yet the pay was too low for most people to buy the basic food, bread, which cost 60 percent of the average person's wages. The French Parliament in Paris presented King Louis XVI with a list of grievances from the peasants and townspeople, but the king's response was less than enough to appease the hungry people, who were convinced that the king and the aristocracy were profiting at the people's expense. A revolution was in the making as angry working people joined one of the various organizations that were trying to take control of the government and food supply. Violent skirmishes led to all-out war within the country as the two main revolutionary groups, the Girondists and the Jacobins, organized and armed themselves against their oppressors.

Although the French Revolution (1789–1799) began in an attempt to create a constitutional monarchy that would give equal power to Assembly members representing the people and the royal rulers, it did not work out that way. Riots were commonplace in Paris, where starving citizens banned together against the monarch. In 1789, the French Assembly adopted a Declaration of the Rights of Man, entitling every citizen to liberties similar to those instituted by the English Bill of Rights (1689) and the U.S. Declaration of Independence (1776). Fearing for their lives, the royal family attempted to escape the country on June 20, 1791, but King Louis XVI was brought back from Varennes, held as a prisoner, and forced to accept the new constitution. By 1792, the monarchy was essentially abolished, and the First Republic of France was established. King Louis XVI was tried, declared guilty by a vote of 683 to 38, and instead of being banished or imprisoned, he was beheaded on January 21, 1793, cheered on by Jean Paul Marat and his leftist friends, members of the Jacobin and Cordeliers clubs.

With Louis XVI out of the picture, the crisis intensified. Not only were the Girondists and the Jacobins fighting each other for control, but France was at war with other countries, many were a result of displaced French nobles forming alliances with neighboring governments and their troops.

Jean Paul Marat, who became known as the strong arm for the Jacobins, was arrested by the Girondists and brought to trial. When he was acquitted on April 24, 1793, he immediately set out with his Jacobin coleaders, Georges Jacques Danton and Maximilien François Marie Isidore de Robespierre, to weed out any threat to the new government and to overthrow the Girondists. A Committee of Public Safety was formed by the Jacobins, with Marat at its head, and a bloody Reign of Terror began. On May 30, 1793, most Girondist leaders were either arrested or forced to flee for their lives. Tens of thousands of citizens—anyone who was even suspected of being a traitor—were executed. Although the guillotine had become the official executioner's tool of the Assembly of France in 1789, it was used only on 10 percent of the traitors, mostly nobility. The other 400,000 people slaughtered during the Reign of Terror were mostly shot, burned, or drowned.

Most Girondists fled to the outer province of Normandy. There, word spread quickly that the Jacobin Reign of Terror was threatening to exterminate everyone in its path unless someone could eliminate Jean Paul Marat. Charlotte Corday was incensed. She strongly identified with the intensely bourgeois Girondists and had been in favor of the constitutional monarchy. She became very upset when King Louis XVI tried to escape the country in 1791, and she was appalled when he was executed in 1793. This recent news about the Reign of Terror was the final insult to Corday's beliefs. She decided that since no one else had done it, she was going to stop Jean Paul Marat.

EVENT: Corday walked the two hundred miles to Paris. On the afternoon of July 13, 1793, she went to the home of Jean Paul Marat and asked to have a brief interview with him in order to render a great service for the country of France. Unknown to Marat's close companions, Corday was immediately turned away. She returned later that evening and demanded to see Marat. This time he agreed to see her.

Corday saw Marat, the bare-chested fifty-year-old hero of the masses, soaking in a medicinal bath to ease the discomfort of his festering skin condition and wearing a vinegar-soaked bandanna around his head to relieve his headaches. He was writing with a quill pen on papers atop a plank of wood set across the middle of a rusty old bathtub of water—he often worked in this way. Sitting nearby on the floor of his squalid room were two loyal female companions. They were folding copies of Marat's popular hand-printed newspaper, *L'Ami du peuple,* dated July 14—Bastille Day. This was a commemorative issue on the fourth anniversary of the day the French monarchy was toppled.

Corday, an aloof virgin with an alluring, somewhat horsy face and retiring backcountry gentlewoman manners, approached Marat, explaining that she had just come from the city of Caen. There, she told Marat, a number of his enemies, exiled leaders of the Girondists, were organizing an armed assault on Paris, and she began to list their names. Marat motioned for Corday to sit on a stool next to the bathtub and wrote down the names of Corday's fictional traitors as she said them. When she was finished, Marat put down the pen, smiled at Corday, and assured her that he would have the traitors sent to the guillotine in a few days.

Corday's gray eyes blazed as she pulled a six-inch butcher knife out of a sheath hidden under her stylish white muslin summer dress. Before Marat could react, Corday plunged the knife deep into his chest, cleanly penetrating a lung and cutting into the aorta. She pulled the blade out of her victim and dropped the bloody knife onto his writing board.

Marat's blood was turning his bathwater deep red by the time his companions cornered his assailant as she tried to escape the room. Upon hearing the commotion, a porter came running, knocked Corday down with a chair, and tied her hands behind her back with a handkerchief. Soon the police and Marat's Jacobin associates arrived to question the pale, totally composed twenty-five-year-old assassin, who said, "Having seen civil war on the verge of blazing out all over France, and persuaded that Marat was the principal author of this disaster, I preferred to make a sacrifice of my own life in order to save my country."

PUNISHMENT: At her trial, Corday got little help from the Girondists who had never heard of her before Marat's assassination. Despite attempts to humiliate her in court by tearing away her dress to expose her breasts to all those attending, Corday met her death on July 17 with womanly virtue. However, it is said that after her head was chopped off and fell into a basket, an attendant lifted it by the hair and slapped her across the face.

AFTERMATH: The assassination of Marat did not accomplish what Corday had hoped. The Reign of Terror thrived as the Committee of Public Safety fought domestic and foreign enemies. Only after the execution of Danton and Robespierre by guillotine in 1794 did the Reign of Terror stop and the National Convention get on with the work of drawing up a new constitution for the country of France. The final count of lives that were sacrificed during the French Revolution numbers in the hundreds of thousands, but the Revolution preserved France, and France was preserved in Europe.

 MARCH 24, 1801

PAUL I (1754–1801)
CZAR OF RUSSIA

Paul I succeeded to the throne following the death of his mother, Catherine the Great, and immediately set out to wipe away any memory of her by destroying statues, paintings, and coins that contained her image. As a ruler, Paul was a petty tyrant who was considered mentally unstable, and he pursued an erratic foreign policy that was detrimental to the great Russian empire his mother had built.

ASSASSINS: A group of military and civil officials, headed by Count Nikita Panin, the vice-chancellor, Count Peter von Palen, the governor-general of Saint Petersburg, and General Leonty Leontyevich, with the blessing of the czar's son and heir, Alexander.

HISTORY: After having her husband, Peter III, assassinated in 1762 so she could rule Russia, Catherine the Great was so busy establishing the great Russian empire and philandering about with her sexual partners that she evidently had little time or energy to devote to her son Paul. The neglected young man was never allowed to participate in government affairs, and by all reports Catherine never intended for him to become czar, planning instead to name Paul's son Alexander to succeed her. For whatever reason, this never happened, and when Catherine died in 1796, at age sixty-seven, after suffering a massive stroke, her forty-two-year-old son became Czar Paul I.

Upon taking the throne, Paul's disdain for his mother compelled him to attempt to undo much of the work she had done. Politically, he reversed many of Catherine's policies in an attempt to strengthen his own power and limit the authority of the nobles, and he alienated most of the army by insisting on harsh discipline. His cruelty toward peasants shocked even his devoted supporters, and his inability to maintain consistency in foreign relations threatened the peace. By 1800, he had managed to get Russia into a real mess. The country was officially at war with Napoleon, unofficially at war with England, not on speaking terms with Austria, and preparing to invade India.

About this time, Paul's military and political advisers came to their wits end and decided they had to get rid of this insanity they called a czar. Count Nikita Panin, Count Peter von Palen, General Leonty Leontyevich, who headed the committee plotting Paul's assassination, did not want to be in disfavor with Paul's son and successor, Alexander, so they approached him with their plan, asked his approval, and got it.

Perhaps Paul suspected an assassination attempt was in the works, or maybe not. In any event, he moved from the Winter Palace to Saint Michael's Castle outside Saint Petersburg. Inside the gloomy castle, Paul felt totally safe, as it was a seemingly impregnable fortress of massive gray stones surrounded by a moat. Outside, a large contingent of Paul's favorite Gatchina regiment guards patrolled the castle's five draw-bridges. What Paul may not have figured was that his assassination might be plotted by some of the most powerful men in Russia, who would have no trouble bribing the guards to sacrifice the czar.

EVENT: On the night of March 24, 1801, only one loyal guard remained, an elderly hussar who slept in front of Paul's bedroom. Upon being approached by the nine assassins, he challenged their intrusion but was swiftly cut down by their swords. When they burst into Paul's room, where he was sleeping fully dressed in his uniform and boots, he quickly awakened, jumped to his feet, and desperately fought for his life with the closest defense he could grab, a chair that he used to block sword-thrusting attackers. Paul was easily maneuvered against a window where, trapped and pleading for his life, he promised to abdicate or, better yet, to make all his attackers princes of the realm and endow them with grand estates. The offer stopped them for a moment as they considered their options, but then one man shouted, "We have passed the Rubicon. If we spare his life, before the setting of tomorrow's sun we shall be his victims." That said, a sash was produced and Paul was strangled to death.

AFTERMATH: The assassins quietly left the castle and went home. Alexander became czar, and none of the assassins was ever punished.

 APRIL 14, 1865

ABRAHAM LINCOLN (1809–1865)
SIXTEENTH PRESIDENT OF THE UNITED STATES, FROM 1861–1865

Born in a log cabin in Kentucky, Abraham Lincoln was self-educated; he began practicing law in Springfield, Illinois, in 1836. He was elected to the state legislature in 1834, served ten years there and became known as Honest Abe. In 1856, he joined the new Republican party and was elected U.S. president in 1860 by a minority vote.

ASSASSIN: John Wilkes Booth, a Confederate sympathizer and actor, had a strong attraction for real-life drama. His dark hair and mustache enhanced his handsome good looks and agility on stage, but he could not live up to the reputation of his insanely brilliant father, famed English Shakespearean actor Junius Brutus Booth, or his brother, noted actor Edwin Booth. John Wilkes Booth was a recruit in Colonel Robert E. Lee's Richmond Grays when the troops defeated John Brown at Harpers Ferry. But when Brown was hanged for treason on December 2, 1859, Booth became ill and shed his uniform, opting instead to help the cause of the Confederacy—and earn money for himself—by smuggling bandages, morphine, quinine, and other medicines from the North to the South.

HISTORY: In December 1860, South Carolina adopted an Ordinance of Succession in protest of Lincoln's election. The Civil War began officially in April 1861 when Lincoln refused to concede to Confederate demands that Union troops evacuate the federal garrison at Fort

Sumter, South Carolina. On September 22, 1862, Lincoln announced in his Emancipation Proclamation that, beginning in January of 1863, all black slaves in states still engaged in rebellion against the federal government would be emancipated. The Union victory at the Battle of Gettysburg in July of 1863 marked a decisive turning point in the war. Lincoln delivered his now-famous Gettysburg Address while dedicating a national cemetery there in November. In the election of 1864, running on a National Union ticket, Lincoln advocated a reconciliatory policy toward the South and was reelected by a large majority. In April 1865, General Robert E. Lee surrendered to General Ulysses S. Grant, ending the Civil War, but Lincoln's victory was short-lived. He was assassinated five days later.

LINCOLN'S FOREBODING DREAMS: While campaigning for his election as president, Lincoln had a startling vision. Preparing to lie down for a rest, he looked at his face in a mirror and saw a double image of himself. One face was pale, Lincoln said, "like a dead man's." A few days later, when the double image appeared again, Lincoln described it to his wife, who interpreted it to mean that he would serve two terms as president and die during his second term.

On the evening of April 11, 1865—three days before his assassination—President Lincoln and his wife were enjoying an evening of conversation with Colonel Ward H. Lamon, a lawyer and presidential aide, and two other friends, when the president began to describe a haunting dream he had had about ten days earlier. He spoke sadly of retiring very late after waiting for dispatches to arrive from the front. Feeling tired, he soon fell asleep and began to dream. Around him he felt a deathlike stillness, and then subdued sobs could be heard, as if a number of people were weeping. He rose from his bed and wandered downstairs, where the sobs grew louder, but no one was visible to him. He went from room to room, but still no one was in sight, though the mournful sounds followed him. He was puzzled and alarmed to see that each room contained objects familiar to him, and the sound of invisible people grieving as

Abraham Lincoln

NATIONAL PORTRAIT GALLERY, SMITHSONIAN INSTITUTION

though their hearts would break. Determined to find the source of the sounds, he continued on to the East Room and entered. There he came upon a sickening surprise: A corpse wrapped in funeral vestments was lying in a catafalque, with soldiers posted all around it. A large group of mourners, some weeping pitifully, were gazing upon the corpse, whose face was covered. He demanded of the soldiers, "Who is dead in the White House?" "The president," one answered. "He was killed by an assassin!" A loud burst of grief then came from the mourners, and Lincoln woke up from his dream. He was so disturbed by the vision that he could not sleep at all the rest of that night.

Lincoln was still troubled by that dream on the day of his assassination, when he described it again in a cabinet meeting, adding that he had seen himself "in an indescribable vessel and moving rapidly toward an indistinct shore."

EVENT: On April 14, 1865, as Good Friday and the end of the Civil War were being celebrated in Washington, D.C., President Lincoln's schedule was full. He worked in the Oval Office until 8 A.M., ate breakfast, received business callers, met with the cabinet at 11 A.M., ate lunch, conducted interviews in his office, took a brief drive with Mrs. Lincoln, met with friends from Illinois, and visited the War Department. An evening was planned at the fashionable playhouse, Ford's Theatre, where the Lincolns would watch a performance of *Our American Cousin*. When evening came, the president was tired and considered not going to the theater. But he remembered that Mrs. Lincoln had invited General and Mrs. Grant to be their guests, and it had been announced to the press that they would attend. At the last moment, Mrs. Grant, who had become annoyed by frequent hysterical outbursts by Mrs. Lincoln, canceled their plans but substituted the daughter of Senator Ira Harris and her fiancé, Major Henry Rathbone, to accompany the presidential couple.

John Wilkes Booth also had a full schedule on April 14, 1865. He began drinking at the Kirkwood House bar at three in the afternoon, then moved on to Deery's saloon, where he ordered a bottle of brandy at 4 P.M. Two hours later he was drinking whiskey at Taltavul's, next door to Ford's Theatre.

That evening, the presidential party went to the theater as planned, entered the building, and proceeded to a door leading to a small vestibule separating the presidential box from the first balcony. Earlier that day the president had asked the War Department to post a special guard in the vestibule at the theater for his protection, but his request was denied. Instead, a member of the Washington police force was to be posted outside the president's box. The door leading to the vestibule was supposed to be locked, but it was unsecured because the lock had been broken. Still, the presidential party went through the door into the vestibule, then proceeded through another set of doors to enter the box, making an official entrance in full view of the theater audience. The play, which had already begun because the Lincolns arrived an hour late, was stopped so that the president could be applauded as he entered the large, flag-adorned state box sitting twelve feet above and at the right end of the stage. Major Rathbone sat on a small plush couch, and the women, wearing billowing, stiff-hooped skirts, sat on simple armless wooden chairs. The bearded fifty-six-year-old president, wearing his usual plain black suit, sat in an upholstered black walnut rocking chair with his back to one of the two doors leading into the double box. No one seemed to notice that a peephole had been pierced in the door earlier that day.

When the performance resumed, the president's official protection, an alcoholic Washington policeman named John Parker, left his post outside the president's box door and went to a nearby tavern, leaving only Lincoln's coachman, Charles Forbes, outside the vestibule for security.

Shortly after 10 P.M., John Wilkes Booth left Taltavul's and headed toward Ford's Theatre. He stopped momentarily to get a chew of tobacco from a ticket taker he knew, then he was seen in the foyer by Jeannie Gourlay, an actress, who said he appeared ill and distraught, with an odd look in his eyes. Booth slipped unnoticed into the hallway leading to the presidential box, and upon encountering the president's coachman, Booth convinced him he was an official messenger and was allowed to pass. He entered the vestibule and blocked the entrance door with a long bar he had brought along for that purpose. He peered through the peephole he had drilled earlier that day in the door leading into the president's box. Seeing that the president was sitting in the box, Booth was ready to make his entrance, but he delayed, waiting for a particular moment in the third act of the play when an outrageous bit of comedy usually brought a laugh from the audience that would be loud enough to cover up the sound of his pistol shot. The laugh came, Booth opened the door directly behind the president, stepped inside the box, raised his brass derringer pistol five feet from Lincoln's head, and fired a lead ball into the back of the president's head just behind the left ear. As Lincoln slumped over, Booth took a moment in the spotlight, dropped the gun, and shouted, "*Sic semper tyrannis!*" ("Thus be it ever to tyrants!"), the official motto of Virginia, capital state of the Confederacy.

Major Rathbone jumped up and lunged toward Booth, who pulled out a knife and slashed the soldier's arm. Booth shouted, "The South is avenged!" He climbed up on the railing around the president's box and leaped from the box onto the stage, twelve feet below. In the process, Booth caught a spur on one of his boots in the decorative flag draped on the railing, throwing him off balance, so that when he landed, his left shinbone was fractured and he almost fell on his face. But he managed to keep his footing and hobbled offstage, dragging the broken leg. After exiting the theater into an alley, Booth mounted a horse he had waiting and rode away into the night.

Doctors rushed to the president's side and immediately saw that he was mortally wounded. He was carried across the street to a simple boardinghouse, where he hovered near death for nine hours. At one point, during the death vigil, Mrs. Lincoln became hysterical, and Edwin Stanton, the secretary of war, ordered her to leave the room. President Lincoln died at 7:22 A.M. on April 15, 1865. Stanton was heard to say, "Now he belongs to the ages."

CONSPIRACY THEORY: It soon became apparent to the authorities that Booth was not an insane lone gunman out to kill the president. Indeed, they believed there had been a conspiracy by Confederate sympathizers to wipe out the men holding top positions in the Union government, and that the plan was to kill not only Lincoln but also General Grant.

Booth had been boasting for some time about a plot that entailed kidnapping Lincoln and taking him to Richmond in chains, where he would become a pawn to get the North to recognize the Confederacy, stop the war, and return all Confederate prisoners. In fact, three weeks before the president was assassinated, Booth and a small group of con-spirators had been waiting to ambush the president's carriage but were disappointed when there was a change in Lincoln's schedule. After the fall of Richmond and Lee's surrender at Appomattox, Booth knew that the Confederacy was finished and that the only remaining course of action was for him to kill the president and Grant, while his coconspirators simultaneously did their part. Lewis Paine was to murder Secretary of State William Seward, and George Atzerodt would kill Vice-President Andrew Johnson.

At 10 P.M. on April 14, 1865, as Booth coolly set out to execute his part of the plan, Paine was across town entering the home of Seward, who was confined to his bed after a carriage accident. Paine savagely attacked Seward, but several deep knife wounds to the Secretary of State's face and neck were not fatal. Atzerodt, in another part of town, lost his nerve and decided not to kill Vice-President Johnson; he got drunk instead.

AFTERMATH: Booth rode his horse across the Potomac, unobtrusive in the confusion of soldiers being demobilized because of General Lee's surrender, and met up with another conspirator, David Herold. With Herold's help, Booth, who was by now in great pain, found a doctor—a Maryland physician named Samuel Mudd—to set his broken leg. The two men then crossed the river into Virginia, believing they had gotten away with assassinating President Lincoln.

Lincoln's body was carried by train from Washington, D.C., to his hometown of Springfield, Illinois. As the funeral train rolled westward, at each railway station a crowd of mourners gathered, displaying the most memorable outpouring of grief in the history of America to that date. Lincoln was buried in Springfield's Oak Ridge Cemetery.

Meanwhile, the president's assassin still had not been found, and the authorities were beginning to feel the pressure. On August 20, 1865, Secretary of War Edwin M. Stanton issued a wanted poster with photographs of Booth, Herold, and a third conspirator, John H. Surratt. It advertised a reward of $100,000 for all three conspirators or $50,000 for Booth alone and $25,000 for each of the others.

Although nearly two thousand people were arrested in connection with the investigation, most were quickly released. Finally, on April 26, 1865, Union troops cornered Booth and Herold in a tobacco shed on a farm outside Port Royal, Virginia. When the two fugitives were ordered to surrender or prepare to be burned out, Booth called out, "Let us have a little time to consider it." A few moments later Booth gave his answer, "I am a cripple. I have got but one leg; if you withdraw your men in one line one hundred yards from the door, I will come out and fight you."

The officer in charge refused Booth's request only to hear him call out, "Well, my brave boys, prepare a stretcher for me."

Soon the troops heard loud voices inside the shed arguing. "You damned coward, will you leave me now? Go, go; I would not have you stay with me," Booth said, then called out to the troops, "There's a man in here who wants to come out."

Herold emerged from the shed, shaking with fear. The troops got near enough to set the shed on fire and could see a dark figure hobbling around inside. Then they heard a shot. No one knows for sure whether it was Booth shooting himself or a soldier who claims to have shot Booth. In any event, the soldiers rushed the shed, went inside, retrieved Booth and pulled him from the burning building. As Booth lay paralyzed and dying from a bullet wound to the neck, his last words were, "Tell Mother I die for my country."

Booth's body was taken back to Washington and secretly buried in an old prison, but four years later it was returned to his relatives, who arranged for his burial in a family plot in Baltimore.

PUNISHMENT: After Booth's death, eight people were brought to trial before a military court for conspiracy in Lincoln's murder. They included: George A. Atzerodt (who got drunk instead of killing Vice-President Johnson, as planned); Lewis Paine (who had been assigned, along with Herold, to kill Seward); David Herold; Samuel Arnold; Michael O'Laughlin; and Edward Spangler, a stagehand at Ford's Theatre, all known companions of Booth. Also tried were Dr. Samuel Mudd, the physician who set Booth's leg, and Mary Surratt, the owner of a boardinghouse in Washington where the conspiracy was supposedly devised. A ninth person, John Surratt, the son of Mary Surratt, escaped the country. Also tried in absentia was Jefferson Davis, president of the Confederacy, who was already in prison.

The trial, from May 9 to June 30, was strongly influenced by postwar hysteria, resulting in something short of fair and impartial justice. John F. Parker, the Washington police officer who was supposed to have been guarding the presidential box but went drinking instead, was not called to testify. The only evidence that implicated Mary Surratt as a conspirator was given by a known liar and drunk. Still, all defendants were convicted on July 6, 1865. Spangler was given a six-year prison term. Dr. Mudd, Arnold, and O'Laughlin were sent to prison for life. Herold, Paine, Atzerodt, and Mary Surratt were hanged the next day, making Surratt the first woman in U.S. history to be hanged.

Mary's son John Surratt, who had escaped to Europe, was later captured in Italy, where he was serving in the Swiss Guard. By the time he was brought back to the United States for trial in 1867, the hysteria of 1865 had passed, and Surratt, tried before a jury instead of a military court, was found not guilty. John Surratt's trial seemed to illustrate the inequity of the original military trial. Michael O'Laughlin died in prison of yellow fever in 1867. Jefferson Davis was released from prison in 1868 and went overseas to tour Europe. By March of 1869 President Johnson had granted a pardon to Dr. Mudd and Samuel Arnold, the only two men still imprisoned for the conspiracy.

EPILOGUE: Major Rathbone, who fought Booth in the theater box the night of the assassination, and his companion, Clara Harris, were married, but he went mad, murdered her, and died in an asylum. Mary Lincoln lived in Springfield, Illinois, where she also went mad. She outlived three of her four sons and died in 1882.

After his assassination, Lincoln was enshrined as a martyr, and his reputation as one of the greatest presidents of all time was ensured, but he did not rest undisturbed. In 1876, a foiled attempt was made to steal his body for a $200,000 ransom. Lincoln's coffin was then hidden between the walls of his tomb for safekeeping. In 1900, the old tomb was torn down and replaced with a new one, and a burglar alarm was connected to the coffin. Still, Robert Lincoln worried that his father's grave would be robbed and ordered the remains to be buried in a hole ten feet deep inside the tomb and covered with twenty inches of concrete. Abraham Lincoln's final burial was September 26, 1901. Robert, who was not present, ordered that the coffin not be opened, but local officials had heard persistent rumors that Lincoln's remains were not in the coffin and decided to check. Inside the tomb twenty-three people gathered as workers pried open the lid. A pungent odor filled the room as the onlookers moved closer and saw the body of the former president. His skin had mysteriously turned black, and chalk applied to his face by the undertaker had taken on a grayish chestnut color. His clothes were mildewed, the French gloves on his hands had rotted away, but his beard, hair, and famous wart were preserved.

CONSPIRACY THEORIES: Various conspiracy theories regarding the assassination of President Abraham Lincoln have surfaced over the years.

One of the most controversial is contained in the 1977 book *The Lincoln Conspiracy*, by David Balsiger and Charles E. Sellier. The authors contend that Booth was not just working for the Confederacy but was being paid by a group of northern cotton and gold speculators and some radical Republicans, including Secretary of War Edwin Stanton. The group was determined to prevent Lincoln from implementing a moderate program of reconstruction for the South. Their idea was that if Booth could kidnap Lincoln, as well as Vice-President Johnson and Secretary of State Seward, they would have time to discredit the Lincoln administration and seize control of the government. The book claims the northern speculators removed from Booth's diary eighteen incriminating pages with key facts about their broad conspiracy. The authors claim to have found the pages. They also say that Booth had tried to kidnap Lincoln three times in 1865, and that after his third failure, he was fired and replaced by James William Boyd, a captured Confederate spy conveniently released from prison to kill President Lincoln. Being fired is said to have inspired Booth to move quickly and get to Lincoln first.

Although the body of the man killed in the Port Royal, Virginia, tobacco shed was officially identified as John Wilkes Booth, there are those who are convinced that it was, in fact, Captain Boyd, who resembled Booth. Some historians claim to have traced Booth to England or India after he supposedly died. Some claim the real Booth hid out for several months on his small farm in Harpers Ferry before traveling to Pennsylvania, Canada, and England. It was even reported that in 1900 a dying California man claimed to be John Wilkes Booth. Because of his claim, the mortician preserved his body instead of burying him, and the body is said to be part of a private collection today.

Stanton is the pivotal character in this conspiracy theory, as evidenced by the following facts. On the day of his assassination, President Lincoln had asked Stanton to give him special protection at the theater that night, but Stanton refused. Instead, John F. Parker, a Washington police officer, was assigned to the job, but he left his post during the play, giving Booth the opportunity to reach the president's box with little trouble. Parker was not dismissed or prosecuted for his breach of conduct, nor was he ever reprimanded. After the assassination, Booth was allowed to ride his horse across the Anacostia Bridge from Washington to Maryland without being questioned by troops posted there. Perhaps they did not know of the presidential shooting because the telegraph wires in Washington were crossed and out of commission for two hours, almost from the moment Booth entered the president's theater box. Boston Corbett, the Union soldier who claims to have shot Booth in the tobacco shed, is reported to have been in the exclusive service of Stanton. Corbett supposedly found the diary on Booth's body and gave it to Stanton instead of to investigators. When the diary was finally given to investigators, eighteen pages were missing.

Stanton has been described as a truculent, seething man who violently opposed Lincoln's plans for reconstruction of the South. After the assassination, it was Stanton who saw to it that the nine conspirators were speedily tried by a military commission, on the grounds that as commander in chief, Lincoln had died in actual service in a time of war. Stanton made sure Mary Surratt was hanged immediately, and he confiscated the only photo taken of Lincoln in his coffin and ordered that the master plate and all prints be burned (although one copy of the photo did resurface eighty-seven years later). Stanton also acted strangely in the handling of the case against John Surratt, the son of Mary. Several times while Surratt was a fugitive, authorities knew his whereabouts and reported them to Stanton, yet Stanton refused to have Surratt arrested. When Surratt was apprehended and returned to the United States in 1867, it was against the wishes of Stanton. At the subsequent trial, during which Surratt was acquitted, he was represented by adept lawyers who were friends of Stanton.

In 1866, a House select committee was formed to investigate the assassination of President Lincoln. One member, Congressman Andrew J. Rogers of New Jersey, filed a report accusing the government of falsifying evidence and testimony during the trial of the conspirators. A few years after Lincoln's assassination, when his son Robert was caught burning many of his father's papers in the fireplace, his explanation was "These papers contain the documentary evidence of the treason of a member of my father's cabinet. . . . It is best for all such evidence to be destroyed." Although Robert was in Washington the night his father was assassinated, he did not go with his parents to Ford's Theatre, but he said later that had he gone he might have been able to avert the violent act. Robert Lincoln would be on the scene when President Garfield was shot in 1881 and when President McKinley was assassinated in 1901.

 MARCH 13, 1881

ALEXANDER II (1818–1881)
CZAR OF RUSSIA FROM 1855 TO 1881

Alexander II enjoyed all the luxuries of the ruling class, but he was more liberal than his predecessors—his grandfather Paul I, son of Catherine the Great, had been assassinated in 1801 after only four years of insane rule. Alexander II partially emancipated the serfs (enslaved farmers) by allowing them to buy their own land, but he also made them pay huge taxes on that land. This and other reforms he prompted were viewed as feeble compared to the poverty and persecution still suffered by the common people. In response, numerous revolutionary organizations formed, some advocating violence, others nonviolent socialists, all outspoken against Alexander II's totalitarian rule.

ASSASSINS: Ignaty Grinevitsky and members of a populist group of terrorists, Narodnaya Volya (The Will of the People), commanded by Sophia Perovskaya.

HISTORY: In January 1878, General Trepov, the Saint Petersburg chief of police, was shot in an assassination attempt by Vera Zasulich, a young typesetter for the underground paper *Land and Liberty*, in retaliation for severe maltreatment of political prisoners. General Trepov survived to see his attacker's trial in March 1878 be turned into a vigorous indictment of police brutality. Vera Zasulich was acquitted and set free. Alexander II was furious. He immediately ordered that Zasulich be arrested again, but an enthusiastic crowd of antigovernment supporters helped her escape Russia and settle in Germany. Vera Zasulich's actions were considered heroic to other militant groups and inspired numerous plots to assassinate the czar himself.

ATTEMPTS: In August 1879, leaders of the militant group Narodnaya Volya (The Will of the People) set their plan in motion. They divided into two groups, disguised themselves as shopkeepers, and rented two buildings along the railway route traveled by the czar. By day they established businesses, by night they dug tunnels and planted explosives along the railway tracks. On November 18 two death traps had been prepared. The second, insurance if their first assassination attempt failed, was twenty-four hours down the railway line, where they were prepared to attack again.

As the czar's train approached the first death trap, members of the Narodnaya Volya waited for the signal from their respected leader, Andrei Zhelyabov, a born serf who was educated at the University of Odessa on a scholarship. The train rolled into position and the signal was given, but the explosives failed to detonate. Although Zhelyabov and his conspirators were disappointed, they sent word to commander Sophia Perovskaya at the backup death trap. She was told there were two trains in the imperial entourage heading their way, the first to test the safety of the tracks, the second believed to carry the czar.

Perovskaya and her comrades waited for the trains to arrive. As instructed, she allowed the first train to pass unharmed, then detonated the explosives, derailing the second train. Again the members of Narodnaya Volya were disappointed. Although the second train derailed, no one was seriously injured, and they discovered that the czar had actually been riding in the first train.

This setback did not dissuade the revolutionaries, who set in motion a series of elaborate assassination attempts during the next two years. The most dramatic attempt was a huge bomb exploded underneath the dining room of the Winter Palace, but the timing was miscalculated, and the bomb exploded minutes before the czar was to enter the dining room for his meal. Although the czar was lucky once more, nine soldiers were killed, and the czar's nervous advisers demanded that he not leave his quarters.

In 1880, when the empress died, sixty-one-year-old Czar Alexander immediately married his thirty-four-year-old mistress, Ekaterina. Alexander II and Ekaterina had first met when he was thirty-eight. One look at Ekaterina, the ten-year-old daughter of prince Mikhail Dolgorukiv, and Alexander was captivated. He took responsibility for her, having her educated in a school for young ladies on the Finnish coast, where he would visit her often. Ekaterina became the czar's mistress when she turned seventeen; he was forty-five. During the twenty-six years they were lovers, they had three children together.

After he married Ekaterina, being confined to the Winter Palace to preserve his safety became unacceptable to the czar. He revolted against his advisers, screaming at his guards, "I am a man. I will go and come as I please. I will eat and drink what I like, and do as I choose. If I am to be murdered in the end, that is the destiny which God himself has reserved for me. I have already lived longer than any of my race; as to death, I do not personally fear it."

EVENT: Sophia Perovskaya and her comrades in the Narodnaya Volya learned that the czar would be viewing a military parade in Saint Petersburg on March 13, 1881. Four men armed with bombs took up positions along the route the czar's carriage usually followed when traveling to or from the Winter Palace, while Perovskaya stood at the site of the parade. When she saw that the czar was taking an alternate route, Perovskaya instructed the assassins to hurry over to new positions on Nevsky Prospect near a bridge by the Michael Palace.

Once there, they hid among the crowd of people waiting to see the czar. As the carriage carrying the czar and his family came by, people began waving, and a nineteen-year-old student named Rysakiv, dressed as a peasant, pushed his way through the crowd, rushed forward, and tossed his bomb. It exploded behind the czar's carriage, shattering it, wounding several soldiers and killing two guards, an errand boy in the crowd, and several horses.

The czar was not harmed and emerged from the carriage to survey the wreckage. He began helping the wounded, but was told by guards to get into another carriage. Just then, Ignaty Grinevitsky ran toward the czar carrying a nitroglycerin bomb enclosed in a glass ball and threw it at the czar's feet. It landed squarely between Alexander's legs. Glittering snow and fragments of wood and glass rose into the air. The ground was dyed red with the czar's blood, the blood of the assassin, and twenty men either killed or wounded. The czar's legs were in shreds, one eyeball was blown from its socket, and his clothes were in tatters.

Grand Duke Michael rushed to the czar's side. "Cold . . . cold . . . to the palace, quick . . . die there," the czar said. The czar died a few hours

later at the Winter Palace, surrounded by his family, including his thirteen-year-old grandson, Nicholas, who would become the last czar of
Russia in 1895 and be assassinated in 1918.

PUNISHMENT: Ignaty Grinevitsky died from wounds inflicted by his
own bomb. The other principal conspirators were arrested, convicted,
and executed.

AFTERMATH: The revolution the conspirators had envisioned didn't
materialize after the czar's assassination, as the revolutionary organizations soon fell apart from lack of leadership. Government oppression
became worse when Alexander III turned Russia into one of the first
modern police states. A radical group tried to assassinate Alexander III
in 1887, but the attempt was aborted when the conspiracy was discovered. One of the conspirators who was hanged was Alexander Ilyich
Ulyanov, older brother of Vladimir Ilyich Ulyanov, who would become
known as Lenin.

During his reign, Alexander III made Jews the scapegoats for his
father's assassination. He vowed to kill a third of Russia's Jews, drive
another third out of the country, and convert the rest. As a result, millions of Jews emigrated from Russia during the following thirty years.

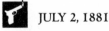 JULY 2, 1881

JAMES ABRAM GARFIELD (1831–1881)
TWENTIETH PRESIDENT OF THE UNITED STATES

Garfield served for only 199 days (a little more than six months) before
becoming the second president to be assassinated and the fourth president to die in office.

Born in a log cabin in the pioneer town of Orange, Ohio, Garfield did not let his boyhood poverty limit his future. He worked hard and graduated from college with honors, then went on to become a college president and lawyer. After joining the Republican party, he was elected to the Ohio Senate in 1859, where he denounced slavery and called for the preservation of the Union. In 1861, he volunteered to fight for the Union in the Civil War and was elevated to the rank of major general for his bravery in battle. By then a radical Republican, he was elected to the U.S. House of Representatives in 1862. He served as Republican minority leader in Congress from 1876 to 1880, when he was elected to the U.S. Senate. After serving four months as a senator, he was a compromise choice for president at the Republican National Convention and won a narrow victory at the polls in the November election. On that day, November 2, 1880, forty-nine-year-old James A. Garfield was a member of the House, a senator-elect, and president-elect all at the same time. On March 4, 1881, Garfield's mother was the first president's mother to attend her son's inauguration. During his short tenure as president, Garfield mostly occupied his time with power struggles within the Republican party and the appointment of cabinet posts.

ASSASSIN: Charles J. Guiteau was an unbalanced Chicago lawyer turned religious journalist, who believed Garfield would appoint him ambassador to France. When this did not happen, Guiteau claimed God told him to kill Garfield so that he could be replaced by Vice-President Chester Arthur.

GARFIELD'S PREMONITION OF DEATH: Some historians believe Garfield had a premonition that he would die in office. It is reported that two days before he was shot, Garfield asked Robert Lincoln, the son of the late president, to meet with him and recount any memories he had of the assassination of his father. Garfield listened intently as Robert Lincoln talked for over an hour.

James A. Garfield

HISTORY: During Horace Greeley's presidential campaign in 1872, Charles Guiteau was an active Democrat who became a familiar presence at campaign headquarters. He had handbills printed proclaiming himself "the Eloquent Chicago Lawyer," but in fact most people tried to avoid the nervous little man who was constantly composing speeches that no one would deliver—except Guiteau himself, to his wife, who had to endure long sessions of him practicing his diplomatic speeches. If Greeley were elected president, Guiteau believed that he would be appointed minister to Chile.

When Greeley lost the election, Guiteau became depressed for months. He shifted his allegiance from the Democrats to the Republicans and left his wife for a teenage prostitute. The 1880 presidential election was a hopeful time for Guiteau, who wrote a speech, "Garfield vs. Hancock," which he was certain would win Garfield the election. Guiteau had the speech printed at his own expense and gave it to as many Republicans as would take it. Although not one person, besides Guiteau, ever delivered the speech publicly, when Garfield was elected president, Guiteau was convinced that Garfield's victory was due to his speech. Guiteau was convinced, as well, that now he would be appointed ambassador to Austria or maybe consul to Paris. He wrote to Garfield saying that Secretary of State James Blaine had approved him for the Paris position, and at the same time wrote to Blaine saying that Garfield had approved him. When he received no response from the president or the secretary of state, Guiteau, feeling angry and abused, decided to kill the president.

Guiteau purchased a .44-caliber pistol and practiced shooting at trees along the Potomac. Then he started stalking the president. If he was not sure of Garfield's schedule on any given day, he would simply go to the White House doorman and ask where the president would be. One time he got close enough to shoot Garfield in church but decided against it because Mrs. Garfield was within range, and he believed her to be "a dear soul."

In July of 1881, Guiteau read in the newspaper that Garfield would be taking the train to his alma mater, Williams College, to deliver an address. This, he decided, was his chance.

EVENT: On July 2, 1881, Guiteau went to the Baltimore and Potomac railroad station and waited in the men's room until he heard that the presidential party had arrived. He left the men's room and stood behind a bench in the waiting room gripping his white bone-handle five-shot British bulldog pistol in his right hand. In his left hand was a note addressed to General William Sherman, asking for troops to protect the jail where he would be taken. Before long, President Garfield entered the room with Secretary Blaine and, as they walked by, Guiteau ran forward and fired at the president, missing the first time but hitting President Garfield in the back with a second shot.

Guiteau was grabbed by security guards and taken away to jail as Garfield was rushed from the scene, still alive. At first, the president was nursed at the White House, where doctors repeatedly probed the wound with nonsterile instruments, trying to locate and remove the bullet. Garfield lingered at the White House an agonizing two months as a result of blood poisoning, and when it was obvious that he would not recover, he asked to be moved from Washington to a summer resort cottage in Elberon, New Jersey, to enjoy the sea air with his family. During his long struggle for life, Garfield did not leave his sick bed, but it was never revealed by his aides whether he was "incapacitated" in the constitutional sense. President Garfield died at Elberon on September 19, 1881, and was buried in Cleveland, Ohio.

PUNISHMENT: Two months after Garfield's death, Guiteau was brought to trial and acted as his own defense attorney, often cursing at the judge and jury, accusing witnesses of being "dirty liars," and calling the prosecutor "a low-livered whelp" and an "old hog." At other times, he would show the utmost courtesy. When confined to his jail cell, he would strut back and forth so that crowds outside the building could gawk at him. In closing arguments, he told the jury that God had told him to kill Garfield. "Let your verdict be, in the Deity's act, not mine," he said.

Although he might have been ruled insane by today's judicial standards, he was judged a deluded religious zealot in 1881, found guilty of the murder of the president, and sentenced to be hanged. His response to the verdict: "You are all low, consummate jackasses!" he snarled, shaking an angry finger at the jury.

As his date of execution approached, although Guiteau seemed unrepentant and relaxed when awake, he constantly moaned while asleep and complained of having nightmares. On June 30, 1882, he ate a large meal and memorized a poem he had composed to recite on the scaffold. A crowd of spectators gathered outside, snacking on cake and drinking lemonade as they waited to witness the first execution of a presidential assassin—some had paid as much as three hundred dollars for the privilege of viewing the event. In his cell, Guiteau prepared himself to give a speech to an audience, at last. He brushed his hair and carefully trimmed his bushy beard, polished his black shoes to a high gloss, and gave a shrill whistle of satisfaction at their shine.

Just after 12:30 in the afternoon Guiteau walked to the scaffold, softly sobbing, while presenting a brave appearance. At the foot of the scaffold, he told witnesses he had shot the president by divine order of God. Once in position, with the noose ready to be placed around his neck, Guiteau was given the opportunity to speak. First saying, "I predict that this nation will go down in blood, and that my murderers from the executive to the hangman will go to hell," he then recited his poem:

> *I am going to the Lordy, I am so glad . . .*
> *I saved my party and my land; glory, hallelujah.*
> *But they have murdered me for it,*
> *and there is no reason*
> *I am going to the Lordy . . .*

As the hangman put the hood over his head, Guiteau was still talking. His last words before he was hanged, at 12:40 P.M., were "Glory, glory, glory."

AFTERMATH: President Garfield was succeeded by Vice-President Chester Alan Arthur, age fifty, who continued Garfield's policy of avoiding party favoritism in his appointments.

A large sum of money was collected by the friends of Garfield and given to his widow and five children. One son, James R. Garfield, would later become secretary of the interior in the administration of President Theodore Roosevelt, and a second son, Harry A. Garfield, became president of his father's alma mater, Williams College.

1901 – 1950s

 SEPTEMBER 6, 1901

WILLIAM McKINLEY (1843–1901)
REPUBLICAN POLITICIAN AND THE
TWENTY-FIFTH PRESIDENT OF THE UNITED STATES,
FROM 1897 TO 1901

Born in Niles, Ohio, William McKinley practiced law before entering politics. He was elected to Congress in 1876, served two terms as governor of Ohio beginning in 1892, and went on to become president largely because of his loyalty to business interests. This period of prosperity for the country was marred by its engagement in foreign conflicts—the Spanish American War in 1898 and the annexation of the Philippines— largely against the wishes of McKinley, although he did implement an open-door policy with China.

ASSASSIN: Leon Czolgosz, a twenty-eight-year-old Polish-American anarchist, whose difficult childhood because of his family's immigrant status turned him against the U.S. government. Czolgosz was born in Detroit in 1873 shortly after his parents arrived in the United States from Poland. His father worked in sewers to support the family, which eventually included eight children. Leon's childhood was normal, and although he was the best educated of his brothers and sisters, he began working at age sixteen in a bottle factory. Soon his family moved to

William McKinley

Cleveland, hoping for a brighter future. Leon got a job in a wire mill and was considered a good, steady worker whose earnings helped the family buy a fifty-one-acre farm.

A turning point and political awakening came in Leon's life in 1893 when the mill workers went on strike. He and his brother Waldek, his only friend, began to rebel against the Catholic church, which they decided had tormented them during their childhood. When Leon met a Cleveland upholsterer named Anton Zwolinski in 1894, he was ready to act on his changing beliefs. Zwolinski was a leader of a Polish educational group that openly discussed socialism and anarchism. Although Leon was a silent member of the discussion group, which met regularly, he had adopted the beliefs of anarchism: opposition to government, rulers, voting, religion, and marriage. In 1898, one of the most brutal and shameful incidents in American labor history occurred, deeply affecting Czolgosz. A large number of coal miners staging a peaceful protest in Mt. Olive,

Illinois, were massacred. In reaction, Czolgosz apparently had some kind of breakdown. He stopped working, retired to his family's farm, and sullenly spent his time reading and making pottery.

But in July of 1900, Leon Czolgosz was inspired by the actions of other anarchists, especially Gaetano Bresci, who was being glamorized in Czolgosz's mind by accounts of his actions in Italy. Bresci was an Italian-American weaver from Patterson, New Jersey, who saved his wages to travel to Italy. There, on July 19, 1900, Bresci watched as Humbert I, king of Italy, stood on a carriage distributing prizes to athletes at Monza, near Milan. When his chance came, Bresci calmly stepped forward, pointed his revolver, and shot the king four times. The elimination of a tyrannical monarch who had treated his subjects and associates as slaves during his twenty-two-year reign was seen by many members of Italian political parties as a necessary and humanitarian sacrifice. Leon Czolgosz saw Bresci as some kind of hero. Bresci was sentenced to life in prison but served only a short time before committing suicide.

HISTORY: Leon Czolgosz decided to go to Chicago, where he would become more active in anarchist circles. But soon he had alienated the members of Chicago's anarchist organizations, as he had those of the Liberty Club in Cleveland, because of his ignorance of libertarian literature, his anti-authoritarianism, and his indiscreet questions about violence and assassination. In August of 1891, a warning was published in *Free Society,* an anarchist periodical, saying Czolgosz was a spy, a police agent, and a dangerous crank. Emma Goldman, the firebrand anarchist activist, having read the warning, protested to the editor of *Free Society* demanding proof against Czolgosz, but there was nothing solid, and a retraction was printed admitting the accusation had been a mistake. Goldman would later reflect on Czolgosz in her autobiography, saying he was a conscientious student of libertarian literature, always seeking the right books on the subject.

Czolgosz attended a rally where Emma Goldman was speaking. Afterward, he went to her hotel to talk with her, but she was too busy to give him attention. Being rebuffed by Goldman made Leon Czolgosz feel totally alone. He decided to leave Chicago and go to West Seneca, New York, a small town near Buffalo, where he took a room in a boardinghouse. Some say he chose this location deliberately as part of a conspiracy, knowing it would give him access to the president of the United States; others say it was merely a coincidence. In any event, when it was announced that President McKinley would be making an appearance in a few days at the Pan-American Exposition in Buffalo, Czolgosz devised a plan.

EVENT: On September 6, 1901, at 4:07 in the afternoon, President William McKinley, wearing his usual sparkling white vest and dark suit, greeted a line of well-wishers in a line moving past him in the Temple of Music at the Pan-American Exposition in Buffalo, New York. As each person stopped to shake the president's hand, fifty soldiers and Secret Service agents patrolled the premises, but no searches were made as the crowd was carefully scrutinized. Seeing that the crowd was growing larger and time was running out, President McKinley and his aides— including cabinet member Robert Todd Lincoln, son of Abraham Lincoln—asked several agents to speed up the line so that the president could shake more hands. Leon Czolgosz stepped toward the front of the line with a large white handkerchief wrapped around his right hand. A Secret Service agent tapped him on the shoulder asking, "Hurt your hand?" Czolgosz nodded yes. "Maybe you better get to a first-aid station," the agent said. "Later," Czolgosz muttered. "After I meet the president. I've been waiting a long time." As the president came near, Czolgosz said to him, "Excuse my left hand, Mr. President." McKinley shook Czolgosz's left hand and moved on. Several people later, the president again encountered Czolgosz, who had moved down the line. As he stepped close to the president, Secret Service agent Samuel Ireland grabbed Czolgosz's shoulder to move him along, but Czolgosz brushed away Ireland's hand. Czolgosz then lunged forward to within three feet of the president, aimed the Iver Johnson .32-caliber revolver that was concealed under the white handkerchief wrapped around his right hand, and fired two bullets into McKinley. One bullet struck the president's breastbone, the other ripped through the left side of his abdomen, perforating both the front and rear walls of the stomach, and lodged somewhere in the gristle of his back muscles. McKinley shuttered, stiffened, and stared at Czolgosz in astonishment before being caught as he collapsed, still conscious. "I done my duty," Czolgosz said, the handkerchief set on fire by the pistol shots. Eight or nine men knocked Czolgosz to the floor, leaped upon him, and began to beat him, one of them later saying, "We thumped him and slapped his face, and I took a knife out of my pocket and started to cut his throat, but he never flinched." Just before he lost consciousness, President McKinley stopped the assault against his would-be assassin, saying to the men, "Be easy with him, boys."

McKinley, his clean white vest stained with gunpowder, was put in an ambulance and rushed to an emergency hospital. A medical team struggled to locate the bullet but finally decided it could not be retrieved and sutured up the stomach walls and the abdominal wound. President McKinley was taken to the home of John G. Milburn, chairman of the exposition and the president's official host in Buffalo. During the next few days, he seemed to get better, then he rapidly deteriorated. On September 14, at 2:15 A.M., eight days after he was shot, fifty-eight-year-old President William McKinley died of gangrene of the pancreas. Today it is believed the president's wounds would not have been fatal if he had had adequate, sterile surgery and medical attention.

PUNISHMENT: Czolgosz was interrogated by police, who asked his name. "Fred Nieman—Fred Nobody—nobody killed the president," he said. When asked why he killed the president, Czolgosz simply shrugged, saying, "I thought it would be a good thing for this country to kill the president." Later, in his handwritten confession, he said he didn't believe "one man should have so much service and another should have none," and complained that "McKinley was going around the country shouting about prosperity when there was no prosperity for the poor man."

Czolgosz was indicted for first-degree murder, and his trial began September 23, 1901. Declared legally sane after medical examinations, he refused to talk to the two elderly attorneys assigned to represent him, saying he didn't believe in courts or lawyers; he showed no interest in his trial and refused to testify. The trial lasted only eight hours and twenty-six minutes. Czolgosz showed no emotion when declared guilty.

Leon Czolgosz was strapped into the electric chair at Auburn State Prison on the morning of October 29, 1901. He appeared calm and self-possessed, with his head erect, his face showing defiant determination. In his final statement, he said, "I killed the president because he was the enemy of the good people—the good working people. I am not sorry for my crime. I am sorry I could not see my father." At 7:12 A.M., 1,800 volts of electricity charged through his body for seven seconds, then 300 volts for twenty-three seconds, then 1,800 volts for four seconds, then 300 volts for twenty-six seconds more. When contact was broken, the attending physician ordered another five seconds of 1,800 volts before Czolgosz was pronounced dead.

Leon Czolgosz's brother tried to claim his body for burial, but his request was refused. Instead, Czolgosz was buried in a prison grave, and sulfuric acid was poured into his coffin. Doctors estimated it would take twelve hours for his body to decompose.

AFTERMATH: The day after President McKinley died, a plaster cast of his head was taken by Edward L. A. Pausch, an experienced artisan from Hartford, Connecticut. Pausch then labored in secret for a month perfecting the final mask—not the usual face-only death mask but the entire head—which would end up weighing twenty-five pounds. Each night, Pausch locked the work-in-progress in a vault for safekeeping. When it was finished, McKinley's plaster head was exhibited in the Smithsonian Institution under heavy guard. Sculptors then remodeled the mask in marble, with the final product exhibiting McKinley's features in accurate proportion.

McKinley was the third American president to be assassinated. His successor, forty-two-year-old Theodore Roosevelt, became the youngest president in U.S. history. One of his first actions as chief executive was to have the Secret Service assigned full responsibility for protecting the president.

CONSPIRACY THEORY: After McKinley's assassination, there was a wave of arrests and attacks on anarchists, including Emma Goldman. Since Czolgosz had attended Goldman's lecture in Chicago, authorities tried to connect her to Czolgosz in a conspiracy to assassinate the president. Prosecutors even resorted to doctoring testimony, but they failed to make the charges stick. Still, the press continued to imply that Goldman was guilty, especially since she had publicly defended Czolgosz as a demented unfortunate who at least deserved a fair trial. Goldman was attacked by mobs in dozens of American cities and towns; she was beaten and jailed.

In 1903, Congress passed a law enabling the government to deport alien anarchists. Although many legislators also wanted to deport citizen anarchists, that provision was not passed into law. Emma Goldman was deported to Russia in 1919.

After McKinley's assassination, Goldman speculated that the denunciation of Czolgosz in *Free Society* had provoked him into assassinating the president in order to prove his devotion to the cause. Czolgosz would never know that his actions significantly inflamed public hostility against the cause he was trying to advance.

 JUNE 28, 1914

FRANZ FERDINAND (1863–1914)
ARCHDUKE OF AUSTRIA AND
HEIR TO THE AUSTRO-HUNGARIAN THRONE

Although Franz Ferdinand grew up as a distant heir to the Austro-Hungarian Empire, he mostly spent time hunting animals to excess and living the life of the idle rich. His marriage to Countess Sophie Chotek in 1900 did not enhance his position in the family, because Emperor Franz Joseph, Ferdinand's uncle, considered the Chotek family commoners. Still, by 1908, when Franz Joseph annexed Bosnia-Herzegovina, Ferdinand had moved up the ladder of succession because of the death of his father, Archduke Karl Ludwig, and the suicide of his cousin, Crown Prince Rudolf. Becoming next in line to the Austrian throne inspired Ferdinand to take a more visible role in government, and he began serving as inspector general of the armed forces of the empire.

ASSASSIN: Gavrilo Princip, a young Serbian student who became part of a terrorist conspiracy by two groups of Serbian nationalists, Young Bosnia and the Black Hand. Gavrilo Princip was a member of the illegal nationalist organization Young Bosnia, which wanted to separate Bosnia-Herzegovina from the Austro-Hungarian Empire.

HISTORY: As 1914 approached, the countries of Europe were divided into well-armied pockets of alliances ready to attack one another, with assurances that their partner nations would come to their aid. All-out war had not broken out, but with every nation ready to come to the aid of its allies, the world held its breath, wondering what would happen next and if whatever it was would cause the smoldering European hostilities to burst into flames.

U.S. president Woodrow Wilson sent Colonel Edward M. House to Europe with instructions to observe the conditions and report on the likelihood of war. Soon House reported back that the situation "is militarism run stark mad. . . . It only needs a spark to set the whole thing off."

When it was announced that Archduke Franz Ferdinand, now heir to the Austrian throne, was planning a visit to the recently annexed Bosnia-Herzegovina, groups of oppressed Serbian conspirators began to form their plans.

THE PLOT: The Green Garland restaurant in Belgrade was a daily meeting place for some three hundred students who talked of getting back their territory, including Bosnia, from Austria. Ferdinand's visit was of particular interest to three Bosnian-Serb high school students, Nedeljiko Cabrinovic, Trifko Grabez, and Gavrilo Princip, who had decided to kill an Austrian as a show of defiance, but they didn't know who. Now they decided their target should be the archduke. Their plotting was overheard by an officer of Serbian military intelligence, Captain Vagislav Tankosic. Tankosic reported what he had heard to his superior, Colonel Dragutin Dimitrijevic, who was also the head of the Black Hand, a Serbian terrorist organization whose goal was to take back Serbian lands seized by other nations. Dimitrijevic, known in the Black Hand as "Apis," was described by some people as a primitive savage and by others as a genuine patriot. He had arranged the assassinations of Alexander and Draga (king and queen of Serbia) in 1903. That he was focused on Black Hand goals was never in question. Upon hearing of the three young students talking about assassinating the archduke, Apis decided that even if they did not succeed, they could cause an impressive disturbance and political embarrassment for Austria during the archduke's visit. He instructed Tankosic to bring the young men to meet with him.

The three teenage would-be assassins were led into a dark, candlelit room. Apis was seated behind a table, on top of which were a skull, a pistol, a bomb, and a vial marked "poison." The boys were instructed to place their hands on the skull and repeat after Apis the Black Hand oath: "By the sun which warms me, by the earth that feeds me, by God, by the blood of my ancestors, by my honor and my life, I swear my fidelity to the cause of Serbian nationalism, and to sacrifice my life for it."

Each boy was then given a pistol and a grenade; later they would be supplied with six bombs, four Browning revolvers, and doses of cyanide with which to commit suicide in the event they were caught. Then they were smuggled across the border into Sarajevo. There they hid in the house of Danilo Ilic, another Black Hand member, who served as their instructor while he recruited other assassins to join the three boys from Belgrade.

News of the Black Hand's assassination plan reached Dr. von Bilinski, a confidant of the emperor. Although von Bilinski disliked Archduke Ferdinand, he discussed the information with one General Potiorek, who agreed that nothing should be done. Their dilemma: Emperor Joseph, who disapproved of Ferdinand's marriage and had disinherited his children, would oppose the pomp and ceremony that would accompany troops being sent to Bosnia to protect the archduke and his disfavored wife.

By the date of Archduke Ferdinand's arrival in Bosnia, the assassination plan had been refined so that as many as seven pro-Serbian Black Hand assassins were planted in the crowd.

EVENT: After leaving Vienna, the archduke, his wife, and their entourage stopped for four days in a small village near Sarajevo. While there, one of Ferdinand's aides learned of the assassination plot and urged the archduke to return to Vienna. Although the archduke's group was nervous, he proceeded with his plans. Arriving in Sarajevo by rail on June 28, 1914, he was met at the station and transferred to a motorcade to ride in a parade entering the city. The archduke and archduchess climbed into a dark green open car—a large Graf und Stift phaeton, with a four-cylinder engine, the first automobile produced in Austria. Archduchess Sophie was wearing a white dress and a wide-brimmed hat; Archduke Ferdinand wore a light blue tunic, black pants, and a cocked hat decorated with ostrich plumes. Both wore amulets to ward off danger. As they passed through, the crowd gathered beside the road waved and hollered "Zivio!"

Posted in the crowd were 120 policemen. Also in the crowd were the students, who had been trained to shoot and throw bombs, but no one had warned them of the hazards of shooting at moving targets through a crowd of people. One of the would-be assassins realized he was standing too close to a policeman to risk shooting. Another was too hemmed in, and another took one look at Sophie and could not shoot because he was sympathetic to her. Yet another simply lost his nerve. Cabrinovic did manage to knock the detonator off his bomb against a water hydrant and throw it at one of the cars. One story says the bomb fell under the wheels of the car directly behind the archduke's. Another story says the bomb landed on the hood of the archduke's car, and Ferdinand knocked it off, after which it rolled under the wheels of the car behind him. Either way, the bomb exploded under the car behind the archduke's, wounding an army officer. Cabrinovic then swallowed the cyanide he had been given, but it did not work, so he jumped into the nearby Miljacka River in an attempt to escape. The river was nearly dry because of the summer heat, and he was captured. When Princip heard the bomb explode, he assumed their assassination plot had been completed and went to a nearby café to celebrate, spending his last coin to buy a cup of coffee.

The archduke's procession reached the town hall, where they were met by the mayor, who delivered a welcoming speech. Although Ferdinand also delivered a short address, he refused to participate in further ceremonies and insisted on going to the hospital to see the injured officer. The driver of the lead car did not know of the change of plans and proceeded as planned along the Appel-Quai, turning into a narrow street. When the archduke's driver followed, he was told to stop and go instead to the hospital. Doing as instructed, the driver began backing out of the narrow road onto the quay where, as it happened, Princip was standing drinking his coffee. Seeing that the archduke was still alive and approaching in his car, Princip pulled his revolver, walked directly up to the archduke's car, and shot Ferdinand in the neck, the bullet slicing through his jugular vein and lodging in his spine. Princip then pointed the gun at General Potiorek. As he did, Sophie rose in her seat. Just as Princip fired his weapon, someone grabbed his arm, causing the bullet intended for the general to hit Sophie. She lay dying with her head in Ferdinand's lap, the archduke crying, "Soferl, Soferl, don't die. Live for my children." She died within moments, and Ferdinand was dead by the time his car was driven into the courtyard of the governor's residence.

PUNISHMENT: Princip took his cyanide, but it only made him sick. Officers grabbed him, beat him over the head with the flat of their swords, knocked him down, kicked him, scraped skin from his neck with the edge of their swords, and tortured him but did not kill him. He was put in a cell next to the one holding Cabrinovic.

In the middle of the night, Princip was awakened to be moved to another prison, but he pleaded with the prison governor, saying, "There is no need to carry me to another prison. My life is already ebbing away. I suggest that you nail me to a cross and burn me alive. My flaming body will be a torch to light my people on their path to freedom."

Twenty-five conspirators were brought to trial for the assassination of Archduke Ferdinand and his wife Sophie. Nine were acquitted, and sixteen were found guilty, three of which, including Princip, were sentenced to serve twenty years in prison. All three were mistreated during their incarceration and died within four years, Princip died of tuberculosis in 1918. Danila Ilic was hanged. Apis was tried later and sentenced to death.

AFTERMATH: Although Emperor Franz Joseph did not make a big deal of the burial of his nephew Archduke Franz Ferdinand and his wife, Sophie (whose grave was marked with two white gloves, a symbol of her position as a mere lady-in-waiting), the Austrian government made a huge statement about the assassinations. Believing that the Serbian authorities were behind the killings, they delivered a harsh ultimatum to Serbia on July 23, demanding the suppression of all pan-Slavic propaganda, the dismissal of Serbian officials named by the Austrians, and a rigorous joint Austrian-Serbian inquiry into the assassination. Serbia was either unable or unwilling to comply with the demands, and five days later Austria used the assassinations as an excuse to declare war on Serbia. Soon the great European powers became involved: Austria-Hungary invoked its alliance with Germany, while the Serbs called for help from the Russian Empire. By year's end, Britain, France, and Belgium were all drawn into the fray. By late 1918, four and a half years later, World War I had ended, but some 20 million people had died, and the shape of Europe was forever changed, making the assassination of Archduke Franz Ferdinand one of the most momentous acts of political terrorism in twentieth-century history.

The Graf und Stift phaeton automobile in which Ferdinand and Sophie were assassinated would be owned by fifteen private parties during the following dozen years. During that time it would be involved in six major accidents in which thirteen people would die. In 1926, it was retired to Vienna's Museum of War History.

   DECEMBER 29, 30, OR 31, 1916
(EXACT DATE DISPUTED)

GRIGORY EFIMOVICH RASPUTIN
(1871–1916)
SIBERIAN EASTERN ORTHODOX MYSTIC

Though illiterate, Rasputin acquired so much influence over Czarina Alexandra, wife of Nicholas II, czar of Russia, that he was able to make political and ecclesiastical appointments. Because of his abuse of power and notorious debauchery (which reputedly extended to the czarina), he was viewed by royal loyalists as a threat that must be eliminated.

Born in Pokrovskoye, Tobolsk, a Siberian province, to a peasant family and given the name Novykh, Rasputin earned his nickname—which
means licentious or debauched one—during his libertine youth. He
became a farmer at age twenty but soon joined the Khlysty (flagellants), a
religious sect condemned by the Orthodox Church of Russia when it
became well known as a sex cult. Rasputin made a pilgrimage to Mount
Athos in Greece, reappearing two years later claiming to be a mystic and
holy man with powers to heal the sick. During his association with the
Khlysty sect, Rasputin (who was married and had three children) earned
a reputation as a ringleader of the cult's orgies. His sexual appetite was
reputed to be such that he could have nonstop sex with as many as thirty
women every night.

When the Orthodox Church condemned the activities of the Khlysty
sect, Rasputin was branded a heretic and tried by the church, but his odd
hypnotic power saved him when no witnesses could be found to testify
against him. After being released, Rasputin escaped to western Siberia by
going on another pilgrimage, this time to Saint Petersburg. He stopped
frequently along the way to act as a roving holy man, or *starets*. In 1904,
after walking more than a thousand miles, Rasputin reached Saint
Petersburg, a destination that offered him influential and affluent society
women who would soon fall under his spell.

Careful not to antagonize the powerful men of Saint Petersburg by
wantonly taking their wives sexually, Rasputin developed a technique
that was more refined than the flagellation and frenzy of the Khlysty sect.
He saw that mysticism was in fashion and presented himself as a monk
and a hypnotist who could perform miraculous cures. Soon the society
ladies became convinced that they would be healed and purified merely
by coming into physical contact with Rasputin. Sexual intercourse
assured complete purification. Because Rasputin refused to bathe, claiming his supernatural powers would be washed away, society women
dowsed themselves in perfume so that their smell would overpower his
during their purification liaisons.

A larger-than-life character, Rasputin even proved hard to kill.

Grigory Rasputin

CORBIS

When poison had no effect, his assassins shot him and dumped him in the river Neva.

ASSASSINS: A group of aristocrats loyal to the monarch, which included Prince Felix Yusupov, the czar's nephew by marriage.

HISTORY: By 1905, Rasputin's reputation as a healer had reached the royal palace, where Czar Nicholas II and Czarina Alexandra were faced with a serious health problem. The youngest of their five children, Alexis, their only son and heir to the most powerful throne in Europe, had been born with hemophilia. The royal couple consulted the finest doctors in Europe, but no cure was found for Alexis. Even prayers had not helped his condition, and their son grew more delicate with each passing year. Alexandra found new hope when she heard of the mystic healer

Rasputin, and she summoned him to the Royal Palace in 1905. As it happened, just before Rasputin arrived, Alexis had taken a fall and was bleeding uncontrollably. Rasputin went to the boy's room. There he used a candle flame to hypnotize the child into a trance. The empress gasped in amazement as the boy stopped bleeding. Rasputin became a mainstay in treating Alexis's condition. He would place his hand on the boy's forehead, pray, and recite endless Siberian fairy tales about humpback horses and legless riders. Alexis would always respond; his pain and swelling would subside, and his mood would become bright.

The superstitious Czarina Alexandra was so grateful that her son was being helped by Rasputin that she gave him free access to the royal palace. Seizing an opportunity, Rasputin opened a redemption center in Saint Petersburg, where his personal quarters were usually filled with women seeking purification. From time to time, a woman would accuse Rasputin of rape, but the secret police would ignore the claims, knowing the czarina would tolerate no persecution of this monk who was saving her son.

Czarina Alexandra trusted Rasputin completely and allowed him to have a say in church matters, including appointments of bishops. For a while Czar Nicholas tried to keep Rasputin's influence in check, but because of the positive effect Rasputin had on the czar's son, Nicholas allowed Rasputin more and more power, eventually involving him in decisions of government as well as religion.

By then, Rasputin had become popularly known as the Mad Monk, and his influence over the royal household did not help the already deteriorating position of Czar Nicholas in Russia. While lavish parties were thrown at the royal palace, severe food rationing was instituted among the people; during the war Nicholas saw to it that massive numbers of men were drafted into the military to supply the front. Meanwhile Rasputin continued his sin and redemption program with the women, preaching as a holy man that salvation could be achieved through penitence, and stipulating that they must commit indiscriminate sexual acts before he could redeem them.

Loyalists who warned the royal couple to get rid of the insane monk were banished. Newspapers that attacked Rasputin for being immoral and insane were forced out of print. By the end of 1916, Russia was involved in World War I, and the czar went to the front, leaving Alexandra in charge of domestic affairs. Rasputin took full advantage of the situation. He believed himself to be the most powerful man in all of Russia because he controlled the empress and therefore the government. It is certain that Rasputin had the most powerful reputation in all of Russia and that there were many who wanted him dead. With Czar Nicholas away at war, royal loyalists who were tired of Rasputin's influence on their government, and their wives, saw this as the perfect time to take care of the Mad Monk once and for all. Late in December of 1916 (probably the night of either December 29 or December 30) a party was held in Rasputin's honor.

EVENT: Prince Felix Yusupov, Grand Duke Dimitry Pavlovich (the cousin of Czar Nicholas), and other nobles prepared a room in the basement of the prince's castle. They baited their trap by sending word to Rasputin that Yusupov's beautiful wife, Princess Irene Alexandrovna, was eager to see him. Rasputin was not aware that she had actually been sent away to the Crimea.

Rasputin arrived drunk and is said to have immediately asked to see Irene Alexandrovna. As the others waited in another room, Yusupov took Rasputin into an empty banquet hall where a long table stood littered with dirty dishes. Yusupov told Rasputin that he had missed the feast but that his wife would be right down from her room upstairs. Invited to sit at the table and eat specially prepared brown cakes placed before him, Rasputin complied. He popped one after another of the brown cakes into his mouth, not knowing they had been laced by a coconspirator named Dr. Lazovert with enough cyanide to kill ten men.

Yusupov could not believe his eyes as he watched Rasputin rapidly eat all the cakes, belch in satisfaction, and ask for more. The cyanide seemed not to affect him at all. Becoming afraid of the Mad Monk's powers, Yusupov, trembling, went into the adjoining room and told his coconspirators that Rasputin was not made ill by the cakes. Dr. Lazovert told him to have Rasputin drink the wine from a jug that had been laced with several ounces of cyanide, and assured Yusupov that only a sip would kill most men instantly.

Back in the banquet room with Rasputin, Yusupov watched as Rasputin drank six goblets of the wine, showing not the least sign of discomfort. What the conspirators did not know was that Rasputin suffered from dyspepsia, a condition that prevented his stomach from secreting the hydrochloric acid necessary to activate the cyanide.

Asking again for Yusupov's wife, Rasputin became restless, got up from the table, and paced back and forth before a large fireplace. Prince Yusupov was amazed that Rasputin did not fall dead from the poison. When Rasputin urged him to bring the princess now, since he did not like waiting, Yusupov panicked. He drew a large dagger and rushed toward the Mad Monk from behind, stabbing him several times until Rasputin fell. Yusupov then grabbed a rope, tied Rasputin's hands and feet, and went to get the others.

The group of assassins entered the room and gathered around Rasputin's seemingly lifeless form lying on the floor. Bending closer to have a good look, they were startled when Rasputin suddenly came back to life, his pawlike hands grasping Yusupov's neck, his fierce eyes ablaze with vengeance. One of the others drew a pistol and fired six shots into Rasputin, who finally collapsed.

Quickly the men tied the Mad Monk's body with more ropes, adding chains to be sure he would be powerless against them should he come to life again. They then transported his body to the frozen Neva River. Six men chopped a hole in the ice and kicked the body through the hole into the icy cold water, believing that was the end of the Mad Monk.

The next day the men learned that the poison had not killed Rasputin, nor had the stab wounds, nor had the six bullets. While in the freezing water under a layer of ice, Rasputin had somehow gotten free of the ropes and chains and smashed through the ice with his head. However, in the process he had swallowed too much water and drowned.

Rasputin's body was found on the opposite shore of the Neva from where he had been dropped the night before.

AFTERMATH: Millions of Russian peasants were shattered by the news of Rasputin's death, as were Nicholas and Alexandra. The empress was loyal to Rasputin to the end. She ordered a chapel built on the czar's estate near Pushkin to house Rasputin's body, and pressured the private guard to investigate the circumstances of his assassination. Prince Yusupov and his wife swiftly left Russia. By then it was apparent that either a palace coup or a popular revolution would topple the powerful Romanov dynasty.

When leaving his apartment the evening of his death, Rasputin, believing he was soon to die, wrote a last letter to the royal family which said in part, "If I am killed by common assassins, especially by my brothers the Russian peasants, you, czar of Russia, will have nothing to fear for your children, they will reign in Russia for hundreds of years. But . . . if it was your relations who have brought about my death, then none of your family, that is to say none of your children or relatives, will remain alive for more than two years. They will all be killed by the Russian people." With Rasputin's body barely cold in the ground, the winds of 1917 blew even colder on the royal family.

 JULY 16, 1918

NICHOLAS II (1868–1918)
AND ALEXANDRA (1872–1918)
CZAR AND CZARINA OF RUSSIA FROM 1894 TO 1917

Alexandra (the former Princess Alix of Hessen and granddaughter of Britain's Queen Victoria) was a dominating force over her husband, especially after 1907, when Rasputin came on the scene. Even before Rasputin's influence, Nicholas proved to be an ineffective ruler. His mismanagement of the Russo-Japanese War and the internal affairs of the country led to the revolution of 1905, which he ultimately suppressed only by granting limited constitutional reforms. In 1914, Nicholas went to the front and led Russia into World War I, but by 1917 he was forced to abdicate the throne.

ASSASSINS: Professional executioners who were members of the newly formed Soviet secret police, the Cheka, led by Jacob Yurovsky.

HISTORY: Russia did not fare well during World War I. The country suffered a shattered economy, near-famine conditions, and popular discontent, not to mention the palace intrigue of Rasputin and his assassination. By February 1917 the government had collapsed under the weight of a revolution that began with strikes in Petrograd (formerly Saint Petersburg), food riots, and mass army desertions. Nicholas, who was powerless to correct the situation and dearly loved his country, believed there was only one way to save Russia: He abdicated his throne.

A provisional government took charge under the leadership of Alexandr Kerenski, who immediately put the royal family under house arrest, at first with friendly though restrictive overseers. By October, the Bolshevik Revolution had resulted in responsibility for the royal family being transferred to less sympathetic souls. Nicholas, Alexandra, their children, and their personal servants were moved from their elegant palace to the gloomy town of Ekaterinburg in the eastern Urals. Nicholas was under the impression that they would receive a public trial and then be banished, but Russian leaders Lenin, Trotsky, and Jacob Sverdlov (known as the "butcher" of the Bolshevik Revolution) could not agree about what to do with the Romanovs. Lenin, not happy about having to make such a decision, observed that although French and English revolutionaries had executed their monarchs, Russian revolutionaries had been slow to take such actions. Trotsky was eager to face the problem head on, proposing that Nicholas be put on trial, with Trotsky as the public prosecutor. Lenin disagreed for practical reasons: Such a trial would take too much time, and there were more important matters requiring their attention. Beyond that, Nicholas, who had not been a popular monarch, was gaining sympathy from the public, as well as his jailers, because of his poise and fortitude as a prisoner.

As the civil war proceeded, a decision was forced upon Lenin and Trotsky. Anti-Bolshevik White forces were approaching Ekaterinburg, where the royal family was being held, and it was time to show a strong and unified front. Trotsky prevailed, saying it was necessary to execute the czar and his family in order to frighten, horrify, and dishearten the enemy and at the same time shake up the ranks, showing them there was no turning back. Realizing that it was all or nothing and choosing victory over ruin, Lenin agreed with Trotsky.

EVENT: It was the night of July 16, 1918. The royal captives were resting in their odd prison, the Ipatiev House. Although it was the finest home in town (built by a successful merchant named N. N. Ipatiev), it was still a two-story prison, called "the House of Special Purpose" by those in charge. Guards awakened the czar and told him and his family to get dressed, that they were being moved because the Czech Legion and the White Army would soon be approaching in an attempt to free them. Once dressed, Nicholas, Alexandra, and their children were led downstairs into a small room in the basement, where they were told to wait for cars to arrive and carry them away. Nicholas asked for chairs for

Czar Nicholas, Czarina Alexandra, and family

CORBIS-BETTMANN

his wife and son Alexis, who was at that moment ill from his hemophilia. The empress sat on one chair; Nicholas, holding Alexis, sat on another; and the four daughters—Tatiana, Olga, Marie, and Anastasia—stood behind their parents, along with the family physician, Dr. Eugene Botkin; the empress's maid, Demidova; the czar's valet, Tropp; and the family cook, Charitonov. Soon the eleven captives heard men marching toward the entrance of their small room. Jacob Yurovsky appeared in the doorway with ten uniformed men, members of the new Soviet secret police, the Cheka, all professional executioners who stood with rifles pointed at the royal grouping. Although an explanation would not have been necessary, Yurovsky offered one, indifferently saying, "Your relations have tried to save you. They have failed. We must now shoot you."

Nicholas could not believe what he had heard and started to rise from his chair, still holding his son in his arms, saying, "What?"

Nothing more was said before the assassins opened fire on the helpless royal family and their servants. At first, the maid escaped by rushing away from the group into a corner of the room, but one assassin followed her and quickly killed her with his bayonet. Checking each person to make sure they were dead, the assassins discovered that Alexis was still alive. Yurovsky leaned over and fired two bullets directly into the young man's ear. The guards began to leave, believing their job was complete, when they noticed Anastasia move. Evidently she had only fainted during the first shots. Quickly they finished her off with bayonets and rifle butts.

The bodies were taken to a nearby mine shaft and dumped into it. Next to go in was a lighted stick of dynamite, which exploded with a fury. After this, more than a hundred gallons of gasoline were poured onto the bodies and set afire to burn for hours. When cooled, the body parts were chopped and sawed into small pieces, then shoved further down the shaft with any remaining clothes and jewelry. To finish the job and in an attempt to eliminate all traces of the Romanovs forever, four hundred pounds of sulfuric acid were dumped in the hole to thoroughly dissolve the remains.

PUNISHMENT: Although the new Soviet government denied for a long time that the Romanovs had been assassinated, in 1919 the White Army took control of Ekaterinburg and, sifting through the remains of several bodies in the mine shaft, found one slender, manicured finger of Empress Alexandra intact. In order to save face, even though Lenin and Sverdlov had secretly ordered the executions, the government claimed the assassins were social revolutionaries trying to discredit the new government and immediately ordered the arrest and trial of twenty-eight people for the conspiracy to murder the royals. Only five men were found guilty and executed.

AFTERMATH: The Bolsheviks set out to assassinate every member of the Romanov family they could find. The Grand Duchess Elizabeth, Alexandra's sister, was being held in the Urals town of Alapayevsk. On July 17, 1918, the day after the assassination, she was led by her captors to a peasant car, where she joined other members of the Romanov family already collected: Grand Duke Sergei Mikhailovich; three sons of Grand Duke Constantine, Ivan, Constantine, and Igor; and the son of Grand Duke Paul, Prince Vladimir Paley. They were taken to the mouth of another abandoned mine shaft and, still alive, thrown in. Heavy lumber and hand grenades were thrown down the shaft on top of them, and the assassination squad left the scene believing their work was done.

Soon a peasant came along and looked into the pit, hearing hymns being sung from down below. By the time the White Russian opponents of the Bolsheviks arrived, all the Romanovs in the pit had died. When the bodies were recovered, Paul's head had been carefully bandaged with Elizabeth's handkerchief.

 FEBRUARY 22, 1913

FRANCISCO INDALECIO MADERO
(1873–1913)
PRESIDENT OF MEXICO

Now considered a martyr of the Mexican Revolution that began in 1910, Francisco Indalecio Madero incited the revolution and is credited with unseating dictatorial Mexican president Porfirio Diaz after thirty-five years in office.

The son of a wealthy liquor-distilling family, Madero was known as a teetotaler, as well as a vegetarian with liberal political views. His defenders say he was a dedicated democrat and social reformer; his critics believe he was an ineffectual idealist and dreamer. There is no question that Madero was keenly interested in political issues; in a book he published in 1908, he agreed with President Diaz that Mexico had a sizable middle class capable of assuming political responsibility and that the country was ready for democracy. He urged the people to organize political parties and institutions, saying that was the only way to guarantee peace and continuity of government programs, because while men perish, institutions are immortal. But as these opinions began to be embraced and acted upon by the populace, Diaz appeared to change his

Francisco Madero

mind. Diaz proposed the presidential term of office scheduled to begin in 1910 be increased from four to six years, while Madero set about putting his ideas into practice. He organized the Anti-Reelectionist Party and began campaigning (something never before done in the history of Mexico) with his wife by his side. Madero visited much of the country, speaking before groups of citizens. Government officials at first ridiculed him, then became alarmed, and finally tried to repress him. To the many Mexicans he would personally meet on his campaign tour, Madero, a man of small build, soon came to symbolize a little David defending the people against the Goliath figure of Diaz and his government.

ASSASSIN: Major Francisco Cardenas.

HISTORY: Small disturbances began to break out in various parts of Mexico as the people began to feel the power of Madero's encouragement.

In an effort to control the people and ensure his reelection, Diaz saw to it that Madero was imprisoned before the election in June 1910. On October 4, Porfirio Diaz was officially declared by Congress to be president for six more years. On October 5, Madero was freed on bond. He immediately crossed the border, seeking refuge in the United States. From there he issued his revolutionary plan, denounced the June election as fraudulent, and refused to recognize the government. He proclaimed himself provisional president until new elections could be held, and proposed legally redressing the abuses committed during Diaz's thirty-five years in office. Finally, Madero summoned the people to rebellion on November 20. Despite a shaky start, Madero soon gained the support of Pascual Orozco and Francisco "Pancho" Villa, who would become his first military leaders, and the revolution had begun.

Although Diaz's forces counterattacked, they were defeated in four major battles in northern Mexico, followed by insurrections throughout the country and an uprising in southern Mexico led by Emiliano Zapata. After failing in his military efforts, Diaz turned to political negotiations and tried to shore up his position by changing officials. Again he was unsuccessful. Faced with a mutiny in the capital itself, Diaz finally resigned as president and fled to the United States. Madero, wanting his new government to get off to a democratic start, negotiated through the Treaties of Ciudad Juarez to place some of his men in the interim government. He then traveled to Mexico City, was triumphantly welcomed, and was declared president in 1911.

Soon President Madero found that he was unable to satisfy the many divergent interests that were placing demands on his government. There was the old regime, the military, revolutionaries such as Zapata who demanded immediate land reforms to benefit the peasants, the hostile conservative press, and U.S. Ambassador Henry Lane Wilson. In fact, Wilson may have been a major contributor to Madero's downfall. As the national situation became more and more complex, those forces controlling the economy began to panic. Their prosperity, and very existence, depended on peace and security within Mexico, and Madero was proving unable to ensure those things. Madero's fatal mistake was trying to correct the illegal situation enjoyed by some foreign investors who had been given an exemption from paying any taxes at all in Mexico. Meetings to discuss the situation were held at the U.S. Embassy in Mexico City. Those in attendance included the foreign investors Madero was threatening to tax, Mexicans defeated by the revolution, and leaders of the Porfirian army, which had survived almost intact. Meanwhile, Madero had jailed a number of military leaders who had helped him rise to power. Two of them, General Felix Diaz and General Bernardo Reyes, plotted behind bars against Madero. In February of 1913, Madero was forced to release Diaz and Reyes from prison, and soon they became key players in a plan to overthrow the Madero regime.

EVENT: General Diaz and General Reyes organized a military assault on the National Palace using the Porfirian army. The assault lasted ten days and is called "Mexico's Ten Tragic Days" by historians. Madero relied on General Victoriano Huerta to stop the assault, but Huerta had secretly joined with Diaz and Reyes. His unimpassioned efforts mainly consisted of firing cannonballs at the attackers, resulting in more innocent victims than legitimate casualties, although Reyes was shot to death. Huerta finally showed his true allegiance, demanding that Madero resign. When Madero refused, Huerta arrested both President Madero and Vice-President Pino Suarez on February 17, 1913. That same day, Gustavo Madero, the president's brother, was seized, tortured, and brutally murdered. The president's wife was frantic, knowing her husband was being held prisoner in the National Palace, and she appealed to Huerta for mercy.

Madero and Suarez officially resigned on February 20 after being assured that they would be released and allowed to go into exile. Ambassador Wilson held a meeting on February 22, Washington's birthday, at the U.S. Embassy, at which Huerta asked him whether they should commit Madero to an insane asylum or exile him. It is reported that Wilson replied simply that Huerta should do what was best for the peace of Mexico.

Later that day, Madero and Suarez, believing they were being exiled, were put into automobiles and driven toward the railroad station. When the vehicles did not stop at the station, it became obvious to them that their fate was not as they had expected. About 11 P.M., they reached the penitentiary of Calle Lecumberri, and the two men were shoved out of the cars as the drivers and guards screamed obscenities at them. One of their escorts, Major Francisco Cardenas, pulled out a gun and shot Madero in the back of the head, killing him instantly. He then turned, pointed the gun at a stunned Suarez, and shot him too.

AFTERMATH: The official explanation for the deaths of Madero and Suarez was that they were shot while attempting to escape during their transfer to prison.

Huerta took control of the Mexican government, but his regime lacked a social base not only because of the brutal way it had seized power but also because opposing interests created by the revolution made real restoration impossible. Despite the support Huerta received from intellectuals and politicians who tried to give his government principles and programs that responded to the problems of the time, Huerta was ineffective. Soon the U.S. government, which had strongly supported Huerta, changed course, leaving him on his own as Mexican revolutionaries were regrouping. With Venustiano Carranza as their leader, the revolutionaries attempted to restore constitutional order to the government Huerta had shattered. By 1914, the extent of Huerta's crimes and international conflicts were exposed, and his reputation was ruined. Huerta resigned and Carranza became the next president of Mexico.

Emiliano Zapata and his men

CORBIS-BETTMANN

 APRIL 10, 1919

EMILIANO ZAPATA (1879–1919)
MEXICAN REVOLUTIONARY LEADER

Emiliano Zapata is considered one of the noblest heroes of the Mexican Revolution and the civil wars of 1910 to 1920. He was a Native American and a working-class man who inspired his ragtag followers by saying, "Men of the south, it is better to die on your feet than to live on your knees."

Zapata's high cheekbones, dark eyes, and swarthy complexion, characteristic of Morelos Indians, were set off by thin black hair and a mandarin mustache. During his youth, while working as a stable hand on a large hacienda, Zapata no doubt noticed that the tiled stable floors on which the horses stood were much nicer than the dirt floors of the housing provided for himself and the other workers. His observations of the inequality of Mexican life must have been enhanced while working as a sharecropper in southern Mexico. As the revolutionary movements in

Mexico gathered strength, Zapata used his natural leadership abilities and strong roots with the poor to collect his own group of fellow farmers who were willing to put their lives on the line to improve their bleak futures. In order to stand out as a person in authority, Zapata chose to wear a uniform, but one that identified him with the people. Selecting attire similar to that worn by village chiefs on special occasions, Zapata could be easily recognized in his enormous black sombrero, black jacket, and tight black charro pants studded with silver buttons.

Zapata's influence spread, perhaps in part because he was able to combine guerrilla tactics with a reputation for honesty and fairness which the peasants admired. Although cruel to his enemies, Zapata tried to avoid bloody excess. When his forces occupied Mexico City without widespread violence and looting, his Zapatista reputation was enhanced. Even when their meager rations were depleted, Zapata's men humbly knocked on doors and asked for food or approached people passing by on the street and asked for a peso or two. For Zapata, the revolution had a nonmilitary goal: the return of the Indians' land, which had been appropriated by plantation owners. He was careful to keep the roots of his revolution planted in the countryside. As haciendas fell, the Zapatistas tore down their fences and redistributed the property among the poor. His philosophy was outlined in the Plan of Ayala, in which Zapata advocated seizure of all foreign-owned land, along with that taken from the Indians, and confiscation of all property owned by *hacendados* who opposed the revolution.

ASSASSINS: Government troops led by Colonel Jesus Guajardo.

HISTORY: By 1897, eighteen-year-old Emiliano Zapata had became a leader of the peasants protesting against the *hacendados* who had appropriated their land. He was arrested, then released, and continued his activities until he was drafted into the army. Zapata's revolutionary ardor did not cool during his army service. In 1909, as president of the board of defense for his village, he led peasants on campaigns to seize hacienda lands and restore them to the people. When Francisco Madero launched a revolution against the reactionary national government of Porfirio Diaz, Zapata eagerly joined his efforts, although he never abandoned his own rebellion. Zapata's army of southern farmers helped to overthrow dictator Porfirio Diaz in 1910.

Although it soon became apparent to Zapata that Madero's reform programs were far too moderate, he still played a key role in defeating General Victoriano Huerta's counterrevolution. After Huerta resigned, Zapata notified the more moderate revolutionaries under Venustiano Carranza and Alvaro Obregon that he and his forces, known as the Liberation Army (numbering fifteen thousand men), were going to continue their own revolutionary struggle, supported by the often savage Pancho Villa.

By 1915, Zapata was thirty-one years old and tired of fighting. With his troops in control of their state of Morelos, he wanted to forget about fighting and get back to farming the land they had fought to regain. As Zapata tried to relax, President Venustiano Carranza tightened his grip on the rest of the country. In a campaign to eliminate all rebel opposition, he sent General Pablo Gonzalez and his army to Morelos to disempower Zapata. At first Gonzalez tried to buy off Zapata, who refused, choosing land over money. Carranza would not give up, however, and enlisted the independent Obregon forces to gain a military advantage. He had weakened both Zapata and Villa by separating them, Villa having gone home to northern Mexico and Zapata to southern Mexico. Although Zapata was weakened, he remained in control of his own territory by reverting when necessary to military matters instead of land reform. In the process, Zapata's people suffered as Gonzalez and his government troops burned villages, destroyed crops, hanged peasants, and herded their families into detention camps. Zapata fought back, torching haciendas and battling desperately, until the two armies eventually settled into a bloody stalemate: Gonzales controlled the major cities, and Zapata ruled the hills.

In March of 1919, Gonzalez quarreled with one of his officers,

Colonel Jesus Guajardo, and threw him in jail. Guajardo was a Yaqui half-breed and probably the best cavalry officer in the south. Zapata learned of Guajardo's arrest and sent him a note asking him to join his ranks, but Gonzalez intercepted the message. Unable to overcome Zapata's masterful guerrilla tactics, Gonzalez decided on another approach, seeing an opportunity to trap Zapata. Gonzalez gave Colonel Jesus Guajardo a choice: face the firing squad or do as I say. As directed by Gonzalez, Guajardo sent word to Zapata that he wanted to join his forces and would bring along eight hundred men and a supply of rifles and ammunition. To convince Zapata of his sincerity, Guajardo staged a mutiny and occupied the government-held town of Jonacatepec. Among Guajardo's prisoners were a detachment of former Zapatistas, who had gone over to the government side and provided valuable information that was used against Zapata. As a final act of allegiance to Zapata, Guarjardo had these fifty men executed on the spot.

That evening, Zapata and Guajardo met for the first time. They exchanged *abrazos*, the embrace of friendship, and Guajardo gave Zapata a handsome sorrel stallion. Throwing aside his normal caution, Zapata agreed to meet his new convert the next day at the hacienda of San Juan Chinameca near Cuautla to discuss their plans. Zapata's last night was spent in the hills that he loved.

EVENT: The next day, April 10, 1919, Zapata mounted the sorrel stallion, named the Golden Ace, and rode with a bodyguard of 150 men to the Chinameca hacienda. Leaving all but ten men outside as sentries because federal forces were believed to be in the area, Zapata rode through the gate at 2 P.M. Bugles sounded and drums thrumped as an honor guard of two hundred of Guajardo's soldiers lined up to welcome Zapata. Guajardo stood at one side of his ranks, smiling. Zapata rode directly in front of the troops to accept their salute. Drawing his sword, Guajardo commanded, "Present arms!" The bugle sounded three times, and then the massive formation of his men turned their guns, firing at Zapata. He fell from the sorrel stallion, riddled with bullets, and died on the spot. The ten men with him were all killed or wounded, and his soldiers outside fled for their lives.

PUNISHMENT: Gonzalez rewarded Guajardo with fifty thousand pesos and a promotion to the rank of brigadier general. With a new reputation for ruthlessness and hatred toward the agrarians, Guajardo became one of Gonzalez's closest followers.

AFTERMATH: That night, Guajardo and his soldiers strapped Zapata's body to a mule and took it to the city of Cuautla to prove the assassination had been carried out. Gonzalez identified the corpse and had photographers snap some pictures of it at the police station. General Gonzalez notified President Carranza of the success of the ambush he had planned that resulted in Zapata's death.

Zapata's body lay on display for two days before burial, with thousands of peasants flocking to the city to see their slain hero. He was buried at the Cuautla cemetery.

Shortly afterward, Gonzalez sent Guajardo to northern Mexico to fight bandit leader Pancho Villa. General Alvaro Obregon removed President Carranza from office with a successful coup, and Gonzalez, caught in the power shift, was arrested. Within days, Guajardo was also arrested by federal troops, who charged him with plotting a revolt to free Gonzalez. Smoking a cigar, at 6:30 on a bright July morning in 1920, Guajardo was executed by a government firing squad.

Some say the movement for immediate land reform died with Zapata, but his death gave birth to a legend. It is said that even today some villagers in southern Mexico see their invincible leader still riding in the Sierras, watching over his beloved people of Morelos.

Zapata's slogan has long survived him—"*Tierra y libertad*" ("Land and Liberty")—and his name is inscribed in gold in the Mexican Chamber of Deputies.

 MAY 1920

VENUSTIANO CARRANZA (1859–1920)
PRESIDENT OF MEXICO,
AND ONE OF THE MOST CONSERVATIVE
LEADERS OF THE MEXICAN REVOLUTION

The son of a powerful landowner, Venustiano Carranza became politically active in 1877. He would later be linked to the reactionary government of Porfirio Diaz, but he joined Francisco Madero in his fight against Diaz in 1910. When Madero was assassinated, Carranza joined the more radical revolutionaries, such as Emiliano Zapata, Pancho Villa, and Alvaro Obregon, in their successful attempt to force General Victoriano Huerta out of Mexico. Carranza established a provisional government in 1914 and defeated Pancho Villa's army in 1915 with the aid of General Alvaro Obregon.

When Carranza was officially declared president in 1917, he was faced with carrying out the provisions of a new Mexican constitution. It called for reforms in land ownership, natural resources, labor organizations, and other social programs. Carranza had difficulty implementing these changes and faced growing social unrest during his term of office, while continually being threatened by the opposition of Pancho Villa and Emiliano Zapata. When Zapata was assassinated, no one doubted that it was with Carranza's approval.

ASSASSINS: Rebel forces led by Rodolfo Herrera.

HISTORY: Under the new constitution of Mexico, the president could serve only one four-year term of office, without the option of reelection. As the end of Carranza's term of office approached, in December of 1920, he decided to ensure his place would be taken by his ambassador to Washington, Ignacio Bonillas. Carranza's efforts set off violent eruptions throughout the country, with many followers of Obregon imprisoned, shot, or executed. A failed attempt was made to assassinate Obregon

Venustiano Carranza

himself in Mexico City. As a result, Obregon called for an all-out civil war, and a number of more radical generals supported him. During the rebellion that followed, Carranza got word that rebel forces were within thirty miles of the capital, and he was forced to flee on May 5, 1920. Before leaving, however, he emptied the entire Mexican national treasury and confiscated the dies from the mint and the national archives, intending to set up his own government in Vera Cruz. As many as ten thousand people learned of Carranza's plans and rushed to the railway station in Mexico City, intending to follow their leader to Vera Cruz. When the train convoy reached the state of Pueblo, near the city of Rinconada, it was brought to a halt because the train tracks had been destroyed. Meanwhile, Vera Cruz had been secured by the rebels.

EVENT: Carranza and a handful of his followers escaped the train and rode on horseback into the mountains. A fierce rainstorm forced them to stop in the small village of Tlaxcalantonga, where Carranza was invited to take refuge in a small mud hut. Resting there, Carranza had no warning that informers had sent word to Rodolfo Herrera of his whereabouts. Just before dawn, Herrera and his troops arrived at Carranza's hideaway and opened fire to shouts of "*Muerta Carranza! Viva Obregon!*" Unable to put up a fight, Carranza was immediately shot to death on the spot.

AFTERMATH: Ten years after the Mexican Revolution began, Madero, Zapata, and Carranza, the three leading figures, were dead. It was 1920, and a new generation of revolutionary *caudillos* advanced triumphantly to the forefront of political life to inaugurate a national reconstruction and an era of peace.

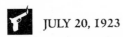 JULY 20, 1923

PANCHO VILLA (1878–1923)
MEXICAN REVOLUTIONARY

Francisco "Pancho" Villa, a dedicated revolutionary and a brutal bandit, became one of the most sentimental yet savage figures of the Mexican Revolution and the civil wars of 1910 to 1920. Considered a military genius and a bloodthirsty marauder, Villa was recognized worldwide for his courage and his guerrilla activities. He and his troops plundered the estates of the rich, often sharing their property and possessions with the poor, making him a real-life Robin Hood in the eyes of many.

Born in 1878 to peasant parents, he was christened Doroteo Arango, and later took the name Francisco Villa (nicknamed "Pancho") in admiration of a feared bandit in Mexican history. Legend has it that the sixteen-year-old Villa, already an orphan, turned to a life of crime when he left his home in 1894 after killing the wealthy owner of an estate where he worked, as revenge for the sexual assault of his sister Mariana. Supposedly he became the leader of a gang of cattle thieves, in addition to robbing foreigners, mostly Chinese merchants living in Mexico, looting trains and mines, and murdering scores of innocent people. Arrested in 1903, Villa avoided a lengthy prison sentence by volunteering for the Mexican cavalry.

Later, when Villa left the military, he put his cavalry training to good use, proving to be a bold military strategist. He also aligned himself with Mexico's revolutionaries. Although it is said his deepest desire was to become president of Mexico, Villa's reputation was distinguished on the battlefield. He was also reputed to be a ruthless leader devoid of social consciousness, once killing eighty women and children living in his own camp because they slowed his troops' movements.

ASSASSINS: Government agents led by Mexican congressman Jesus Salas Barranzas.

HISTORY: By 1909 Villa, already a hero of the poor of northern Mexico, became a devoted follower of the liberal revolutionary Francisco Madero. He offered the entire division of trained soldiers he commanded to assist Madero in his efforts to drive longtime dictator Porfirio Diaz out of power. Even after Diaz had left Mexico and Madero was president, Villa remained in the service of an irregular army, ready to go to battle against insurrectionists attempting to bring down Madero.

Madero showed his appreciation for Villa's support by saving his life in 1912. That year General Victoriano Huerta, who was secretly plotting against Madero, declared Villa a traitor, had him arrested, and ordered his execution. At the last moment, as Villa stood before Huerta's firing squad, Madero ordered a stay of execution. Villa then escaped prison, fleeing to the United States. After Madero was assassinated in Huerta's coup of 1913, Villa returned to Mexico seeking, along with Emiliano Zapata and Venustiano Carranza, to restore the revolution and eliminate Huerta.

Pancho Villa

It was during this time that Villa's reputation for ruthlessness was established. Although bloodletting was common during this period of Mexican history, Villa was a terror to his enemies, hanging or shooting any and all he would capture.

As late as 1916, Villa, though no longer a major player in the Mexican civil war, was still prepared to defend the Mexican people. Antagonized when the U.S. government formally recognized the Carranza government, Villa and fifteen hundred men crossed the United States border into Columbus, New Mexico, on March 19, 1916. There they killed nine civilians while gathering much-needed supplies and rode off toward Mexico, stopping along the way only long enough to kill eight U.S. soldiers. U.S. troops pursued Villa as he escaped, killing fifty of his men on the U.S. side of the border and seventy more during a fifteen-mile penetration into Mexico. Upon hearing of Villa's actions, President Woodrow Wilson knew that although the United States had recognized the Carranza government, Carranza could not be expected to take action against Villa, so the United States needed to act. Brigadier General John "Black Jack" Pershing was sent into Mexico with six thousand soldiers to capture Villa and bring him back to the United States to stand trial. A three-hundred-mile chase ensued through the mountains of northern Mexico, with Villa outwitting Pershing by splitting up his men and sending them off in small groups into the wild mountains where they could not be identified or captured.

To complicate matters further, although Carranza hated Villa, he could not risk the wrath of the Mexican people (who still loved Villa), and was thus forced to declare Pershing's invasion of Mexican soil a hostile act. In June, a detachment of Pershing's troops was confronted near Carrizal by the Mexican army, and twenty-three U.S. soldiers were captured. The men were held prisoner until July, when they were released at the International Bridge in El Paso, Texas, totally naked because Mexican bandits had taken their uniforms. Finally, General Pershing was ordered out of Mexico on February 5, 1917. The unsuccessful invasion had cost the United States $130 million and a tremendous loss of prestige and friendship with almost all of Mexico.

Villa's legend grew with the singing of the "Ballad to Pancho Villa," which derided the United States for ending its pursuit of Villa in shame. While Villa regained much of his prestige and power during 1917 and 1918, it was limited to northern Mexico, where he continued his guerrilla campaign against Carranza. When Carranza was overthrown and assassinated in 1920, Villa was tired of warfare. After ten years of violence, he reached an agreement with provisional president Huerta to lay down his arms in exchange for some land and a year's pay for each of his soldiers. Villa was given $2 million in gold as a pension, a twenty-five-thousand-acre ranch at Canutillo, Durango, and a fifty-man bodyguard from the ranks of his *dorados*. Villa's ranch became a monument to national reform. He bought the latest American farm equipment to be used on his property and built a hospital, a chapel, a school, and a telegraph office in the nearby town of Parral. Although Villa was content, the government was unsure about him.

Obregon, who had masterminded the elimination of Carranza in order to became the new constitutional president, established a number of reforms. Nevertheless, he had been threatened by several coup attempts by revolutionary generals. With the elections of 1924 approaching, Obregon wondered if Villa would make trouble. Although Obregon had no concrete reason to believe Villa was planning a comeback, a group of gunmen directed by Mexican congressman Jesus Salas Barranzas prepared to put an end to Obregon's worries about Villa.

Jesus Salas had two reasons for planning to assassinate Pancho Villa. Years earlier Villa and his men had massacred the residents of the small village of El Oro, in Salas's region of Mexico, the state of Durango, and Salas sought to avenge Villa's cruelty. Also Salas was coming up for reelection and felt certain that killing Villa would make him a hero in the eyes of the voters of Durango.

Salas spent months planning the assassination of Villa and assembling a group of men to help him execute it. In April of 1923 he rented a house at the corner of Benito Juarez and Balbino Barredo Streets, knowing Villa routinely passed the location on trips from his ranch in the hills to the village of Parral. The house was used as a command post, where Salas and six assassins studied Villa's habits, the routes he rode and walked, and the best positions from which to shoot at him.

One day Salas and his men were all set up and ready to assassinate Villa as he passed by, but the attack was foiled at the last minute when a group of schoolchildren ran between the assassins and Villa.

EVENT: On July 20, 1923, Pancho Villa, then fifty-five years old, and his four heavily armed aides and bodyguards got into his massive 1919 Dodge touring car (given to him by the government) for his regular visit with his mistress Manuela Casas in the town of Parral. Two other bodyguards jumped on the running boards of the Dodge as it drove away from Villa's ranch. Not far from town, Salas and his men picked an ideal location, positioning themselves on either side of the road at dawn, then readied their guns and watched for Villa's Dodge to come into sight. When the car came near, the assassins opened fire. A blast of over a hundred bullets sprayed the walls of the houses lining Benito Juarez Street, with forty penetrating Villa's car. Nine shots hit Pancho Villa himself, who was so surprised by the onslaught that he had no time to fire his famous twin pistols, which he always carried with him. Also unable to defend themselves were Daniel Tamayo, Villa's assistant, Rosario Rosales, Villa's chauffeur, and an unidentified civilian. They all died instantly. Only one of Villa's bodyguards survived, although wounded, and escaped.

The assassins then jumped onto horses and rode into the hills. Salas would say later, during his confession, that it was not necessary for them to run from the scene because there were plenty of sympathetic citizens of Parral who would have given them shelter.

PUNISHMENT: A few days later, Salas left his hideout in the hills and surrendered to authorities. He was taken to Mexico City for trial and, he assumed, to receive the reward previously offered by the U.S. government for the capture, dead or alive, of the notorious bandit, Pancho Villa. During his trial, Salas announced that the reward money would be used to establish a charitable institution for the many families of Villa's victims.

Although Salas was convicted of the assassination of Pancho Villa and sentenced, on September 20, 1923, to twenty years in prison, he served only a few months before being freed by President Obregon on the grounds that he was in mortal danger while in prison. All the other men who participated in Villa's assassination, except one, died violent deaths. One was even murdered in an ambush at the exact spot where he had helped to assassinate Villa.

AFTERMATH: Villa was buried in the small town of Parral. Forty years later, he would join other heroes of the Mexican Revolution when the Mexican Congress voted to preserve their names in gold on its chamber walls. Pancho Villa's body was moved in 1976 from its original burial place to Mexico City, where it was placed in a crypt at the Revolution Monument.

 JULY 17, 1928

ALVARO OBREGON (1880–1928)
PRESIDENT OF MEXICO

Although a man of simple background and little formal education, Obregon, before becoming president of Mexico, was one of the most successful generals of the Mexican Revolution.

ASSASSIN: José de León Toral, a cartoonist who, as an ardent Catholic, resented Obregon's anticlerical dictates.

HISTORY: Obregon was not active in the 1910–1911 revolt by Francisco Madero, but he joined the movement in 1912, supporting Madero. After Madero's assassination by General Victoriano Huerta, Obregon aligned himself with the diverse groups of Venustiano Carranza, Emiliano Zapata, and Pancho Villa. When Huerta was defeated, Obregon joined the more conservative Carranza against Zapata and Villa.

Obregon's relationship with Villa was extremely conflicted; at times Obregon expressed genuine hatred for the rebel leader, and at other times the two men showed genuine affection for each other. Each plotted to assassinate the other, and during one three-day period Villa ordered Obregon's killing at least four times but always changed his mind. Obregon proved to be militarily superior to Zapata and defeated Villa in 1915 at Celaya and León, which significantly reduced Villa's power.

Considered a radical compared to Carranza, Obregon incorporated political maneuvers into his military campaigns. With harsh anticlerical

Alvaro Obregon

THE BANCROFT LIBRARY

policies and a prolabor stance, Obregon dominated the Mexican constitutional convention of 1917. When Carranza became constitutional
president, the programs Obregon had pushed through were forced on
him. Afterward, Obregon served for a short time in Carranza's cabinet,
then retired to farming life, ignoring politics for two years. But by 1920,
Obregon could no longer ignore Carranza's increasing reactionary policies, his abrogation of the constitution, and his attempt to install a puppet successor. Obregon led an uprising against Carranza, which led to
Carranza's assassination. Obregon then became president of Mexico.

Obregon's presidency brought considerable prosperity and peace to
Mexico, improving the economic conditions of both peasants and laborers, but his regime was considered too radical by the United States, which
refused to recognize his government until 1923, when Obregon agreed
not to expropriate American oil companies. That year, as his nonrenew-
able term of office was about to end, Obregon became obsessed with

picking his successor. He favored Plutarco Elias Calles but worried that Pancho Villa might interfere with the election process. Although Villa was retired and probably incapable of launching a full-scale insurrection, Obregon resolved to have Villa eliminated, and Villa was assassinated.

Plutarco Elias Calles did become the next president of Mexico, and when his term of office was about to end, in 1928, he went about the business of securing the position for his successor. Calles insisted that the constitution be amended so that the one-term-of-office limitation would apply only to immediate succession, and that the presidential term be increased from four to six years. Only two generals opposed the idea, but they were quickly seized and executed. Soon the constitutional amendment passed, and Obregon overwhelmingly won the election, becoming president again. Although many intellectuals, labor leaders, and young politicians were dismayed with the prospect of power alternating indefinitely between Calles and Obregon, they felt powerless to stop it.

EVENT: On July 15, only days after his new election, Obregon attended a small victory banquet in a restaurant called *La Bombilla* (the Little Bomb). José de León Toral, a newspaper cartoonist and fervent Catholic, also happened to be in the restaurant and sketched the president-elect. It was well known that, as an ardent Catholic, Toral resented the anticlerical actions of both Obregon and Calles, but no one seemed to be alarmed as Toral approached Obregon, presumably to show Obregon his sketches. Instead, Toral drew a pistol and shot Obregon three times at point-blank range. Obregon was killed instantly, probably not even aware of what had happened.

AFTERMATH: Rumored links between Toral and a Catholic nun led some to say Obregon's assassination was arranged by the church, but popular opinion was that Calles himself was behind the murder. When Obregon joined Madero, Zapata, Carranza, and Villa as revolutionary martyrs, Calles became the only living man with enough power to rule Mexico. He announced pompously that the era of the *caudillos* was over;

it was time, Calles said, "to pass from the country of one man to a nation of institutions and laws." Still, between 1928 and 1935, Calles ran the country from his luxurious mansion in picturesque Cuernavaca, becoming known as *Jefe Maximo*, and his rule as the *maximato*. At the end of his term, the nation was astonished when Calles stepped down from the presidency.

 FEBRUARY 15, 1933

FRANKLIN D. ROOSEVELT (1882–1945)
THIRTY-SECOND PRESIDENT OF THE UNITED STATES, FROM 1933 TO 1945

WOULD-BE ASSASSIN: Guiseppe Joseph Zangara, a political malcontent.

HISTORY: Born into a wealthy family in Hyde Park, New York, Franklin Delano Roosevelt was educated in Europe, then at Harvard and Columbia universities, before becoming a lawyer. He was elected a New York state senator in 1910 and left that office in 1913 to serve as assistant secretary of the navy under Woodrow Wilson, effectively increasing the efficiency of the navy during World War I. In 1921, Roosevelt was stricken with polio, but he had recovered enough to return to politics by 1929, when he was elected governor of New York. FDR, a Democrat, was governor of New York from 1929 to 1933, when he was elected president of the United States.

EVENT: Before his inauguration on March 13, 1933, President-elect Roosevelt took a twelve-day fishing vacation on a yacht owned by Vincent Astor. On the evening of February 15, when he come ashore in

Miami, FDR decided to stop at a nearby park to give a short speech. Sitting atop the right rear seat of a convertible in bright light, he concluded his 132-word address, slid down into the seat, and motioned to Chicago mayor Anton J. Cermak, seated in a nearby bandstand, to join him in the car. As Cermak reached FDR's car, Guiseppe Zangara stood up on a chair about twenty-five feet away and opened fire with a .32-caliber revolver he had purchased for eight dollars in a downtown Miami pawnshop. Five rapid shots rang out. Five people were hit: three men in the head, a woman in the abdomen, and Mayor Cermak by a bullet that smashed into his body under his right armpit and entered his lung.

Realizing he had been shot, Cermak cried out, "The president, get him away!" And he told Roosevelt, "I'm glad it was me instead of you." Roosevelt cradled the wounded mayor as the car sped away. Later, FDR would say, "I held him all the way to the hospital and his pulse constantly improved. . . . I remember I said, 'Tony, keep quiet—don't move—it won't hurt you if you keep quiet and remain perfectly still.'"

PUNISHMENT: Guiseppe Zangara was put to death by electrocution on March 21, 1933. He went to his execution without remorse, saying, "If I got out, I would kill him [Roosevelt] at once."

Upon being taken into the death chamber, Zangara said, "There is no God. It's all below. . . . See, I no scared of electric chair." He sat down in the electric chair and glared at the witnesses with contempt, saying, "Lousy capitalists." His last words were "Good-bye. *Addio* to all the world. Go ahead. Push the button."

AFTERMATH: Mayor Cermak lingered for three weeks. From his deathbed he suggested that he, not Roosevelt, was the intended assassination victim. Although many believed Cermak's theory was nonsense, others thought there was an element of plausibility to it. Cermak was feuding with the Capone gang in Chicago at the time, and despite Zangara's confession to the contrary, he could have been a hired hit man using FDR as a cover for his real assignment. Judge John H. Lyle, not a

Mafia member but generally recognized for his knowledge of Chicago crime, stated without doubt that Zangara was a Mafia killer who had been brought to the United States from Sicily to assassinate Mayor Cermak. However, records show that Zangara had actually lived in the United States for some ten years.

CERMAK ASSASSINATION PLOT THEORY: Although Cermak was elected as a reformer who would take control of Chicago back from Capone, maybe the general public didn't realize he would replace Capone's gangsters with his own. Cermak was known in political circles as Ten Percent Tony, because 10 percent was the standard amount he would skim in kickbacks and other graft deals. Some say Cermak even tried to remove Frank Nitti, Capone's successor while Capone was in prison, sending some tough cops to assassinate Nitti. He had been handcuffed, then shot three times in the neck and back. When Nitti miraculously recovered, Cermak supposedly got scared and left Chicago on December 21, 1932, for an extended vacation in Florida. By February 15, 1932, the day Zangara shot Cermak, the mayor had not returned to the Windy City even once, leading some newsmen to speculate that he never intended to return at all. As the theory goes, Nitti had Cermak's top man in Chicago murdered, then sent Zangara to Florida with orders to eliminate the mayor himself.

The Cermak assassination-plot theory has never been proved, and some Mafia experts say a Mafia hit man would never use a handgun to shoot his target twenty-five feet away. Still, some question why Zangara, who was said to have been an expert shooter in the Italian army many years earlier, missed FDR. Press accounts credit his failure to the alert reaction of fearless spectators who grabbed his arm and shoved it upward as he began firing, but Zangara told a different story to his lawyers. He said no one grabbed his arm until after he had fired all his shots. A police officer who helped subdue Zangara said he was not a good shot at all, since he hit four bystanders as well as Cermak.

In his book, *American Assassins*, James W. Clarke disputes the conspiracy theory, describing Zangara as a man with severely distorted emotions and an obsessive antisocial perspective. Although Zangara raved against capitalists, no records indicate he was a socialist, communist, anarchist, or even a fascist; in fact, he was a registered Republican. According to Zangara's confession, he had rallied against presidents after coming to America in 1923, and he considered killing King Victor Emmanuel III before leaving Italy. Further, he said he was just as likely to kill Calvin Coolidge or Herbert Hoover, but FDR just happened to be in Miami when he was there. "I see Mr. Hoover first, I kill him first," Zangara said at his trial. "Make no difference, presidents just the same bunch—all same." When asked why he shot Cermak, Zangara said, "I wasn't shooting at him, but I'm not sorry I hit him."

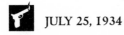 JULY 25, 1934

ENGELBERT DOLLFUSS (1892–1934)
AUSTRIAN STATESMAN

Although a devout Catholic, Austrian statesman Engelbert Dollfuss was appointed chancellor, of Austria in 1932 as a member of the Christian Socialist party. But as chancellor, he became a politically isolated figure, opposed by both the Socialists, who bitterly attacked him because of his right-wing authoritarian mode of government, and the Nationalists (Nazis) because of his determination to maintain Austrian integrity.

ASSASSINS: Otto Planetta and Franz Holzweber, leading a group of SS men.

HISTORY: As Hitler gained control of Germany, a strong Nazi movement grew in Austria, with many Austrians believing a union with

Germany was necessary for economic security. Still, Dollfuss was determined to maintain Austria's independence. On March 7, 1933, as antigovernment agitation increased in Austria, Dollfuss attempted to take control of his country. He proclaimed a dictatorship and dissolved the Bundersversammlung (parliament). Although Austrian citizens were prohibited from holding parades and assemblies as of March 8, Austrian Nazis staged a huge demonstration and rioted on March 29. Dollfuss countered by forbidding any member of a political party to wear a uniform. Hitler retaliated, imposing a tax of one thousand marks on any German who visited Austria, effectively ruining Austria's tourist business.

Dollfuss then sought the support of his friend Benito Mussolini in Italy. Mussolini was willing to guarantee Austrian independence if certain conditions were met: The Austrian constitution must be altered to include a fascist style of corporate government; the Socialists must be destroyed; and Austria must break from the League of Nations. In February 1934, Dollfuss announced that Austria had a new constitution, and issued a decree dissolving all political parties except for his own Fatherland Front. He antagonized Vienna's working class by ordering police to raid Socialist headquarters and bombard a Socialist housing unit, the Karl Marx Hof. When Socialist workers protested, Dollfuss ordered the Austrian army to take charge of the situation, which led to fierce fighting and the deaths of some one thousand men, women, and children, and the wounding of another four thousand.

By that time, the forty-one-year-old chancellor, nicknamed "Millimeternich" because of his small stature (he stood less than five feet tall), had become popular throughout Europe for steadfastly resisting the Nazis. Because he opposed Hitler, it was generally overlooked that Dollfuss himself was guiding his country toward a fascist dictatorship at the urging of Mussolini. Although Dollfuss managed to suppress all political parties other than his own, including the Austrian Nazi Party, Hitler secretly urged the Austrian Nazis to attempt a violent takeover.

EVENT: On July 25, 1934, the Austrian Nazis attempted a coup. Putting their plan into action that morning, 154 members of the SS Standarte 89, dressed in Austrian army uniforms, seized Vienna's main radio station and important government buildings, including the chancellery. Because Austrian leaders had been warned about the coup minutes beforehand, they had all fled the chancellery except Dollfuss, who was preparing to leave, when a small group of SS men led by Franz Holzweber and Otto Planetta burst in. They found Dollfuss in the Yellow Salon, his private office. Dollfuss tried to convince the men to give up the idea of taking over the government. Planetta raised his pistol. Dollfuss put his hands up to shield his face. Planetta fired two shots directly at his hands. One bullet penetrated Dollfuss's throat; the other passed through his spinal column. Dollfuss, still alive but paralyzed from the hips down, begged the men to call a doctor to help him.

As the assassins tried to keep control of the chancellery building, they came under siege by government troops. The siege lasted for several hours, while Dollfuss, still breathing, continued to plead with his attackers to summon medical aid. They ignored his pleas.

Dollfuss died at about 6 P.M. after saying, "Children, be good to one another. I always wanted to do only the best."

As the coup attempt progressed, Hitler received updates by telephone while attending a performance of *Das Rheingold* at the annual Wagner Festival at Bayreuth. But Hitler was not yet ready to openly support the Austrian Nazi Party in its efforts to hold control of the government that day. After the coup was easily smashed by Austrian forces, Hitler denied any knowledge of the event and denounced the assassination of Dollfuss.

PUNISHMENT: Thirteen of the Austrian Nazis who murdered Dollfuss were tried for their crime, found guilty, and executed by hanging.

After Planetta and Holzweber were led to the scaffold, they stood to attention, faced Germany, and shouted, "Heil Hitler!"

AFTERMATH: The murder of Austrian chancellor Engelbert Dollfuss is believed to be German dictator Adolf Hitler's first attempt to use assassination as a method of conquest. Though Hitler refused to acknowledge any connection to this attempt to unify Austria with Germany, four years later when the Nazis easily took control of Austria without bloodshed, Hitler immediately ordered the release of all the SS men involved in the attempted coup who were still in prison.

 OCTOBER 9, 1934

ALEXANDER I (1888–1934)
KING OF YUGOSLAVIA

Alexander Karageorgevich served as regent of Serbia from 1912 to 1921 for his father, Peter I, the king. When his father died in 1921, Alexander became king of the territory then known as the Kingdom of the Serbs, Croats, and Slovenes. His country had been formed in 1918 following World War I, mostly from the defeated Austro-Hungarian Empire, and included Serbia, Croatia-Slovenia, Montenegro, Bosnia, and Herzegovina. As king, Alexander faced the huge challenge of trying to pacify various forces producing political chaos in his country, including the Croatians at home and the Italians abroad.

ASSASSIN: Vlada Chernozamsky, a young Croatian nationalist and professional assassin hired by Ante Pavelic in a conspiracy of Croatian nationalists.

HISTORY: King Alexander's problems worsened in 1928 when Stefan Radich, the Croat leader, was assassinated in Parliament. In response,

Alexander, a hardline militarist, dissolved Parliament, abolished the constitution, and established himself as dictator, renaming his kingdom Yugoslavia ("Nation of the South Slavs"). A new constitution was proclaimed in 1931, but Alexander was unable to enact many of its terms as bitter feelings toward him, especially among the Croats, undermined his efforts. At the same time, Croat nationalists, led by Ante Pavelic and with the secret support of Benito Mussolini of Italy, were conspiring to assassinate Alexander.

EVENT: On October 9, 1934, Alexander was in France working out the details of an alliance of peace. Riding through the streets of Marseilles in a limousine, along with Foreign Minister Louis Barthou and French general Alfonse Georges, Alexander was surprised to see a man bolt from the crowd toward his car. Vlada Chernozamsky, a professional assassin hired by Croatian nationalist Ante Pavelic, jumped on the running board of the limo and emptied his pistol, striking King Alexander twice and hitting Barthou once. General Georges, who received only four superficial wounds, watched as Alexander died within two minutes. Also watching was a newsreel cameraman, who was the first to capture a live assassination on film.

Forty people in the crowd were injured when the mounted guards charged them, trying to capture the assassin. Barthou died hours later from loss of blood and inadequate medical attention.

PUNISHMENT: Chernozamsky was smashed to the ground by the crowd, captured by police bodyguards, severely beaten, and shot in the head, probably by a policeman. He was dead within hours. Several others were captured, charged in a conspiracy to assassinate King Alexander I, and later sentenced to life in prison. Ante Pavelic, who had planned the assassination, escaped to Italy and was never charged in the crime.

AFTERMATH: The assassins of King Alexander and Louis Barthou are considered one of the first of the modern terrorist groups. Well funded and highly mobile, they were provided with false passports and efficient firearms and had a well-placed organization to support them.

Although it was later declared that Mussolini's government had instigated the assassination, the French Sûreté decided it was the result of a conspiracy of Croatian nationalists. Still, international outrage resulted, and the League of Nations (forerunner of the United Nations) was prompted to address the problem of international political terrorism. In 1937, it established two international conventions designed to combat political terrorism: the Convention for the Prevention and Punishment of Terrorism, which criminalized attacks on heads of state and other internationally protected persons, and the Convention for the Creation of an International Criminal Court, which was designed to impose international law on terrorist networks. But the league's provisions would prove to be a failure when few nations would ratify the conventions, and the measures were eventually abandoned.

SEPTEMBER 8, 1935

HUEY P. LONG (1893–1935)
U.S. DEMOCRATIC POLITICIAN

Huey P. Long served as governor of Louisiana from 1928 to 1931, and U.S. senator from Louisiana from 1930 to 1935.

A powerful and flamboyant politician, Long established his southern dynasty by fighting for popular social reform and increasing welfare, while enjoying the personal and political benefits of government corruption. He was a Democrat who hated big business and loved big politics. The man and his career got so much attention nationwide that there have been numerous novels, movies, and nonfiction studies about him. Called everything from a dictator to a radical, Huey P. Long was a U.S.

senator hoping to become president when he was shot to death. Even today the events surrounding his death are blurred by a debate that keeps alive his memory.

Born in Winnfield, Louisiana, in 1893, Long worked as a farm boy, then a salesman, before attending Tulane University, where he earned a law degree. After being admitted to the bar, he served as an attorney for the state of Louisiana. Long's first try at political office failed when he ran for governor of Louisiana, but in 1928 he tried again and won. His winning political platform of reforms that would benefit working-class families was enacted early in his term: State-owned hospitals were expanded, schools were built in rural regions, and badly needed roads and bridges were constructed. At the same time, he indulged in extravagances, including a new state capital building in Baton Rouge made of bronze and marble. The money to pay for these projects was collected mostly by heavily taxing big business, especially oil companies.

Although some claim that Long used ruthless and demogogic methods to establish dictatorial power and to push through his social and economic reforms as governor, he remained popular with the people. His election to the U.S. Senate in 1930 was proof of his continued popularity. Still, unwilling to relinquish control of the government of his home state, Long handpicked his successor, and Oscar O. K. Allen became the figurehead governor of Louisiana under Senator Long's control.

While Long essentially still controlled the government of Louisiana from Washington, D.C., he also caused problems in the nation's capital. President Franklin D. Roosevelt was trying desperately to gain control of the nation's failing economy during the Great Depression with his New Deal economic program, but Senator Huey P. Long had another idea, which gained considerable popular support: his Share the Wealth program.

As the 1936 presidential election approached, it looked like Long's economic proposals would play a significant role in undermining FDR's reelection. Poor white voters idolized Long for his Share the Wealth program, which called for massive redistribution of wealth by significantly increasing inheritance taxes and confiscatory taxes on high incomes. President Roosevelt was counted among the wealthy businessmen and conservative politicians who detested Huey P. Long, whose slogan was "Every man a king, but no man wears a crown."

ASSASSIN: Carl Austin Weiss, twenty-nine years old, was considered a brilliant doctor and a calm, sensitive family man. Born in Baton Rouge, Dr. Weiss interned at the American Hospital in Paris and Bellevue Hospital in New York before entering into practice with his father back home in 1932. When he married Yvonne Pavy, the daughter of Judge Benjamin H. Pavy, a minor political opponent of Huey Long, Weiss automatically took the side of his father-in-law. As the leader of an anti-Long faction in Saint Landry Parish of Opelousas, Louisiana, Judge Pavy strongly opposed a bill that was scheduled for passage during a special session of the Long-controlled Louisiana Legislature. The bill was designed to gerrymander judicial districts in a way that would make Judge Pavy's reelection the following January almost impossible. It would add to Pavy's district the parishes of Acadia, Lafayette, and Vermillion, where Long held strong majorities.

Weiss's dislike of Huey P. Long apparently stemmed more from loyalty to his family (his own parents hated Long) and his wife's family than from his own interest in politics. It is reported that he never talked politics or got involved in political activities. When he wasn't seeing patients or operating, Weiss spent time with his family and designed medical instruments. He was considered to be one of the most highly trained young ear-nose-and-throat specialists in Louisiana, a genuine "doctor's doctor."

On the day Huey P. Long was shot, Weiss appeared to go about his usual routine, and even confirmed an operation he was scheduled to perform the following morning.

HISTORY: There seemed to be no middle ground when it came to an opinion about Huey P. Long. He was considered by some to be the most

Huey P. Long

UPI / CORBIS-BETTMANN

beloved man in his state and the nation, a true friend of the poor, while those who opposed him called him a demagogue, a madman, and the destroyer of constitutional government.

On the surface, Long appeared to have noble intentions as a politician, but working through normal channels didn't seem expedient enough for him. Circumventing established procedures for change became his mode of operation, and the source of assistance for his programs seemed irrelevant if a quick end result was achieved. Long even used organized crime to his advantage.

When Fiorello La Guardia, mayor of New York City, went on a campaign to rid his jurisdiction of a crime syndicate's slot-machine empire, the mobsters needed a new location for their operation. Mafia kingpin Frank Costello accepted an offer from then-governor Long to set up shop in Louisiana. Soon the underworld shipped thousands of one-armed bandits to New Orleans, and Louisiana became the illegal slot-machine center of the United States. In exchange, millions of dollars in payoffs by the crime syndicate kept Long's political machine running.

It was not unheard-of for Long to use strong-arm tactics to get what he wanted, and most of the time they worked. Still, every now and then the democratic process would prevail. A special session of the Louisiana Legislature was called by Long in 1929 in order to pass a new tax on the oil industry. During the debate fistfights broke out on the floor of the Louisiana House of Representatives, and the bill was thrown out. Further, the House tried to impeach Governor Long for the crimes of bribery and gross misconduct, but he was never convicted.

In 1930, when Long was elected to the U.S. Senate, he refused to vacate the governorship and take his Senate seat in Washington, D.C., for nearly two years. Lieutenant Governor Paul N. Cyr would have become the new governor of Louisiana, and Long believed Cyr would dismantle the political machine he had worked so hard to establish. When Cyr swore himself into office twice during that time, national guardsmen were dispatched by Long to surround the highway commission, the capital, and the executive mansion, preventing Cyr from becoming governor. It was one and a half years after he was elected U.S. senator before Long assumed his duties in Washington.

Although he supported Roosevelt's New Deal policies early in his senatorial career, it soon became apparent to Long that with FDR intending to serve multiple terms in the White House there would be no room for him to move up. Suddenly Long became a fierce opponent of FDR, devising his own Share the Wealth program of social and economic reforms. Long's plan, introduced early in 1934, called for a national and social overhaul. It proposed to guarantee family income and a homestead allowance for each and every family in the United States. Voters suffering during the Great Depression loved Long's Share the Wealth program and threw their support behind the senator.

That same year, Long decided Louisiana's state government needed to be restructured so that he would have ultimate power. He saw to it that the election districts were redrawn on the state's map to guarantee that anti-Long candidates would be defeated in the next election. Some say the redistricting would have created for Long a virtual dictatorship in his home state. One of the districts that was gerrymandered would have politically disabled Judge B. H. Pavy, the father-in-law of Dr. Carl Weiss.

When Weiss learned that his wife's father would be unseated in his district if Long's redistricting plan passed the Louisiana Legislature, something inside the well-respected doctor must have snapped. On the evening of September 8, 1935, Weiss dressed in a white linen suit, told his wife he was going to make a few house calls, and left his home. He drove to the $5 million statehouse that Long had built while he was governor. After parking his car, Weiss went up the building's steps, then inside, where he stationed himself outside the office of Long's handpicked successor, Governor Oscar O. K. Allen. Witnesses would later swear that Weiss seemed agitated as he paced up and down the hallway, muttering, "It won't be long now."

EVENT: There are various versions of the events that took place in the magnificent capitol building on the night of September 8, 1935.

OFFICIAL VERSION: While Huey P. Long attended a special session of his puppet Louisiana House of Representatives, he strutted up and down the aisles interrupting the speakers, making jokes, and generally bullying and cajoling the members into passing his ideas and programs into law. Around 9:30 P.M., as the legislators prepared to recess, Long left the House chamber, shouting, "Everyone be here in the morning. Tell everybody to be here." He then walked with his armed bodyguards and Supreme Court justice John B. Fournet through the capitol building and into the governor's suite of offices, leaving five bodyguards waiting outside. Soon Long emerged, and his bodyguards followed as he strode down one of the corridors in his usual aggressive manner. Trying to keep up with Long and spread out behind him, guarding his rear, the bodyguards could not anticipate what would happen in front of the senator.

Suddenly, a man dressed in a white linen suit walked out from behind a recessed pillar and stepped up beside Long, taking a few steps with him. It was Weiss, and he was carrying a Belgian .32-caliber automatic pistol, which he pressed into Long's right side. Weiss said nothing and fired the gun once, striking Long in the lower right abdomen.

Long cried out, staggered, and clutched his right side, then escaped down the hall with blood streaming from his mouth. He staggered down a stairway and fell into the arms of James O'Connor, the public service commissioner saying, "Jimmy, my boy, I'm shot." O'Connor drew his gun and helped the wounded senator into an automobile, which headed for the nearest medical facility.

Meanwhile, Justice Fournet struck at Weiss's arm while Murphy Roden, one of Long's bodyguards, dived at the assassin. Immediately Weiss was disarmed and wrestled to the floor, and a fusillade of bullets was discharged by Long's bodyguards and state troopers arriving at the scene. When it ended, Weiss had been shot sixty-one times: Thirty bullets entered his chest, twenty-nine entered his back, and two struck him in the head. The dead assassin lay on the polished marble floor, his white linen suit red with blood.

The most skilled surgeons in the area were dispatched to Our Lady of the Lake Sanitarium, where Senator Long lay bleeding profusely but still conscious. Informed that the wound must be cleaned, Long said, "Go ahead and clean it," and gritted his teeth to bear the pain without anesthesia. It was decided that surgery must be performed, but first a blood transfusion was required. The doctors considered ten men from the large number of volunteers who offered to give their own blood to save Long. Lieutenant Governor James A. Noe, a close friend of Long, was finally chosen, and the transfusion began one and a half hours after the shooting.

At two o'clock on the morning of September 9, the surgeons issued the following news bulletin:

Senator Long was wounded by one bullet entering the upper right side, emerging from the back. The colon was punctured in two places. The first blood transfusion has been given the senator, with good results. The condition of Senator Long is thoroughly satisfactory. It will be seventy-two to ninety hours before further developments can be expected. Another bulletin will be issued at 7 A.M.

During the emergency operation, surgeons sutured veins to stop Long's internal bleeding and cleaned the wound to prevent infection. They found that the bullet had made two puncture wounds in Long's stomach and pierced a kidney. One more blood transfusion was given to the senator, but he died at 4:20 A.M. on September 10, thirty hours and forty-four minutes after being shot.

OFFICIAL-VERSION CONTROVERSY: According to one version of the events of September 8, Weiss never had a chance to fire a shot before Long's bodyguards themselves opened fire, accidentally killing their own boss while trying to protect him. Another version claims that Weiss never intended to kill Long but went to the statehouse to confront him publicly; Weiss then approached Long and punched him in the mouth, inciting the guards to open fire. (Indeed, Long did have an unexplained cut on his mouth, and he supposedly said, "That's where he hit me.") In the excitement, the scenario goes, one of the bodyguard's bullets accidentally hit Senator Long, who staggered from the scene. The bodyguards then searched Weiss, found his gun, and fired it, implicating Weiss as the assassin. Because the bullet that killed Long passed through his body entirely, there was no way to prove it was not from Weiss's gun.

At the coroner's inquest, the only eyewitness testimony came from Long's bodyguards and close associates, who all mostly agreed with the official version of the events. Some minor contradictions did arise, but they were not pursued at that time. Only later did other evidence about the assassination come to light in two heavily documented books: *The Huey Long Murder Case*, by Hermann B. Deutsch, and *The Day Huey Long Was Shot*, by David H. Zinman.

AFTERMATH: The next day, several of Long's aides, along with Assistant Attorney General George Wallace, made sure the Louisiana Legislature passed every piece of legislation Senator Long had wanted—although later much of it was ruled unconstitutional and reversed.

The following day the funeral held for Dr. Carl Weiss was attended by thousands of people, including many prominent in political circles.

Huey P. Long was laid to rest later that week, with a state funeral that attracted thirty thousand mourners. He was buried on the landscaped grounds of the magnificent capitol he had built.

There was some speculation by a small fringe group of Long loyalists that their hero's assassination had been engineered by President Roosevelt to ensure that Long would not cause him problems in the 1936 election.

Ironically, despite all the money that had passed through Long's hands during his political career, he died a relatively poor man. He left no will. He had a few oil stocks of uncertain value, his home in New Orleans was heavily mortgaged, and his life insurance policies were worth only about $130,000. The question was asked, What did he do with the rest of the millions he had made over the years? It has been theorized that the money must have been used to promote Long's image in preparation for his presidential campaign and to finance his newspaper, *The American Progress*.

A U.S. Senate inquiry was convened to determine the true cause of Long's assassination, but no conspiracy was ever proved.

In 1946, a masterful novel entitled *All the King's Men,* written by Robert Penn Warren and modeled on the life of Huey P. Long, became a best-seller and won a Pulitzer Prize. A film version of the novel won an Academy Award in 1949.

 AUGUST 20, 1940

LEON TROTSKY (1879–1940)
RUSSIAN REVOLUTIONARY LEADER
AND COFOUNDER OF THE BOLSHEVIK PARTY

Leon Trotsky organized the Red Army and played a key role in the Russian Revolution as the second most powerful man in the Soviet Union. When his opposition to Joseph Stalin resulted in his exile, he used his mighty pen to continue his attacks on Stalin from afar, until Stalin finally had him eliminated.

Leon Trotsky was named Lev Davidovich Bronstein at birth by his Jewish parents in Yelisavetgrad, Ukraine. The son of a farmer, Lev was educated at a local Jewish school before attending schools in Odessa and Nikolaev, graduating in 1897. He showed early leadership abilities when, at the age of ten, he was expelled from secondary school in Odessa, Russia, for inciting his classmates to laugh at their teacher. Because he was the school's best pupil, he was allowed to return the following year.

In 1900, Lev Bronstein, who had been active in the Marxist South Russian Workers Union, was banished to Sibera. Two years later he escaped. Then twenty-three years old, Lev took the name of his head jailer, officially becoming Leon Trotsky. He joined Lenin in London, where he waged a war of propaganda, writing for *Iskra*, while waiting to carry the revolution back to his homeland. When a general strike occurred in Saint Petersburg in October of 1905, Trotsky hurried back to Russia from Finland. Now home, Trotsky followed Vladimir Ilyich Lenin's lead, supporting the Menshevik faction of the Russian Social Democratic Workers party against the Bolsheviks. During the revolution, Trotsky was elected to the executive committee as speaker for the Mensheviks in Saint Petersburg (later renamed Leningrad).

By 1907, the revolution had collapsed and Trotsky was again exiled to Siberia, this time for life; but on the way to Siberia he escaped. During the next ten years Trotsky lived in Paris, Vienna, Zurich, and finally New

Leon Trotsky

UPI / CORBIS-BETTMANN

York City, all the while working with Lenin to bring about the Russian Revolution of 1917–1918.

By May 1917, when the revolution was three months old, Lenin abandoned the Mensheviks and rejoined the Bolsheviks. Trotsky followed his lead, returning to Saint Petersburg in time for the Sixth Party Congress in July. Trotsky and Lenin organized the October revolution and the overthrow of the provisional Soviet government in the civil war of 1918 to 1920. Lenin became leader of the new Soviet government when the Bolsheviks came to power and named Trotsky commissar of foreign affairs. Trotsky led negotiations with the Germans at the Brest-Litovsk Peace Conference. As minister of war, he built up the Red Army from fewer than ten thousand men to five million, and directed the campaign against the White Army during the civil war that followed the revolution.

It was during this time that a great hatred and competition was established between Trotsky and Joseph Stalin (who became secretary general of the Soviet party in 1922). Stalin wanted socialism within the country, and Trotsky was outspoken in his belief that socialism within Russia was not possible until a revolution occurred in Western Europe. These public statements by Trotsky, as well as his rapid advancement in power, created bitter enemies for him. He and Stalin battled to retain power within the Soviet government, each working toward becoming its leader as Lenin's health declined.

By the time Lenin died in 1924, Stalin had enlisted the support of all the enemies Trotsky had made while strong-arming himself into power. At Lenin's funeral, which Trotsky did not attend, Stalin declared himself Lenin's successor and immediately had Trotsky expelled from the Communist party. Trotsky tried to form an alliance against Stalin with two other prominent Bolshevik leaders, Lev Kamenev and Grigory Zinoviev, but they were defeated. In 1929, Stalin had Trotsky banished from the USSR to Alma-Ata in Central Asia. He stayed there only a short time, then went to Turkey, where he was granted asylum. In 1933 he moved to France, and on to Norway in 1935. Under pressure from Stalin, Norway expelled Trotsky in 1936 and he settled in Mexico, where he lived the remainder of his life.

While in exile, Trotsky did not forget about his country and continued his campaign for revolution, writing and speaking out against Stalin. His best-known publications include *My Life* (1930), *The History of the Russian Revolution* (three volumes, 1932–1933), and *The Revolution Betrayed* (1937).

ASSASSIN: Jaime Ramon Mercador del Rio Hernandez (a.k.a. Jacques Mornard and Frank Jacson), born in 1914 in Barcelona, Spain. Mercador was the son of a middle-class businessman and an unstable, passionate Cuban beauty who was an ardent supporter of Stalin. His mother fought in the Spanish civil war and became the mistress of a Soviet secret police general who later organized the conspiracy to kill Trotsky.

Ramon Mercador was of average intelligence but so dominated by his mother that he was strongly influenced by her beliefs.

Some historians believe Mercador was not the first choice to be the assassin of Trotsky but he put himself in a position to succeed when other attempts failed.

HISTORY: While Stalin was busy in the Soviet Union purging dissent and dissenters, Trotsky was busy in Mexico City writing fierce anti-Stalinist tracts that made their way back to his own country. In 1936, Stalin accused Trotsky of treason and had him tried in absentia.

By 1940, Joseph Stalin, as dictator of the USSR, had carried out a mass extermination of "old Bolsheviks" that he considered potential threats to his power. After the Great Purge, only his rival Trotsky remained.

Stalin and Trotsky agreed on one thing: When World War II ended there would be a total disruption of capitalism in the West and an international wave of socialist revolution. Both men wanted to head that revolution. Stalin had at his disposal all the resources of the Soviet Union, while Trotsky had only a few thousand followers, plus a potent weapon, his mighty pen. From Mexico, Trotsky worked feverishly to organize the Fourth International, a small but articulate group of revolutionaries who advocated worldwide revolution and pure communism. Still, that did not concern Stalin as much as the political propaganda Trotsky was writing and distributing. Perhaps Stalin regretted exiling Trotsky in 1929 instead of having him executed in the Soviet Union.

Since his exile, Trotsky had intensified his literary attacks on Stalin with such works as *Stalin's Crimes, the Real Situation in Russia* and *The Stalinist School of Falsification.* Then, while living in Mexico, the sixty-year-old banished revolutionary began working on a full-length "antibiography" called *Stalin.*

ATTEMPT: In the early hours of May 24, 1940, twenty men, led by the famous painter and Stalinist David Alfaro Sequeiros, dressed in fake Mexican police uniforms, overpowered Trotsky's guards and burst into Trotsky's Mexico City home. Once inside, the band of attackers set off dynamite, flung open Trotsky's bedroom door, and sprayed the room with several dozen rounds of machine-gun fire. Miraculously, Trotsky and his wife escaped serious injury by hiding under their bed. When the attackers fled, they took with them one of Trotsky's guests, a wealthy twenty-three-year-old New Yorker named Sheldon Harte, who was devoted to Trotsky and his ideals.

Considering the attack a failure, Communists in Mexico claimed the raid had been a fake, staged by Trotsky. But then the truth came out. Harte was traced to a house where Sequeiros and his men had taken him after the raid. There they apparently murdered him in his sleep, then dumped his body in a lime-filled grave.

With this new evidence revealed, the Soviets blamed Mexican Communist leaders for the raid, while the Mexican Communists claimed the men involved had recently been ousted from office. Sequeiros was denounced as an uncontrollable fringe element of the party. He joined his accomplices, and all of them fled Mexico.

ALTERNATE PLAN: During the late spring and early summer of 1940, Trotsky had his home transformed into a fortress with three-gun pill-boxes mounted on fifteen-foot-high brick walls, a steel door added to the front entrance of the villa, and an army of guards patrolling the grounds. While Trotsky was well protected from strangers, he seemed to have little thought of protecting himself from his friends.

In March of 1940, Sylvia Ageloff, an American girl from Brooklyn and an ardent Trotskyite, introduced Trotsky to Frank Jacson, a young man she had met in Paris two years earlier. Ageloff didn't know Jacson's true identity: Ramon Mercador, an agent of the GPU, Stalin's secret police. Trotsky and Mercador seemed to enjoy each other's company. Mercador was a willing listener, an eager student, and a skilled flatterer. While he became a regular dinner guest in Trotsky's home and a member of his inner circle of acquaintances, Ageloff returned in April to her job as a welfare investigator in New York. It is reported that no one questioned how Mercador earned a living or why he had a seemingly inexhaustible supply of money. Apparently he was an extraordinarily skilled fake and charmer. Sylvia Ageloff returned to Mexico City on August 1 to spend her vacation with him.

Mercador earned Trotsky's trust by doing small errands and totally agreeing with Trotsky's opinions. In time, Mercador would come and go from Trotsky's villa almost at will, without drawing suspicion from his guards. During one discussion with Trotsky, four days after the May 24 raid on Trotsky's home, Mercador even suggested, without batting an eyelash, that "in the next attack, the GPU will use other methods."

When he wasn't visiting Trotsky's villa, Mercador spent time building his strength and learning to properly use an ice ax while climbing volcanoes near Mexico City. He also wrote political pieces he hoped Trotsky would publish.

EVENT: At 5:30 P.M. on August 20, 1940, twenty-six-year-old Mercador entered Trotsky's villa armed with a revolver and a dagger and hiding a short-handled mountaineer's ice ax beneath his raincoat. He found sixty-year-old Leon Trotsky feeding his pet rabbits and asked for his help with an article he had written. Trotsky agreed, and the two men talked for a while, then entered the dining room, where Mrs. Trotsky sat reading. Mercador asked for a glass of water. Mrs. Trotsky got it for him, and the two men, still talking earnestly, entered Trotsky's paper-littered study. Trotsky sat down at a long wooden table he used as a desk to read Mercador's article. Mercador, still holding his raincoat, positioned himself to Trotsky's left, where he could block the alarm button Trotsky could push to summon the guards.

Within a few minutes, guards in an adjoining room heard loud arguing in the study, then several thuds. The guards and Mrs. Trotsky ran to the study and flung open the door to find a scene of bloody mayhem. Mercador later described what had happened:

> I put my raincoat on the table on purpose so that I could take out the ice ax which I had in the pocket. . . . I took the *piolet* [ice ax] out of my raincoat, took it in my fist, and, closing my

eyes, I gave him a tremendous blow on the head. . . . The man
screamed in such a way that I will never forget as long as I live.
His scream was . . . very long, infinitely long, and it still seems
to me as if that scream were piercing my brains.

Because the ice ax sank deeply into Trotsky's brain, the assassin
apparently expected his victim to die silently and instantly, but Trotsky
remained standing. He whirled around, grabbed his assailant's arm, and
bit his hand to make him drop the weapon. As Trotsky staggered toward
the study door, Mercador pulled out his revolver and aimed. Before he
could fire a shot, the door of the study burst open. Two of Trotsky's
guards rushed in, knocked the revolver from Mercador's hand, slammed
him to the floor, and beat him mercilessly. The guards asked Trotsky, who
was bleeding profusely but still conscious, if they should kill his attacker.
With difficulty Trotsky answered, "Impermissible to kill, he must be . . .
forced . . . to . . . talk."

Trotsky then staggered into the dining room and collapsed. Mrs.
Trotsky cradled her husband's head while a guard called an ambulance.
Both Trotsky and his attacker were rushed to the central hospital in
Mexico City, where they were treated on the same floor. Mercador recov-
ered quickly. Trotsky lingered for twenty-six hours, then died at 7:25 P.M.
on August 21, 1940.

PUNISHMENT: Only after the assassination of Leon Trotsky did Sylvia
Ageloff realize her boyfriend, Frank Jacson, was actually a Soviet assassin
named Ramon Mercador and that Mercador's mother, who held the
Order of Lenin for masterminding Stalinist assassinations, had convinced her son that assassinating Trotsky was a necessary and glorious
mission.

Sylvia Ageloff was arrested as an accomplice to the crime and put on
trial with Mercador in Mexico City. Eventually all charges against her
were dropped when the court was convinced that she had been an innocent victim seduced by the charms of Ramon Mercador.

During his trial, which took years, Mercador first identified himself as Jacques Monard van den Dreshd, a native of Tehran and the son of a Belgian diplomat. He said the money he always carried was an inheritance. He also claimed he killed Trotsky because the revolutionary had prevented his marriage to Ageloff. But Mercador's real identity and his true motives for the assassination slowly emerged. It was revealed that Mercador's mother, Caridad, the great Soviet heroine, was waiting in a car outside Trotsky's compound to help her son escape after the assassination. Finally, in 1943, Mercador was sentenced by a Mexican court to twenty years in prison for the assassination of Leon Trotsky.

During Mercador's incarceration, there were negotiations between Mexico and the USSR, first to make Mercador's stay in prison more comfortable and then to secure his early release. When Mercador was set free in 1960, he went to communist Czechoslovakia, where he lived for a while. There both he and his mother were declared heroes of the Soviet Union. By the 1970s, Mercador had emigrated to Cuba, where he died on October 18, 1978, in Havana.

AFTERMATH: After Leon Trotsky's assassination, it was announced by his wife and his family attorney, Albert Goldman, that the former Russian revolutionary leader's body would be taken to New York for a memorial service and burial. But that same day, the U.S. State Department issued an order barring his entrance, dead or alive, into the United States. Goldman said the State Department's order would immediately be appealed, but Mrs. Trotsky apparently had neither the heart nor the stomach to go through protracted legal proceedings. Five days later, on August 27, Leon Trotsky's body was cremated in Mexico City.

Not until 1989 did the Soviet Union officially recognize that the GPU was responsible for the assassination of Leon Trotsky almost fifty years earlier.

MAY 27, 1942

REINHARD TRISTAN HEYDRICH
(1904–1942)
NAZI OFFICIAL

A German Nazi, Heydrich, as head of the party's security service and Heinrich Himmler's deputy, was instrumental in organizing *Endlosung der Judenfrage,* "the Final Solution." This was the policy that led to the Holocaust: the annihilation of an estimated six million Jews by the Hitler regime between 1933 and 1945. An additional ten million non-Jews died during imprisonment or were executed; among them were Ukrainian, Polish, and Russian civilians and prisoners of war, Gypsies, socialists, homosexuals, and others labeled "defective." The victims were starved, tortured, and worked to death; millions were executed in gas chambers, shot, or hanged.

Before becoming chief of the Nazi Security Police and deputy chief of the Gestapo, Reinhard Heydrich was an unemployed German navy intelligence officer who had been court-martialed for having an affair with a teenage girl. He was a man of considerable personal accomplishments, among them playing the violin and fencing. Heydrich reveled in flying volunteer sorties with *Luftwaffe* fighter pilots. Once he was shot down over the Russian front and, though wounded, still managed to make a forced landing in German-held territory. Some of his contemporaries were convinced that such stunts were part of Heydrich's plan to undermine Heinrich Himmler and take his place as one of Hitler's top advisers. Walter Schellenberg, the Nazi intelligence expert, writes about Heydrich in his memoirs: "This man was the hidden pivot around which the Nazi regime revolved. The development of a whole nation was guided indirectly by his forceful character."

Reinhard Heydrich was considered the ideal of Nazism. It is said that Adolf Hitler himself viewed the charismatic icy-eyed, ambitious young man as his possible successor. Heydrich had joined a Free Corps band at the age of fourteen and was schooled in street fighting and terrorism. He enlisted in the navy in 1922 and rose in rank to first lieutenant before being forced to resign in 1931 because of sexual indiscretions. From that time on he devoted every waking hour to the Nazi cause.

By age thirty-eight, Heydrich had become the Nazi "protector" of Bohemia and Moravia and was known as the "hangman of Europe" because of his brutal treatment of civilians there and elsewhere on the continent.

ASSASSINS: Jan Kubis and Josef Gabcik, two Czech freedom fighters of the Czech underground.

HISTORY: Shortly after Hitler came to power, Heydrich was named chief of the political department of the Munich police, which controlled, among other things, the notorious Dachau concentration camp. In 1934 he was elevated to the position of SS chief for Berlin, and later became deputy chief of the SS under Heinrich Himmler.

After being put in charge of police matters in Austria following the Anschluss in 1938, Heydrich played a key role in fabricating Polish "atrocities" against Germans to justify the invasion of Poland. He was made *Reichsprotektor* of Bohemia-Moravia in 1941, and ordered the execution of three hundred Czechs within five weeks of his arrival in Prague. Heydrich performed his duties so well that his territory was extended to Norway, Holland, and occupied France. Wherever he visited to put down outbreaks of sabotage and terrorism there were always mass executions, resulting in his notorious nickname, "Hangman Heydrich." Finally, he took charge of the establishment and operation of the extermination camps that would liquidate millions of Jews and other "undesirables." The details of this "Final Solution" to the Jewish problem had been decided upon during a Nazi conference in a Berlin suburb on January 20, 1942. Heydrich saw to it that every European Jew who could be identified was rounded up, packed into a ghetto, and finally herded into the gas ovens of specially designed extermination camps.

EVENT: By May 27, 1942, the Czechoslovakian government in exile felt Reinhard Heydrich had become too popular in their country as its "protector." Two members of the free Czechoslovak army in England, John Kubis and Josef Gabcik, were enlisted to board a Royal Air Force bomber with specific orders to assassinate Heydrich. As the bomber flew low over the target area of Czechoslovakia, Kubis and Gabcik jumped out, parachuting home with a mission. They made their way to the Prague suburb of Holesovice and waited, with two other freedom fighters who joined them on the ground, alongside the Dresden-Prague road near the Troja Bridge. This was the route taken daily by Heydrich as he was driven from his villa to his headquarters in Hradschin Castle.

Soon Heydrich's green Mercedes convertible approached and slowed to take a hairpin curve. The Czechs aimed their guns and opened fire at the Mercedes while Kubis hurled a grenade, which struck the back of the car, blowing it apart. Heydrich stumbled, swerving out of the smashed automobile, his pistol in hand, firing it at his assailants. Then he suddenly grabbed his hip, staggered, and fell. The steel springs from the car's seat had been driven into the thirty-eight-year-old Nazi's ribs and stomach. He died of his wounds on June 4, 1942.

The assassins escaped under cover of a smoke screen and were given sanctuary by priests of the Karl Borromaeus Church. But they were soon betrayed and killed, along with every other member of the resistance, by attacking SS troops.

AFTERMATH: The Nazis, unaware that Kubis and Gabcik were dead, gathered German troops and entered the Bohemian village of Lidice, seeking the assassins of Reinhard Heydrich. In the process, they burned the village to the ground and liquidated 1,331 Czechs, slaughtering every male citizen of Lidice over sixteen years of age, and some women, and deported the remaining women and children to concentration camps. Four of the women were pregnant and about to give birth, so they were sent to a maternity hospital in Prague. When the babies were born, they were killed, and their mothers were sent to concentration camps. Although many of the children of Lidice were murdered, others who could pass muster by SS "racial experts" were raised as Germans. The officer responsible for the obliteration of Lidice was hanged in 1946.

Meanwhile, in Germany, Josef Goebbels, hearing that Heydrich had been attacked, ordered that five hundred of the few Jews still living in Berlin be rounded up and held prisoner. When Heydrich died eight days later, 152 of the Berlin Jews were executed, and some three thousand Jews from the ghetto of Theresienstadt were sent to concentration camps to be executed.

Historians have speculated about the reasons why Heydrich was assassinated. Since the Czechs appeared to be acting on British orders, some people believe Heydrich was silenced because he knew too much about the treasonable activities of England's duke of Windsor. But in his book *The Killing of SS Obergruppenführer Reinhard Heydrich*, Callum MacDonald argues persuasively that Heydrich's assassination was a desperate gamble by Eduard Benes, the head of the Czechoslovak government in exile. MacDonald theorizes that Benes wanted to prove to England and Russia that the Czech underground was a viable force. Further, Benes wanted to gain personal prestige, to the detriment of the Czechoslovak Communists, and ensure that the Czechoslovak people would not compromise by making peace with the Nazis. If this thesis is viable, it would follow that both Benes and the allies knew beforehand that the assassination would have disastrous consequences, with rivers of blood spilled after Heydrich was killed.

JULY 20, 1944

ADOLF HITLER (1889–1945)
CHANCELLOR OF GERMANY AND NAZI LEADER
FROM 1933 TO 1945

Adolf Hitler was one of the most powerful and evil figures in world
history. As head of the National Socialist German Workers party, or
Nationalsozialistische Deutsche Arbeiterpartei (the shortened name *Nazi*
is derived from the syllables *Nat* and *zi*), he made a serious attempt to
dominate the world. The Nazi dictator's Third Reich conquered 1.37 million square miles of territory from 1933 to the fall of 1942, taking control
of most of continental Europe, from the English Channel to the outskirts
of Moscow and from North Africa to Norway. Hitler's infamous reign of
ruthless violence, torture, extermination, and discrimination lasted for
thirteen years, ultimately resulting in the deaths of millions of people.

WOULD-BE ASSASSINS: German military officers and aristocrats.

HISTORY: Adolf Hitler was born at Braunau am Inn, Austria-Hungary,
the son of a customs official. As a young man, he dreamed of becoming
an artist, but he flunked the entrance exams for Vienna's Academy of
Fine Arts in 1907 and 1908. Supporting himself by painting postcards
and posters, he frequently moved from place to place in the Austrian
capital to evade military service. When World War I began, he enlisted
in a Bavarian infantry regiment and served as a lance corporal with distinction, being awarded the Iron Cross twice (during four years of front-
line combat he was gassed and wounded). In 1920, when Hitler joined
the German Workers party, his leadership soon turned the tiny, ineffective group into a formidable paramilitary organization. On November
8, 1923, in Munich, he tried to force the Bavarian government into a
full-scale revolution against the Weimar Republic, but his beer-hall
putsch failed. Charged with high treason, Hitler was sentenced to serve

five years in Landsberg prison. During that time, the future Nazi leader dictated to his secretary, Rudolf Hess, a rambling manuscript outlining his plan for Germany's domination of the world. Upon his release from prison, Hitler published the document, entitled *Mein Kampf* (*My Struggle*), which became the Nazi party's bible.

By 1933, as Germany's economic condition deteriorated and the country fell into a state of chaos, Hitler's popularity was growing. With his hypnotic oratories winning him the adoration of the masses, he used their enthusiastic support to scheme his way into a position of authority, first being named chancellor. When President Paul von Hindenburg died in 1934, Hitler saw the opening he had been waiting for. Moving quickly, he used devious political maneuvers to combine the offices of president and chancellor, naming himself Der Führer (the leader). With the support of right-wing industrialists and bankers throughout the country, Hitler rearmed Germany. He eliminated German democracy and his political opponents, having them permanently jailed or brutally murdered. Recognizing a potential threat to his leadership from within his private army of one hundred thousand men, the brown-shirted Sturmabteilung (Storm Troopers), Der Führer purged his forces with a bloody massacre on June 30, 1934, which become known as the Night of the Long Knives.

As Hitler prepared a series of military moves, he introduced a fanatical anti-Semitic policy of Aryan supremacy and whipped up emotional support for his regime through elaborate propaganda. Films were made of mass meetings he held during which his audiences appeared to be hypnotically obedient to him and his doctrines. With Germany readied to take over the world, Hitler reoccupied the Rhineland and established the Rome-Berlin Axis in 1936. He annexed Austria and Sudetenland in 1938 and Czechoslovakia in 1939. His foreign minister, Joachim von Ribbentrop, negotiated a nonaggressive pact with the Soviet Union in 1939, which enabled Hitler to invade Poland, bringing Germany into a state of war with Britain and France. With World War II under way, France fell under Hitler's power in 1940, and the rest of continental

Europe was not far behind. Overall military strategy was personally
directed by Der Führer himself, who often rejected any advice given by
his experienced top military commanders.

Hitler's momentum was stopped when he invaded the Soviet Union
in 1943, suffered disastrous losses at Stalingrad, and was forced to retreat.
By 1944, Germany's battlefield casualties began to number in the millions, and some of Hitler's close advisers devised new plans to assassinate
Der Führer and try to save their country.

CONSPIRACY TO ASSASSINATE: Within the German army a large-
scale conspiracy had tried for several years to assassinate Hitler, without
success. Time bombs placed on Hitler's plane failed to explode. Three
young officers modeling new Nazi uniforms volunteered to carry bombs
under their coats and blow up Hitler, as well as themselves, but Der
Führer left the room before the plan could be executed. Time bombs
were hidden in new military packs presented to Hitler, but they failed to
detonate. And an assassination attempt in an art gallery failed when
Hitler departed earlier than scheduled.

Because Hitler expected attempts on his life, he was not an easy target. He frequently changed his schedule at the last minute and stayed out
of sight. Whenever possible, he hid in his remote fortress-headquarters.
His travel plans were known to as few people as possible and were usually
changed at the last minute. He would arrive early, depart early, and rarely
appeared where he was most expected.

Keeping himself safe from the army was his greatest challenge, Hitler
believed, because the army was the only power structure in Germany that
he did not create and totally control. He would constantly move high
officers from one command to another in order to prevent them from
devising conspiracy plans. Personally, Hitler surrounded himself with tall
sharpshooters. He wore a bulletproof vest and his military cap was lined
with steel plate. Around 1941, Hitler ordered at least two 770-K
Mercedes-Benz cars to be specially equipped for his personal use. An
armor plate one and a half inches thick was added to their twenty-foot

chassis, as well as bulletproof glass one and a quarter inches thick. The modifications, along with five hundred pounds of fuel, oil, and radiator fluid, added two thousand pounds to each vehicle's existing weight of ten thousand pounds. Hitler was a skilled marksman who always carried a revolver. And if all these precautions failed, he depended on his intuition to detect danger and believed himself to be protected by Divine Providence.

Although many plots apparently were devised to assassinate Hitler, only two reached the overt stage: the first on November 8, 1939, and the second on July 20, 1944.

ATTEMPT OF NOVEMBER 8, 1939: Every year Hitler commemorated this day, the anniversary of the Munich putsch in 1923, by delivering a speech in the beer cellar where the attempted coup had originated, and he would linger afterward to reminisce with old beer-drinking party comrades. But in 1939, Der Führer's speech was much shorter than usual, and he did not follow his custom of staying around afterward. Twelve minutes after Hitler and his entourage left, a bomb that had been planted in a pillar directly behind the speaker's platform exploded, killing seven Nazis and wounding sixty-three others.

AFTERMATH: It is reported that the assassination attempt had been carried out by a thirty-six-year-old cabinetmaker, electrician, and all-around tinkerer named Johann Georg Elser. After the bomb exploded, he left Munich and traveled to the Swiss border, where he planned to escape Germany.

Elser was captured at the Swiss border and intensely questioned. He admitted that he had engineered the attack on Hitler. He confessed that he had built an explosive mechanism into one of the wooden pillars in the beer cellar, then set an ingenious timing device that could run for three days. At first Elser said he carried out the entire operation alone, but later he claimed to have had two coconspirators, whose names he did not know but who had promised him a refuge abroad afterward.

The Gestapo, convinced Elser could not have masterminded the scheme, used torture, drugs, and hypnosis on the suspect but could not get Elser to alter his story. He was outraged that his interrogators thought he did not have the expertise to carry out the plot on his own, and insisted on being given access to a carpenter's shop, in which he reconstructed the bomb. Finally, Hitler's henchmen, Heinrich Himmler, Reinhard Heydrich, and Walter Schellenberg, were satisfied that Elser was a fanatic with an abnormal need for recognition, and solely responsible. But Hitler did not agree. He believed the British secret service had tried to kill him and insisted Elser be kept alive in a concentration camp for further questioning.

Over five years later, when all hope for Germany was lost, Elser was murdered by the Gestapo at Dachau Prison on April 9, 1945, under cover of an Allied air attack. Hitler outlived his attempted assassin by only three weeks.

ATTEMPT OF 1944: The events of this assassination conspiracy have been called the most important unsuccessful assassination in history. Members of the German army who planned this attempt had by this time lost faith in their leader and realized Germany could not win the war. Their hope was that by eliminating Hitler they could negotiate an agreement with the Allies and save Germany from destruction, while maintaining the integrity of German territory or, at least, the German army. The plan was to kill Hitler, seize control of the government, imprison or kill all other leading Nazis, and seek peace.

The army had attempted to blow up Hitler many times before and had always failed. This time, thirty-seven-year-old Lieutenant Colonel Klaus Schenk von Stauffenberg was in charge. Stauffenberg, known as a capable officer with liberal political views, had never hidden his hatred for Hitler. As early as 1936 in private conversations he had referred to Hitler as "the buffoon" and "the enemy of the world." It was Stauffenberg's intention that after the coup, when peace was secured, Germany would have a freely elected government, with socialist leader Julius Leber as minister of the interior.

As the assassination plot developed, many participants enlisted for a variety of reasons. Rumors were circulating that after Hitler's victory there would be a wave of executions of German aristocracy, so many who joined the conspiracy were aristocrats or high-minded military officers who held middle-rank staff positions. Their class status provided a common bond, as did their mistrust of the Nazis, their conviction that Hitler was destroying their country, and their disgust at the blatant immorality of Hitler's actions.

Among those at the center of the long-term assassination conspiracy were highly placed military officers. There was Colonel-General Ludwig Beck, chief of the army's general staff until 1938, when he resigned in protest against Hitler. Before the Nazis rise to power, Beck had been the effective head of the resistance against Hitler. Also a key player was Admiral Wilhelm Canaris, chief of military intelligence from 1935 to 1944; legal adviser Hans von Dohnanyi; and chief of staff Major-General Hans Oster.

Those working closely with Stauffenberg also included Colonel-General Friedrich Olbricht, Lieutenant Fabian Schlabrendorff, and Major-General Henning Tresckow, all of whom had unsuccessfully attempted to bomb Hitler. Add to these men scores of other military officers and civilians in support of the opposition and a picture develops not of a group of fanatics but of an organized conspiracy of responsible Germans who tried for years to regain control of their country.

Agents of the resistance met with Winston Churchill in 1939 to inform him of their plans. One of the conspirators met with U.S. intelligence leader Allen Dulles in 1943, requesting that there be active contact between the resistance and the Allies. General Erwin Rommel, the "Desert Fox," was approached in 1944 to join the coup, or at least support them afterward, but he declined, electing instead to protect his men by insisting that Hitler be taken alive and put on trial. (Rommel generated little support for his idea, however, since most people believed it would never succeed.) Many German generals chose to wait and see if the coup succeeded before committing themselves to anti-Hitler forces.

EVENT: By July 20, 1944, the June 6 invasion of Normandy had assured Germany's defeat, and the conspirators now feared a national suicidal mania when Hitler finally fell. Stauffenberg had gained access to Hitler's headquarters in June of 1944 when he was named chief of staff to General Friedrich Fromm, head of the reserve army. Because of war injuries, Stauffenberg went through lighter security checks than normal when coming into contact with Hitler, and so numerous plans were made to have him carry in a bomb and detonate it while Hitler, Hermann Göring, and Heinrich Himmler were together. When this could not be arranged, the conspirators decided it might be necessary to kill Hitler alone.

On July 20, at half-past noon, Stauffenberg, carrying a prewired bomb in his briefcase, arrived at Wolf's Lair (Hitler's retreat headquarters in Rastenberg, East Prussia) to meet with Hitler and two dozen high officers. Although the meeting was scheduled for one o'clock, it started early because Hitler planned to meet with Mussolini at three o'clock. Stauffenberg talked briefly with Hitler's aids in the compound's guard bunker, then sneaked into the bathroom and activated the silent acid fuse attached to two pounds of British plastic explosives in his briefcase. He had twenty minutes until the bomb would explode.

The usual conference room, a heavy concrete bunker, would be the ideal place for the bomb's lethal effects because it was a tightly enclosed area, so Stauffenberg was disappointed to learn that the meeting was instead taking place in the Lagebaracke, a lighter structure with three open windows. Still, he easily gained access to the conference room without raising suspicions. Three minutes had passed. General Adolf Heusinger was assessing the overall military situation as Stauffenberg entered the small room almost filled by a massive oak table supported by two huge oak slabs. Sitting around the table were Hitler and twenty-three important Nazis; others stood around the room.

Taking his seat about five or six feet to the right of Hitler, Stauffenberg placed his briefcase on the floor against the inner side of one of the oak supports, then muttered something about a telephone call and abruptly left the room while General Heusinger continued to give his report.

Colonel Brandt, who was seated three chairs to the right of Hitler, moved Stauffenberg's briefcase to the outer side of the oak support, probably because it was in his way. When Stauffenberg did not immediately return, one of Hitler's top aides, Field Marshal Wilhelm Keitel, became concerned that he would not return in time to give his report and sent a subordinate to find Stauffenberg. Soon the man returned, saying he could not locate him.

Hitler was leaning across the heavy oak table, looking at a map, when the bomb exploded. Bodies flew in all directions as the walls and ceiling were blasted apart. Four people were killed and several badly injured. Hitler suffered from shock, minor burns, and injury to his eardrums, but the heavy oak table had protected him from serious harm. Two hours later he was sufficiently recovered to meet with Mussolini.

Stauffenberg watched the explosion from a hundred yards away, then quickly managed to leave the compound and board an airplane, assuming Hitler was dead. It was 3:42 P.M. For two tense hours Beck, Olbricht, and other conspirators had waited in Berlin for word from Wolf's Lair, but no word came. Finally, while Stauffenberg's plane was still in the air, the planned coup was set in motion. Units of the reserve army were supposed to move in and surround the Berlin Administrative Center, then follow orders from the conspirators, who would take over the government as the new military command.

When the conspirators announced that Hitler was dead, confusion followed. The conspirators made arrests; the loyalists made counter-arrests. Stauffenberg finally arrived in Berlin around 5 P.M. to confirm Hitler's demise, setting off a flurry of activity in the War Office (the conspirators' headquarters). They telephoned the European commands to confirm the death of Hitler, then arrested more Nazis; but already their reports of Hitler's death were being challenged. The conspirators had made a serious error: They moved too slowly, not taking over the propaganda ministry and central broadcasting facility.

At 6:45 P.M., Goebbels's voice was heard by the nation, officially announcing that Hitler was, indeed, still alive. The conspirators continued desperately to contact the European commands, but the Nazis were swiftly closing all doors the conspirators had opened. Late that night the coup attempt was completely halted when SS commandos shot their way into the War Office and arrested everyone inside.

PUNISHMENT: Stauffenberg was among the group of several conspirators who were immediately court-martialed and sentenced to death. Ludwig Beck, the former chief of the general staff, was given the choice of committing suicide or being executed. He chose to kill himself. Stauffenberg and the others were led into a courtyard, placed in front of a wall, then executed by firing squad.

During the following days and weeks, Canaris, Oster, Schlabrendorff, Tresckow, and other principal conspirators were arrested. Some sources estimate that there were seven thousand arrests, resulting in two thousand death sentences handed down by the Nazi "people's court," which allowed no evidence to be presented by the defendants on their own behalf.

Hitler sadistically condemned a number of the conspirators to a slow, deliberately prolonged death by piano-wire strangulation as they were hanging like carcasses of meat. Eight officers were herded into a small room at the Ploetzensee prison, where eight meat hooks awaited them. One by one, each was stripped to the waist and strung up by a noose of piano wire attached to a meat hook. Repeatedly, just as the men were about to die, they were cut down, revived, and then rehung. In the process their trousers fell down as they struggled to die, leaving them naked in their final agony. Hitler ordered that this gruesome spectacle be filmed in graphic detail and that the films be sent immediately to his personal viewing room so that he could watch and rewatch them later. It has been reported that Joseph Goebbels covered his eyes with his hands to keep himself from fainting while watching the ghastly films. Eventually Hitler's revenge reached even those who were not directly involved in the coup attempt but had knowledge that it was taking place. Rommel was offered the choice of committing suicide or facing a grand show trial. If he took poison, he was told, it would be announced that his death was a tragic accident, and he would receive the full honors of a German hero, leaving his reputation and family unscathed. Rommel complied, taking the poison.

One of the last to be punished was General Friedrich Fromm, who, although involved in the plot, had turned against it when word came that Hitler was still alive. He was executed in March of 1945 for cowardice.

AFTERMATH: In 1945, when Germany's army faced total collapse on both the eastern and western fronts, Hitler fled to a concrete bunker beneath the Berlin Chancellery. In the final days of the war, as British, U.S., and Soviet troops advanced on Berlin, Hitler reportedly married his mistress, Eva Braun, then committed suicide on April 30, 1945, ending a reign he once boasted would last for a thousand years. By that time, Hitler's policy of Aryan supremacy had sent at least six million European Jews, Gypsies, and political dissidents to the gas chambers and crematoriums.

 APRIL 18, 1945

BENITO MUSSOLINI (1883–1945)
FASCIST DICTATOR OF ITALY FROM 1921 TO 1945

Benito Amilcare Andrea Mussolini was idolized by his countrymen and dreamed of building a new Roman Empire, but his military alliance with the Germans proved to be his downfall. When it became clear that Italy faced certain defeat by the Allies during World War II, Il Duce ("the leader") was forced by the Fascist Grand Council to resign, abruptly ending his reign of more than twenty years and ultimately leading to his public assassination.

ASSASSINS: Italian partisans.

HISTORY: Mussolini was born in the northern Italian town of Dovia in the province of Forli. His father was a blacksmith, his mother a school-teacher. He showed an aggressive personality early in life and was expelled from two elementary schools after attacking other students with his penknife. Although unruly, he was an intelligent young man who earned a degree in primary education in 1901 at a school in Forlimpopoli. Mussolini briefly taught school in Gualtieri Emilia, then emigrated to Switzerland in 1902. He lived there until 1904 but was forced to leave when it was discovered he carried a false passport. During the next few years, Mussolini became active in socialist politics, as a labor leader, and an editor of *La Lotta di Classe* (*The Class Struggle*), a provincial newspaper. By the time he reached the age of twenty-six, his skills as a socialist orator, a journalist, and an instigator had earned him some fame and six visits to jail for inciting violence against authority. In 1912 he was elected director of the Socialist Party and editor of its news-paper, *Avanti*. He used this position to advocate the unpopular position that Italy should enter World War I, and was expelled from the party in 1914. Mussolini then founded an independent newspaper, *Popolo d'Italia*, supported by the Autonomous Fascist Party.

When World War I began, Mussolini enlisted in the army and served at the front until he was wounded by shrapnel. In 1919 he organized a new fascist party called the Fighting Fascists, or Blackshirts, originally a group of intellectuals opposed to Bolshevism, and quickly accumulated some three hundred thousand followers. He was elected to parliament as head of the National Fascist Party in 1921.

The following year he had gained enough power and admiration as a party leader to inspire a march on Rome that intimidated King Victor Emanuel III into appointing Mussolini, then thirty-nine, the youngest prime minister in Italy's history. The country prospered under Mussolini's control. He developed a powerful militia and secret police, reorganized the country into a "corporate state," stabilized the economy, and started public works programs. By abolishing representative gov-ernment, Mussolini made himself a virtual dictator. In 1929 he signed

Hitler with Mussolini

UPI / CORBIS-BETTMANN

the Lateran Treaty, initiating the most empowering development in the Catholic Church in nearly a thousand years. It granted the pope sovereignty over a newly created Vatican City within Rome. With this act, Mussolini eased all tensions that had existed between himself and the Roman Catholics.

Although three assassination attempts had been made on his life by the early 1930s Mussolini held a large measure of popular support and had crushed virtually all opposition to his regime. However, before long, the theatrical and arrogant dictator began to lose the support of the people when he involved the Italians in a series of military measures. He invaded Ethiopia in 1936, provoking worldwide protest, including a feeble attempt by the League of Nations to impose sanctions on Italy. Although Mussolini showed his initial antagonism toward Hitler by blocking the Brenner Pass in 1934 in order to prevent Hitler from annexing Austria, in 1937 Mussolini formed the Rome-Berlin Axis with Hitler.

This alliance, some say, was Mussolini's way of assuring the Italians that they did not stand alone in the world. It is also said that Mussolini emulated the Nazis, hoping some of their success might rub off on him. He introduced anti-Semitism and a number of other measures that were popular in Germany, but only a hooligan element in Italy was attracted to such things. Mussolini succeeded only in alienating the majority of peace-loving Italians.

As World War II began, Mussolini invaded Albania in 1939, and after the German invasion of France in 1940, he declared war on the Allies. Soon it became clear that Mussolini had thrown his support behind the wrong side, and by 1943 the Italians had suffered disastrous military losses. After controlling Italy for more than twenty years, Mussolini's desire for expansion, which had led to an alliance with Hitler, proved to be ill-fated. In July of 1943, Mussolini's government was overthrown, and Il Duce was imprisoned. Still, two months later, he was freed by German paratroopers, and with Hitler's support, set up a puppet government in northern Italy. But when German forces collapsed in April of 1945, Mussolini and his mistress, Clara Petacci, fled.

EVENT: Mussolini, previously known for his flamboyance, donned the uniform of a German soldier hoping not to be recognized. He, Petacci, and an entourage of fifteen political supporters and various members of their families hid in the back of a truck traveling in a convoy north toward the border to escape into Switzerland. On April 24, as the convoy approached the town of Como, Italian partisans stopped the trucks, searched them, and immediately recognized Mussolini. He and Petacci were taken to a three-story farmhouse on the outskirts of the village of Bonzanigo, held prisoner, and assured that they would not be harmed. But when word of Mussolini's capture arrived at partisan headquarters in Milan, another future was decided for the couple. Palmiro Togliatti, head of the Italian Communist party, wanted Mussolini kept out of the hands of the Allies, who would certainly subject both the man and Italy to a war crimes trial, involving themselves in Italian postwar affairs. It was imperative, Togliatti declared, to dispose of Mussolini as expeditiously as possible. Walter Audisio, also known as Colonel Valerio, a dedicated Communist, was sent to assassinate Mussolini.

On April 28 Valerio and his men arrived at the farmhouse and encountered strong opposition from the partisans guarding Mussolini, many of whom were not Communists. But Valerio's threats quickly ended the confrontation. Around four o'clock in the afternoon, Valerio burst into the bedroom where Mussolini and Petacci were confined. "Hurry, I have come to rescue you," Valerio announced.

"Really?" Mussolini replied, not believing him.

Mussolini and Petacci were rushed out of the farmhouse into a waiting automobile, then driven through the village with two partisans riding on the running boards. Leaving the village, they drove toward the town of Azzano and stopped at the gate of a villa. Valerio told Mussolini and Petacci to get out of the car and hide in the bushes near the gate while he went inside to see if the coast was clear. Although Mussolini seemed hesitant, he went toward the gate. After a moment of silence, Valerio declared, "By order of the general headquarters of the Volunteers for Freedom Corps, I am required to render justice to the Italian people!" Mussolini did not move, but Clara Petacci became hysterical, throwing her arms around Mussolini's neck, pleading for his life.

"Move away if you don't want to die too," Valerio told Petacci. She stepped to the right side of Mussolini. Valerio aimed his machine pistol and pulled the trigger, but the weapon did not fire. He pulled out a smaller pistol, aimed, and fired, but it also jammed. Valerio grabbed a Max 7.65 machine pistol from one of his men, aimed, and fired a third time. Mussolini fell to the ground after being hit by five shots. Valerio then turned the gun on Clara Petacci and fired.

That night the bodies of Mussolini, Petacci, and fifteen other Fascists who had been executed were thrown into a van and driven to Milan. There they were dumped in front of a partially built garage in the Piazzale Loreto, the exact spot where fifteen hostages had been killed by the Nazis the year before. Although the bodies were left in a pile, the next morning they were arranged in a row, Mussolini positioned so that his head rested on Petacci's breasts. Soon crowds formed, kicking and mutilating the bodies. Eventually Mussolini's feet were tied with a rope and the corpse hung from a girder by the feet. Clara was hung beside him, also upside down, with her dress falling down over her face, revealing her undergarments. Finally, a woman climbed up on a box, lifted up Petacci's skirt, and secured it around her legs.

Still the public was not appeased. The people of Milan forced their way through a cordon of three hundred soldiers to take revenge for all they had suffered because of Mussolini. The corpse of the once powerful dictator was kicked in the head; a woman fired five more bullets into the body, one for each of her sons who had been killed in the war.

The site where the bodies of Mussolini and his mistress were hanged is ironic in view of an encounter that once took place between Petacci and Mussolini's wife. Mussolini loved and enjoyed women from the time he became a man until his assassination. His socialist ideology forbade him to marry, though he did eventually marry Rachele Guidi, who had been his mistress for several years. But in the end, the woman he most favored was Clara Petacci, his mistress for ten years. Despite his love for Clara, he was legally bound to Rachele and his family and refused to break their permanent bond. To appease Clara, Mussolini always provided her with luxurious apartments where they could be together. One day Clara opened the door to find Rachele standing before her. Although their meeting was brief, Rachele made her anger clear to Clara and observed the luxuries surrounding her. Calling Clara her husband's whore, Rachele told her, "[Someday] they'll take you to Piazzale Loreto," a well-known gathering place for down-and-out prostitutes. It was in the Piazzale Loreto where the bodies of Mussolini and Clara Petacci were hanged by their feet after their assassination.

AFTERMATH: Mussolini and Petacci were buried on May Day in paupers' graves in Milan's Musocco Cemetery. One year later Mussolini's body was moved to the Capuchin monastery cemetery in Cerro Maggiore, where it remained in secret until 1957. Then, once again, he was disinterred and reburied, this time in the family vault at the Cassiano Cemetery, in Predappio.

 JANUARY 30, 1948

MOHANDAS KARAMCHAND GANDHI
(1869–1948)
INDIAN SPIRITUAL LEADER

Known lovingly as Mahatma ("Great Soul"), Mohandas Gandhi never held a government office, yet he is regarded as the father of modern India. The small, frail man wearing a loincloth and metal-rimmed spectacles was a revered political and spiritual leader who pioneered the use of nonviolent resistance and inspired his countrymen to achieve independence from British rule.

Although it is reported that Gandhi once said he wanted to live to the age of 125, shortly before his assassination he remarked, "I do not want to die . . . of creeping paralysis of my faculties . . . a defeated man. An assassin's bullet may put an end to my life. I would welcome it."

ASSASSINS: Nathuram Godse led at least seven men in a conspiracy to assassinate Mahatma Gandhi. Godse was the polite and reserved editor of a Marathi-language daily newspaper, *Hindu Rashra*, in Poona, India. The son of a small-town bureaucrat with meager earnings, Godse received little formal education. As a young man he struggled financially, working as a tailor, and at age twenty decided to devote his life to the Hindu Mahasabha, a fiercely anti-Muslim political-religious organization that hated Gandhi for tolerating non-Hindu faiths. The Mahasabha was, for a time, the second-largest political party in India, led by its president, Vinayak Savarkar.

Gandi

The other main conspirators eventually included Gopal Godse, Nathuram's younger brother; Narayan Apte, a former teacher at the American Mission High School and the production manager of Godse's newspaper; Mandan Lal Pahwa, a young man who had watched a Muslim mob murder his father and aunt and was considered a significant action man; Pahwa's employer, Vishnu Karkare, a former restaurant owner and official Mahasabha representative in Ahmednagar; Digambar Badge, a bookseller and weapons supplier; Shankar Kistayya, the illiterate youngest member of the group, who mainly transported their illegal weapons; and Vinayak Savarkar, the charismatic former leader of the Hindu Mahasabha party and political opponent of Gandhi. Although Savarkar had retired from political office, he was suspected of collusion because of his ruthless and antagonistic history. While his direct involvement in the assassination conspiracy was not definitively established, there is evidence that Godse and others of the group visited Savarkar at crucial times while planning Gandhi's assassination.

HISTORY: Mohandas Gandhi's family belonged to the Vaishya cast of farmers and tradesmen in the coastal town of Porbandar near Bombay. His paternal great-grandfather was a grocer and Mohandas's father, Karamchand, took the name Gandhi, which means grocer in Gujerati, when the British, who then governed India, demanded Indian citizens' names be simplified for census purposes. Karamchand Gandhi, also called Kaba, held the position of *dewan* (chief minister) of Porbandar and was an astute official, blessed with natural tact in dealing with the British.

Born when his father was forty-seven years old, Mohandas, as the youngest, smallest, and favorite child, shared a close relationship with his father as well as his mother, Putlibai, Kaba's fourth wife. A frail, shy, sweet-tempered, and solitary woman, Putlibai was devoutly religious, honoring her vows by fasting as prescribed for self-purification and spiritual clarity. Kaba arranged for Mohandas's marriage to Kasturbai Makanji when both groom and bride were thirteen, according to Hindu tradition. As Kaba traveled to their wedding, his carriage overturned, and his injuries left him bedridden for the last three years of his life. Mohandas appeared to have a normal married life during those three years, until a traumatic event occurred. As the story goes, Mohandas was having sex with his pregnant wife at the exact moment his father died. When Mohandas realized the two events had occurred simultaneously, the knowledge had a dramatic impact on him. At eighteen years of age, he took a vow to abstain from wine, women, and meat, then went alone to England for three years to study law.

Upon his return to India, Gandhi's home life was less than peaceful. Not only had his mother died while he was away, leaving a serious void in his life, but he created problems for his family by insisting his wife and children adopt English dress and eating habits, as many returning Indian students would do after studying abroad. Gandhi worked as a lawyer for two years but considered himself a failure because he was unfamiliar with Indian laws. Finally, in 1893, he was offered a job with a Muslim firm established in South Africa. He gladly accepted, ultimately staying in that country, with his family, for twenty-one years.

Gandhi quickly recognized mass discriminatory practices against his own countrymen in South Africa. Large settlements of Indians who had come over as contract laborers were living in virtual slavery. They could not move around the country freely and were not protected under the law if they left their employer. Gandhi soon became involved as an attorney representing Indian laborers' rights, calling this his "public work" and accepting no pay. He unified Indians of all religious sects into an Indian Congress and organized protests against discrimination. While he became a leader in the Indian community in South Africa, his own thoughts and actions solidified into a political philosophy he called satyagraha. Describing it, Gandhi said: "Truth (satya) implies love, and Firmness (agraha) engenders and therefore serves as a synonym for force. I thus began to call the Indian movement satyagraha; that is to say, the force which is born of truth and love or nonviolence."

Gandhi established two cooperative communities in order to promote Indian unity in South Africa—the Phoenix Settlement and the Tolstoy Farm—and studied Leo Tolstoy's The Kingdom of God Is Within You and Henry David Thoreau's essay on civil disobedience to strengthen his own convictions. He believed that the means determined the end, and renounced violence or threat of force. Teaching his followers to love those who hated them, he organized civil-disobedience campaigns and symbolic protest demonstrations. Later there would be dramatic public fasts. Gandhi believed fasting was a form of prayer and self-purification that would strengthen him for the moral struggle. He sought a balanced life to feed the soul, saying simplicity was the most favorable environment for spiritual growth. He believed people should not take more than they needed or produce more than they could use.

Attempting to train his senses for the service of the body, he dressed simply and chose a vegetarian diet, not only for its nourishment but because it protected animal life. He abhorred artificial birth control, saying it interfered with nature, and encouraged married couples who already had enough children to practice chastity. Because controlling his own sexual desires had been difficult for him, Gandhi took the Hindu vow of *brahmacharya* (celibacy) when he was thirty-seven. Gandhi had radically changed the lives of Indians living in South Africa, as well as his own life, before taking his family back to live in India in 1915.

This homecoming was completely different from the previous one. He rejected all Western influences and established a simple, austere lifestyle in ashrams (communal retreats).

Leading a protest in 1919 after the April 13 massacre of Amritsar— when hundreds of Indian nationalists who had gathered to protest a ban on public meetings were gunned down by British-controlled troops— Gandhi was established as the leader of the Indian National Congress, soon instituting his policy of noncooperation and nonviolent civil disobedience against British rule. He initiated a boycott of British products so that India's village industries could gain financial independence. He traveled around India campaigning against the degradation of the untouchables. He encouraged friendship between the Hindus and Muslims. In 1930, he made his famous two-hundred-mile walk from Ahmedabad to the sea, where he distilled salt from seawater to protest the government's salt monopoly, and was arrested and sent to prison.

Between 1922 and 1944, Gandhi was arrested and jailed numerous times, in South Africa as well as in India. Still, his belief in nonviolent protest and religious tolerance was unshakable. Frequently he was released from jail when he vowed to fast until death.

In 1944 Gandhi joined Jawaharlal Nehru (the man who would become the independent country of India's first prime minister) and played a crucial role in negotiations that resulted in his country's independence. When India finally became an independent republic in 1947, Gandhi was gravely disappointed when it was partitioned into Hindu India and Muslim Pakistan, and violence became rampant. An ethnic cleansing, accompanied by murder, torture, and rape on both sides, occurred as Muslims sought refuge in Pakistan, and Hindus and Sikhs fled to India.

Hindu nationalists became furious when Gandhi urged his Hindu followers not to retaliate against Muslim atrocities. When mass rioting broke out between Hindus and Muslims, resulting in thousands of deaths, Gandhi visited troubled areas, vowing to fast until his death if the violence did not stop. Once more he was successful, and the riots subsided.

Although many viewed Gandhi as a hero, his actions were viewed by some as a threat to their very existence. Nathuram Godse, for one, was afraid Gandhi's plan to unite India's Hindus and Muslims would eventually lead to a Muslim takeover of the country. He decided Gandhi must be stopped.

ASSASSINATION CONSPIRACY: By August of 1947, Godse began plotting Gandhi's assassination. Recognizing that an armed group of assailants would have better chances of success than a lone executioner, Godse spent the next several months organizing his small group of conspirators and collecting weapons. Obtaining weapons that worked took a while, but eventually the conspirators secured two pistols, five hand grenades, and two slabs of guncotton explosives. Their first attempt to assassinate Gandhi was on January 20, 1948, at Birla House, his ashram outside New Delhi. They planned to set off one slab of guncotton explosives during a garden prayer meeting in order to cause a panic, then during the confusion, kill Gandhi with guns and grenades. But as they made last-minute preparations, they couldn't decide who would carry guns and who would carry hand grenades, whether to shoot through spaces in the thin back wall or to move inside the garden itself, and whether to attack Gandhi from the front or the rear. Before leaving for Birla House, they tested the guns, discovered they didn't work, and forgot, until the last minute, to disguise themselves.

Finally, when the disheveled group of would-be assassins arrived at the prayer meeting, again they changed their plans, then took their positions around the garden. Pahwa detonated the mild guncotton explosives within full view of witnesses, but the uproar they expected did not occur. The meeting continued as though nothing had happened, until a woman grabbed Pahwa and he was arrested. The other conspirators quietly escaped the garden.

Of the conspirators, not one had stayed behind to help Pahwa; they all left town, hurrying back to Bombay. Although the police were obviously aware that an assassination attempt had taken place, Godse was determined to try again. He regrouped. Badge and Kistayya bowed out, and Godse decided it was best that his brother Gopal no longer be involved, because he had a wife and children. Godse was calm and happy as he gave the remaining two conspirators a pep talk, explaining to Apte and Karkare that it was his destiny to be Gandhi's actual assassin, and it was their responsibility to finish the work of the Mahasabha if he was captured or killed.

EVENT: On January 30, 1948, at 5:13 P.M., seventy-nine-year-old Mahatma Gandhi emerged from his sanctuary quarters at Birla House to conduct a prayer meeting in the gardens, where several hundred people were waiting to pray for Hindu-Muslim unity. Weakened by a long fast, Gandhi was supported by one grandniece at each of his sides, joking with them as they walked along the covered corridor adjacent to the gardens. They climbed the brick stairs leading up to the grounds and stopped there while Gandhi smiled at the crowd, which parted, opening a pathway for him to enter.

Suddenly, thirty-seven-year-old Nathuram Godse, wearing a khaki tunic, his hands clasped in a traditional Hindu greeting, approached Gandhi, bowed briefly, then pulled a gun from his jacket and shot the pacifist spiritual leader three times: once in the abdomen and twice in the chest.

"Hai Rama! [Oh, God!] Hai Rama!" Gandhi cried out. He fell to the ground, his eyes held on his assassin, then gave Godse the sign of forgiveness.

Godse was immediately grabbed by onlookers, beaten, and dragged away.

Gandhi was quickly carried back to his quarters in Birla House, where he was placed on a sofa with his head resting in the lap of his sixteen-year-old granddaughter, Mani. He soon died.

The next day Gandhi's body was taken through the streets of both Old Delhi and New Delhi. The five-hour funeral procession was followed by a cremation ceremony that was witnessed by nearly one million people. It was reported that another two or three million later watched Gandhi's son place some of his father's ashes in the sacred waters of the Ganges and Jumna Rivers. The remainder of Gandhi's ashes was placed in fifty other holy rivers throughout India, enabling as many as ten million people to participate in the last rites for their revered leader.

PUNISHMENT: On May 27, 1948, a trial, which would continue several months, was convened before a judge at the Red Fort in Delhi to prosecute the eight primary conspirators. Godse remained totally detached as the conspiracy was gradually revealed to the court. Finally, on November 8, 1948, he took center stage, taking five hours to read a ninety-two-page handwritten statement saying he was fully and solely responsible for Gandhi's assassination. Godse said he decided Gandhi had to be assassinated because he was responsible for the partition of August 1947 and that he feared Gandhi's actions would lead to Muslims taking over India, with Hinduism being emasculated and destroyed. Without denying his own willful actions, Godse cited Hindu legends and mythological characters who had also used violence, to illustrate man's subjugation to greater forces and meta-destinies. But finally Godse added, "My respect for the Mahatma was deep and deathless. It therefore gave me no pleasure to kill him."

On February 10, 1949, the verdicts were handed down. Vinayak Savarkar, the retired political leader who continually denied any involvement and had offered elaborate legal arguments during the trial to prove his innocence, had successfully convinced the judge. Savarkar was acquitted. Shankar Kistayya was sentenced to seven years of rigorous imprisonment. Four of the other conspirators were also found guilty and given life sentences, although Karkare and Kistayya were later acquitted on appeal. Godse and Apte were found guilty and sentenced to death.

With all their appeals finally rejected, on the morning of November

15, 1949, the two were walked to the gallows shouting, "India united!" Godse thanked his jailers for treating him kindly and asked their forgiveness for any inconvenience he and Apte might have caused them. The floor dropped beneath their feet, and the ropes around their necks held the full weight of their bodies. Apte died instantly of a broken neck. Godse took fifteen minutes to strangle to death. After the two assassins' bodies were cremated, their ashes and bones were secretly discarded in a shallow river, but enthusiastic young supporters later recovered the bones, distributing them among their friends.

AFTERMATH: An inquiry into the assassination of Mohandas Gandhi was conducted in 1967, resulting in the conclusion that it was possible the police had been aware of the conspirators' identities and intentions from the time of the first assassination attempt. One account suggests the police decided to allow the conspirators to carry out a "permissive assassination" because Gandhi had created so much trouble for them.

Today, many believe Gandhi ranks with Jesus Christ and Buddha as a great religious teacher, prophet, and spiritual force who transformed the lives of his followers. His political gospel of militant nonviolence not only helped to bring about India's independence, as well as Gandhi's own assassination, but ultimately influenced other nationalist revolutions of the twentieth century.

NOVEMBER 1, 1950

HARRY S. TRUMAN (1884–1972)
THIRTY-THIRD PRESIDENT OF THE UNITED STATES, FROM 1945 TO 1953

While he was president, Truman gave the go-ahead for U.S. pilots to drop the atomic bombs on Japan, thus ending World War II. He launched the Marshall Plan to restore Western Europe's economy after the war and nurtured the European Community and NATO. Because of Truman's support of the United Nations, he offered to send U.S. forces to join U.N. troops in North Korea when it was invaded by South Korea in 1950, thus involving American troops in the Korean War.

Harry S. Truman was born into a farming family in Lamar, Missouri. As a young man, he was awarded a place at West Point Military Academy, but bad eyesight kept him from attending. He served as an artillery captain in France during World War I, and after the war was a partner in a clothing store that went bankrupt during the Depression. Truman entered politics at age thirty-eight, when Thomas J. Pendergast, the Kansas Democratic leader, arranged for him to be elected as a county judge. Pendergast was so impressed with Truman's honesty and ability as a judge that he selected him as a candidate for the U.S. Senate in 1934. In the Senate, Truman was a reliable supporter of Roosevelt's New Deal, and after being reelected in 1940 he served as chairman of a committee to investigate wasteful military spending. The committee succeeded in cutting millions of dollars from the defense budget. When FDR needed a vice-presidential candidate in 1944, Truman was his choice.

WOULD-BE ASSASSINS: Oscar Collazo and Griselio Torresola were long-standing members of the Puerto Rican Nationalist party, an organization that agitated for Puerto Rico's independence from the United States, although neither man had a record of criminal activity or violence.

Collazo, an extremely mild-mannered thirty-six-year-old family man, was kind, likable, and dependable. Born in Puerto Rico, he automatically became a U.S. citizen with passage of the Jones Act when he was three years old. When he was a young child, Collazo's family was fractured by the death of his father, and an older brother became his guardian. Collazo was self-educated, a voracious reader of history and literature, especially the heritage and culture of his native island. He went to New York at age seventeen and worked at miscellaneous unskilled jobs, such as washing dishes in the Army and Navy Club. He moved back and forth between New York and Puerto Rico, always finding work. Gradually he became active in the independence movement. Eventually Collazo settled in New York, worked as a metal polisher, and gave English lessons to his coworkers. He also made it a habit to go to the docks and meet ships of Puerto Rican immigrants in order to assist them in the transition from their peaceful native island into life in the often hostile environment of New York.

Collazo married, divorced, then remarried Rosa Mercado and lived with her and their two daughters in a Bronx tenement. He was a leader and speaker in the nationalist movement, as well as a union leader in his factory, where he was respected by workers and management alike.

Not as much is known about twenty-five-year-old Griselio Torresola. Although the two men were both passionate about the cause of independence for their native Puerto Rico, apparently they were more acquaintances than close friends. Torresola arrived in New York in 1948 and lived on welfare in the Bronx with his daughter and various women. Torresola procured the guns that would later be used in an attempt to assassinate President Truman.

HISTORY: President Franklin D. Roosevelt suddenly died of a cerebral hemorrhage on April 12, 1945. Although there are various stories of how Harry S. Truman learned that he had become president, one has it that Eleanor Roosevelt summoned Vice-President Truman to the White House. When he arrived, Mrs. Roosevelt greeted him saying, "Mr. President, my husband is dead."

President Truman was sworn into office at a critical time in American history. World War II was just about to end, and the Cold War with the Soviet Union was just beginning. President Truman assumed his duties, making difficult and important decisions with the down-to-earth directness the country had known him to possess. The first few weeks of Truman's presidency were dominated by foreign affairs. While attending the Potsdam conference in July of 1945, he authorized the use of atomic bombs against Hiroshima and Nagasaki in order to end the war with Japan. His postwar foreign policies included the Truman Doctrine to restrain communist expansion and the Marshall Plan to aid war-devastated countries. He acted swiftly to halt a Soviet blockade of West Berlin, established the CIA, supported the establishment of NATO, then cooperated with NATO's efforts to stop communist aggression in South Korea. Truman was unable to take the same kind of control over domestic affairs, and during both of his terms as president, Congress blocked much of the legislation required to implement Truman's Fair Deal program of social reforms, which addressed U.S. citizens' needs for greater employment opportunities and increased civil rights for minority groups. Truman's second term was overshadowed by a communist victory in China, allegations of communist subversion at home (culminating in Senator Joseph McCarthy's anticommunist purge), and charges of corruption and incompetence in his own administration.

EVENT: In the fall of 1950 the White House was undergoing restoration, and President Harry Truman was residing across the street in Blair House. On the evening of November 1, Donald Birdzell, a uniformed presidential guard stationed at the bottom of the outside stairs, heard a faint metallic click. He turned his head in the direction of the sound and saw a dark-skinned man, neatly dressed in a blue-green pinstriped suit, pointing a German F-38 automatic pistol at him. Birdzell jumped toward the street—standard operating procedure designed to draw gunfire away from the president's residence—and as he did so, he heard the gun go off. This was the first time a U. S. president was attacked at his residence in Washington, D.C.

Harry S. Truman

From the streetcar tracks on Pennsylvania Avenue, Birdzell returned the gunman's fire. The attacker shot him in the leg, forcing Birdzell to drop to one knee. Then he was hit by another bullet, this one penetrating his good leg, forcing him to fall forward onto his face. At that moment, other presidential guards and Secret Service agents got involved in the action, but their attention was drawn to a second gunman who was running toward Leslie Coffelt, the lone guard in the west sentry booth. The second assailant opened fire on Coffelt at point-blank range, toppling him with bullets in his chest, stomach, and legs. Coffelt would die a short time later. Joseph Downs, a plainclothes guard, was the next victim, shot in the stomach, but he would survive.

Although wounded and stretched out prone on the pavement, Birdzell could see that the first gunman was frantically trying to reload his weapon. Birdzell aimed his gun at the assailant and fired, hitting him in the chest. The would-be assassin fell down hard. The other guards opened fire on the second gunman, who was propelled backward over a low boxwood hedge. He was killed by a bullet through his head.

Suddenly it was silent. Secret Service agent Floyd Boring looked at the president's upstairs window and saw Truman in his undershirt peering out. "Get back, Mr. President!" Boring frantically yelled. "Get back!" Truman stepped back.

One group of Secret Service agents converged on the assailants while others remained at their posts, alert for further attacks.

The would-be assassin who was wounded was identified as Oscar Collazo. The dead man was Griselio Torresola. In Torresola's pockets were two letters from the president of the Nationalist party in Puerto Rico, Pedro Albizu Campos.

Some experts say that attempting to assassinate the president in his official residence was an insane idea. Even the outermost defenses were not penetrated by Collazo and Torresola. An armed Secret Service agent was positioned in the window of a nearby office building with a clear view of Blair House. His responsibility was to protect other agents stationed in front of Blair House, not to shoot down an attacker, so he had not even fired his weapon. Even if Collazo and Torresola had made it past the front door of the president's residence, they would have come face to face with an agent stationed just inside the entrance, holding a submachine gun in his lap. Another agent was positioned on the stairway, one in front of Truman's door, and numerous others stationed in surrounding rooms. The assassins would have had to shoot their way past at least twenty agents to reach the president.

CONSPIRACY THEORY: Although U.S. government officials believed the attempt to assassinate President Truman on November 1, 1950, was a conspiracy, it could never be proved. Their theory was that the attack was timed to cause chaos and possibly a revolution at the exact moment that a large-scale rebellion was supposed to erupt in Puerto Rico. (The revolt was quickly crushed by authorities.)

Torresola had met with Harvard-educated Pedro Albizu Campos, president of the Nationalist party in Puerto Rico, two months before the assassination attempt at Blair House. The letters signed by Campos that were found in Torresola's pocket at the time of his death contained provocative information but did not directly implicate Campos in an assassination plot.

PUNISHMENT: Collazo recovered from his wounds and maintained during his trial that he and Torresola had concocted the assassination plot entirely on their own as a show of solidarity with the rebels in Puerto Rico. Collazo's wife, Rosa, was also arrested, then released. (Several years later, she was one of thirteen people convicted in an unrelated case, for conspiracy to overthrow the government, and was sentenced to six years in prison.)

Collazo used his trial to express his passionate views on the cause of freedom for his beloved Puerto Rico. He condemned the U.S. government's exploitation and political manipulation of the Puerto Rican people, saying, "Anything that I have done I did for the cause of the liberty of my country, and I still insist, even to the last, that we have the right to be free. . . . I didn't come here to plead for my life. I came here to plead for the cause of the liberty of my people." Still, he expressed no personal feelings toward Truman.

Collazo was sentenced to death for the murder of Coffelt, and as he was led from the courtroom, his wife cried out, "Good-bye, my dove!" Even though Collazo refused to plead for clemency, a few days before his scheduled execution, President Truman commuted his sentence to life imprisonment.

On September 10, 1979, Collazo's life sentence was commuted by President Jimmy Carter to time served, "for humane reasons," and he was released from federal prison.

AFTERMATH: President Truman did not believe the attempt to assassinate him had any special significance, and only a few hours later, as though nothing had happened, he presided at the unveiling of a statue before a large crowd in Arlington, Virginia.

After his first full term as president, Truman decided not to run for reelection. He left office in January 1953 and returned home to Independence, Missouri. For the remainder of his life, he traveled widely, published his memoirs in a two-volume set in 1955 and 1956, and enjoyed the status of an elder statesman. Truman died on December 16, 1972, and was buried in Independence.

1960s

MARCH 13, 1961

FIDEL CASTRO (1927–)
PRESIDENT OF CUBA

Fidel Castro served as his country's prime minister from 1959 to 1976 and its president from 1976 until today. His vision for his country has guided it through almost forty-five years of change and struggle, during which education, housing, and health care have improved for most Cubans. But in the process, Castro has lost support of the middle class, and hundreds of thousands have fled the country, most emigrating to the United States. Viewed as a threat to the United States because of his allegiance to the USSR during the 1960s, Castro became the target of CIA assassination operations. But he was not easy to kill because of the friendships he nurtured with the very people who were sent to eliminate him.

Born in Biran, the son of a sugar planter, Fidel Castro was educated in Jesuit schools and studied law at the University of Havana, where he gained a reputation for assisting poor clients. Opposed to the right-wing dictatorship of Fulgencio Batista, Castro and his brother Raul took part in a disastrously unsuccessful attack on Batista's Moncada Barracks at Santiago de Cuba in 1953. Captured and tried for his involvement, Castro received a fifteen-year prison sentence but was given amnesty after serving twenty-two months. Upon his release, Castro lived in exile for a time in the United States, then Mexico, where he organized a small band of guerrillas and publicly announced plans to invade Cuba. (He said making the public announcement was an essential psychological-warfare tactic.)

On December 2, 1956, Castro sailed from Mexico with his army of eighty-two men on a dilapidated American yacht named the *Granma*. As his troops waded ashore on the swampy coast of his native Oriente Province, government forces waiting in ambush killed all but Castro and twelve of his rebels, who escaped into the Sierra Maestra mountains. While the Batista government announced the rebels' defeat, Castro invited *New York Times* correspondent Herbert Matthews to his camp to conduct an interview with the rebel leader that would astonish the world. Eventually Castro gathered an army of about two thousand men, conducted raids, and became a sort of Cuban Robin Hood, fighting Batista's army of some forty thousand. On January 1, 1959, Castro's hearty band of rebels, led by Argentine Ernesto "Che" Guevara, captured Cuba's provincial capital of Santa Clara. Batista gave up without a fight, packed his bags with cash, and fled to the Dominican Republic. Triumphantly Castro claimed his country like a hero, marching into Havana at the head of a victory parade on January 8.

Castro set up his headquarters in the Havana Hilton instead of Batista's presidential palace, and began to transform his country. He appointed his brother Raul minister of the armed forces; introduced a centrally planned economy based on the production for export of sugar, tobacco, and nickel; and nationalized, without compensation, Cuban property owned by wealthy Cubans, Americans; and other foreigners in 1960.

WOULD-BE ASSASSIN: The U.S. Central Intelligence Agency (CIA).

HISTORY: After Castro seized control of his country in 1960, the United States immediately severed diplomatic relations with Cuba and devised plans to subvert Castro's government. Organized during Eisenhower's administration but enacted a few months after John F. Kennedy took office, the Bay of Pigs invasion was an embarrassing mistake for the U.S.

Fidel Castro

government. Beginning on April 17, 1961, the three-day fiasco involved 1,500 U.S.-sponsored Cuban exiles, who attempted to invade Cuba by going ashore on the south coast of the island at the Bay of Pigs inlet. Not only was the escapade a complete failure, which ended with 1,173 of the exiles being taken prisoner, but it pushed Castro into a closer relationship with the USSR. He declared Cuba a communist state at the end of the year. In 1962, when most of the Cuban prisoners were ransomed by the United States for $53 million in food and medicine, Cuba was expelled from the Organization of American States (OAS), and a full political and economic blockade was enacted against Cuba.

Soon the USSR supplied missiles with atomic warheads to be installed at a former U.S. military base in Cuba. When U.S. intelligence learned Soviet nuclear missiles were in place within miles of the continental United States, President Kennedy reacted strongly. A naval "quarantine" was placed around the island of Cuba, and Kennedy demanded that Soviet leader Nikita Khrushchev immediately dismantle and remove the missiles. The situation placed the entire planet under threat of a full-scale nuclear war. With only days to make a decision, Khrushchev finally backed down because his country's nuclear capabilities lagged far behind those of the United States, and Khrushchev believed President Kennedy would follow through on his threat to take military action against both Cuba and the USSR.

ASSASSINATION PLOTS: Operation Mongoose, the supersecret CIA plot to assassinate Fidel Castro, was a fascinating real-life saga that has provided more intrigue for investigative reporters than any mystery writer could ever invent.

Records indicate that as early as December 1959 the CIA discussed eliminating Fidel Castro, and that special meetings on this matter took place in January and March of 1960. During the 1960s, the CIA recruited almost two thousand Cubans in Miami and trained them as commandos for Operation Mongoose. After the 1961 Bay of Pigs fiasco, the CIA launched a succession of commando raids against the tiny island. At the same time, a succession of clandestine operations were tried, among them several assassination attempts against Castro, some carried out with the help of organized crime.

Evidently, the CIA had no way to penetrate Cuba and get to Castro, so creative minds got together and decided the best way to pull off their mission without implicating the U.S. government would be through the Mafia, whose gambling empire had just been confiscated by Castro. Not only could the assassination be made to look like a gangland killing, but it could be accomplished by recruiting former Mafia gambling contacts in Havana. The cast of characters was bigger than life: Sam Giancana, Mafia boss of Chicago; Santos Trafficante Jr., crime boss of Tampa; Johnny Roselli, flamboyant mobster; Meyer Lansky, mastermind; billionaire Howard Hughes; and Robert Maheu, executive officer of Hughes's business.

Some reports say that Howard Hughes was considered the perfect conduit to initiate contact between key players because of his Las Vegas connections and a long-suspected relationship with the CIA. When approached about the matter, Hughes is said to have ordered Maheu to find suitable Mafia members to assassinate Castro. Maheu recruited Johnny Roselli, the Chicago mob's overseer in Las Vegas. Roselli got his boss, Giancana, involved, and they apparently brought Tampa's Trafficante into the operation. As this theory goes, the Mafia used the opportunity to scam the CIA, and the CIA and Howard Hughes were the only participants who believed the plot to assassinate Castro was for real.

The CIA came up with various creative ways in which Mafia killers could eliminate Castro: He could be injected with deadly poison from a specially prepared pen; he could smoke a poisoned cigar; he could be blown up while deep-sea diving; or he could be given a deadly illness by wearing clothing contaminated with fungus spores and tubercle bacilli.

Trafficante was put in charge of executing various plans agreed upon by the CIA and the Mafia but did nothing, though he reported back with dramatic stories about the adventures of hit men who were supposedly trying to carry out the assassination. He said, for instance, that every time the hit men's boats would sneak close enough to Cuba for them to go ashore, they would be suddenly detected and the boats shot out from under them. When a liquid poison that would kill Castro in two or three days after he consumed it was concocted by CIA scientists and given to Trafficante, he flushed it down the toilet instead of getting it to his Cuban contacts. Apparently none of the money, poison, guns, explosives, boat radar equipment, or radios supplied to the Mafia by the CIA every reached Cuba.

Eventually, some government agents began to suspect that Trafficante had sold out the CIA and taken up with Castro, keeping him abreast of the assassination plots against him, as well as supplying him with intelligence information about anti-Castro movements in Florida among Cuban refugees. U.S. agents believed Trafficante, who had controlled a small piece of the Cuban casino business before Castro's takeover, thought ingratiating himself to Castro would put him in a favorable position if Castro ever allowed gambling to return to his country.

Finally, Operation Mongoose was called off when the CIA decided their Mafia cohorts, as well as Maheu, were using them to keep other government investigators, including the FBI, off their backs and out of their illegal activities.

AFTERMATH: President Lyndon Johnson put an end to the CIA's assassination plots in 1965. "We had been operating a damned Murder, Inc., in the Caribbean," Johnson commented. Still, many Cuban exiles continued to mount independent raids, and eventually established a violent Cuban terrorist movement.

On May 3, 1967, investigative journalist Jack Anderson's daily column, which appeared in one thousand newspapers and was read by as many as 60 million people, broke a story revealing details of the CIA assassination scandal. Anderson was the first to inform the American masses that the assassination of Fidel Castro was supposed to kick off the failed 1961 Bay of Pigs invasion. Senator George Smathers, a close friend of President Kennedy during his administration, told Anderson the president complained to him that he could not control the CIA. Smathers is quoted: "I remember him saying that the CIA frequently did things he didn't know about, and he was unhappy about it. He complained that the CIA was almost autonomous." Smathers also said President Kennedy had suspected that the shooting of Dominican Republic dictator Rafael Trujillo in 1961 and South Vietnam's Ngo Dinh Diem in 1963 had been arranged by the CIA. But John McCone, who headed the CIA in the early 1960s, told Anderson that although the subject of assassinating Castro had come up from time to time, it was never taken seriously. McCone denied that the CIA ever attempted to assassinate any foreign leaders.

Anderson did not give up on this story, reporting updates on January 18 and 19 and February 23, 1971. He questioned whether these activities had backfired on President Kennedy, who by then had himself been assassinated. In response to Anderson's persistence, in 1975 President Gerald Ford created the Rockefeller Commission, a Senate select committee, to investigate the activities of the CIA. During closed hearings, the CIA and the Justice Department presented some sixty-two secret documents on political assassinations that they claimed to have just found in their files.

Sam Giancana was murdered in 1975, shortly before he was expected to appear before the Rockefeller Commission. Johnny Roselli was murdered in 1976. There is speculation that these two men were not just the victims of another gangland killing but were wiped out by the CIA so that they could not reveal embarrassing details of the government's failed attempts to assassinate Fidel Castro through Operation Mongoose.

The Rockefeller Commission released a document in November of 1975 saying U.S. officials had ordered the assassinations of Fidel Castro and of Patrice Lumumba, prime minister of the Belgian Congo (whose death in 1961 has been characterized as an assassination, although it was officially attributed to an airplane accident). The document also asserted that the CIA had been involved in assassination plots against three other foreign officials: Rafael Trujillo of the Dominican Republic; Ngo Dinh Diem of South Vietnam; and General Rene Schneider of Chile. The report concluded that although four of the five men had been killed, none of their deaths was a direct result of U.S. assassination plots.

 MAY 30, 1961

RAFAEL LÉONIDAS TRUJILLO (1891–1961)
DICTATOR OF THE DOMINICAN REPUBLIC
FROM 1930 TO 1961

Generalissimo Rafael Léonidas Trujillo Molina ruled his country with an iron hand, using his ruthless police force to cruelly repress, torture, and murder the people at will.

Born into a poor family in San Cristóbal, Trujillo joined the army in 1918 and was trained by U.S. marines, who occupied the republic from 1916 to 1924. In 1921 he graduated from the Haira Military Academy, then quickly rose through the ranks, becoming a general in 1927, chief of staff in 1928, and president of his country in 1930. Although officially the president for two periods of time—1930–38 and 1942–52—he maintained absolute power for thirty-one years, even while not an officeholder, with the help of puppet governments. During his regime, Trujillo improved his country's social services and increased material benefits for his people, but he also crushed all opposition, allowing only one political party to exist, and controlled his command of the army through nepotism. Toward the end of his dictatorship, the middle classes and Roman Catholic church became increasingly more opposed to his rule, as did neighboring states, especially Cuba.

ASSASSINS: A group of conspirators encouraged by U.S. intelligence agencies, including members of the de la Maza family, Pedro Cedeño, and Lieutenant Amado Garcia.

HISTORY: During his thirty-one-year regime, Trujillo was sometimes supported by the U.S. government, and at other times he was threatened by U.S. efforts to undermine his power. In 1961, while attempting to eliminate Fidel Castro, the U.S. government apparently thought it was necessary to demonstrate to other Latin countries that U.S. policy opposed right-wing elements as well. It was rationalized that removing Trujillo would be an impressive act because his dictatorship was considered terrorism at its most horrific. By all accounts, Trujillo considered human life a cheap commodity, and his actions caused observers to compare him to the Roman emperor Caligula.

Finding people in his own country who were willing to assassinate Trujillo was not difficult. The CIA and members of the U.S. diplomatic corps were in close contact with anti-Trujillo conspirators. Right-wing military figures, libertarians, and members of the close-knit and affluent old Dominican family the de la Mazas were counted on to join an assassination plot. The de la Mazas had a reputation for volatile behavior. Although they had once cooperated with Trujillo and his enforcers, the dreaded secret police known as the SIM, something had happened that shifted their support away from the Generalissimo.

Wittingly or not, Tavio de la Maza had helped the Trujillo regime kidnap and later assassinate Jesus de Galindez, an exiled professor of international law at Columbia University. When Galindez's death sparked an investigation, Trujillo saw to it that Tavio "committed suicide" while in custody, throwing suspicion away from Trujillo himself. As a result, the de la Mazas became the most dedicated of all anti-Trujilloists, reinforcing the beliefs and actions of others fighting against his regime.

By early May of 1961, the United states was much less determined to depose Trujillo than it had been one month earlier, before the Bay of Pigs debacle. Now, unable to constrain Castro and the Latin left, some government officials thought it unwise to demonstrate opposition toward the right. But by this time the CIA had devised a way to supply machine guns that the conspirators needed to assassinate Trujillo. Still, U.S. charge d'affaires Henry Dearborn made it clear that the Dominican dissidents were not prepared to carry out any type of revolutionary activity in the near future, except to assassinate their enemy Trujillo.

While U.S. intelligence agencies and the White House were occupied with more pressing matters during the hectic days of May, Dearborn and the CIA pushed to continue supplying weapons to the anti-Trujilloists. On May 5, 1961, President Kennedy, apprised of the plot, told National Security Council members that the United States should not initiate the overthrow of Trujillo before knowing what kind of government would succeed him. Dearborn cabled Washington on May 16, requesting the release of machine guns and hand grenades already in the Dominican Republic, saying the assassination attempt was set for that evening (although it was later postponed to May 30) and that the machine guns might increase the chances of success beyond the estimated 80 percent. Washington's answer was, "Negative," thus establishing credible deniability. On May 21 Dearborn sent another communiqué to Washington, saying State Department officials in the Dominican Republic had been "nurturing the effort to overthrow Trujillo and had assisted the dissidents in numerous ways, all of which were known to the Department." He also cabled that it was "too late to consider whether [the] United States will initiate [the] overthrow of Trujillo."

EVENT: On May 30, 1961, Trujillo dressed in an elegant army uniform, in preparation for a visit to one of his mistresses, on his sprawling ranch in his hometown of San Cristóbal. As the Generalissimo's chauffeur-driven blue-and-gray sedan traveled along the road just outside Ciudad Trujillo, a car filled with dissidents pulled alongside. Before Trujillo or his driver realized what was happening, the assassins pumped dozens of bullets into his vehicle.

"I am wounded!" Trujillo shouted at his driver. "Let's stop and fight!" Both vehicles came to a stop. Trujillo pulled out his revolver and fired at the other car as his driver fired a machine gun. By the time his driver could glance into the backseat, Trujillo was slumped over, dead. The assassins overpowered the driver, pulled Trujillo from his vehicle, mutilated his face, then stuffed his body in the trunk of their own car. They drove back to Ciudad Trujillo and abandoned the vehicle with Trujillo's body still in the trunk.

PUNISHMENT: Eventually the conspirators—including members of the de la Maza family as well as the actual assassins, Pedro Cedeño and Lieutenant Amado Garcia—were caught, tortured, and murdered.

AFTERMATH: Although the dissidents planned to seize power, fear of reprisal caused them to delay, giving remnants of the Trujillo family months to carry on the Trujillo tradition of strong-arming and vengeance, but the Trujillo regime was as good as finished.

Although the CIA has always denied any involvement in the assassination of one of the Western Hemisphere's most ruthless dictators, journalist Bernard Diederich is quoted as saying, "The CIA lists the end of the Trujillo era as one of the Agency's successes."

 AUGUST 22, 1962

CHARLES DE GAULLE (1890–1970)
FRENCH GENERAL, STATESMAN, AND PRESIDENT FROM 1958 TO 1969

Charles-André-Joseph-Marie de Gaulle was legendary as the embodiment of the spirit of France. During and after World War II, he had the distinction of being called, in popular publications, one of the "great survivors" of all time, because he survived no fewer than thirty-one documented assassination attempts. He attracted the enmity of members of the political left, right, and center and was attacked during the war by pro-Germans, anti-British, and Frenchmen alike.

Born in Lille, the son of a teacher, de Gaulle was educated at the Ecole Militaire of Saint Cyr, graduating in 1912. During World War I, as part of an infantry regiment, he was wounded and taken prisoner during the 1916 Battle of Verdun. He became a lecturer at the Staff College in 1923, and during the 1930s he wrote several books and articles on military subjects. When World War II began, de Gaulle was appointed commander of an armored division, and he briefly held the office of undersecretary of state for war in 1940 before escaping to England. There he organized the French resistance as leader of the Free French movement, which refused to recognize the Vichy regime led by Philippe Pétain. In 1943, he headed up the French Committee of National Liberation in Algiers, then triumphantly entered Paris in 1944.

Although he was elected president of the provisional government, the constitution adopted by the Fourth Republic was not to his liking, so he resigned in 1946. De Gaulle founded the moderately successful Rassemblement du Peuple Français, a non-party constitutional reform movement, in 1947 but retired from politics in 1953 to concentrate on writing. Still, he could not say no when asked by the Fourth Republic to form a new government in 1958, as France faced a severe economic crisis at home and civil war in Algeria. A new constitution, which provided for a presidential system, enabled him to take office as president in December 1958. During the early 1960s, de Gaulle presided over France's economic recovery and the solving of the Algerian crisis, and granted independence to African colonies. Reelected in 1965, he pursued an assertive foreign policy. He opposed British entry to the European Economic Community, withdrew French contingents from NATO (1966), and maintained development of the French nuclear deterrent. After overcoming student-worker protests in 1968, he proposed constitutional changes that were rejected by the electorate, and resigned in 1969.

WOULD-BE ASSASSINS: Charles de Gaulle was probably more hated than loved by his countrymen, many of whom believed he was a dangerous dictator whose political policies were leading France to ruin. He antagonized many members of his own government, including members of the French army whom he had dismissed, imprisoned, and even executed; businessmen; bankers; and a powerful and wealthy group of Catholic industrialists. But perhaps his most dangerous enemies were those who had strong feelings about the traditionally French colony of Algeria. The two main groups were the National Resistance Council (CNR), which opposed de Gaulle's vision of independence for French Algeria, and the Organisation Armée Secrète (OAS), a subversive organization that comprised military men, civil servants, veterans of Indochina, students, and Algerian colonists, who pledged to fight for French Algeria. The most serious attempts on de Gaulle's life occurred while he was president because members of the political right in France, including many French Algerians, held de Gaulle responsible for Algerian independence.

FIRST ASSASSINATION ATTEMPT: As the symbol of free France during the years of Nazi occupation, de Gaulle was leading the West African port city of Cakar in a celebration after the liberation of his homeland. Standing at attention on the deck of the cruiser *Georges Leygues* as the band played the *Marseillaise*, a French sailor raised his rifle, aiming it directly at de Gaulle. The sailor, a petty officer in the French

Charles De Gaulle

UPI / CORBIS-BETTMAN

fleet who considered de Gaulle a yes-man of the British (as did many Frenchmen), didn't get a chance to shoot. A fellow officer saw where the weapon was aimed, disarmed the sailor and knocked him down.

This was the first of thirty-one documented attempts to assassinate Charles de Gaulle. (Although de Gaulle's triumphal return to Paris in 1944 was marred by gunfire at Notre Dame Cathedral, there is no conclusive evidence that the shots were aimed at de Gaulle.) The fact that he survived so many assassination attempts has been credited partly to his great courage and his ability to remain calm during any crisis.

ATTEMPT OF SEPTEMBER 8, 1961: Traveling that night with his wife, Yvonne, to their country home, La Boisserie, in Colombey-les-Deux-Eglises, 150 miles east of Paris, de Gaulle was not aware that a bomb made from a propane cylinder stuffed with almost one hundred pounds of plastic explosives was buried in an innocent-looking sandpile alongside the road in the Pont-sur-Seine district, near the village of Crancey. Along with the bomb, there was a canister holding fifteen liters of napalm waiting to be detonated by wires strung to a nearby thicket.

As de Gaulle's car, a Citroen Deesse driven by his favorite chauffeur, Francis Marroux, approached the sandpile traveling at around seventy miles per hour, the sand exploded, causing the Deesse to lurch sharply and throw a sheet of flame across the roadway. De Gaulle ordered Marroux to drive straight through the flames. "Faster!" he commanded, as the car plunged straight for the inferno. No one was harmed, and de Gaulle continued on his way, stopping only to change cars at a military barracks nearby.

No one was convicted of the assassination attempt, although it was suspected to be the work of the OAS.

ATTEMPT OF AUGUST 22, 1962: Once again, President and Madame de Gaulle were being driven to Colombey in their Citroen Deesse by their favorite chauffeur. But this time an identical dark Citroen with secret service agents was traveling in front of them, and they were being followed by a number of motorcyclists. Cars loaded with a handpicked fifteen-man OAS sharpshooting team armed with submachine guns, grenades, and Molotov cocktails were stationed on the Avenue Petit-Clamart. Because it was a dark night, the would-be assassins did not see de Gaulle's approaching convoy in time to block the road. As the Deesse sped past, they desperately opened up with a volley of machine-gun fire, shooting out a front tire and the Deesse's rear window and causing the vehicle to skid out of control, nearly colliding with an oncoming automobile. Once again de Gaulle's chauffeur, Marroux, was able to gain control of the Deesse and quickly drive away to safety. Although twelve bullets pierced de Gaulle's vehicle, and one missed his head by mere inches, the only injury was to de Gaulle: a small scratch on his finger sustained when he brushed splintered glass off his coat.

PUNISHMENT: Following a massive investigation of hundreds of OAS members, several conspirators were arrested. Before a military court at the fort at Vincennes, fifteen defendants, nine were present, and six in absentia, were found guilty. Their defense had been that they merely intended to take de Gaulle prisoner and put him on trial for illegal acts. Six of the defendants (three of those absent) were sentenced to death; the other nine were given prison terms varying from three years to life. Later, two of the three in custody had their sentences commuted to life by de Gaulle, but he refused to commute the sentence of air-force lieutenant colonel Jean-Marie Bastien-Thiry. De Gaulle had personally awarded Bastien-Thiry the Knights' Cross of the Legion of Honor only two years earlier. One week after his sentence was set forth, Bastien-Thiry was awakened in his prison cell at 4 A.M. and informed by his lawyers that he was going to be executed. "Am I the only one to be executed?" he asked. Yes, he was told. "Are the others pardoned?" Yes, he was told. Bastien-Thiry was served coffee, then died before a firing squad on March 11, 1963.

LAST KNOWN ASSASSINATION ATTEMPT: On July 1, 1966, de Gaulle was being driven to Orly Airport, where he would board a plane and fly to the Soviet Union. A group of students, formerly of the National Resistance Council, planted a car holding almost a ton of dynamite on the Boulevard Montparnasse within inches of where President de Gaulle actually passed. The dynamite did not detonate, however, because the night before, the young students were arrested following a robbery. They had been trying to steal money with which to disappear abroad following the planned assassination.

AFTERMATH: Algerian independence was acknowledged by Paris on July 3, 1962, after a national referendum in which the people of Algeria voted nearly 6 million to 16,534 for their independence.

    Charles de Gaulle died of a heart attack on Monday, November 9, 1970, at 7:25 P.M., while sitting in his armchair at La Boisserie watching television.

JUNE 12, 1963

MEDGAR W. EVERS (1926–1963)
U.S. CIVIL RIGHTS LEADER

During his nine years as field secretary of the Mississippi chapter of the National Association for the Advancement of Colored People (NAACP), Medgar Evers became a principal leader of the growing civil rights movement in his home state.

Born July 2, 1925, outside the small central Mississippi lumber town of Decatur, Medgar Evers was the son of a hardworking, taciturn sawmill worker named James Evers and his deeply religious wife, Jessie. During his rural childhood, Evers enjoyed freedoms black children in urban areas were not allowed. He and his older brother, Charles, were taught self-discipline and Spartan ways early on by parents who were both loving and rigid. Although they were poor, Medgar's father owned his own house and some land, making him more independent than many blacks and able to avoid much of the disrespect blacks suffered in a white world. Still, he understood the realities of living as a black person in the South. Medgar's mother was ambitious for her children, and Medgar's brother Charles remembers Medgar as the saint of the family, performing mundane farm and household chores ungrudgingly. The most studious of his friends, Medgar did not join in teenage drinking or swearing, and when the other boys got into fights, Medgar would try to settle the disputes. He was a figure of respect among his peers and had an unusually deep appreciation of the humiliations that white supremacy inflicted on blacks.

Medgar quit school at age seventeen to sign on with a segregated unit of the Army Transportation Corps. He was sent to England, then to the Continent after the Normandy invasion. Although the officers were white, many of them racists, and the worst jobs, such as cleaning latrines, were reserved for blacks, Medgar saw another side of life. He was treated by white Europeans like he'd never been treated by white people before, and he served under a sympathetic white lieutenant who recognized his intelligence. He also encountered Nazism, which left an indelible impression on him. Medgar's sister said, "He was altogether different" when he returned from the war. Back in Decatur, where he could not even sit in the downtown restaurant, he told her, "Something's going to need to be done."

After finishing high school at a state-supported laboratory school for blacks, Medgar entered Alcorn College. There he was a studious and disciplined campus leader, and a member of the debate team, the college choir, and the football and track teams. He served for two years as the editor of the school newspaper and edited the yearbook in 1951. Medgar even made it into *Who's Who in American Colleges.*

By the time Medgar graduated from college he had married Myrlie Beasley and decided not to leave Mississippi, as many blacks in his position would do. The Magnolia Mutual life-insurance company, one of the few black-owned companies in Mississippi, offered the promising young Medgar a job, and he grabbed it. Aaron Henry, the company's secretary, who had been a member of the NAACP for years, and the company's founder, T.R.M. Howard, saw Evers's job as twofold: promoting the interests of Mississippi's major black-owned company and doing civil rights work. Evers began selling insurance and NAACP memberships, quietly but firmly explaining the urgency of the NAACP cause. Although the NAACP was a tough sell among black teachers, the prime targets of the NAACP's contribution drives, Evers was good at his job. He assured potential members that their names would be kept strictly confidential. At that time, the national office of the NAACP, which was operated for and by America's tiny black middle class, had two main objectives: antilynching legislation and abolition of the poll tax. Mississippi, a state that accounted for nearly 13 percent of the country's 3,786 lynchings between 1889 and 1945, was considered a lost cause. If transformation in Mississippi was a possibility, it would require someone of unusual toughness and dedication. Evers was proving his mettle through his recruiting efforts. In the fall of 1954, when talk arose that the NAACP would be filling a new position, field secretary for the state of Mississippi, Evers's bosses enthusiastically backed the courageous and impressive young man. He was hired five days later to open an office in Jackson, the state capital. The governor of Mississippi and the mayor of Jackson were invited to the office's grand opening, but they did not attend.

During the next eight and a half years, Evers sent hundreds of pages of reports to New York headquarters from the sparsely furnished two-room office in Jackson. Enthusiastically, and perhaps naively, he reported that the NAACP was having a tremendous influence in Mississippi and in America, even though he himself was in considerable personal danger much of the time. He was harassed and vilified at every level, from the common citizen to the police officer to state legislative committees, but he was not cowed. Evers was dedicated to his organization, his job, and the larger cause he served. He took seriously the work of finding and interviewing witnesses of crimes against blacks, particularly lynchings, and meticulously recorded evidence, even when it seemed futile. In the first year alone, Evers traveled over thirteen thousand miles on the narrow two-lane highways of Mississippi.

In 1955 he went to Money, Mississippi, to investigate the murder of a fourteen-year-old Chicago boy, Emmitt Till, who had been beaten, shot, bound to a cotton gin fan with barbed wire, and dumped in the Tallahatchie River for whistling at a white woman. Although it was the first Mississippi lynching to receive the full glare of national publicity, Evers proudly reported that he had come up with two new witnesses. That same year, he went to Belzoni, Mississippi, to look into the murder of George Lee, a preacher and NAACP member who had struggled to put ninety-two blacks on the voting rolls. Someone fired two shotgun blasts in Lee's face while he drove on a downtown street. The local sheriff said the lead pellets in Lee's mouth and face were dental fillings, and no arrest was ever made. Later that year, Evers went to Brookhaven, Mississippi, where a prosperous farmer named Lamar Smith had been killed on the lawn of the county courthouse for encouraging blacks to vote. During his one-man NAACP investigations, Evers literally inspected the mangled bodies of Mack Charles Parker, lynched in 1959 after being dragged from

Medgar Evers

his cell in southern Mississippi, and Edward Duckworth, shot in 1956 by a white man who claimed self-defense.

While Evers depended on local blacks to talk to him (when they did not, he had no report), fear of retribution from angry whites shut the mouths of blacks and forced people out of the NAACP. Whites saw any gathering of blacks, even three or four, as a threat. As time went on, Evers became both more widely known and more isolated, because blacks were afraid to associate with him.

Still, Evers downplayed the constant danger he faced. In 1958 he was beaten up when he tried to integrate a Trailways bus as he returned home from Meridian. In 1960 he was menaced by a white mob in Winona, Mississippi, while trying to get a young NAACP man out of jail. In 1961 Evers was beaten by policemen outside a court hearing for the so-called Tougaloo Nine, the first civil rights demonstrators in Mississippi. In Jackson, police watched his house constantly. During the height of civil rights demonstrations in Jackson in the spring of 1963, a firebomb was tossed into the Evers carport. After that, Evers taught his children to drop to the floor at the sound of passing cars.

Nobody remembers Evers complaining or making plans to leave Mississippi. Offered a transfer to California, he declined. Evers's job was his life. The ideal he fought for was indistinguishable from the work he was paid to do. In the late 1950s, the NAACP put these qualities, as well as the Mississippi story itself, on display by sending Evers around the country to make speeches.

The added notoriety ignited more anger toward Evers, but he maintained a mild demeanor. When the most vile abuse came at him over his office telephone, Evers remained calm. Sometimes there were death threats. "I remember distinctly one individual calling with a pistol on the other end, and he hit the cylinder, and of course you could hear it was a revolver," Evers told a CBS correspondent in June 1962. "He said, 'This is for you.' And I said, 'Well, whenever my time comes, I'm ready.'"

ASSASSIN: Byron de la Beckwith, a forty-two-year-old fertilizer salesman and member of the Citizens Council of Mississippi, was orphaned at the age of eleven and raised in Greenwood, Mississippi, by uncles who were not happy to have such a responsibility. A poor student in the various schools he attended, Beckwith had an enduring interest in collecting and trading guns. After Pearl Harbor, Beckwith put his passion for guns to good use. He enlisted in the Marine Corps and was part of the first bloody assault on Tarawa Atoll in November 1943. He served well, providing machine-gun cover for landing troops, but was hit in the thigh by a bullet and spent four months recuperating in a hospital in Memphis. There he met a Wave named Mary Louise Williams and married her in September 1945. Back in Greenwood, Beckwith struggled as a salesman to support his wife and a newborn son while living in the family's dilapidated mansion. While some reports of Beckwith's activities and attitudes say he was an excellent salesman, good with people, and friendly to black employees of the stores where he hawked his goods, other reports say he had violent eruptions against blacks.

A turning point in Beckwith's life evidently came in 1954 after the Supreme Court decision to desegregate schools. In May of that year, Tom Brady, a Mississippi circuit-court judge, gave his famous "Black Monday" speech (in which he likened blacks to chimpanzees) to the Greenwood chapter of the Sons of the American Revolution. Beckwith, the organization's state treasurer, was in the audience. After this event, Beckwith suddenly seemed to be filled with purpose. In May 1956, he wrote a letter to Mississippi Governor J. P. Coleman saying he was "rabid on the subject of segregation" and pleaded for a spot on the new Sovereignty Commission. Beckwith assured the governor that he was "expert with a pistol, good with a rifle, and fair with a shotgun." When his request was denied by the governor, Beckwith began his own personal campaign against integration, writing letters to newspapers in Jackson and Memphis and to government officials.

Beckwith's anti-integration campaign won him the attention and admiration of people with similar views. He sold copies of Judge Brady's speech and spent his own money on anti-integration handbills. In the spring of 1961, when the COLORED sign was removed from the Jim Crow waiting room at the Greenwood bus station after the Interstate Commerce Commission banned segregated interstate bus travel, Beckwith stood in a doorway to block blacks from entering the room designated for whites only.

HISTORY: Although President Abraham Lincoln's Emancipation Proclamation of 1863 officially freed the slaves (about 4 million), it could not be enforced until the Union victory in 1865 and the period after the Civil War known as Reconstruction. Even then, freed slaves, who were often viewed by poor whites as economic competitors, became the victims of vigilante groups in the South, such as the Ku Klux Klan. To make matters worse, although the Fourteenth Amendment to the Constitution entitled freed slaves to full U.S. citizenship and all its attendant rights, including the right to vote, state and local governments imposed such obstacles as poll taxes and literacy tests. In a step backward, a "separate but equal" policy was established in 1896 when the U.S. Supreme Court ruled that segregation was legal if equal facilities were provided for both blacks and whites. It was not until 1954 that that ruling was overturned, and segregation in public schools was outlawed. Still, despite that ruling, Arkansas governor Orval Faubus tried to prevent black students from entering Central High School in Little Rock, leading to an historic confrontation when President Eisenhower sent federal troops to the scene to enforce the right of blacks to attend the public school.

In 1955, Rosa Parks refused to give up her seat on a public bus to a white passenger, and the Montgomery, Alabama, bus boycott became another landmark in blacks' struggle for civil rights. It was during this time that Martin Luther King Jr., who led the Montgomery bus boycott, first received national attention. Although moderate groups such as the NAACP had been active since early in the century, large numbers of whites didn't join the civil rights movement until 1957, when King founded the Southern Christian Leadership Conference (SCLC), a coalition advocating nonviolence.

On January 1, 1963, Martin Luther King Jr. gave his inspired "I have a dream" speech at a ceremony held at the Lincoln Memorial in Washington, D.C., to commemorate the centennial of the Emancipation Proclamation. Still, most of the 11 million black Americans living in the South continued to be routinely deprived of their constitutional right to vote. Poll taxes were still imposed, and blacks were made to take trumped-up literacy tests, with questions as arbitrary as "How many bubbles are there on a bar of soap?" Black children in both the North and the South were still confined to segregated schools that usually did not prepare them to compete as adults in the job market. But things were beginning to change. Many Americans came out in support of the nation's black citizens, serving notice that these circumstances were no longer acceptable. This dramatic emergence was activated in two massive phases: first, the crusading nonviolence movement, and later, a militant campaign.

At this time, Greenwood, Mississippi was the headquarters of the Citizens' Council and had no visible local NAACP representation. The town had somehow remained untouched by what Beckwith called "the evils of integration." Although blacks outnumbered whites three to two in Greenwood and the surrounding Leflore County, fewer than 2 percent of adult blacks were registered to vote. But all that changed on Saturday, August 11, 1962, when the integration movement came to town. On that day, two Student Non-Violent Coordinating Committee (SNCC) organizers led a parade of twenty-five blacks down the street to the neo-classical courthouse in downtown Greenwood, where they were determined to register to vote. (Beckwith's grandmother had modeled for the monument to Confederate mothers that stood by the courthouse steps.) Because nothing like this had ever happened before, it took stunned Greenwood segregationists a few days to react, but when they did, their response was brutal. The following Monday, one of the young SNCC men, twenty-five-year-old Sam Block, was pulled from his car downtown and severely beaten by three white men. Civil rights workers were routinely shot at, attacked by police dogs in the streets, and beaten in the jails, in the alleys, and as they were coming out of movie theaters. With the police department closely allied with the roving band of thugs, some of whom were ostensibly "respectable" citizens, there was no civil protection. Local judges and lawyers did everything they could to put the civil rights workers in jail and keep them there. When questioned by the press about what was happening in Greenwood, the city fathers asserted that the attacks were staged hoaxes or communist plots, or both. The handful of whites who were opposed to the onslaught stayed silent.

The climax of the campaign came in the spring of 1963. To show that the SNCC would not be cowed by the shooting of civil rights worker Jimmy Travis, the SNCC targeted Greenwood for intensive voter-registration efforts. For over a week, at the end of March and the beginning of April, there were mass meetings and marches to the courthouse to register black voters, all in full view of the national media. As the story of Greenwood appeared on the front pages of newspapers across the country, civil rights celebrities poured into Greenwood: James Farmer of the Congress of Racial Equality (CORE), social activist Dick Gregory, and Medgar Evers.

Some Greenwood whites went down to the courthouse to watch the blacks picketing, but whites who considered themselves respectable stayed away from downtown. It is reported that Beckwith was seen at the edge of some of these crowds, hanging back, watching; and indeed Beckwith could not have missed the protests, because his dilapidated old house was just up the street from the courthouse.

In January of 1963, Beckwith wrote to the National Rifle Association: "Gentlemen, for the next fifteen years we here in Mississippi are going to have to do a lot of shooting to protect our wives, children and ourselves from bad niggers."

By February of 1963, Beckwith had taken a new job, selling fertilizer for the Delta Liquid Plant Food Company, based in Greenville. During that late winter and early spring, he drove throughout the Delta's rutted gravel roads in the company-owned white Plymouth Valiant that had a long radio antenna for two-way communication trailing in back. Beckwith liked to travel with shotguns and rifles on the front seat of his car.

By mid-April, the Greenwood movement was stifled when the U.S. Justice Department struck a deal with city officials that left the civil rights workers hanging: Eight SNCC workers would be released from Greenwood's jail, and in return, the federal lawsuit demanding that the city stop harassing (or start protecting) blacks seeking to vote, would be dropped. The action shifted to Jackson, and to Medgar Evers.

In May and June, Evers orchestrated demonstrations in Jackson, an undertaking that left him feeling pulled in opposite directions by the clamoring student demonstrators, who looked up to him, and by NAACP officials in New York, who were reluctant to be associated with demonstrations. The outside media that had descended on Jackson to cover the demonstration that had turned bloody saw Evers as a confident, undisputed spokesman, while people inside the movement saw an increasingly troubled and weary man.

Although things had suddenly changed after Martin Luther King Jr.'s triumph in Birmingham, the NAACP's caution seemed to make it incapable of committing itself to protests, a policy previously not endorsed. With rumors that Jackson might be next on King's SCLC agenda, NAACP executive secretary Roy Wilkins let it be known that he was suddenly "extremely interested" in what was happening in Jackson. Thus began an emotional roller-coaster ride for Medgar Evers, with the NAACP alternately backing off plans for demonstrations, then agreeing to move forward. Reporters saw Evers urge the growing crowd forward into the streets and then watch in disgust as they were beaten and herded into paddy wagons and a makeshift barbed-wire stockade at the Jackson Fairgrounds.

On May 20, the Supreme Court ruled that convictions by lower courts in cases of sit-ins to protest discriminatory practices by retail establishments were unconstitutional. Later that day, Evers made a daring move and appeared live on television. In answer to Jackson's mayor's bumbling attempt to calm the city, Evers's speech detailed all the things black citizens were still being denied. He demanded an end to segregation in parks, playgrounds, libraries, and downtown stores and restaurants. The bloody protests continued. On June 1, Evers and Roy Wilkins were arrested along with demonstrators on Capitol Street.

Throughout all of this, Evers arrived at his office every morning at 7 A.M., rushed all over the city to arrange bail bonds for jailed students, attended mass meetings, and met with reporters. People remember Evers being exhausted and at an emotional and physical breaking point. Death threats against him continued. Police cars followed him constantly.

At around 4 P.M. on Saturday, June 8, 1963, cabdriver Herbert Richard Speight was sitting with Lee Swilley, a fellow cabbie, in his White-Top cab in front of the old Trailways bus station in downtown Jackson, waiting for a fare. A white man came up to the cab, leaned down, and asked Speight, "Do you know where the Negro NAACP leader Medgar Evers lives?" The veteran cabbie said no, he didn't. The man, who seemed calm, went into the bus station and came back with a map, apparently torn out of the phone book. He asked if this Negro could live on Lexington Street? Speight knew the man was an out-of-towner because Lexington Street was in a white neighborhood, which is what he told the man. "I got to find where he lives in a couple of days," the man said, then went back into the station. The cabbies saw him check the phone book, then come back out. "Buena Vista Street?" he asked. No, another white neighborhood. Again, he went to the phone book and came out with another address. He was wrong this time too. Just then, Speight got a fare, drove off, and thought no more of it.

Later that evening, the family of B. L. Pittman was gathered in Pittman's modest grocery store on Delta Drive, barely 350 yards from Medgar Evers's house on Guynes Street. When a car pulled up by the side of the store, Bob Pittman, the grocer's seventeen-year-old son, saw that it was a late-model white Plymouth Valiant, with a long antenna trailing in back. Young Pittman also saw what looked like a Shriners emblem hanging on a chain from the rearview mirror. When a man got out of the car, Pittman thought it was strange that he was wearing white shoes, a hat, and sunglasses, even though it was dark. The man walked up and down in an adjoining field for a while, then got back into the car and drove away.

Byron de la Beckwith was relaxing at home in Greenwood on Sunday, June 9. The company-owned white Plymouth Valiant, with a Shriners emblem hanging on a chain from the rearview mirror, was parked in his driveway. He decided to do a little target practice, and took out a vintage 1918 .30/06 Enfield rifle he had gotten a few years earlier in a trade with a local farmer. Although it was not the best gun in his collection, it was a serviceable weapon. Beckwith invited a few high school students who were employed by his company for the summer to go with him so that he could show off. The next day at work, the teenagers showed their boss the target Beckwith had used. "They were just dumbfounded he could shoot that good," Beckwith's boss, DeWitt Walcott said. The boys told Walcott that Beckwith had set the sight on his rifle so it was "deadly accurate."

Tuesday evening, June 11, was warm and dry in Jackson. Around nine o'clock, Bob Pittman was playing outside his father's grocery store when he noticed the same white Valiant he had seen on Saturday slowly drive back and forth across a vacant lot on Missouri Street five or six times. On the other side of the lot from the store was Guynes Street, where Medgar Evers lived. Business was slow that night at the nearby Joe's Drive-In, one of a strip of businesses on Delta Drive, the road leading out of town. The drive-in was a familiar landmark for the young Evers family, who lived within easy walking distance. Martha Jean O'Brien, a seventeen-year-old carhop at the drive-in, was standing around that night talking to her friend and ex-coworker Barbara Ann Holder. Both girls saw a white Plymouth Valiant, which they thought was a police car because it had a long radio antenna in back, pull up behind the drive-in. The car was very dirty, as though it had been on some rough roads recently. The strange thing about this customer was that he did not blink the car lights for service, as other customers did. Instead, the driver got out of the car. He was wearing sunglasses, even though it was dark out. He walked to the drive-in's bathroom, and Holder thought he carried himself in an unusual way. "Well, he walked straight," she said later, "because most of those people out there don't walk straight, and he did, he walked erect and straight." When she left her friend at 11:30 that night, she noticed that the car was still there behind the drive-in. A few hundred yards away was the Evers house. The lights were still on.

EVENT: On that same evening, Myrlie Evers was at home watching President Kennedy's breakthrough civil rights speech on television. The speech was in response to that day's heated showdown with Governor George Wallace at the University of Alabama, as well as demonstrations and beatings in Virginia and the ongoing crisis in Jackson. Medgar Evers was at a rally, struggling to prop up the faltering Jackson civil rights campaign. The three Evers children were waiting up for their father; lately, their only chance to see him came late at night. Myrlie, reclining on the bed, drifted off to sleep as the children argued over which television program they were going to watch.

At midnight, Myrlie woke up to the sound of tires in the driveway.

Medgar was home. His car door slammed. Then she heard a much louder sound. People all over the neighborhood heard it in the hot, quiet night. The Evers children hit the floor, as they had been taught to do. Myrlie knew the sound was gunfire, and that it must have been aimed at her husband. She rushed to the door, turned on the light, and saw Medgar lying facedown. She saw the keys in his hand. She saw the trail of blood left behind as he had managed to drag himself thirty-nine feet from his car to his front door. The sweatshirts he had been carrying, which were printed with JIM CROW MUST GO, were scattered all over the driveway. Myrlie screamed. Her husband did not move. The Evers children— eleven-year-old Darrell, ten-year-old Reena, and four-year-old James— rushed outside to join their mother hovering over their father's body. "Daddy! Daddy! Please get up, Daddy!" they screamed, but their father did not move.

Wearing a white shirt, Medgar Evers had been an easy target for the sniper. Neighbors helped the police lift the dying man onto a mattress and load him into a station wagon. "Sit me up," Evers said. "Turn me loose." Those were his last words.

As police looked over the scene, they were shocked by the large amount of blood on the driveway and the flesh spattered on the car. The bullet struck Evers in the back, exited through his chest, crashed through his living room window, went through another wall into the kitchen, ricocheted off the refrigerator, shattered a glass coffeepot at the sink, then landed on a cabinet, where detectives found it.

A neighbor up the street had heard a "crunching sound," then the unmistakable noise of someone running. Another neighbor had heard leaves and branches crackling as though someone was running, fast.

When Evers died at University Hospital in Jackson, Myrlie did what her husband had done after seeing such atrocities: She called the press. Cliff Sessions, a reporter for United Press International, got Myrlie's call. Before Sessions could reach the scene, more police arrived, the same police who had followed Medgar Evers for months. Myrlie screamed at them in anger: Medgar's blood was on their hands. Twenty-five neighbors had gathered on the lawn of the Evers house by the time Detective John Chamblee arrived.

THE INVESTIGATION: The Jackson Police Department, riddled with violence-prone racists who had made a habit of harassing Evers and others in the civil rights movement, surprised everyone. In the early morning hours of June 12 and throughout the day, Jackson police, notably Detective John Chamblee and Captain Ralph Hargrove, conducted a thorough investigation. Their first break came when Chamblee shined his flashlight from the spot where Evers had been shot, to retrace the trajectory of the bullet. Through the night, for six hours, the officers searched the path of the bullet. Chamblee's flashlight beam illuminated a clump of bushes two hundred feet away, across Guynes Street from the Evers house, which was directly visible through a ten-inch hole someone had torn in the foliage. This dense area of sweetgum trees and honeysuckle bushes was a perfect place for an assailant to hide. Upon inspecting the area, the detectives found that some of the vines had been trampled and a tree branch had been broken off. At around 11 A.M. the detectives found a perfectly clean, well-cared-for, vintage 1918 .30/06 Enfield rifle hidden in some honeysuckle vines about 150 feet from the bushes. Attached to the rifle was a steel-blue Japanese telescopic sight called a Goldenhawk. This standard-issue six-power sight would prove to be critical evidence. Three hours later Captain Hargrove was able to lift a good fingerprint from the Goldenhawk, a fresh fingerprint, one that contained moisture along the ridges. The FBI had been called in, and that night an agent left Jackson for Washington with a bundle of evidence: a photograph of the fingerprint, the gun and scope, the bullet, an empty cartridge case, and six live rounds found in the rifle.

After Evers's painful, grief-filled funeral, as angry emotions erupted into a riot of blacks in Jackson, pieces of the FBI's case began to fall into place. The Goldenhawk's importer, located in Chicago, told the FBI that fifteen thousand of the sights had been sold to over two hundred dealers across the country; sixty of them had gone to the Mississippi area.

Working day and night, FBI agents traced thirty-five of the sights sold in an area extending from Memphis south to Jackson. When they found out that five sights had been sold to a gun dealer in the northern Mississippi town of Grenada, agents tracked down all but one of the people who had purchased a Goldenhawk. That man was Byron de la Beckwith of Greenwood.

Nine days after Evers's assassination, on the morning of Friday, June 21, FBI agent Sam H. Allen Jr. arrived in Greenwood. He stopped to join forces with Walser Prospere, the FBI's resident agent in town, then drove to Beckwith's house. Nobody was home, so the two men waited in their car until 7:45 P.M., when Beckwith's white Valiant with the long radio antenna drove up. Beckwith spotted the agents sitting in their car, walked over, and cordially inquired, "Are you looking for me?" When the agents tried to question him about the scope, Beckwith's tone changed. "I have no comment," he said sharply, then walked away, into his house.

The FBI could take no further action until the next day, when the fingerprint lifted from the Goldenhawk scope was compared at the FBI lab in Washington to Beckwith's fingerprint samples in his military records. In fourteen points of comparison the print in the photograph matched the print of Beckwith's right index finger. Prospere and Allen searched for Beckwith while teams of agents watched his house. Alerted by a neighbor, who called him at work, that FBI agents were swarming his property, Beckwith called his lawyer and old Citizens' Council associate Hardy Lott and decided to turn himself in. He was driven that night to Jackson for a 2 A.M. preliminary hearing.

When cabdriver Swilley saw a report of the event in the newspaper, he called the police station to give them the details of his encounter with the stranger at the Trailways bus station. Ten days later, Swilley looked at a lineup of suspects and identified Byron de la Beckwith.

In Beckwith's hometown of Greenwood, a White Citizens Legal Fund was set up to pay his legal fees and provide legal aid to other whites in civil rights matters.

THE TRIALS: In the days after his arrest, Beckwith talked amiably with detectives about hunting and fishing and other manly topics, but when questioned about Medgar Evers's assassination he gave only a steely, "No comment." Beckwith maintained his nonchalance at all times from the moment he turned himself in, through psychiatric examinations, and his first trial. Old newsreels show him confident, relaxed, and apparently in control; immaculately dressed, with his hair slicked back, he conferred with members of his defense team in the courtroom and smiled for the camera as he breezed out of the courtroom. Two days before his trial began, he even wrote a letter to the editors of *Outdoor Life* magazine, saying, "Sir, I have just finished an article on garfish hunting at night, which is sure to be of interest to the reader, along with several ideas I have on shooting at night in the summertime for varmints."

During his trial, there was testimony about Beckwith's gun being the murder weapon; witnesses testified that they kept seeing him and his white Valiant with the long radio antenna in Jackson; and the two cabdrivers identified Beckwith as the man who had approached their cab in Jackson, asking where Medgar Evers lived. (The cabdrivers were fired for being backstabbers two days after the trial ended.)

Despite the fact that the prosecutor, a Mississippi white man, presented an exceptionally strong murder case against him, Beckwith appeared relaxed and seemed to enjoy being the center of attention. His team of attorneys offered only a minimal defense, hardly bothering to refute the eyewitness testimony and the FBI's evidence, although they did produce two Greenwood policemen who swore that they saw Beckwith in a filling station around 1 A.M. the morning of June 12, 1963. The defense capped off its case, knowing that no all-white jury had ever convicted a white man of killing a black person, by having Beckwith speak for himself. Wearing a dark suit with a Masonic emblem on the lapel, Beckwith walked his distinctive erect-military walk to the witness stand. Once seated, he tugged at the monogrammed cuffs of his shirt. Respectfully he answered, "Yes, sir," and "No, sir," to his attorney's questions. He said "No, sir," when asked if he had shot Medgar Evers. Given the rifle to examine,

Beckwith practiced aiming it over the jury box and suggested that the day before the murder the rifle had been stolen from his bathroom closet.

As the prosecuting attorney cross-examined Beckwith, he knew that all the physical evidence in the world was not going to convict this man, and that he needed to establish a motive for the crime. But he wondered if Beckwith's actual motive would make the all-white Mississippi jury more sympathetic to the defendant. At first Beckwith was calm, but when the prosecutor read him his 1957 letter to the Jackson newspaper, the one in which he said he would "bend every effort to rid the U.S.A. of the integrationists," and asked Beckwith if this was the way he felt, the defendant was indignant. "Of course I feel that way, sir," Beckwith replied. "It is a cause, sir, the cause of white supremacy."

In the jury room, the twelve men argued politely for seven hours the first night and four hours the next morning before reporting to the judge that they were hopelessly deadlocked, seven for acquittal and five for conviction.

On the morning of February 7, after the jury's announcement that they could not reach a verdict, the mayor of Jackson, expecting a riot, sent three hundred policemen to block off the roads leading to the Jackson State College campus. Although no riot occurred, the jumpy police shot into the crowd of students and wounded five of them. Whites in Jackson had nervously expected black rage over the outcome, but instead of anger, blacks were astonished. On the other hand, as one reporter put it, "The whole state, including the prisoner, was stunned by the mistrial. Everyone had expected acquittal."

Beckwith was kept in jail for two more months while all the evidence against him was heard by a second set of white jurors. This time he looked bored and glum. Still, the outcome was no different. The new all-white jury also deadlocked, this time reportedly split with eight for acquittal and four for conviction. When the second mistrial was declared, there seemed little reason to pursue a third trial. Beckwith was released.

Arriving home in grand style, Beckwith was chauffeured by the sympathetic sheriff of Hinds County, Fred Pickett, leading a sizable motorcade. As his car entered the Delta, a WELCOME HOME sign was posted in the village of Tchula. When they reached the courthouse in Greenwood, the local newspaper reported on the front page the next day, "well wishers rushed up to him and greeted him." There were balloons, and honking horns, and people waving from the street to greet their favorite son. Beckwith told a reporter that it all "brought tears to my eyes." That night, he was treated to a steak dinner at one of the best restaurants in town; his friends were going to take care of him. Flat broke and "starving to death" when he got out of jail, Beckwith went back to his old job selling fertilizer. The Greenwood police department made him an auxiliary policeman, allowing him to ride up front in police cars, with his own gun and club, during trips through the black neighborhoods.

In December of 1990, more than a quarter century after Beckwith's two mistrials, a singular event in Southern history occurred. Without any prodding from the federal government, the state of Mississippi reached back into its own past and indicted Beckwith once again for the murder of Medgar Evers. Legally, it was a relatively simple matter; the case could still be reopened because no statute of limitations applied to murder. Still, this was an unheard-of event in the long catalog of unpunished Southern civil rights murders. As the months dragged on toward Beckwith's third trial, Mississippi whites grumbled and Mississippi blacks were cynical. The judge moved jury selection to Panola County, 140 miles north of Jackson, at the request of Beckwith's lawyers, in hopes of finding jurors who had not read about the case (although the testimony was still heard in the courthouse in Jackson). Most potential jurors, black as well as white, looked at the seventy-three-year-old defendant and wondered if he was even worth it. What they didn't know was that the old man sitting there in the courtroom had been involved with numerous white supremacist groups, including the Ku Klux Klan, and had served time at the infamous Louisiana State Penitentiary for carrying a bomb, which he was transporting in his car to use on behalf of the KKK. After eight days of jury selection, the lawyers finally agreed on eight blacks and four whites to be on the panel;

eight of them had been infants when Medgar Evers was assassinated.

Beckwith's third trial began on January 27, 1994, thirty years to the day after his first trial. Myrlie Evers was the first witness, as she had been in the other trials. Initially, all the same evidence was presented and all the same witnesses testified—those that were still alive, that is. Everything looked old, outdated, undramatic—even the scraggly defendant, who appeared mostly disinterested. Then came new evidence: gruesome autopsy photographs of the victim's body, exhumed for a second medical examination, and the testimony of five witnesses who said they had heard Beckwith brag about assassinating Evers. Beckwith was reindicted mainly on the basis of new testimony from witnesses who said they had heard Beckwith brag to people attending a Ku Klux Klan rally in the mid-1960s, and to two women in 1966 that he had murdered Medgar Evers. Although the court-appointed defense team privately said they were disgusted by Beckwith, they defended him well by discrediting those witnesses: Two had been KKK informants, two had drinking and psychiatric problems, and the fifth could not remember the exact words Beckwith had used. As the prosecution's case wound down, some observers were worried.

Then a new and credible witness suddenly emerged. Mark Reiley, a red-haired junior executive from Chicago, had seen a report of the trial on CNN and remembered something he thought could help the case against Beckwith. That same day, he called the district attorney's office in Jackson. Reiley would be their final witness. Fifteen years earlier he had been a young guard at the Louisiana State Penitentiary while Beckwith was incarcerated there. Beckwith had befriended the twenty-one-year-old guard, calling him "Young Blood," and Reiley, being away from his family and lonely, initially got along with Beckwith. But as Reiley got to know Beckwith better, he saw the true nature of the man, characteristics he didn't like. He remembered that Beckwith had called blacks "beasts of the field," and one day Beckwith angrily demanded a black nurse be taken out of his sight, saying, "If I could get rid of an uppity nigger like Medgar Evers, I can get rid of a no-account nigger like you." Further,

Beckwith tried to convince Reiley that he was a man of importance, as Reiley testified: "He told me that if he was lying and didn't have the power and connections he said he had, he would be serving time in prison for getting rid of that nigger Medgar Evers."

In his closing remarks on February 5, 1994, the prosecuting attorney, Bobby DeLaughter, said to the jury, in part, "Why was Medgar Evers assassinated? For his beliefs. To go in a restaurant. To vote. For wanting some degree of equality for himself and his fellow human beings." The jury deliberated for five hours the first evening before wearily returning to their hotel without a decision. The next morning they agreed: Byron de la Beckwith was guilty. He was sentenced to spend the rest of his life in prison.

AFTERMATH: Medgar Evers's assassination was the first civil rights killing to have a truly national impact. The next day it was the lead story in the *New York Times*; hundreds of people demonstrated at the courthouse in Wichita, Kansas, and hundreds more turned out on the steps of the state capitol in Topeka; blacks marched through downtown Fresno, California; church bells tolled in Plymouth, New Hampshire; and blacks and whites gathered together under the statue of Abraham Lincoln in Springfield, Illinois. A crowd of mourners gathered at the train station in Atlanta to sing and pray as the train carrying Evers's body to Washington, D.C., passed through. In the nation's capital, eight hundred people followed Evers's casket from Union Station to the McGuire Funeral Home. "Men bared their heads and women wept openly as the hearse rolled by," the *Washington Post* reported; hundreds of people, mostly whites with their heads bowed solemnly, lined the streets as the procession carried him to Arlington National Cemetery.

In death, it seemed, Evers inspired the kind of idealism he had fought for and believed in. As his colleague John Salter remembered, "[He] always envisioned a genuinely integrated society." The entire nation was awakened by Evers's assassination to the unfolding drama in the South. His murder was un-American and shocking, and it inspired speeches on the floor of Congress. An editorial of "revulsion universally felt" appeared in the *New York Times*. And in a message to Evers's widow, President Kennedy spoke of "the justice of the cause for which your husband gave his life."

On June 19, 1963, President Kennedy asked Congress to enact far-reaching civil rights legislation. On August 18 more than 200,000 black and white Americans marched on Washington to demonstrate support for civil rights. But violence against blacks continued in the South.

Kennedy would not live to see the Twenty-fourth Amendment to the Constitution take effect on February 24, 1964 (making U.S. poll taxes unconstitutional). Later that same year the National Labor Relations Board ruled that racial discrimination by a labor union constitutes an unfair labor practice.

Twenty-eight years after his assassination, Medgar Evers's body was exhumed for examination by forensic pathologist Michael Baden for Beckwith's third trial. Evers's son Darrell, who was barely four years old at the time of his father's assassination, wanted to be present during his father's autopsy. As Baden explained, when Evers's casket was opened, everyone present was amazed at what they saw. Evers's body looked like he had been dead only one or two days, not twenty-eight years. Darrell Evers, who looks exactly like his father, entered the autopsy room, looked down at his slain father, whom he barely remembered seeing alive, and the entire room was transformed.

NOVEMBER 2, 1963

NGO DINH DIEM (1901–1963)
PRESIDENT OF SOUTH VIETNAM

Elected the first president of South Vietnam in 1955, Ngo Dinh Diem quickly established a virtual dictatorship that lasted until his government was overthrown in 1963. A devout Roman Catholic and fervent national-ist, Diem gradually alienated both domestic and international support for his regime. His own military leaders plotted his assassination, some say, with help from the CIA.

Diem was of royal descent; his ancestors were among the first Vietnamese to be converted to Roman Catholicism in the seventeenth century. Ngo Dinh Diem spent his youth mostly associating with the imperial family. Working in government, as his father had done, during the 1930s Ngo Dinh Diem was minister of the interior for Emperor Bao Dai. In 1945 Diem was taken prisoner by the communist forces of Ho Chi Minh, who hoped Diem would secure Catholic support for the communists and asked Diem to join his government in the north. Diem refused, then fled to the United States, where he lived in exile for almost a decade. In 1954 Diem returned to South Vietnam as prime minister under the sponsorship of the United States. He ousted the monarchy in 1955, declared South Vietnam a republic, and became president. A tyrannical ruler, Ngo Dinh Diem survived almost a decade in power, despite making enemies of every major element of Vietnamese society and the United States as well. Regarded as a bigot, a despot, and an incompetent, Diem disregarded demands from a growing guerrilla movement in the countryside for land reform, ignored government cor-ruption, and ordered savage crackdowns on his critics, some of whom were thrown into airless prison cells.

In addition to continuing his opposition to communism, Diem scorned the French and was fiercely independent of the Americans who supported him. Though he promised to make land reforms and eliminate corruption, he succeeded mostly at nepotism, promoting members of his family and fellow Catholics while ruthlessly suppressing his opposition. His fatal error was persecution of the Buddhists, who comprised an overwhelming majority in South Vietnam. This led to withdrawal of U.S. support for his regime and a military coup in 1963.

ASSASSINS: The actual assassin was a major in the tank corps, who at one time was affiliated with the Dai Viet party, a minority faction opposed to both the communists and Diem. It has been reported that the major had wanted to kill Diem ever since the ruler had one of his close friends executed.

The mastermind of the coup was Duong Van Minh (called Big Minh by Americans), a general who had been educated in France, as many of his fellow generals had been, where he was an outstanding student at L'Ecole de Chartres. When Big Minh returned to his native land, he joined the army, working for a French-influenced Vietnam. When it became clear that the Diem regime was antagonistic toward his goals, Big Minh engineered a takeover of Diem's government.

HISTORY: A number of attempts were made to oust Diem from power. In November of 1960, paratroopers and other elements of the air force tried to seize the presidential palace but were repelled, with Ngo Dinh Diem regaining power on November 12. Following this coup attempt, dissident groups, collectively called the Vietcong (Vietnamese communists), met secretly on December 20 to organize the National Front for the Liberation of South Vietnam. In 1962, fighter planes flew in low over the palace and sprayed Diem's ground troops with machine-gun fire, badly damaging the palace building. Although Diem survived the assault and maintained control of the government, he became suspicious of even his closest advisers. He grew increasingly isolated and more reliant on his brother, Ngo Dinh Nhu, chief of the secret police. Because Diem was widowed and never remarried, Madame Nhu, his sister-in-law, acted as the official first lady of South Vietnam, but she did not enhance his popularity and hurt him politically. Noted for her harsh views and callous remarks, Madame Nhu was dubbed "the Dragon Lady" by American reporters. When Buddhist monks burned themselves to death to protest the Diem government, Madame Nhu provoked worldwide outrage by accusing the monks of staging "a barbecue with imported gasoline." By the summer of 1963, antigovernment riots were becoming more and more common, and Buddhist monks were immolating themselves in the streets of Saigon much too frequently. Leading Vietnamese generals, who had for months been discussing ways to oust Diem and his brother, stepped up their efforts to rescue their country from its despotic ruler.

Evidently, Diem's brother realized he was on the verge of losing everything, so he devised an ingenious plan to purge anti-Diem forces within his brother's government. Nhu decided he would stage a full-scale revolt, then dramatically crush it in order to demonstrate Diem's muscle and righteousness. He figured this one event could eliminate the opposition and solidify his and his brother's power. The scheme, called Operation Bravo, was scheduled for November 1, All Saints' Day. Nhu arranged with Le Quang Tung, a Diem loyalist and special forces commander, to join with dissident police officers and initiate the phony coup. It was assumed that spontaneous violence would explode in the streets, at which time Diem and Nhu would flee the capital. Tung would then proclaim a rebel government to replace the fallen tyrants, and during the following twenty-four hours of chaos, Nhu and his troops would amass on the city's outskirts, then move in on Tung and company, smother the revolt, and reinstate Diem.

While Nhu was solidifying his plans, Big Minh and other Vietnamese generals were plotting to overthrow Diem with the sanction and advice of the U.S. government. They viewed Nhu's mock coup as a stroke of luck because it would provide an ideal cover for the real thing. Big Minh asked General Ton That Dinh, who had been put in charge of martial law in Saigon, to pretend to go along with Nhu's plan, but then take his side instead. Big Minh promised Dinh that he would be given a ministerial position in the new government, as well as various material rewards.

Although Dinh had no particular ideological bias toward Diem, he was an opportunist determined to be on the winning side and would not commit himself to Minh's cause until the last possible moment.

EVENT: During the early morning hours of November 1, 1963, in Saigon, General Ton That Dinh directed marine battalions, paratroopers, tanks, and other contingents into position in and around the city, but few of those troops knew for sure whether they were supposed to lay siege to the presidential palace or protect it. It also appears that at this point the Americans didn't know what was happening either.

At 1:30 P.M. the attack began as scheduled: Marines rushed in, and blood flowed as Ngu and Diem watched from the cool rooms of the palace, assuming everything was going as planned. Their first clue that something was amiss came when General Dinh did not answer their phone calls to him at staff headquarters. When the gunfire came perilously close to palace windows, Ngu and Diem began to realize that they had been duped. That evening they packed a suitcase full of U.S. currency and escaped the palace through an elaborate maze of tunnels. A car waiting outside quickly took them to the home of a Chinese businessman.

The next morning the brothers left that house and took refuge in the church of Saint Francis Xavier. There they telephoned General Dinh and agreed to surrender. Within minutes the rebels arrived, tied their hands behind their backs, and led the two men out of the church to an armored personnel carrier. As they rode in the backseat with a headstrong tank corps major, harsh words were exchanged between Nhu and the officer, who drew his bayonet and stabbed Nhu. The major then pulled out his revolver and shot Diem in the back of the head, then looked at Nhu, who was lying on the floor twitching, and shot him in the head too.

General Dinh and his lieutenants at staff headquarters in Saigon were shocked when they were told that both men had been assassinated. He claimed publicly that both men had died by their own hand, later saying it had been "accidental." The identity of the Vietnamese major was never made public.

AFTERMATH: Word of the downfall of Diem's government set off widespread exuberance throughout Saigon. The generals who had enacted the coup, intent on concealing the circumstances under which the brothers had died, buried the men's bodies in an unmarked grave in a prison cemetery near Saigon airport. They were identified on their death certificates not as high-ranking government officials but as "Chief of Province" and "Chief of Library Services," respectively, the ranks to which they had risen during the French presence in Indochina.

Big Minh's junta was ineffectual and soon overthrown by a rival faction led by General Nguyen Khanh, although Minh was retained as head of state until 1964, when he was replaced by a civilian and forced into exile. In 1966, Big Minh ran for president but was disqualified because he was not a current resident of his country. He tried again in 1971 but withdrew from the presidential race, claiming his opponent, Nguyen Van Thieu, was making a travesty of the supposedly free election. Thieu ran unopposed and became president.

At the time of the coup, which resulted in the deaths of her husband and brother-in-law, Madame Nhu was on a speaking tour of the United States. Upon learning of the events back home, she accused the United States of engineering the downfall of Diem and her husband. The vengeful widow immediately left the United States and went to Paris, where she lived only a couple of years before moving to Italy. There she was ensconced in a high-walled villa on the southeast outskirts of Rome.

The CIA had become active in Vietnam during the early 1950s, engaging in psychological warfare, military training, and guerrilla raids, as well as helping Diem eliminate his political enemies. Diem is only one of a list of many foreign leaders who have been implicated as recipients of CIA subsidies through the years, with Diem's successor, South Vietnamese president Nguyen Van Thieu, also joining the list. After Diem's elimination, the U.S. presence in Vietnam increased, as did the CIA's. Among their operations was the Phoenix Program, run by William Colby (who later would become director of the CIA), which reportedly resulted in the execution of over twenty thousand suspected Vietcong during the course of the operation.

NOVEMBER 22, 1963

JOHN F. KENNEDY (1917–1963)
THIRTY-FIFTH PRESIDENT OF THE UNITED STATES FROM 1961 TO 1963

John Fitzgerald Kennedy was the youngest man and the first Roman Catholic ever elected to the office of president, and he lived a shorter life than any other president. Although some say Kennedy's youth, brilliance, and glamour—enhanced by the charm and good looks of the first lady— brought more style than substance to the White House, his administration inspired a generation of idealists and a new emphasis on activism. JFK's wit and charisma combined with his political shrewdness to disarm many of his critics.

Born in Brookline, Massachusetts, the second son of Joseph P. Kennedy, millionaire banker, business tycoon, and U.S. ambassador to Britain in the 1930s, John F. Kennedy was educated at Harvard, then served during World War II in the Pacific as a navy lieutenant. Commanding the torpedo boat *PT-109* on patrol near the Solomon Islands, Kennedy became a hero when his vessel was struck by a Japanese destroyer and broken apart. Despite receiving a severe back injury during the event, Kennedy ensured the escape of his crew and would later receive an award for gallantry. Back home, influential family connections helped him win election to the House of Representatives in 1946, then the Senate in 1952. The next year he married socialite Jacqueline Lee Bouvier. While recovering from back surgery, Senator Kennedy wrote a book about his experiences during the war; *Profiles in Courage* was published in 1956, became an instant best-seller, and went on to win Kennedy a Pulitzer prize. His increasing prominence in Democratic politics won him a narrow victory over Richard Nixon in the presidential elections of 1960.

During his term of office, President Kennedy created the Peace Corps in 1961, and Lieutenant Colonel John Glenn became the first American to orbit the earth in 1962. Although the Bay of Pigs invasion of Cuba in 1961 was an embarrassing failure for Kennedy, the Cuban missile crisis in October 1962 ended successfully for the United States. The following June, the United States, Britain, and the USSR signed the Nuclear Test-Ban Treaty, which prohibited atmospheric weapons testing. When President Kennedy appointed Robert Kennedy as attorney general, he became the only president to appoint his brother to a cabinet post. In domestic policy, President Kennedy, closely assisted by his brother Robert, championed the civil rights movement and supervised a crackdown on organized crime.

ALLEGED ASSASSIN: The man named as President Kennedy's assassin was Lee Harvey Oswald, but numerous other theories have been proposed as to who assassinated Kennedy and why.

Lee Harvey Oswald, born in New Orleans on October 18, 1939, has been described as a solitary child whose fatherless family often moved around the country while he was growing up. At the age of seventeen he enlisted in the U.S. Marine Corps. After completing his training, he was barely an average marksman. He was sent to a U.S. air base in Japan and given a "hardship" discharge in 1959 because his mother had suffered an injury and required his help back home. Once there, though, Oswald did not stay long. Instead, he traveled to the Soviet Union. It has been reported that Oswald applied for Soviet citizenship, and although initially it was refused, eventually he was permitted to stay. In Minsk, where Oswald was sent to work in a transistor-radio factory, he met and married Marina Pruskova, said to be the daughter of a KGB colonel. After two-and-a-half years, he evidently grew tired of drab Soviet life. Although Oswald's discharge from the marines had been changed from "hardship" to "dishonorable," he secured a loan from the State Department to purchase passage for himself and his pregnant wife to return to the United States They were settled in New Orleans by the time their daughter was born in June 1962. Later that year, Oswald became a member of Fair Play for Cuba, a pro-Castro organization, but it is said that he associated with Guy Bannister, a known CIA operative involved in providing money, arms, and munitions to anti-Castro forces preparing for a second invasion of Cuba (in direct violation of President Kennedy's executive orders). Bannister, it is reported, was a close friend and associate of David Ferrie, a former Eastern Airlines pilot who flew weapons to Cuba for the CIA. In turn, Ferrie was connected to Carlos Marcello, the New Orleans Mafia boss.

In 1963, Oswald moved his family to Dallas. By that time Marina was pregnant again, and Oswald found work at the Texas School Book Depository. He was hired on October 16, 1963, to fill book orders, and paid a salary of $1.25 an hour. Oswald took a room in town to be near his job, and continued to spend weekends with his wife in the suburban home of Ruth Hyde Paine.

HISTORY: The U.S. civil rights movement gained a foothold in 1963, when the year began with a ceremony at the Lincoln Memorial to commemorate the centennial of the Emancipation Proclamation. The highlight of that event was Martin Luther King Jr.'s inspiring "I have a dream" speech. Protests in the South led to violence, including the June 12 assassination of Medgar Evers and the deaths of several black schoolchildren in the bombing of a Birmingham, Alabama, church in September. When President Kennedy was called upon to take a stand on the civil rights issue, he and his brother Robert upheld the law, calling for a halt to discrimination and segregation.

Also on the two brothers' agenda was an all-out assault on organized crime. Even though J. Edgar Hoover, FBI director since 1924, refused to cooperate with Robert Kennedy, the attorney general and his aides in the Justice Department drew up a list of some forty priority targets among Cosa Nostra bosses, under-bosses, and Mob-influenced labor union leaders. Teamsters president Jimmy Hoffa was at the top of the list, followed by crime bosses Carlos Marcello of Louisiana and Texas, Santos Trafficante Jr. of Florida, Sam Giancana of Chicago, and Angelo Bruno of Philadelphia. During the first year, 121 Mob defendants were indicted,

John and Robert Kennedy

and 73 were convicted; by the end of 1962, 350 had been indicted and 138 convicted; as the end of 1963 neared, 615 had been indicted and 288 convicted. This was the first time in its history that organized crime was on the run.

While domestic matters sizzled, foreign affairs seemed to make great strides, after the false start between President Kennedy and Soviet president Nikita Khrushchev in 1962, during the Cuban missile crisis. With the Nuclear Test-Ban Treaty in place, a hot-line between Washington and Moscow designed to avert an accidental war went into effect on August 30, 1963. Still, President Kennedy reportedly confided to his advisers that he could not control the CIA, which was then implicated not only in assassination attempts on Cuba's Fidel Castro but also in a coup that overthrew the government of South Vietnam (resulting in the assassination of Ngo Dinh Diem and, ultimately, an escalation of U.S. involvement in the Vietnam War).

In November of 1963, the Kennedy presidential reelection campaign, looking toward the 1964 election, wanted to get an early start on securing the vote in Texas, a state they had lost to Nixon in 1960. Plans to visit the state had begun in April, but as the departure date neared, the president seemed reluctant to make the trip. U.N. ambassador Adlai Stevenson had recently visited Dallas, where he was attacked by a small crowd of demonstrators who regarded the United Nations as a communist front; they spat at him and pelted him with eggs. Stevenson was concerned about the president's visit, as were Senator William Fulbright and Robert Kennedy, and Stevenson suggested that the president and the first lady change their plans. But the president knew this trip was as much about money as it was about votes, because serious financial support for the next year's campaign could come from Texas. Finally, the official itinerary was announced in October: The presidential party was scheduled to visit the five major cities of Texas, with its final stop being the vice president's ranch, where he planned to hold a huge home-style barbecue and a horseback ride on the range. The exact route of the president's motorcade was printed in Dallas newspapers four days before the president's arrival.

The president's first stop was San Antonio, where his speech dedicating a new research facility, part of the Aerospace Medical Center at Brooks Air Force Base, was received enthusiastically. Next, the presidential party was greeted warmly in Houston, where Jackie gave a short speech in Spanish to the League of United Latin American Citizens and the couple attended a testimonial dinner at the Coliseum for Congressman Albert Thomas. Afterward, they flew to Fort Worth, arriving at the Texas Hotel after midnight. The next morning they would fly to Dallas.

At the end of his workday on Thursday, November 21, 1963, Lee Harvey Oswald varied his usual routine, catching a ride with a coworker who lived in the same neighborhood as Oswald's family; he claimed he needed to pick up something and would spend the night there. The next morning, the day of Kennedy's assassination, Oswald rose without waking his wife, placed $170 in cash and his wedding ring on top of the dresser, picked up a brown package about four feet long, then left for work. Getting a ride from the same coworker, Oswald placed the package in the backseat of the car. When asked what was in the package, Oswald replied simply, "Curtain rods." At the book depository, Oswald was seen several times looking down from the windows onto Dealey Plaza. He asked a coworker why crowds were gathering in the area, and when told that President Kennedy's motorcade would be passing by in a couple of hours, Oswald replied, "Oh, I see."

EVENT: When Air Force One landed at Dallas's Love Field on November 22, 1963, the president and first lady stepped off the plane into the brilliant, crisp sunshine and greeted the crowd before everyone proceeded to their assigned vehicles in the motorcade. The Secret Service had lined up the vehicles, marking each with a number indicating its position in the upcoming parade. A 1961 Lincoln Continental limousine carrying the president and first lady was supposed to occupy the number-seven position, but there was a mix-up, placing them up front. JFK climbed into the presidential position, the right rear seat, with Jackie on his left. Texas governor John B. Connally sat directly in front of the president, in the jump seat, with his wife, Nellie, beside him in front of the first lady. A Secret Service agent sat up front with driver William Greer. A Secret Service car followed directly behind the president's limousine. The press car, which would usually be close to the president's, ended up fourteenth, last in the procession, too far behind the president's vehicle to get coverage of the events that would take place that day.

During the planning of this trip, there had been much discussion about whether the president's car should have the bubble top in place. The Secret Service wanted it for security reasons, but JFK wanted the car open if weather permitted.

The motorcade drove away from Love Field at 11:55 A.M. The first vehicle in the procession contained Dallas police chief Jesse Curry and Sheriff Bill Decker. It was followed by a police motorcycle escort, then the big Lincoln carrying President and Mrs. Kennedy, and Governor and Mrs. Connally. Destined for the Trade Mart, where JFK was scheduled to speak, the entourage drove for more than thirty minutes, smiling and waving at the large, friendly crowds, before reaching the central part of Dallas. At the corner of Elm and Houston Streets the motorcade almost stopped as it negotiated a 120-degree left turn onto Elm Street, where the road heads down an incline toward an underpass. The crowds were thinner at this point but still enthusiastic as, at 12:30, the motorcade entered Dealey Plaza, passing directly in front of the Texas School Book Depository.

With bright sunlight in their eyes, the president and first lady continued to smile and wave as Mrs. Connally turned to the Kennedys, saying, "Mr. President, you can't say that Dallas doesn't love you." Then, suddenly, shots rang out, echoing through Dealey Plaza. The president, who was waving to the crowd with his right hand, was hit by the first bullet and reacted immediately, reaching for his throat with clenched fists, his elbows pointing out in opposite directions. The first lady leaned forward, looking to see what was wrong with her husband. The driver slowed the limousine almost to a standstill and turned to see what was happening. Governor Connally also turned, looking over his right shoulder. Another shot struck the president in the head, creating a viscous cloud of his blood and brain tissue as the bullet blew away the right rear quadrant of JFK's skull. Governor Connally was also injured, a bullet wounding him in the chest, the right wrist, and his left thigh. "Oh God, they are going to kill us all!" the governor cried out. Nellie pulled her wounded husband into her lap and out of the line of fire, then bent down over him with her own body.

The assault had lasted six to eight seconds by the time the president slumped down into the seat. During those violent seconds, the extensive training of what was touted as the world's most efficient enforcement agency—the United States Secret Service—should have gone into practice; instead, uncertainty seemed to prevail. The president's driver, who was trained to immediately speed away from danger, apparently was uncertain about which direction to go. Finally, as the president slumped down into the seat, Mrs. Kennedy turned to her right and scrambled out onto the trunk of the limousine to retrieve a piece of her husband's skull, just as the Secret Service bolted into action. Agent Clint Hill climbed aboard the back of the Lincoln, clinging to the rear of the car, and Mrs. Kennedy slid back into her seat just as the driver hit the accelerator and sped away down Elm Street. The nearest hospital was four miles away.

At 12:36 P.M., within six minutes of the onslaught, the president's car came to a halt in front of the emergency entrance at Parkland Memorial Hospital. Governor Connally struggled to his feet to make way for medics to reach the president, then collapsed. JFK was placed on a stretcher and rushed inside the hospital. The backseat of the Lincoln was splattered with blood and gore, as were Mrs. Kennedy's clothes.

In emergency room No. 1 a team of surgeons was hastily assembled to save the president's life, although all recognized immediately that he was too badly wounded for there to be any hope. Dr. Paul Peters later recalled: "My first thought was, 'My God, he is dead.' A considerable portion of the skull, of the brain, was gone. It looked like a wound we could not salvage."

When Dr. Malcolm Perry, acting chief resident in surgery, stepped into the narrow room with gray-tiled walls and a cream-colored ceiling, he saw the president of the United States lying on his back on an aluminum hospital cart, a huge lamp shining on his face. The president had already been stripped of his jacket, shirt, and T-shirt, and a staff doctor had started to place an endotracheal tube down his throat so that they could get oxygen into his lungs.

The president was not breathing. There was no heartbeat. The wound in his throat was small and neat, with blood running out of it. The back of his head had a huge loose flap of skull and brain matter with blood flowing out onto the floor. Before doing the tracheotomy, Dr. Perry asked that Doctors Clark, McClelland, and Baxter be called in to help.

The tracheotomy was completed. A chest tube was put in place to suction out the blood and air packed in JFK's chest and prevent his lungs from collapsing. A transfusion was begun by the time Dr. Kemp Clark, chief neurosurgeon in residency, entered the room. One look at Dr. Perry's face, and he knew there was no hope.

Dr. Perry still could feel no heartbeat, no evidence of breathing; JFK's body was motionless but still bleeding. With no time to open the chest and massage the heart to stimulate it to beat, Perry began external massage. The aluminum cart was too high for him to get into the proper position, and so, standing on his toes, he proceeded and called for somebody to get him a stool. Now perched on the stool, Perry massaged the chest of the president's body in front of him, hoping to get a heartbeat but knowing it was futile. In a corner of the room, Dr. Clark watched an electrocardiogram for any sign that Dr. Perry's efforts were successful. After ten minutes, Dr. Clark said to Dr. Perry, "It's too late, Mac." Dr. Perry stopped. The doctor controlling the oxygen flow stopped, then reached for the edges of a white sheet and pulled it over the face of John F. Kennedy. It was 1 P.M.

Father Oscar Huber was in the rectory at Holy Trinity Church when he heard the news. He had rushed over, entering the room as Dr. Perry was leaving. The priest offered Mrs. Kennedy his sympathy, then the two of them approached JFK's body. Pulling back the white sheet, Father Huber administered last rites, and he and Jacqueline Kennedy prayed together for fifteen minutes. Then Mrs. Kennedy slipped the ring off her finger and placed it on her husband's finger.

Shortly after one o'clock Vernon B. Oneal answered the telephone at his funeral home. A man who said he was with the U.S. Secret Service asked Oneal to bring the best casket he had to Parkland as quickly as humanly possible. "It is for the president of the United States," the man said.

Although word had already reached the press waiting outside the hospital, Malcolm Kilduff, the acting press secretary for the Texas trip, made the official announcement at 2:31 P.M.: President Kennedy was dead.

THE APPREHENSION: As soon as the shooting started, chaos broke out in Dealey Plaza. Two uniformed motorcycle officers who had flanked the presidential limousine ran up a grassy knoll that faced the motorcade route, in search of a gunman. They were followed by many bystanders. Other witnesses claimed the shots came from the upper floors of the Texas School Book Depository, which officers immediately entered in search of the shooter. In the second-floor lunchroom, Officer Marrion Baker, accompanied by the building superintendent, Roy Truly, came across Lee Oswald, calmly sipping a soda. "Does this man work for you?" Baker asked Truly. When Truly said Oswald did, Baker, evidently not suspecting Oswald, continued up the stairway to search the other floors of the building. Eventually officers found a "sniper's nest" on the sixth floor: A 6.5-millimeter bolt-action, clip-fed 1938 Mannlicher-Carcano rifle, with three empty bullet shells nearby, was hidden behind some boxes stacked near a window overlooking Dealy Plaza. Deputy Sheriff Roger D. Craig said that by this time he had seen Oswald calmly exit the back of the building and get into a light-colored 1959 Rambler station wagon, although other accounts say Oswald left the building through the front door on Elm Street, after being asked by a newsman where to find a telephone.

Within fifteen minutes of the assassination, the first description of a suspect was broadcast by Dallas police: an unknown white male, approximately thirty years old, slender build, height five feet ten inches, weight 165 pounds. The police had gotten this description from eyewitness Howard Brennan, who said he saw a man in the window of the book depository at the time of the shooting.

Lee Harvey Oswald boarded a city bus, but because pandemonium in Dallas made the streets impassable, he got off the bus and walked two blocks to the Greyhound bus station. There he got a taxi that took him to a street corner near his rooming house. Oswald walked to the house, went to his room without stopping to chat with his landlady, who was watching news reports of the assassination on television, changed his shirt, and grabbed a revolver. Leaving his rooming house at 1:04 P.M., he was walking quickly along Tenth Street when patrolman J. D. Tippit, driving by, noticed that Oswald matched the description of the suspect that had been broadcast over the police radio four times during the previous thirty minutes. Although Tippit was a ten-year veteran of the force, he didn't have his service revolver ready as he pulled his patrol car over and got out to speak with Oswald. Reportedly Oswald pulled a revolver from the waistband of his pants, aimed, and shot four times, killing Tippit. At least a half dozen people testified that they either saw Oswald murder Tippit or saw him quickly walk away with the gun in his hands.

Next, Oswald was seen ducking into the Texas Theatre on Jefferson Boulevard without stopping to buy a ticket, which prompted the cashier to call the police. Within minutes authorities arrived, sealed the theater's exits, and had the house lights turned on in order to look for the man they were after. Cornered and asked to stand up as one officer approached him, Oswald punched the officer, then went for his gun, but was subdued before he was able to fire it. As he was dragged from the theater, Oswald shouted, "I am not resisting arrest! Police brutality!"

THE AUTOPSY: Although the Dallas County medical examiner informed JFK's staff that Texas law required an autopsy be performed before the body could be taken back to Washington, D.C., Kennedy's people did not comply. JFK's body was quickly transported to Air Force One, where Lyndon Johnson was sworn in as president before the long flight home.

That evening at Bethesda Naval Hospital, a military autopsy was performed on President Kennedy by military personnel, although apparently it did not meet even minimum military guidelines. Said to be controlled by Robert Kennedy and other members of his family, the physician officially in charge of the autopsy was Dr. James J. Humes, who was not a forensic pathologist. According to Robert J. Groden's book *The Killing of a President,* Humes, who had never before performed an autopsy involving gunshot wounds, was directed by navy admiral George Burkley, JFK's personal physician, not to track the path of the bullet wounds through the president's body. Groden also says that Burkley authorized Humes to destroy his original notes made during the autopsy, about which Humes would later testify that "the original notes, which were stained with the blood of our late president, I felt, were inappropriate to retain." Also missing after the autopsy, were JFK's brain, tissue sections, blood smears, and organ samples. The condition of JFK's brain after the assassination could have answered crucial questions about the entry wound(s) that killed the president, a source of speculation about the actual events surrounding his death. Although JFK's brain was removed, then placed in a stainless steel container of formalin solution, a preservative, until it could be sectioned and examined, no results of such an examination have ever been made public. The FBI had two agents present at all times during the autopsy, but when they were offered the autopsy X rays and photographs, the FBI didn't want them.

It was later determined by the House Select Committee on Assassinations that probably Robert Kennedy had disposed of these and other materials because he was concerned that they would be placed on public display in future years in an institution such as the Smithsonian.

THE FUNERAL: When the autopsy was completed, John F. Kennedy's corpse was taken to the White House and placed on a specially constructed catafalque in the East Room. Flowers were arranged on one side of the casket and an honor guard was posted.

At 10 A.M. on November 23, Father John Cavanaugh, an old friend of the Kennedys, conducted a low mass for family and intimates of the slain president in the East Room of the White House. President John F. Kennedy's public funeral made a lasting impression of his place in history. Some 300,000 mourners lined Pennsylvania and Constitution Avenues to watch the caisson carry their slain leader from the White House to the Capitol. There, another 250,000 people filed past JFK's flag-covered coffin in the Great Rotunda. A million people lined the streets of Washington to view the funeral procession, as millions more watched the solemn ceremonies on live television.

A procession of international dignitaries walked to Saint Matthew's Cathedral behind Jacqueline Kennedy and other members of the immediate family. JFK's coffin was drawn by the same gun caisson that had carried Franklin D. Roosevelt to his grave in 1945. A riderless horse (ironically named Black Jack, Jacqueline's father's nickname) with boots reversed in their stirrups, followed the coffin, as muffled drum rolls marked the way. At the entrance to Saint Matthew's, Jacqueline Kennedy and her two young children were met by Cardinal Richard Cushing, then entered the cathedral for the funeral mass. Afterward, they emerged to the strains of "Hail to the Chief," and at his mother's gentle prodding, little John Kennedy Jr. saluted the American flag atop his father's coffin.

JFK's burial at Arlington National Cemetery followed the mass, and afterward Jacqueline met privately at the White House with President Charles de Gaulle of France, Emperor Haile Selassie of Ethiopia, President Eamon de Valera of Ireland, and England's Prince Philip. Next a procession of 220 representatives from 102 nations, including eight chiefs of state and eleven heads of government, stretched from the Red Room back through the Blue Room and the state dining room, slowly moving along toward the receiving line with Jacqueline Kennedy at its heart.

THE SUSPECT: During the two days that twenty-four-year-old Lee Harvey Oswald was held at Dallas police headquarters, he was questioned extensively about the assassination of President Kennedy. Although Oswald consistently denied having killed either the president or patrolman J. D. Tippit, several witnesses identified Oswald as Tippit's killer, and his palm print was found on the rifle discovered near the sixth-floor window of the Texas School Book Depository.

On Sunday morning, November 24, news reporters gathered in the close quarters of a basement hallway of the Dallas police building and waited for Lee Harvey Oswald to be brought through as he was transferred by police to a safer location. Standing among reporters waiting for the accused assassin of President John F. Kennedy was Jack Ruby, the owner of a sleazy strip joint called the Carousel. Ruby was known to police, having been arrested several times—once for assaulting a police officer—though he'd received no convictions.

Through the doorway they came. Detectives surrounded Oswald, who was in handcuffs, leading him into the tunnel of people, lights, and cameras. As they approached, out of the crowd stepped Jack Ruby. With a snub-nosed .38-caliber revolver concealed by the sleeve of his coat, he walked right up to Oswald, stuck the gun in his left side, and shot him at point-blank range. "You killed my president, you rat!" Ruby screamed.

Oswald was taken by ambulance to Parkland Hospital—the same hospital where President Kennedy had been taken forty-eight hours earlier—and soon died.

INVESTIGATIONS: Since the initial investigation, there have been other official investigations through the years. The first, the Warren Commission, was enacted by President Johnson. Subsequent official investigations were conducted by New Orleans district attorney Jim Garrison, the prosecutor of Clay Shaw for conspiracy to assassinate the president; the Rockefeller Commission (Senate Select Committee on Intelligence Activities), created by President Gerald Ford to investigate illegal intelligence activities of the CIA; and the House Select Committee on Assassinations. Cuba's Fidel Castro and *Hustler* magazine publisher Larry Flynt are among those who instigated their own unofficial investigations.

WARREN COMMISSION INVESTIGATION: When a Gallup poll taken one week after JFK's assassination showed that only 29 percent of Americans believed reports that Oswald acted alone, President Lyndon Johnson appointed a blue-ribbon panel, on November 29, to investigate the assassination. Some say President Johnson hoped this panel would quell rumors that many people suspected he was somehow involved in JFK's assassination. Not only was the relationship between JFK and Vice-President Johnson not a close one, but there was speculation that President Kennedy might replace Johnson on the 1964 reelection ticket. These rumors were fueled by an interview with Richard Nixon that was published in the *Dallas Morning News* on the day of JFK's assassination. Nixon, who had been barely defeated by Kennedy three years earlier, was in Dallas to meet with Don Kendall, president of the Pepsi Cola Bottling

Company. In the newspaper article, Nixon said he believed that Johnson had become a political liability to the Democrats and predicted that Kennedy would drop Johnson from the ticket if JFK was not a shoo-in for reelection.

Johnson gave the seven-member panel, named after its chairman, Earl Warren, chief justice of the Supreme Court, almost unlimited power in hopes it would reach a conclusion that would put the matter to rest, once and for all. Serving on the commission were two ranking senators (John Sherman Cooper and Richard Russell), two senior members of the House of Representatives (Hale Boggs and Gerald Ford), attorney John J. McCloy, former director of the World Bank, and Allen Dulles, formerly with the CIA.

The Warren Commission conducted a massive investigation completely behind closed doors—no public hearings were involved—and submitted an 888-page report to President Johnson in September of 1964. After more than twenty-seven thousand interviews and three thousand investigative reports, the commission concluded that Lee Harvey Oswald acted alone, and that there was no conspiracy of any kind involved in the assassination of JFK. The commission's report placed Oswald on the sixth floor of the Texas School Book Depository, where a 6.5-millimeter bolt-action, clip-fed, 1938 Mannlicher-Carcano rifle, belonging to Oswald and bearing his palm print, was found after the assassination. It was from there, they concluded, that Oswald fired the three shots necessary to kill the president. The official hypothesis was that the first shot struck Kennedy in the back and exited through his throat, then hit Connally twice before settling in his thigh. The second shot went astray, striking the curb near James T. Tague, a bystander, spraying his foot and cheek with fragments of cement and lead. The third shot shattered the right front side of JFK's head.

From the moment it was released, the Warren Commission report was challenged, primarily in two areas: bullet trajectory and time lapse. The assertion that one bullet could have struck Kennedy and Connally a total of four times, then be found in near-pristine condition on Connally's stretcher in the hospital, defied logic, and was promptly dubbed the "magic bullet" theory.

Assuming Oswald was firing from the building's sixth floor, the angle of trajectory was 17 degrees, 43 minutes, 30 seconds, in a downward direction. The bullet apparently entered Kennedy's back 5.5 inches below his collar line, leaving a small slit in the president's throat and no other apparent wound on his body. The Warren Commission theorized that this slit was caused by the bullet's exit as it continued on to strike Connally. Since autopsy reports indicated that the bullet did not strike any bone in Kennedy's body that might have deflected its trajectory upward, how did the bullet change course? Further, could that same bullet have been powerful enough to pass through Connally's body and wrist before lodging in his thigh, and still not be badly mangled?

Regarding the time factor, an 8-millimeter home movie shot by Abraham Zapruder became the single most important piece of evidence. Zapruder was 72 feet from the middle of Elm Street, perched on top of a block of granite, his Bell & Howell movie camera set on telephoto. He filmed Kennedy's limousine as it passed by and captured the president's reaction as he was hit by bullets. After the FBI made copies of Zapruder's film, *Life* magazine purchased it for $25,000, which Zapruder donated to the Fireman's and Policemen's Benevolent Fund. Only the Secret Service and the FBI retained official copies of the film until 1967, when New Orleans district attorney Jim Garrison subpoenaed the Zapruder film as evidence in the trial of New Orleans businessman Clay Shaw, who was accused of conspiracy in the assassination of JFK. Garrison obtained the film and copied it, after which it became available to the myriad of researchers and investigators interested in JFK's assassination.

Careful frame-by-frame analysis of Zapruder's film revealed that ten frames passed between the last moment before Kennedy was hit and the second Connally was struck. It was established that Zapruder's camera operated at 18.3 frames per second, or just over half a second per frame. If the bullet fired from the Oswald weapon passed through the neck of Kennedy, as the Warren Commission claimed, it would have been moving at a speed of 1,772 feet to 1,779 feet per second. Based on that formula, the bullet would have had to pause for approximately one-half second somewhere along the way between Kennedy's body and Connally's.

FBI special agent Robert A. Frazier, who testified as the firearms expert before the Warren Commission, stated that the bolt action of the Italian rifle took at least 2.3 seconds, according to tests run by expert riflemen. He therefore concluded that it was impossible for that weapon to be fired twice within half a second.

Such analyses supported the claims of conspiracy theorists that there were two or more shooters stationed throughout Dealey Plaza, catching the presidential limousine in a hail of gunfire. Still, author Gerald Posner, writing in his 1993 book *Case Closed*, supported the conclusions of the Warren Commission by citing a computer program, created by a firm named Failure Analysis Associates, that he claims verifies the "magic bullet" theory. The program shows that the bullet could have grazed Kennedy's vertebra, then tumbled end over end after it exited the president's throat. As for the bullet's pristine condition afterward, the fact that it never struck a hard object (such as the bones in Connally's wrist) at full speed would have allowed it to keep its shape.

What Posner's book does not say is that Failure Analysis prepared two computer analyses for a 1992 mock trial of Lee Harvey Oswald, staged by the American Bar Association: one analysis for the prosecution, the other for the defense. The purpose of the analyses was not to re-create the assassination but to support the positions of each side. The analysis that Posner cites was the one created to support the prosecution of Oswald.

Regarding the time-lapse problem, Posner says Kennedy was hit a split second or two earlier than was first believed. Saying Kennedy suffered from a condition known as Thorburn's position—where a blow to the spinal column instantaneously forces the victim's arms up and out—Posner theorized that Kennedy may have been reacting to the first bullet when his hands were supposedly going for his throat. This theory has the president being hit as many as 3.5 seconds before Connally, more than enough time for Oswald to recock his rifle and fire again.

Testimony of the Warren Commission's star witness, Howard Leslie Brennan, also troubled many who read the report. Although FBI tests concluded that an assassin in the sixth-floor window would have to be kneeling in order to successfully perform the assassination, Brennan initially said he saw a man standing in a window on the fifth floor. Commission counsel Arlen Specter prodded the witness, and even marked the window for him on an exhibit, before Brennan agreed that, indeed, it had been the sixth floor. After Oswald's arrest, Brennan was brought in to view a police lineup of suspects and later said he had identified the man who "most resembled" the one he saw in the window.

GARRISON INVESTIGATION: On March 1, 1969, New Orleans district attorney Jim Garrison arrested Clay Shaw, a prominent New Orleans businessman, charging him with being part of a conspiracy to assassinate JFK. Shaw, Garrison believed, was one of the CIA agents who had set up Lee Harvey Oswald to be the patsy in the assassination.

Although Garrison first became suspicious of a link between the CIA and Kennedy's assassination in 1963, his investigation did not start in earnest until 1967. The trail of evidence started with David W. Ferrie. Witnesses told Garrison that Ferrie had frequently been seen in New Orleans with Lee Harvey Oswald during the months before JFK's assassination. Garrison learned that Oswald had earlier been a member of the Civil Air Patrol, with Ferrie as his superior officer, and that Ferrie participated in the 1961 Bay of Pigs invasion. Although Garrison brought Ferrie in for questioning on November 25, 1963, the results were not conclusive, and Garrison turned over the information about Ferrie to the FBI, which quickly cleared Ferrie. While his suspicions about Ferrie were not put to rest, Garrison made no further inquiries. When Ferrie died under questionable circumstances in February of 1967, Garrison took another look.

The trail of suspicion about Ferrie always led to a dead end: a man named Clay Bertrand, who Garrison could not find, until one day Garrison's investigative team discovered Bertrand was an alias used by

Clay Shaw. They also discovered that Shaw, under the name of Bertrand, had hired New Orleans attorney Dean Andrews to defend Oswald soon after he was arrested in Dallas. Andrews was also reported to have worked for New Orleans Mafia boss Carlos Marcello.

During Garrison's investigation of Shaw, all evidence pointed to the CIA being responsible for killing President Kennedy. According to Garrison's theory, the CIA, under the direction of Allen Dulles, had virtually a free hand to enact covert military actions during the Eisenhower administration, but when Kennedy became president, their power was suddenly reined in. During the height of the Cold War, Eisenhower had looked the other way because he was happy with the CIA's actions in Iran and Guatemala, but when Kennedy took office he was immediately forced to confront the CIA and make decisions on two plans that were already under way. One was Vietnam. The other was the CIA's plan to overthrow Cuba's Castro. During the Bay of Pigs invasion, the CIA expected the president to give the go-ahead for adequate air support, but when the time came for him to do so, Kennedy refused. While the CIA blamed the president for the Bay of Pigs fiasco, JFK publicly blamed the CIA and subsequently fired Allen Dulles. When Kennedy also ordered the withdrawal of fifteen thousand advisers from Vietnam, the gulf between JFK and the CIA widened almost irreparably.

After his investigation, Garrison came to the conclusion that there was a huge cover-up, saying, "The FBI was in full cooperation with the CIA and the perpetrators of the assassination within hours." Garrison believed Vice-President Johnson was not told because there was no reason to do so.

Garrison's investigative team discovered information that the Warren Commission either hadn't discovered or hadn't revealed. Security around the Dallas motorcade was surprisingly lax, especially considering that previous threats to the president's life had been taken seriously. Just days earlier, a motorcade in Miami had been canceled because police had uncovered a plan to assassinate JFK with high-powered rifles. Further, Garrison said certain members of the Dallas police force cooperated with the conspirators. The motorcade route, published in a Dallas newspaper on Thursday, was changed that night by Dallas police officials, taking it in a more circuitous route past the Texas School Book Depository and the grassy knoll, where, the conspiracy theorists claim, an ambush was planned for JFK.

Despite the Warren Commission's official findings, numerous witnesses said the shots that killed the president came from the area behind the grassy knoll. Motorcycle patrolman Bill Hargis, riding to the left rear of the president's vehicle, was splattered with the president's blood. Jack Ruby was identified in photographs taken in the area during the assassination. During Clay Shaw's trial, Garrison presented what he believed was evidence that Lee Harvey Oswald had been set up to be the fall guy in a conspiracy to assassinate JFK. After Dallas patrolman J. D. Tippet was shot, the cashier of the Texas Theatre called police when a man meeting the vague description of the presidential assassin suspect entered without buying a ticket. Fifteen Dallas police cars were dispatched to the scene, surrounding the theater. When he was arrested at 1:50 P.M., only for killing officer J. D. Tippit, Oswald had on him two different pieces of identification: one for Lee H. Oswald, the other for Alex James Hidell. Without admitting to being either person, Oswald calmly said on press film at police headquarters, "I really don't know what the situation is about. Nobody has told me anything, just that I'm accused of murdering a policeman. I know nothing more than that. I do request for someone to come forward to give me legal assistance." When asked, "Did you kill the president?" Oswald replied, "No, I have not been charged with that. In fact, nobody has said that to me yet. The first thing I heard about it was when the newspaper reporters in the hall asked me that question."

Witnesses surfaced who said Oswald was a CIA operative, not a disloyal American who had defected to the Soviet Union, then returned to the United States. Garrison believed the Warren Commission knew Oswald had been a trained intelligence agent, but that the commission had suppressed this information in its final report. It has been reported that during the late 1970s, when the House Select Committee on

Assassinations looked into Oswald's background, many of his military service records had vanished.

Dallas police claim that while searching Oswald's rooming house shortly after his arrest, they found two photographs showing Oswald posed with two communist newspapers, a rifle, and a pistol. When Oswald was shown the photos during his twelve hours of interrogation by Dallas police, he said they were fakes, and that he could and would prove it in time. Garrison said that during the time Oswald spent in Russia he received extensive photographic training and that he was an expert photographer. In fact, at the time Oswald was arrested, he owned $3,000 worth of camera equipment. A photographic expert, analyst, and investigator for Jim Garrison agreed with Oswald that the photos were fakes.

Also, Garrison believed that because full biographical data on the unknown twenty-four-year-old assassin, Lee Harvey Oswald, was available for newspaper accounts around the world within hours of the assassination, such information had to have been written in advance of the events of that day.

The Warren Commission claimed only one weapon was found in the Texas School Book Depository. When Garrison's investigators interviewed Dallas police officers who were first on the scene, however, the officers said two different rifles were found in the Texas School Book Depository: a 7.65 Mauser and the 6.5 Mannlicher-Carcana, said to be the murder weapon. It was traced to a post-office box owned by A. J. Hidell, Oswald's alias. When the Mannlicher-Carcana rifle was discovered, the Mauser disappeared. Immediately after Oswald's arrest, although the FBI had no legal jurisdiction, J. Edgar Hoover moved in and took over the case. Key eyewitnesses to Tippet's murder did not identify Oswald as the officer's killer.

As Dallas police prepared to move Oswald, the FBI agent in charge of the Dallas office warned the police that an anonymous caller had threatened to kill Oswald. Garrison believes Jack Ruby made that call, as well as one to the Dallas police, because he had been instructed to take out Oswald but didn't want to do it. After Ruby shot Oswald, the police could have taken the injured man directly to the hospital in the vehicle waiting to transport him to a safer location, but they did not. Instead, they took Oswald back into the jail office, called an ambulance, and waited six or seven minutes for the ambulance to arrive and treat his wound. Interns from Parkland Hospital were always on duty at the jail as part of their training, and the intern present at the time of Oswald's shooting began some medical procedures on Oswald, but his actions have been criticized as contributing to Oswald's death. The intern started pumping Oswald's chest, claiming he was in respiratory arrest. Garrison's experts said that anyone with medical training would know not to use this procedure on a person with an abdominal wound, because it only exacerbates the problem.

Garrison attempted to expose a cover-up of the medical evidence of the assassination, but he claimed that Attorney General Ramsey Clark tried to block his inquiries. Further, Garrison said Clark convened the panel of four doctors slated to testify at the Shaw trial and, in a confidential meeting, showed them JFK autopsy photos and X rays. Garrison's investigators were told by the doctors, who had been present at JFK's autopsy, that they were amazed to see that the photos and X rays Clarke showed them indicated JFK's head wound had "traveled" four inches toward the top of the head from where the original autopsy had placed it. When Garrison called Pierre Finck, one of the doctors present at the autopsy, to the witness stand, Finck testified that some high-ranking, powerful officers kept him and the other attending physicians from performing the autopsy according to proper military procedure. He also said that the bullet that caused the wound in JFK's back did not pass through his body, contrary to the Warren Commission's "magic bullet" theory.

Garrison's investigation and prosecution of Clay Shaw was a huge undertaking that unraveled a complicated tale of the CIA planning and then executing the assassination of President Kennedy, implicating Oswald as the assassin, eliminating Oswald, then covering up the crime. During his trial, Clay Shaw testified that he did not know David Ferrie and had never met him, but in addition to the testimony of witnesses that linked Shaw with Ferrie and Oswald, there were also photographs of them together.

In the end, Clay Shaw was acquitted of all charges, but Garrison believed the CIA deliberately undermined his case. Although the jury found Shaw not guilty of the conspiracy charges, they believed Garrison had laid a strong foundation for a conspiracy, and they were convinced that Shaw had lied on the witness stand. Garrison claimed that when he later tried to bring Shaw to trial for perjury, federal authorities blocked his efforts.

Until the day he died, October 21, 1992, Garrison defended his conspiracy theory and insisted that the public had a right to know the truth.

Perhaps the most dramatic result of Garrison's investigation was the first public viewing of the Zapruder film of JFK's assassination, which Garrison showed to the jury. Six years later the American public would have its first look at the horrible reality of what happened on that day in November 1963, when the side of JFK's head was blown off and blood, brain matter, and skull fragments sprayed Jacqueline Kennedy.

SENATE SELECT COMMITTEE INVESTIGATION: In its report of November 20, 1975, the Senate Select Committee on Intelligence Activities said that it found the CIA had plotted to assassinate at least five foreign leaders. Although the focus of its investigation was not JFK's assassination, under the umbrella of this committee was the Schweiker-Hart Subcommittee. Senators Richard Schweiker and Gary Hart hired independent investigators, who conducted one of the most straightforward investigations into the murder of JFK, keeping their activities out of the press until their final report was released. This subcommittee's report said that although it experienced substantial interference from U.S. intelligence agencies and the administration during its investigation, they believed that a conspiracy to kill the president had existed.

ROCKEFELLER COMMISSION INVESTIGATION: On January 15, 1975, President Gerald Ford, who had been a member of the 1963

Warren Commission, created the Rockefeller Commission to investigate illegal domestic intelligence activities of the CIA. Vice-President Nelson Rockefeller was appointed chairman of the committee, and former Warren Commission assistant counsel David Belin was its director.

A photographic expert and author of the book *The Killing of a President*, Robert J. Groden, had spent years enhancing a copy of the Zapruder film from its rough form into a more easily viewed presentation. This evidence of the JFK assassination was viewed in a secured room by the Rockefeller Commission on February 4, 1975. To explain the fact that JFK was obviously pushed backward and to the left after being hit in the head by a bullet, the commission's director, David Belin, produced an unsolicited letter that had been submitted as evidence. The letter, from a physician, made the hypothesis that a neuromuscular reaction, or neurospasm, might have been the reason JFK was pushed backward in his seat, instead of forward, when he was hit by a bullet from behind. In the end, the Rockefeller Commission basically agreed with the findings of the Warren Commission.

HOUSE SELECT COMMITTEE ON ASSASSINATIONS: By the mid-1970s, criticism of the Warren Commission's report prompted the House of Representatives to establish its own committee to pursue the facts of the assassinations of both JFK and Martin Luther King Jr. Headed by Ohio Democrat Louis Stokes, the committee knew it must deal with the serious issues of criminal plots and enormous cover-ups. Using the Warren Commission findings as a starting point, it sought to take each piece of evidence and independently authenticate it or eliminate it.

The House investigation turned up information that linked Lee Harvey Oswald and Jack Ruby and pointed to Ruby's supposed long-standing, although loose, ties to underworld figures. Three weeks before JFK's assassination, Ruby called the New Orleans office of the Tropical Court Tourist Park, which was operated by Nofio Pecora, a lieutenant of Louisiana crime boss Carlos Marcello. Days before JFK's assassination, Ruby, who owed some $40,000 in back taxes, was suddenly flashing

$7,000 in cash and bragging that he had a connection that would bail him out of his tax problems. Further, the House panel concluded that some Dallas police acquaintances of Ruby probably helped slip him into the jail's basement along with reporters stationed there while Oswald was being moved, although they probably didn't realize Ruby intended to shoot Oswald. After killing Oswald, Ruby repeatedly claimed it was a spontaneous act of compassion for Mrs. Kennedy, but when representatives of the Warren Commission questioned Ruby in Dallas, he begged them to take him back to Washington, where he would feel safe to tell the real story of JFK's assassination.

The House panel also received evidence that the CIA and members of the Mafia were involved in plots to assassinate Fidel Castro in Cuba—evidence that the Warren Commission either never got or never revealed. The panel dismissed any involvement by Castro in JFK's assassination and decided the CIA was not involved in a cover-up.

The House panel addressed conspiracy theories by exploring a phenomenon the committee members called the "Mysterious Death Project," which was brought to their attention by a book entitled *Forgive My Grief*. In this book, author Penn Jones tracked and examined the strange and often unexplainable deaths of many key witnesses in the JFK assassination, beginning in 1966. The committee appointed Jacqueline Hess, chief of research, to look into the deaths of only twenty-one of the three hundred witnesses in Jones's book, many of whom had died under odd and often violent circumstances. Although an article in the *London Sunday Times* reported odds of 100,000 trillion to one that so many witnesses would die so soon after the assassination, the committee response was that "our final conclusion on the issue is that the available evidence does not establish anything about the nature of these deaths which would indicate that the deaths were in some manner, either direct or peripheral, caused by the assassination of President Kennedy."

Until the last two weeks of the committee's mandate, it seemed that there would be no outstanding conclusions that would diverge from the Warren Commission. Then things suddenly changed. A Dictabelt recording of the assassination on one of two police radio channels was analyzed by more than one acoustic expert. The first said there was a fifty-fifty chance that there were gunshots coming from the grassy knoll. Other experts said there was a 95 percent certainty that a second gunman had fired from the grassy knoll. With this, the panel decided that although Oswald had shot JFK, there was "a high probability that two gunmen fired at President John F. Kennedy."

Still, a minority of the panel would not agree on record with the acoustics findings, including Congressman Robert Edgar, who complained that the committee had been hindered by "limitations of time and familiarity with the science." Later, a Committee of Ballistic Acoustics of the National Research Council would disagree with the House committee report. The Ballistic Acoustics panel, chaired by Norman F. Ramsey, Higgins Professor of Physics at Harvard, would include Ph.D.s from MIT, the University of California, Columbia, and Princeton; an expert from the Firearms National Laboratory Center of the Department of the Treasury; and experts from the research centers of Bell Telephone Laboratories, Xerox, IBM, and Trisolar Corporation. The unanimous conclusion of this esteemed panel was that there was "no acoustic basis for the claim of a 95 percent probability of such a shot. The acoustic analyses impulses attributed to gunshots were recorded about one minute after the president had been shot and the motorcade had been instructed to go to the hospital."

The House committee's report was issued at the end of 1978 after a two-and-a-half-year inquiry. It addressed most of the theories about JFK's assassination that had been circulating for years. Although it contradicted the Warren Commission in some ways, it agreed in others. The committee concluded that Lee Harvey Oswald had fired three shots at President Kennedy from the Texas School Book Depository, that the second and third shots had struck the president, and the third shot had killed him. It concluded that scientific acoustical evidence established a high probability that two gunmen fired at President Kennedy, that other scientific evidence did not preclude the possibility of two gunmen firing at the president, and that scientific evidence negated some specific conspiracy allegations.

Further, the report said that the committee believed, "on the basis of the evidence available to it, that President John F. Kennedy was probably assassinated as a result of a conspiracy. The committee is unable to identify the other gunman or the extent of the conspiracy." The report specifically stated that the committee believed the Soviet government was not involved in JFK's assassination, nor was the Cuban government. It believed that anti-Castro Cuban groups were not involved but that "the available evidence does not preclude the possibility that individual members of such groups may have been involved." It found that the "national syndicate of organized crime, as a group," was not involved "but that the available evidence does not preclude the possibility that individual members may have been involved."

Finally, the committee mandated that the files from its investigation be locked away and not accessible to the public until the year 2029.

ALTERNATE THEORIES: The "magic bullet" and time-lapse inconsistencies are only two of the Warren Commission conclusions that conspiracy theorists have built upon over the years. Also controversial was Allen Dulles's inclusion on the Warren Commission. Dulles, called a former CIA spymaster who had been ousted by Kennedy, has been accused of being sloppy and disinterested during the investigation, and of spending more time covering up facts than seeking the truth.

Late in 1988, David W. Belin, former assistant counsel to the Warren Commission, in his book *Final Disclosure: The Full Truth About the Assassination of President Kennedy*, wrote that despite some minor defects, historians fifty years from now will agree that the Warren Commission was right. He attacks authors of eight other books on assassinations for ignoring crucial facts, taking quotes out of context, and concocting alluring and deceptive arguments about what happened.

Still, the idea that a lone nut killed President Kennedy with a very lucky shot has remained the most controversial conclusion of the Warren Commission. Thus, an array of other scenarios has been proposed.

SECOND-GUNMAN THEORY: As soon as those in Dealey Plaza real-ized the president had been shot, two motorcycle police officers, Robert Hargis and Bill Martin, who had been flanking the presidential limou-sine, as well as some spectators, ran in the direction of a grassy knoll where they believed the shots had originated. Photographs document that the officers and spectators ran up an embankment and across a grassy knoll located in front of JFK's vehicle, not behind it. Situated at the top of the embankment was a wooden fence, with a very small space between the top of the fence and the lowest foliage on the trees that line the fence. In this area, a gunman would have been hidden from sight. Officers Hargis and Martin peered over the fence, saw a police officer there, and, believing he had the area covered, retreated. In photos taken of that other officer, his uniform and weaponry did not appear to be the same as those of the official Dallas police. Later investigation convinced many that the grassy knoll was an opportune location for a gunman.

A witness named Richard Carr, one of the closest observers of the fatal shot, testified at the Clay Shaw proceeding in 1969. He said that he had told the FBI at the time of the assassination that the fatal shot came over his right shoulder from the grassy knoll, but was then instructed to keep his mouth shut, which he did. Carr was not called to testify before the Warren Commission.

Since there seems to be no question that some shots were fired from the Texas School Book Depository, behind the presidential limousine, the conclusion many have made is that there must have been a second gun-man in the grassy knoll in front of the vehicle. Making this assumption, conspiracy theorists move ahead into cover-up theories, asking, Why were these clues ignored?

MAFIA-HIT THEORY: In this theory, the Mafia ordered JFK's assassi-nation as payback for the brutal crackdown on organized crime enacted by his brother, Attorney General Robert Kennedy. A link is made between Oswald, Ruby, Ferrie, and Bannister, with all finally connected to New Orleans bosses. Oswald was the "patsy," as he insisted from the moment of his arrest, and the murder of Oswald by Jack Ruby was a classic Mafia hit.

There are reports that Chicago Mafia boss Sam Giancana claimed that during the 1960 presidential campaign Joseph P. Kennedy had associates meet with Giancana to seek the crime boss's assistance in getting Kennedy's son elected to the nation's highest political office. Giancana claims to have agreed to do whatever was needed, and in the end took credit for Kennedy's election. Further, the CIA sought Mafia assistance in assassinating Cuba's Castro. The Mafia's reward was to be the return of its gambling businesses in Havana once Castro was out of the picture. When JFK decided not to invade Cuba a second time, the Syndicate's highly profitable casinos and prostitution operations, which Fidel Castro had closed down upon coming to power, remained shut down.

The Mafia-hit theorists claim that after all he did for the Kennedys, Giancana was incensed enough after Attorney General Robert Kennedy went after organized crime to order a hit on President Kennedy, assuming it would take away all of Robert Kennedy's power. This theory is backed up by a number of books, including *The Plot to Kill the President*, written by Richard N. Billings and G. Robert Blakey. Chief counsel to the House Select Committee on Assassinations and a law professor at the University of Notre Dame, Blakey concluded there was indeed a second gunman but that he fired and missed. In *Contract on America*, published in the late eighties, author David E. Schiem compiles evidence to support the Mafia-hit theory.

Those opposing this theory point out that since the national crime syndicate was established in the early 1930s, it has been Mafia policy not to kill police officers, FBI men, prosecutors, or high public officials.

FAREWELL-AMERICA THEORY: A book entitled *Farewell, America*, published in 1968, was reportedly prepared by the British Secret Service and published under the pseudonym James Hepburn. Not allowed to pass through U.S. Customs at the time it was published, the book details the most expensive and extravagant conspiracy theory of all. It begins with a long chapter on the history of the oil industry, particularly the independent Texas and Louisiana oilmen who were more vulnerable to

JFK's economic policies than were well-rooted wealthy Northern oil powers. According to the authors, JFK's assassination and the cover-up cost $5 million to $10 million, money that was raised by at least one hundred people each contributing from $10,000 to $50,000. The plan called for ten men: four gunmen, each with an assistant responsible for his gunman's protection and evacuation, for maintaining radio contact, and for retrieving the shells; one man to be a central radio operator; and a man to create a last-minute diversion so that the gunmen could get into position. A few minutes before the motorcade arrived, a man wearing green army fatigues suddenly had an epileptic fit on Elm Street, drew the attention of people around him, and was taken away by police.

According to the book, the Dallas conspirators got information from FBI agents; former FBI agents, one a member of the Secret Service; Dallas officials; and CIA agents. Further, it says J. Edgar Hoover learned of the conspiracy by mid-October and was privy to many of the details but did nothing until after the assassination, when the FBI accumulated 25,000 investigative reports laying the blame and designating the culprits. In turn, Texas retaliated on January 24, 1964, saying Lee Harvey Oswald had been a paid FBI informant since 1962. Neither the FBI nor the CIA was ever called upon to clear itself.

CENTRAL-INTELLIGENCE-AGENCY THEORY: In this theory, the CIA ordered JFK's assassination in order to keep him from getting too "soft" on communism and/or pulling out of the burgeoning war in Vietnam.

In a 1971 column, writer Jack Anderson speculated about whether CIA assassination attempts on Cuba's Fidel Castro had backfired on JFK. President Kennedy's close friend Senator George Smathers had told Anderson that JFK complained that he could not control the CIA. Further, JFK was angry with the CIA after the Bay of Pigs fiasco and horrified by the agency's involvement in assassination plots (with the help of Mafia chieftains Santos Trafficante and Carlos Marcello) against Castro. In turn, JFK stopped a second planned invasion of Cuba and threatened the CIA, vowing, "I will smash the CIA into a thousand pieces." At the time of the Cuban missile crisis, JFK had made an agreement with Soviet premier Nikita Khrushchev that all U.S. assassination attempts against Castro would be stopped if the Soviets would remove nuclear missile warheads from Cuba. When JFK discovered that CIA top brass had ignored his direct orders to stop all assassination plots against Castro, he sent the FBI and local law enforcement agencies to break up the CIA's training camps on Florida's No Name Key and on Lake Pontchartrain in New Orleans.

THE KGB THEORY: In this theory, Soviet secret police ordered JFK's assassination as payback for the Cuban missile crisis and because he was an avowed foe of communism.

Although Oswald was known to have Marxist sympathies, the idea that the KGB would enlist him to carry out such a big task is hard to believe. Further, leaders of the Soviet Union had more to lose than to gain by Kennedy's assassination. They had put their political careers on the line during the Khrushchev-Kennedy negotiations to curtail nuclear weapons testing, and the agreement between the two leaders had placed them on the same team for world peace for the first time since the Cold War began.

THE CUBAN THEORY: This theory follows two divergent paths: Pro-Castro Cubans ordered JFK's assassination as payback for the failed Bay of Pigs invasion and other attempts to assassinate Fidel Castro; or, anti-Castro Cubans ordered JFK's assassination as payback for the failed Bay of Pigs invasion and for failing to authorize a second Bay of Pigs invasion.

SECRET SERVICE-AGENT THEORY: A Secret Service agent accidentally shot JFK while reaching for his gun in response to Oswald's gunfire.

CHRONICLE: Jack Ruby, the Dallas nightclub owner who claimed it was out of patriotism that he killed Lee Harvey Oswald, was convicted of murder on March 14, 1964, and sentenced to death. When the Warren Commission interviewed Ruby in the interrogation room of the Dallas County jail in June 1964, Ruby pleaded with Earl Warren and several other commission members to take him back to Washington so he could tell them the true story. Ruby said he wasn't safe in Dallas, adding, "I won't be around for you to come and question me again." His pleas were ignored. On October 5, 1966, a Texas Court of Criminal Appeals overturned his conviction, citing judicial error. While waiting in jail to be retried, Ruby became ill and accused officials of systematically poisoning him. Finally, he was transferred to Parkland Hospital on December 9, 1966. Initially diagnosed with pneumonia, Ruby was told the next day that he had terminal cancer. This news was followed by allegations from Ruby that he had been injected with live cancer cells by people who were afraid he would reveal secret information about JFK's assassination. Ruby's team of doctors considered his disease too advanced for surgery or radiation therapy and opted instead to give Ruby a series of injections of 5-fluorouracil to retard the cancer's progress. Jack Ruby died in Parkland Hospital on January 3, 1967.

Shortly before his death, in a filmed interview, Jack Ruby fueled the JFK assassination controversy by saying, "The world will never know the true facts of what occurred—my motives. . . . Unfortunately, the people that had so much to gain and had such an ulterior motive, and who put me in the position I'm in, will never let the true facts come above board to the world."

Jack Ruby's death exacerbated the conspiracy and cover-up theories, as JFK assassination conspiracies became an industry unto themselves. Annual conventions are held in Dallas to swap theories and sell gruesome memorabilia, such as Oswald's coroner's tag, Ruby's gun, and bootleg autopsy photos, and publications act as a clearinghouse for other theories. The John F. Kennedy Assassination Information Center in Dallas publishes its own newsletter.

As the days, months, and years have passed, every aspect of John F. Kennedy's assassination has continued to be questioned. The idea that

Lee Harvey Oswald, acting alone, could have planned to kill the president of the United States, efficiently executed his plan while looking through the telescopic lens of a rifle on the sixth floor of the Texas School Book Depository, then nonchalantly walked away from the scene has been too absurd for many to believe. From time to time, as additional classified documents are released, new fuel is added to a flame of mystery that seems to burn as eternally as the monument on President Kennedy's grave in Arlington National Cemetery.

 FEBRUARY 21, 1965

MALCOLM X (1925–1965)
BLACK MILITANT CIVIL RIGHTS LEADER WHO FOUNDED THE ORGANIZATION OF AFRO-AMERICAN UNITY AND THE MUSLIM MOSQUE, INC.

Malcolm Little was born in Omaha, Nebraska, the son of a Baptist minister. He grew up in Lansing, Michigan, then moved to his sister's home in Boston at age sixteen, and soon became involved in crime. Imprisoned for burglary in 1946, he converted to the Nation of Islam, or Black Muslim faith, led by Elijah Muhammad. Released from jail in 1953, Malcolm X became an active member of the sect and abandoned his surname, which he considered a relic of slavery. He studied the doctrines, mythology, and eschatology of the Nation of Islam, which were devised by Master [Wallace Dodd] Fard, its founder, then passed on to Elijah Muhammad. Traveling around the United States during the next ten years, Malcolm X spoke on behalf of the movement and against the exploitation of black people, while founding Muslim temples. Considered an excellent orator, he made impressive headway, increasing the number of followers of the sect more dramatically than Elijah Muhammad had done with his soft, hesitant speaking style. Malcolm X eloquently told the story that is the basis of Master Fard's theory that the lighter a person's skin, the more likely he is to be evil and to attempt to corrupt others, and that there is a white conspiracy to keep African Americans enslaved.

It was with pride and assurance that Malcolm X spread the word of Islam to middle-class blacks during refined and sedate worship services. His engaging oratories and hard work throughout the country made him a successful and valuable part of the Nation of Islam hierarchy. He also earned an international reputation by traveling to Africa and the Middle East to meet with leaders from those parts of the world. And he became friendly with Fidel Castro during one of his visits to the United States. But while Malcolm X helped to make the Nation of Islam one of the largest and fastest-growing organizations in America, he became more popular than Elijah Muhammad himself and alienated some members of the sect's upper echelon (especially Elijah Muhammad's two sons). When Elijah Muhammad's health problems became worse and Malcolm X made it known that he was Elijah Muhammad's handpicked heir, some members of the Nation of Islam were not pleased. Malcolm X had set himself up as a target for violent reactions, not only from the sect's enemies but also from some within the sect's own ranks.

By this time, violence against blacks in the United States was leaving a bloody trail from one civil rights group to another, with the Nation of Islam being the most militant and retaliatory. On May 26, 1962, Elijah Muhammad surprised civil rights leaders by calling upon them to form a coalition with the Nation of Islam. In *Muhammad Speaks*, the sect's newspaper, he wrote: "There could be no better step taken, to bring about an end to the free killing of our people, than the uniting of the NAACP and the Muslims and all national groups that are for justice for our people."

In 1963, Malcolm X heard rumors that Elijah Muhammad, who claimed to be the prophet of Allah, was involved in a sex scandal. Although at first he refused to believe this story that violated his puritanical Muslim beliefs, Malcolm X talked to three of Elijah Muhammad's former secretaries, and was shocked when each claimed they had had sex with the prophet. On July 3, 1963, the scandal became public when two of the former secretaries filed paternity suits against Elijah Muhammad on behalf of their four children. Also in July, the FBI, which had compiled dossiers on Master Fard, Elijah Muhammad, and Malcolm X, reportedly sent Fard's dossier to several large newspapers. The *Los Angeles Herald-Examiner* took the bait on July 28, breaking the story that Fard's version of his background was false and that his father was a white man. This news was no surprise to members of the Nation of Islam. Fard was often mistaken for an Arab or a Latino because of his straight black hair, swarthy skin, and eyes of an unusual color, almost maroon, and his followers had been taught that Fard had been put on the earth as God in the form of a mulatto so that he could enter both the black and white communities. But the *Herald-Examiner* story, combined with newspaper portrayals of Fard as a con man and convicted felon served to discredit the entire Nation of Islam movement in the eyes of would-be followers. Even though Fard had disappeared decades earlier after proclaiming Elijah Muhammad the sect's leader, Elijah Muhammad, who was quite disturbed by the news story, decided to sue the *Herald-Examiner.*

Malcolm X, who was in Washington, D.C., when the story broke, told reporters, "The source of this slander is the government itself." He said that President Kennedy's administration had "planted the story to enhance the image of the so-called Negro civil rights leaders" who were going to lead an August 28 march on Washington. Soon afterward, President Kennedy told reporters that he was deeply concerned about "growing extremism" among African Americans, particularly citing the Nation of Islam and Malcolm X's comments.

If the FBI had tried to cause a rift between the non-violent civil rights movement and the militant Nation of Islam, it was working, with the added benefit that leaders of the sect were becoming increasingly uncomfortable with Malcolm X. After the assassination of President Kennedy, Malcolm X became even more outspoken. On December 1, 1963, during a Black Muslim rally in New York, he castigated the late president for "twiddling his thumbs" while the Congo's Patrice Lumumba, South Vietnam's Diem brothers, and four little girls in Birmingham were all murdered. Further, Malcolm X said, "Being an old farm boy myself, chickens coming home to roost never did make me sad; they've always made me glad."

The next day, Nation of Islam minister Malcolm Shabazz announced that Elijah Muhammad had suspended Malcolm X for ninety days, saying Malcolm X "did not speak for the Muslims when he made comments about the death of the president. . . . He was speaking for himself and not Muslims in general, and Minister Malcolm has been suspended from public speaking for the time being." In response, Malcolm X abandoned the Nation of Islam, citing differences in the group's theories on race and segregation and criticizing Elijah Muhammad for his alleged immoral lifestyle. This prompted Louis Farrakhan (Louis Eugene Walcott, who became Louis X when recruited by Malcolm X into the Nation of Islam in the 1950s) to write in a December 1964 issue of *Muhammad Speaks:* "The die is set and Malcolm shall not escape. Such a man is worthy of death."

ALLEGED ASSASSINS: Talmadge Hayer/a.k.a. Thomas Hayer/a.k.a. Thomas Hagan, age twenty-two, described by his lawyer as "closed-mouthed," was married, with two children. Although two witnesses said he was a member of the Black Muslims, Hayer consistently denied it, and his brother-in-law, stepsister, and brother all testified that he was not a member of the religious sect. The prosecution was not able to prove whether he was or had ever been a member of the Black Muslims.

Norman 3X Butler, age twenty-seven, a known and admitted Black Muslim, belonged to the Fruit of Islam, the elite Muslim security force. On the morning of the assassination, Butler was treated for superficial thrombophlebitis by Dr. Kenneth Seslowe of Jacobi Hospital, who bandaged his right leg and prescribed some oral medication.

Thomas 15X Johnson, age thirty, a housepainter and father of four children, was a known Black Muslim and companion of Norman 3X Butler. Johnson, Butler, and an unknown third man had been arrested in January of 1965 for assault on Benjamin Brown, a Black Muslim defector.

HISTORY: In 1964, disillusioned with the Nation of Islam, Malcolm X formed a rival organization, the Muslim Mosque, Inc. After another visit to the Middle East and Africa, he also founded the Organization of Afro-American Unity. Earlier in his career he had called himself "the angriest black man in America" and encouraged blacks to defend themselves, but now he altered many of his positions. During a five-week trip to Mecca and Africa he wrote his much-publicized *Letter from Mecca,* in which he reflected favorably on his experiences with Caucasian Muslims and began to reevaluate his position on how whites might help fight racism in America.   ·

As 1965 began, the violent feud that had developed between the Black Muslims and followers of Malcolm X was growing in intensity. Malcolm X stopped calling black integrationists Uncle Toms, but in February, when he visited Selma, Alabama, during the voter registration drive, he told Coretta Scott King that his own militant reputation would cause scared whites to support her husband's campaign. On February 14, shortly after he returned from Selma, Malcolm X's home was destroyed by a firebomb. On February 16, during a private meeting with his friend James Shabazz, Malcolm X said, "I have been marked for death within the next five days. I have the names of five Muslims who have been chosen to kill me. I will announce them at the next meeting." At the time, he knew he was under close surveillance by the FBI and confided in very few people.

Malcolm X prepared to give a speech on February 21, which would be the first of a new series of lectures revealing his expanded awareness and ideology: that the time had come for blacks and whites to coexist in peace. As he told his friend and biographer, Alex Haley, in a telephone conversation the night of February 20, he also felt an urgent need to tell his followers that the Black Muslims alone were not to be blamed for such harassments as the firebombing of his house the week before.

EVENT: On Sunday, February 21, thirty-nine-year-old Malcolm X drove his black 1963 Oldsmobile sedan toward the Audubon Ballroom

Malcolm X

UPI / CORBIS-BETTMANN

in Harlem, where he would be speaking at a meeting of the Organization of Afro-American Unity. Tension within the black community was extremely high, and he was repeatedly receiving death threats. On this day, Malcolm X was so concerned that he initially refused to let his wife, Betty Shabazz, and his four daughters attend this meeting, but later he said they could. He looked in his rearview mirror, and although he saw nothing suspicious, he felt like he was being stalked. Afraid that he might be shot while driving, he parked his car about a mile and a half south of the Audubon Ballroom, got out, and walked to a bus stop.

Moments later, a car with New Jersey license plates pulled up to the bus stop, and one of the occupants rolled down a window and called his name. He looked into the car and was relieved to see the smiling face of his friend, Charles X Blackwell, who offered him a ride. Arriving at the ballroom a few minutes later, Malcolm X hurried backstage. Waiting for special guest speakers to arrive, Malcolm X told Leon 4X Ameer, "I really shouldn't be here today." He also told Ameer, A. Peter Bailey, and other top aides that he felt something evil was in the air. One by one, all the guest speakers called to cancel, as out front, the crowded hall of people became restless waiting. At about 3 P.M., an exasperated Malcolm X finally told an aide, Benjamin X Goodman, to get things under way. Onstage, Goodman gave Malcolm X an accolade, then introduced him to the anxious audience.

"As-Salaam Alaikum [peace be with you]," Malcolm X said, his eyes looking around at the faces in the predominantly black crowd. "Wa-Alaikum-Salaam [and peace be with you]," the crowd replied.

As Malcolm X began speaking, Gene X Roberts, one of the bodyguards standing nearby, subtly signaled that he wished to move from that position. Another guard took his place, and Roberts moved to a position near the front entrance. Suddenly, a scuffle broke out between two young black men seated near the stage. "Get your hand outta my pocket!" one of them shouted. Some of the bodyguards began to move forward. "Hold it! Let's cool it, brothers!" Malcolm X said sympathetically.

When Malcolm X extended his right hand toward the two men, one of them pulled a German Luger out of the other man's overcoat, moved forward to within eight feet of Malcolm X, and blasted buckshot through the plywood lectern and into Malcolm X's chest. In the back of the room, another man threw a smoke bomb into the air, creating pandemonium, as Malcolm X fell backward. A fourth man, armed with a sawed-off shotgun, rose from the third row and shot Malcolm X in the chest. As he fell to the floor, a fifth black man shot him in his left leg and hand. Then, like an outlaw in a Western movie, the fifth man backed toward the entrance of the ballroom, firing shot after shot at Malcolm X. His body hit the dusty stage floor, blood gushing from his wounds.

Reuben X Frances, one of Malcolm X's bodyguards, fired three shots at the fifth assailant, hitting him once in the leg. People from the audience descended upon him, shouting obscenities and kicking and clawing the injured suspect. "Kill that son of a bitch," some shouted. "Kill him!"

The other four suspects used their weapons to hold off the crowd as they escaped through entrances on either side of the stage. Gene X Roberts, the bodyguard who had relocated before the shooting started, ran through the crowd, jumped onstage, knelt over Malcolm X, and appeared to administer mouth-to-mouth resuscitation. "His pulse was weak, very weak," Roberts later recalled. Betty Shabazz, Malcolm X's wife, who was a registered nurse, pulled Roberts away from her dying husband and tried to do something to save his life. Sarah Mitchell, a young black woman, came to her aide. Mitchell quickly loosened Malcolm X's tie and opened his shirt, revealing volcano-shaped wounds in his chest. Yuri Kuchiama, a Japanese American disciple of Malcolm X, held his head upright to prevent him from choking on blood in his throat. As they tried to revive him, everyone knew there was little chance that he would survive.

Several witnesses later said that as Betty Shabazz and others onstage wept in grief and dismay, a black man standing in the left corner near the stage laughed triumphantly; he wore the pin of the Nation of Islam on his lapel.

Hakim A. Jamal and Leon 4X Ameer, two of Malcolm X's aides, told another aide to run across the street to the Columbia Presbyterian Medical Center and get help. When five minutes passed and no help had arrived from the hospital, Jamal and Ameer, enraged, reluctantly left their leader's side and ran to the emergency room. There, they ignored protests from the emergency room staff, grabbed a stretcher and wheeled it over to the Audubon Ballroom. The guards and other people onstage delicately lifted Malcolm X and placed him on the stretcher. Just as they attempted to carry him out of the ballroom, uniformed police officers arrived and ordered everyone to move aside. Four policemen seized the stretcher, carried Malcolm X out of the ballroom, and quickly wheeled him to the hospital.

The people who had been onstage with Malcolm X that afternoon, as well as hundreds who had gone to the Audubon Ballroom to hear him speak, now gathered in the hospital waiting room. Most of them were praying for Malcolm X, some in silence, others loudly pleading with

God to spare his life. Fifteen minutes after Malcolm X was carried into the emergency room, a hospital physician walked into the lobby filled with people and told them, "The gentleman you know as Malcolm X is dead."

The next day, Malcolm X's body was put on display in a glass-topped, wrought-copper casket at the Unity Funeral Home in Harlem. Despite bomb threats and the objections of orthodox Muslims, who argued that the body should be buried before the setting of the second sun, an estimated thirty thousand people came to the funeral home. On February 27, amid tight security and police protection, more than one thousand people wedged themselves into the Faith Temple Church and another three thousand waited outside during Malcolm X's funeral services. Actor Ossie Davis spoke, calling Malcolm X "our own black shining prince," and Islamic rites were performed. Malcolm X was buried in the white robe of a Muslim, his head pointed toward the east and Mecca in Ferncliff Cemetery in suburban Westchester County under his full Muslim name, El-Hajj Malik El-shabazz. Rather than allow white grave diggers to cover their fallen hero, many of his followers, dressed in their best suits and ties, scooped earth over the coffin with their bare hands.

ARRESTS AND INVESTIGATION: The investigation into the assassination of Malcolm X was complicated and confusing. Black hostility toward the police department made it difficult to track down suspects, and informants were afraid that if they talked, Black Muslims would retaliate against them. In addition, detectives and prosecutors apparently ignored or overlooked evidence that might have helped. Still, three men were arrested and charged with the murder.

Malcolm X had never used bodyguards until after the bombing of his home on February 14, when members of his Muslim Mosque took control of his security. Reports say there were six bodyguards onstage at the time Malcolm X was shot. By October of 1965, three of his former lieutenants and members of his bodyguard had vanished. Although everyone entering the Audubon Ballroom had to pass through a security check the day of the assassination, two of the three accused assassins were known Black Muslims and recognizable adversaries.

After the shooting, Charles Blackwell, a bodyguard of Malcolm X, saw one of the assailants run into the ladies' lounge. He didn't pursue him, and this assailant escaped. Talmadge Hayer, the assailant who had rushed toward the stairway exit at the front of the ballroom and was shot by bodyguard Reuben Francis, was rescued from being beaten to death by the crowd by two New York police officers. Sergeant Alvin Aronoff and Patrolman Louis Angelos arrested Hayer and took him to Bellevue Hospital for treatment of his wound (although a .32-caliber bullet in his thigh was not removed until March 8).

Immediate press accounts said a second man was beaten by the audience, then supposedly arrested by Patrolman Thomas Hoy. Jimmy Breslin reported in the *New York Herald Tribune*, February 22, 1965, "The other suspect was taken to the Wadsworth Avenue precinct, where the city's top policemen immediately converged and began one of the heaviest homicide investigations this city has ever seen." Yet, no further information regarding this second man was made available to the press, which seemingly failed to follow up on him. Ultimately, New York police denied that they had arrested a second man, saying it had been a journalistic error.

Reuben Francis, the bodyguard who shot Hayer, also wounded two spectators: William Harris, age fifty-one, was struck in the abdomen, and William Parker, age thirty-six, was shot in the foot. (Neither of them were called to testify in the subsequent trial of Malcolm X's accused assassins.) Francis was indicted for shooting Hayer, posted $10,000 bail, jumped bail, disappeared, but was arrested again on February 2, 1966, in a New York assistant district attorney's office. On February 15, 1966, a spokesman for the district attorney's office told *The Militant*, a weekly socialist newspaper, that "Francis had been picked up by the FBI" and was being held on $25,000 bail. But on that same date, according to *The Militant*, "a spokesman for the FBI denied any knowledge of Francis." Reuben never testified during the trial of the accused assassins, and he has apparently disappeared.

After the assassination, Benjamin X, the man who had introduced Malcolm X to the Audubon Ballroom audience seconds before the killing, also disappeared. The October 1965 issue of *Ebony* magazine said one of Benjamin X's ex-colleagues said, "Only the police know where to find him." Benjamin X did not testify during the trial of the accused assassins.

PUNISHMENT: The trial of Talmadge Hayer, Norman 3X Butler, and Thomas 15X Johnson began on January 21, 1966. Hayer, acting as his own attorney, testified on January 23, and on January 28 he confessed to the assassination of Malcolm X, saying the other two defendants had nothing to do with it. Hayer, who insisted he was not a Muslim, testified that he and four accomplices, whom he would not name, had been hired to carry out the assassination, but he refused to say how much money he had been offered. He also said that the man who hired him was not a Muslim either.

Trial testimony revealed that Hayer's fingerprint was found on a flammable piece of film from which the smoke bomb, set off during the assault, was made, but because Hayer was close to the stage, he could not have set off the smoke bomb in the back of the room. Therefore, another person was needed to create this diversion.

Butler, a known Muslim who was physically handicapped by the thrombophlebitis of his right leg (for which he had been treated by a doctor earlier that day), said he was not even in the Audubon Ballroom at the time of Malcolm X's assassination. Although witnesses claim to have seen Butler at the exit where Hayer was wounded by Reuben Francis, there is evidence that he was not present in the ballroom. Some reports ask if Butler could have been the "second man," who was supposedly arrested at the scene but whose existence was later denied by police.

Johnson also denied being in the ballroom during the assassination, although the prosecution claimed he was the man wielding the shotgun. Eyewitness testimony varied as to which of the three, if any, carried a shotgun. Johnson testified that he was at home that day and denied ever handling a shotgun. His lawyer argued that both Johnson and Butler were well known by the Organization of Afro-American Unity as Black Muslims and would never have been allowed inside the ballroom.

Despite Hayer's testimony that Butler and Johnson were not involved in the assassination of Malcolm X, on March 11, 1965, the jury found all three defendants guilty of murder, and they were sentenced to life imprisonment. But the lack of a complete investigation, the disappearance of key persons involved, and the great deal of conflicting testimony during the trial left many unanswered questions about the true identity of the assassins of Malcolm X.

In 1977, Talmadge Hayer broke his silence and identified four coconspirators, Muslims from the Nation of Islam Mosque Number 25 in Newark, New Jersey. Hayer said Benjamin X Thomas (a.k.a. Ben Thompson), Leon X Davis, William X Bradley, and Wilbur X Kinley had participated in the killing with him. He signed two affidavits, describing in great detail how they cased the Audubon Ballroom, the exact positioning of the gunmen in it, and the strategy sessions that were held. Butler and Johnson, he said, were not involved. Their innocence was further advocated by filmmaker Spike Lee, who said that Captain Joseph, who now uses the name Yusuf Shah, and who was a high official in the Nation of Islam at the time of the killing, confirmed that Malcolm X's assassination and the bombing of his home in Queens were planned at the highest levels of that organization. No further arrests have been made. Although unsuccessful attempts were made to vacate the charges against Butler and Johnson, they were paroled in 1985. During his incarceration, Hayer was a model prisoner and earned two college degrees. He has subsequently been released in a New York City work-release program.

CONSPIRACY THEORIES: Although it was the general opinion of the police, the press, and Malcolm X's supporters that his assassination was committed by the Black Muslims, there are three main theories about a plot to kill Malcolm X: The Black Muslims did it; the Intelligence Community did it; or the Mafia and/or an international drug cartel did it.

The most obvious theory, that Black Muslim *mujaheddin* (Muslim warriors engaged in a holy war) assassinated Malcolm X, was supported by information in Elijah Muhammad's FBI file indicating that members of the sect would have welcomed such an event. In the weeks before Malcolm X's assassination, Black Muslim officials Louis Farrakhan, Joseph X Gravitt of New York, and Jeremiah X Pugh of Atlanta wrote a series of articles for the sect's newspaper saying Malcolm X was a "hypocrite," and that hypocrites "deserve to die."

When Malcolm X left the Nation of Islam on March 8, 1964, Elijah Muhammad was deeply affected. One memo describes a wiretapped telephone conversation about Malcolm X during which Elijah Muhammad mentioned to an assistant that it was time "to close his eyes." Another memo, dated March 23, 1964, has Elijah Muhammad saying that Malcolm X was a "no-good long-legged" hypocrite, and that when you find hypocrites, you should "cut their heads off."

Within thirty-six hours, there was apparent retaliation for the assassination. A firebomb was tossed from an adjacent rooftop through an open window of Mosque Number 7 in New York. The mosque flared into flame and was left a gutted shell. The door of a Muslim temple in San Francisco was splashed with kerosene and set ablaze, but firemen quickly put out the fire. In Rochester, New York, police were tipped off that another mosque was going to be bombed, and they confiscated five sticks of dynamite from a car parked nearby.

On Chicago's South Side, armies of police surrounded Elijah Muhammad's red brick mansion. From the safety of its interior, Muhammad issued a statement: "We are innocent of Malcolm's death. Malcolm died of his own preaching. He preached violence and violence took him away." But after Malcolm X's assassination, Elijah Muhammad needed to take sedatives at bedtime in order to sleep, and his chronic bronchitis forced him to turn over responsibility for running the Nation of Islam to his son, Herbert Muhammad, his son-in-law Raymond Sharrieff, and John Ali, national secretary of the Black Muslims.

Despite irregularities in their trial, there is no question that two of the accused assassins were Muslims. While waiting in prison to be tried, and after his conviction, Johnson strictly adhered to the sanctions of his religion down to the details of his diet. Still, when Butler and Johnson were arrested days after the assassination, they had alibis placing them elsewhere, though these were dismissed by the prosecutor.

In 1970 investigators revealed that prosecutors of the case had withheld legal evidence from defense attorneys, and that there were undercover New York detectives in the organizations created by Malcolm X after his defection from the Nation of Islam. Further, there was an undercover agent guarding Malcolm X when he was killed. This information supported the theory that the intelligence community had Malcolm X assassinated. His half-sister, Ella Collins, expressed this idea while standing in the long line of mourners at Malcolm X's funeral. The theory was repeated by other African Americans interviewed that day, and in editorials of dozens of Third World newspapers, but no one questioned the intelligence community's motive. They believed FBI director J. Edgar Hoover feared an alliance between African American radicals led by Malcolm X and the more moderate followers of Dr. Martin Luther King Jr. While tracking their budding relationship, the FBI uncovered strong links between the two men: Lawyers retained by King also represented the Nation of Islam, and these same attorneys had close personal friendships with both King and Malcolm X.

Declassified CIA documents reveal that the office of the deputy director of plans, the division involved in the overthrow and assassination of several Asian, African, and Latin American rulers, was keeping track of Malcolm X's activities up to the hour of his assassination. They knew that Malcolm X intended to file a petition with the United Nations, accusing the U.S. government of violating the human rights of African Americans. This information, in particular, was considered so potentially damaging to American foreign policy that it was discussed with President Lyndon B. Johnson. Declassified FBI and CIA documents also indicate that the intelligence community was concerned about Malcolm X's friendship with prominent African diplomats, as well as Cuban premier Fidel Castro and his protégé, Che Guevara. But on February 25, 1965, the FBI concluded after a three-day investigation that there were no "international implications" in the murder of Malcolm X.

The third theory, that the Mafia and/or an international drug cartel had conspired to assassinate Malcolm X was initially posed by James Farmer only days after the assassination. Farmer was then director of the Congress of Racial Equality (CORE). He wondered if the international drug merchants may have wanted Malcolm X out of the picture because Malcolm X was having a serious detrimental impact on drug profits in black communities throughout the United States. Although this theory was originally thought to be absurd, it began to look more plausible by 1973, when a series of gruesome murders in New Jersey made it clear that a few Black Muslims were deeply involved with the drug underworld. In 1975, Nathaniel Muhammad, Elijah Muhammad's son, was arrested for drug distribution in the Midwest. He was later convicted and served his sentence at the Federal Correctional Institution in Sandstone, Minnesota. Then, in 1979, the late Edward Bennett Williams, former owner of the Baltimore Orioles and the Washington Redskins and legal counsel for dozens of men with ties to the Mafia, represented Hayer when he appealed his conviction for killing Malcolm X.

Within the black American community today there remains as much controversy about the official findings in the 1965 assassination of Malcolm X as there is among the general population concerning the murder of President John F. Kennedy. Many blacks insist that the police investigation was superficial and although three men were convicted of the crime and imprisoned for life, one or more of the convicted men was unjustly charged. Many believe the assassination was not the work of Black Muslims or at least not of that group alone.

AFTERMATH: In March of 1994, Betty Shabazz publicly expressed her belief that Nation of Islam leader Louis Farrakhan was involved in her husband's slaying. In a speech later that month, Farrakhan said he had nothing to do with Malcolm X's assassination, but "an atmosphere that allowed Malcolm to be assassinated" had been created.

On January 12, 1995, Qubilah Bahiyah Shabazz, the thirty-four-year-old daughter of Malcolm X, was arrested in Minneapolis on federal charges of attempting to hire a hit man to kill Louis Farrakhan. Shabazz, who had witnessed her father's 1965 assassination, was accused of trying to hire a government informer to kill Farrakhan in revenge for her father's murder. She was indicted on January 12 by a Minneapolis federal grand jury. Shabazz appeared in a St. Paul, Minnesota, federal court on January 18 to plead not guilty to the charges.

Authorities said that Farrakhan had been informed several months earlier that there was a plot against him, but after Shabazz was arraigned Farrakhan publicly expressed skepticism about the charges against her. The government informer, thirty-four-year-old Michael Fitzpatrick, had been a classmate of Qubilah Shabazz's at the United Nations International School of New York City in the 1970s. Fitzpatrick, a member of the militant Jewish Defense League, had been arrested in 1977 in connection with the bombing of a Soviet bookstore in New York City. After pleading guilty in that case, he became a government informer, and tape-recorded conversations with JDL members regarding a subsequently foiled 1978 plot to bomb the Egyptian tourist office in New York. After Fitzpatrick's recordings helped to secure convictions of JDL members, he entered the federal witness-protection program. In November of 1993, he was arrested for cocaine possession and faced trial on that charge.

Authorities alleged that Shabazz had moved to Minneapolis from New York City in September of 1994 to arrange Farrakhan's killing in Chicago, the Nation of Islam's home base. Prosecutors said Shabazz was recorded on videotape and audiotape plotting the assassination and giving Fitzpatrick a partial payment for the job. Still, the Nation of Islam and many blacks were skeptical about the charges against Shabazz. Some critics said Shabazz would never take such actions on her own and accused the government of entrapment. Others asserted that Shabazz's indictment was part of a government effort to divide the black community.

On January 17, 1995, in a speech at the Nation of Islam's Chicago mosque, Farrakhan himself addressed the case, calling Shabazz the victim of "a trained setup artist." Qubilah's mother, Betty Shabazz, said the next day that she was "totally surprised" by Farrakhan's remarks and "at the extent of his humanity, of his understanding that my daughter had nothing to do with" the alleged plot against him. On May 1, 1995, a federal district court judge in Minneapolis approved an agreement under which the indictment against Qubilah Shabazz would be dismissed if she accepted responsibility for her involvement in a plot to kill Farrakhan. The terms of the agreement also called for Shabazz to be placed on two years' probation, during which time she was to find employment and undergo a psychiatric and drug-and-alcohol treatment program in Texas. Although she later still insisted that she had been entrapped and had not plotted to kill Farrakhan, in order to avoid going to trial, Shabazz agreed to the terms of the judge's proposal.

 APRIL 4, 1968

MARTIN LUTHER KING JR. (1929–1968)
U.S. CIVIL RIGHTS LEADER

Martin Luther King Jr., the black Baptist minister from Alabama who spearheaded the nonviolent civil rights movement in the mid-1950s, won the Nobel Peace Prize for his efforts. The movement focused national attention on the plight of blacks and resulted in the passage of the Civil Rights Act in 1964 and the Voting Rights Act in 1965.

Born in Atlanta, the son and grandson of Baptist preachers, King graduated with a degree in sociology from Atlanta's Morehouse College at age nineteen. Encouraged by his father to enter the Baptist ministry, he abandoned earlier ambitions to become a doctor or a lawyer and attended Crozer Theological Seminary in Chester, Pennsylvania. His education was completed at Boston University, where he was awarded a Ph.D. in 1955. In the meantime, King was appointed pastor of a Baptist church in Montgomery, Alabama. It was there, on December 1, 1955, that his future took shape. Rosa Parks, a black seamstress, boarded a city bus, sat down in the white section up front, and refused to give up her seat to a later-boarding white man. When Parks was arrested for her actions, Martin Luther King Jr. engineered a yearlong bus boycott to protest racial segregation on public transportation. The end result was a U.S. Supreme Court decision that segregation on public transportation was unconstitutional.

Inspired by the nonviolent resistance principles of Mahatma Gandhi, King led his followers with courage and determination, founding the Southern Christian Leadership Conference (SCLC) in 1957. While lecturing on civil rights throughout the country during the next three years, King discussed with religious and state leaders the problems faced by blacks in their struggle for freedom. He returned to Atlanta in 1960 to share the pastorship of Ebenezer Baptist Church with his father, still devoting time to the civil rights movement.

Martin Luther King Jr. led the Prayer Pilgrimage for Freedom in 1957, the Selma-Montgomery march in 1965, and the Mississippi march in 1966. In 1963 he joined other leaders of the civil rights movement as they marched to the Lincoln Memorial in Washington at the head of some 200,000 Americans of all races and creeds in a peaceful demonstration known as the March on Washington for Jobs and Freedom. On that occasion, King's brilliance as an orator made a profound impression with his now-famous "I have a dream" speech. In time King expanded his focus from campaigns for integration, equal education, voting rights, and fair hiring practices for black Americans to include a general fight against poverty, racism, and war. King was arrested more than fifteen times during numerous demonstrations and always maintained his nonviolent beliefs, even counseling love and forgiveness to his heavily armed neighbors after his house was bombed by segregationists.

In 1963 he was chosen Man of the Year by *Time* magazine, and in 1964, at the age of thirty-five, he was the youngest person to be awarded the Nobel Peace Prize.

Martin Luther King
UPI / CORBIS-BETTMANN

ACCUSED ASSASSIN: James Earl Ray, one of eight children of James Gerald Ray and Lucille Maher, dropped out of school in the tenth grade and worked at menial jobs until 1946, when he joined the U.S. Army. He was discharged on December 23, 1948, for "ineptness and lack of adaptability to military service." After that time, he was arrested for a series of armed robberies, served three years in prison for forgery, and was involved in small-time smuggling and burglary activities.

HISTORY: During the 1960s, King's rising prominence made him a target not only of violence by segregationists but of government harassment as well. The FBI began keeping tabs on King's activities. The bureau began tapping his telephone in 1957, and in 1964 FBI director J. Edgar Hoover, apparently obsessed with ruining King's reputation, ordered his agents to spy on King day and night. Hoover authorized wiretaps in fifteen different hotels where King was staying. He obtained tapes allegedly proving that King had engaged in extramarital sexual activities and supplied copies of the tapes to members of the press, to members of Congress, and to President Lyndon Johnson. News that King was slated to have an audience with the pope in August of 1964 prompted Hoover to send the pontiff derogatory information about King. (The pope went ahead with the meeting as scheduled.) Hoover's attacks on King's character reached a peak while King was preparing to travel to Stockholm for the Nobel Peace Prize ceremony. Hoover freely expressed his feelings about Dr. King, berating his selection as the Nobel Peace Prize recipient, and during a session with reporters, Hoover called King "the most notorious liar in the country."

Reportedly, Hoover authorized illegal harassment of King, seemed obsessed with ferreting out details of King's sex life, and even had a letter sent to King which encouraged him to commit suicide or else his reputation would be ruined by release of the "sex" tapes prior to his attending the Nobel Peace Prize awards ceremony. Hoover had excerpts of the hotel tapes sent to King's wife, Coretta, with an unsigned letter addressed to Dr. King enclosed in the package. The letter said, in part: "King—there is only one thing left for you to do. You know what it is. You have just thirty-four days in which to do it. It has definite practical significance. You are done. There is but one way out for you. You better take it before your filthy, abnormal fraudulent self is bared to the nation."

In addition to threats from the FBI and by segregationists, King's nonviolent approach was increasingly challenged by younger and more militant black activists. Soon he was speaking out on a broader range of issues, including the Vietnam War and conditions of the poor. In 1968 he announced plans for a Poor People's March on Washington, and while they were being finalized, King traveled to Memphis, Tennessee, to lend support to a largely black group of striking sanitation workers. In February, the strike by the city's 1,300 sanitation personnel had erupted into a large-scale disturbance (said to have been instigated in part by undercover law-enforcement infiltrators); one youth was killed and 238 persons were arrested.

King went to Memphis in April to help bring a more peaceful climate to the ongoing strike. Originally he planned to stay in a white-owned hotel, but when a news story criticized this choice, his reservations where changed to the Lorraine Motel. Some believe J. Edgar Hoover was responsible for planting the news story.

EVENT: On April 3, 1968, thirty-nine-year-old Dr. King checked into room 306 of the Lorraine Motel. Employees of the Lorraine later recalled that a white man, made up to appear black, had earlier that day come to check on King's reservation. Although room 202, in a secluded corner location, had been reserved for King, this man requested that King's room be changed to the upper floor, to the more visible room 306. That man was not connected in any way with King's party.

That evening King was greeted with strong support by more than two thousand people at the Mason Street Temple. His speech contained a passage that would later seem prophetic: "We've got some difficult days ahead, but it really doesn't matter with me now. Because I've been to the mountaintop. Like anybody, I would like to live a long life. . . . But I'm not concerned about that now . . ."

The next day, King stayed in his room at the Lorraine Motel. As evening approached, he and his associates stepped out onto the balcony overlooking a parking lot. Looking down, they began a conversation with the Reverend Jesse Jackson and their mutual friend musician Ben Branch, both of whom were standing below.

King's chauffeur, Solomon Jones, called up to him that it was chilly and he should probably wear his topcoat. King agreed, then as he straightened up to leave, a bullet struck him in the right side of the jaw, entered his neck, and severed his spinal cord. Thrown violently backward, his necktie ripped completely off his shirt, King was bleeding profusely as shocked associates and staff members ran to help him. An ambulance arrived within fifteen minutes and took King to Saint Joseph's Hospital, where he was pronounced dead at 7:05 P.M., one hour and four minutes after the shooting.

AFTERMATH: The night of Martin Luther King Jr.'s assassination, riots broke out in hundreds of U.S. cities. Forty-six people died and 21,270 were injured as 55,000 federal troops and National Guardsmen were called in. The biggest disturbances took place in Chicago, Baltimore, Kansas City, and Washington, D.C., where 711 fires were started. President Johnson ordered U.S. flags on all federal buildings to be flown at half-mast, and called for an end to the violence. Dr. King's widow, Coretta Scott King, tried to calm the nation, issuing statements pleading with demonstrators to "join us in fulfilling his dream of a creative rather than a destructive way."

An uneasy peace had settled in by Tuesday, April 9, when memorial services and silent marches were held around the world as a massive funeral for Dr. King was taking place in Atlanta. A shining mahogany coffin holding his body was placed on the green boards of a crude farm wagon pulled by two Georgia mules, as a symbol of Dr. King's identification with the poor. A march, which began at Ebenezer Baptist Church and wound three and a half miles through the streets of Atlanta, was headed by some of the nation's most elevated figures in finance, politics, religion, and government, who walked along with 100,000 others through the blistering, eighty-degree heat of the afternoon. The funeral procession ended at Morehouse College, where an open-air public service was held.

One week later, President Johnson signed into law the Civil Rights Act, which assured racial, sexual, and ethnic fairness throughout the United States.

APPREHENDING THE SUSPECT: Immediately after Dr. King was shot, police found, in front of Guy Canipe's Amusement Company, a zippered satchel, a bedspread, and a cardboard case containing a Remington Gamemaster rifle, model 760, 30.06-caliber, with a 2-by-7 telescopic sight. Although Bernell Finley and Julius Graham, two of Canipe's customers, had seen a man run past and drop the items, no one could give a clear description to Lieutenant Chormley of the Memphis police.

Next door to Canipe's business was a rooming house, whose tenants were perplexed by a man who had locked himself in the fifth floor's only bathroom. He had registered that morning as John Willard, choosing room 5B, located fifteen feet down the hall from the bathroom. Authorities believed the fatal shot had been fired from the window of that bathroom and had traveled 205 feet across the parking lot to the balcony of room 306 at the Lorraine Motel. Willie Anschutz and Charles Stephens, two tenants at the rooming house, said they saw Willard go around the corner at the end of the hall and down the stairs shortly after the shot was fired, but no one could give a good description of the man. No fingerprints were found in Willard's room or in the bathroom, not even on the doorknobs.

Guy Canipe gave the most detailed description of the supposed killer, saying he was "a white man, a little under six feet, pretty well dressed, dark-headed, no hat, and wearing a dark suit." Other descriptions of the suspect varied. Witnesses said not one but two white Mustangs had pulled away from Canipe's store after the shooting, and the cars were going in opposite directions. Police lieutenant Rufus Bradshaw called in a report that one of the cars had been spotted and was being pursued, but when police followed Bradshaw's directions, they found nothing. Later, Bradshaw said he had gotten his information from a young motorist of doubtful credibility.

When the police searched items left behind at the Canipe establishment, they found that the small canvas satchel contained some clothes, a pair of pliers, and a newspaper with the headline "King Challenges Court Restraint, Vows to March." The pliers were traced to the Romage Hardware Store in Los Angeles. Laundry marks on the clothes led to a cleaner two blocks away. From these two pieces of evidence, police came up with a name: Eric Starvo Galt. Meanwhile, an abandoned white Mustang registered in the name of E. Galt was found in Atlanta. Police discovered that Galt had been taking dancing lessons and attending a bartending school while living at the St. Francis Hotel in Los Angeles. The bartending school was able to provide a photo of Galt, who was identified as James Earl Ray.

A single fingerprint on a map was the only one found in the Mustang, and one print was also reportedly found on the rifle left outside Canipe's store. The unusual scarcity of fingerprints added to two other puzzles: Clothes found in the satchel and in the trunk of the Mustang were of different sizes, and though Ray was a nonsmoker, the roominghouse room and the floor of the Mustang were littered with Viceroy butts.

Suspecting that Ray had left the country, authorities began to examine passport information. Royal Canadian Mounted Police discovered that Ray had obtained passports in at least three names: Paul Edward Bridgeman, Toronto policeman George Ramon Sneyd, and Eric St. Vincent Galt (his middle name was signed in a way that it appeared to be "Starvo").

James Earl Ray was arrested at London's Heathrow Airport on June 8, more than two months after Martin Luther King's assassination. While attempting to board a British European Airways flight for Brussels, he had accidentally shown two passports, one for George Ramon Sneyd, a second for George Ramon Sneya. Questioned about the dual passports, security officers searched Ray and discovered a loaded .38-caliber pistol. Ray remained calm until Scotland Yard official Thomas Butler told him that his true identity was known and that he was wanted for murder in the United States. At that point, Ray put his head on his hands and wept.

A search of his criminal record showed that Ray was a minor habitual criminal whose previous offenses included stealing a typewriter, robbing a cabdriver, stealing money orders, and robbing a supermarket. He had been sentenced to twenty years in prison for the last offense, had tried to escape in 1960 and 1966, and had finally succeeded in April 1967 by hiding in a bread truck.

After King was shot, Ray had fled to Canada and the following month to London with a Canadian passport, some say displaying a sophistication in avoiding detection that he had previously never exhibited. He then went to Lisbon, although the purpose of that trip was never established, and back to London, where he was apprehended and returned to the United States on July 19, 1968, via a U.S. Air Force jet.

PUNISHMENT: Ray's original attorneys, the team of Arthur J. Hanes and his son of the same name, spent the next several months interviewing witnesses and developing a case to defend Ray in court. But when an article appeared in *Look* magazine, which presented most of the information the Haneses had compiled, Ray felt his case had been compromised and fired them, hiring flamboyant Texas attorney Percy Foreman. After a cursory examination of the state's case against Ray, which convinced Foreman that his client was in deep trouble, Foreman told Ray that based on the overwhelming evidence that had been assembled against him, there was more than a 99 percent chance he would receive a death-penalty verdict in a jury trial. Foreman advised Ray that the only way he could escape the electric chair was to plead guilty to Dr. King's murder.

On March 10, 1969, more than eleven months after Dr. King's assassination, James Earl Ray pleaded guilty to the crime in a court session before Judge W. Preston Battle. At the same time, Ray waived his right to any appeal or review of his case or to a trial. Ray was sentenced to ninety-nine years' imprisonment. But within twenty-four hours, Ray recanted his confession and attempted to reverse his plea. He insisted on dropping Percy Foreman as his attorney, claiming Foreman and the government had coerced him into pleading guilty to a crime he did not commit. Ray said a shadowy man he called Raoul had given him money and instructed him to buy the white Mustang and the rifle and then go to Memphis in April of 1968 for a gun-running scheme. On the day King was shot, Ray said Raoul took the rifle from him, told him to get lost until 6 P.M., then return in the white Mustang and pick him up at the rooming house. When Ray returned at that time, the presence of police made him speed away from town without retrieving Raoul. Ray insisted he did not know who killed Martin Luther King Jr.

James Earl Ray has been behind bars continually since 1969 except for a three-day escape in 1977. During this brief period of freedom, he exhibited none of the adept planning and generous financing that enabled his flight after Dr. King's assassination, and he was quickly apprehended.

As of February 20, 1997, attorneys for James Earl Ray had taken his claims of innocence to court eight times, requesting that his case be heard, but Ray's requests for a trial have not been granted.

CONSPIRACY THEORIES: Many questions remain about whether James Earl Ray had the ability to assassinate Dr. King, then escape as he did. The question of money has been prominent. An escaped convict with no money of his own, Ray had paid $2,000 for the white Mustang. He had also undergone plastic surgery, attended bartending school, and taken dancing lessons in Los Angeles, and he'd lavishly entertained a Canadian woman who claimed Ray told her, "There's plenty more where that came from." His only benefactor might have been his brother Jerry, but he was a manual laborer who could not have financed Ray's costly pursuits. Still, law-enforcement officials maintained there was no conspiracy in the murder of Dr. King, despite the money issue and the questions about how Ray, who was not known as a savvy criminal, could have escaped authorities for two months. Later, when new reports exposed FBI activities concerning King, the U.S. Justice Department began an internal probe to determine the validity of accusations of a cover-up. An eight-month Justice Department report, costing $2 million, led lawyer-investigators through fifteen cities and two hundred thousand documents (mostly FBI reports), although only forty people were interviewed. This report concluded that Ray acted alone and that there was no evidence that the FBI had been involved in King's assassination. A second investigation, conducted by the FBI itself, also failed to unearth any evidence of a conspiracy or FBI involvement in the crime.

Despite these investigations, there remains much controversy about King's assassination, with a number of details indicating the existence of a broad plot to kill the civil rights leader. There were even charges that the FBI engineered the plan to eliminate King, setting up James Earl Ray as the scapegoat. Arthur Murtagh, a former agent in the FBI's Atlanta office, who was apparently later stricken by guilt over his role in the bureau's harassment of King, has said he believes Ray was framed.

Saying Raoul's behavior was consistent with standard FBI procedures, Murtagh told a *Los Angeles Times* reporter that he thought "Raoul was feeding [Ray] the rifle and . . . making sure . . . that his fingerprints were on [it]. . . . Raoul or some other operative was probably involved in the shooting that killed King." Although this theory has never been proved, it has been reported that some elements within the FBI did not regret King's demise. A retired FBI agent working in the Atlanta office at the time of the killing told the press that deep anti-King feelings existed within the FBI and that one agent literally jumped for joy when he learned of King's assassination. Further, the former agent alleged that his superiors washed out leads that would have pointed to a conspiracy. Years later, the FBI admitted only that it had wiretapped King's home and that it had sent Mrs. Coretta King letters implying her husband was seeing numerous other women.

Many believe that if there was a conspiracy, Memphis police were involved. Memphis police detective Ed Reddit later said that he had been pulled off an assignment in preparation for King's visit after suggesting that the police should plan to seal off a four-block area in Memphis in the event someone tried to shoot King. Reddit was told to remove himself from the case; when he refused, he was placed under virtual house arrest and was not allowed to continue in his duties that day.

In 1978, the House Select Committee on Assassinations investigated the circumstances of King's death. During the hearings, a St. Louis man named Russell Byers said he had been offered fifty thousand dollars to arrange King's death. Byers said the offer came from two men, John Kauffmann and John Sutherland, who said they were acting on behalf of a group of businessmen. The offer was made in the Confederate-flag-decked den of Sutherland, a well-to-do attorney, who was wearing the uniform of a Confederate officer, complete with a colonel's hat. By the time of Byers's testimony, both Kauffmann and Sutherland were dead, of natural causes, but their widows denied that their husbands would have taken part in such a plot. The House committee learned that the FBI had known of Byers's charges in 1973, but the information was never passed along to agents investigating King's assassination. Although the FBI claimed this was a simple case of "administrative error," a spokesman for the bureau called the handling of the information a "violation of established rules and procedures." The agent who had "misfiled" the material had since retired. Byers told House investigators that at the time he suspected Sutherland and Kauffmann were trying to recruit him as a dupe to take the blame for the murder but not to carry it out. This prompted an investigation attempting to link Byers or Sutherland or Kauffmann to Ray's escape from the penitentiary in 1967.

In December 1978, the House committee investigation was concluded with a report saying there was a "likelihood" of a conspiracy in King's assassination. Although the panel cleared all federal, state, and local government agencies of involvement, it called the Domestic Intelligence Division of the FBI guilty of "gross" abuse of its legal authority in its surveillance of King, and it stated that the Justice Department had "failed to supervise adequately" that division.

These conclusions have come under serious scrutiny, most notably by Philip H. Melanson, a professor of political science at the University of Massachusetts. In *The Murkin Conspiracy* (1989), Melanson contends that both the FBI's and the House committee's investigations were seriously flawed. He writes: "A close examination of the fingerprint, ballistics, and eyewitness evidence, reveals . . . gaps and inconsistencies . . . clearly biased toward establishing Ray's guilt." Melanson suggests that even if the FBI did not have King killed, other federal agencies could have been involved. He cites documents such as a May 1965 CIA internal memo that states that an informant "feels that somewhere in the negro movement . . . there must be a negro leader who is 'clean' and who could step into the vacuum and chaos if Martin Luther King were either exposed or assassinated." In his book, Melanson speculates that the assassination may have been the work of a cabal within the CIA and/or U.S. military intelligence, and that its motives would have been rooted less in classic racism than in a widely held perception that King, who had recently begun to speak out against the Vietnam War, was knowingly or unknowingly serving as a conduit for pro-Hanoi propaganda.

Melanson says Ray's story about Raoul is consistent with the methods of a sophisticated covert-operations handler experienced in "tradecraft." Following up on an investigation conducted by a Canadian journalist, Melanson was able to identify a shadowy character named Jules Ricco Kimble, whose movements during the months leading up to King's assassination coincide with the dates and places Ray says he met with Raoul. Finally, the professor says that while Ray may well have killed King, he did not act alone. He concludes, "The best evidence suggests that Ray was an unexceptional criminal who had exceptionally clever help."

The circumstantial evidence suggests that Ray did not act on his own, having neither the resources nor the contacts to supply himself with passports, money, and weapons. The bullet recovered from Dr. King's body has never been scientifically linked with the alleged murder weapon that held Ray's fingerprint. If he did act alone, Ray's motive is not clear, although the House committee received testimony that James Earl Ray hoped to collect a fifty-thousand-dollar bounty by killing Dr. King.

CHRONICLE: In his 1992 book *Who Killed Martin Luther King?*, James Earl Ray tells in detail his version of the events of 1968, explaining how he was set up as a patsy by the mysterious figure he calls Raoul. First contacted in Toronto in 1967 after he had escaped from prison, Ray claims Raoul lured him into a smuggling scheme both in Canada and in Mexico. The following year, Ray met Raoul in various places in the United States where Raoul gave him money and told him to buy a white Mustang and a Remington .30/06 rifle (the one apparently used to kill Dr. King). Raoul then told Ray to go to Memphis on April 3, 1968, to participate in a gun-running scheme. In Memphis on the afternoon of April 4, Ray says, Raoul disappeared with the rifle, allegedly to meet with underworld connections. When Ray later heard that King had been assassinated and police were looking for a man in a white Mustang, he fled. He says no one helped him escape, and that after he was captured, Percy Foreman, his attorney, coerced him into pleading guilty.

Dr. King's assassination and the question of Ray's guilt once again became front-page news in the 1990s. On the twenty-fifth anniversary of the assassination, April 4, 1993, HBO aired a $3 million production entitled *Guilt or Innocence: The Trial of James Earl Ray.* An unscripted mock trial was filmed in a Memphis courtroom, with real attorneys questioning real witnesses. Ray also testified and was cross-examined via a satellite hookup from prison; he was visible on a television monitor in the courtroom during the entire mock trial. In the end, the jury found James Earl Ray innocent.

In 1994, the *Los Angeles Times* published the astonishing story of Betty Spates, a black woman who was working at Jim's Grill, which stood behind the Lorraine Motel, in April of 1968. Spates said she was having an affair with Lloyd Jowers, the owner of Jim's Grill, and that she came into the diner on the afternoon of April 4, 1968, thinking she might catch him with another woman. Instead, she saw Jowers enter through the rear door of the diner, behind which there was a bushy field where three witnesses claimed the fatal shot may have originated. Jowers had mud on his pants, was carrying a rifle, and had a look of terror on his face. When asked why she had not come forward sooner, Spates said she was seventeen years old at the time, entangled in an affair with Jowers, felt conflicting loyalties, and was afraid. All of this, she said, caused her to try to block the image from her mind for twenty-six years. Why did she finally tell what she knew? William Pepper, Ray's newest attorney, convinced her to tell her story.

When interviewed soon afterward by Sam Donaldson on ABC's *Prime Time Live,* Lloyd Jowers said that a friend had approached him and asked him to hire a gunman to kill King, and that that gunman was not James Earl Ray. Jowers would not provide details, but he said that for a promise of immunity from prosecution he would tell everything. An investigation identified the friend who approached Jowers as Frank Liberto, a local produce supplier with ties to the New Orleans Mafia, but Jowers did not name Liberto, who was, by then, dead. It was also learned that back in 1968, a witness named John McFerren had told the FBI about a telephone conversation he had overheard in Liberto's store a few hours before King was shot. McFerren said Liberto was not aware that he was overheard saying, "Kill the S.O.B. on the balcony and get the job done. Don't come out here. Go to New Orleans and get your money. You know my brother." Investigators maintain that McFerren's testimony was investigated in 1968 but that the conversation was found to be "unrelated" to Dr. King's murder.

An eighteen-year investigation by Ray's attorney, William Pepper, confirmed the link between Liberto and the crime. While representing James Earl Ray in his attempts to finally get a court trial, Pepper has written his own book, *Orders to Kill*. Pepper, who worked with Dr. King during the last year of his life, first met with Ray on October 17, 1978, at the request of Dr. King's close friend, Ralph Abernathy. He asked Pepper to go to the prison and interrogate Ray. At the time, Pepper knew nothing about the case and assumed Ray had killed Dr. King. Pepper agreed to take Ray's case ten years later, when he was absolutely convinced that Ray had neither shot King nor knowingly had been involved in his murder. Based on his investigation, Pepper has come up with a theory about why and how Dr. King was assassinated.

During 1967 and 1968, more than a hundred cities in America burned and there was a massive invasion of Washington, D.C., by demonstrators. Pepper says that government authorities were terrified about King's upcoming march, which would bring a mass of alienated Americans—black, white, Hispanic, Asian, Native Americans—into the nation's capitol again. In order to stop King and the march, Memphis was designated as the place for King to be assassinated. Pepper says that on April 4, 1968, as Martin Luther King Jr. stood on the balcony of the Lorraine Motel, there was a contract killer in the brushy area behind Jim's Grill. This killer had taken the contract from the Marcello organization in New Orleans. He fired a single shot that killed Dr. King. At the same time, there was a backup team of assassins: an eight-man Special Forces team. These Green Berets came from Camp Shelby, Mississippi, where they were briefed from 4:30 to 5 A.M. They then set out for Memphis. When Dr. King was shot, there were two teams of snipers in their perches: One team had its guns trained on Dr. King, the other on Andrew Young. Pepper says all of this information came from eyewitness testimony. Members of the Green Beret team provided some of it, someone inside the Pentagon provided documentation and additional information, and a best friend of one of the Green Berets independently corroborated it.

According to Pepper, King was deliberately put in room 306 of the Lorraine Motel. From a bushy area outside the kitchen door of Jim's Grill, someone standing on the balcony of room 306 was an easy target. Lloyd Jowers was in the bushy area when Dr. King was shot. Jowers had been contacted on March 15 by Frank Liberto, an associate of Carlos Marcello, who was given a contract to carry out the logistics of King's assassination. Liberto offered Jowers $100,000 and said he would forgive a gambling debt if Jowers would let his facility be used for the hit on Martin Luther King. While Betty Spates said she saw Jowers run into the kitchen of Jim's Grill carrying a gun after King was shot, Jowers has never admitted to committing the assassination.

After the murder, although police found fresh footprints in the bushy area behind Jim's Grill, they never investigated the area. In fact, the next day, city officials ordered the area cleared and the bushes cut down, destroying any potential additional evidence. Neither police nor investigators ever questioned numerous witnesses who saw someone in the bushy area behind Jim's Grill immediately after Dr. King was shot.

All of these facts support the belief of many that not only was there a conspiracy to assassinate Dr. King, but there was also a cover-up after the crime was committed.

Ironically, many of Dr. King's old friends and colleagues, who have always been convinced that the FBI was involved in his assassination, have taken James Earl Ray's side in requesting a full and public hearing. Jesse Jackson wrote the foreword to Ray's book. The Reverend James Lawson, who had invited King to visit Memphis during that fatal week in April 1968, performed Ray's 1978 wedding ceremony in prison. In December of 1994 Joseph Lowery, president of the Southern Christian

Leadership Conference, formally requested that the Justice Department investigate new information that has emerged concerning a possible conspiracy.

In February of 1997, William Pepper took Ray's case before an appellate court for the eighth time. Pepper claims the rifle that showed one of Ray's fingerprints was actually thrown down in a location where it could be found in order to implicate Ray, but that it is not the actual murder weapon. Citing new scientific techniques that could be used to test the assassin's bullet and the alleged murder weapon, Pepper hopes to finally get James Earl Ray a trial. During this hearing even Dr. King's wife and his family came out, for the first time, in support of a trial for the sixty-eight-year-old Ray, who has already served twenty-nine years in prison. They testified that it was time for the truth to be told, that there are too many unanswered questions that need to be put to rest.

While Ray was not granted a trial, Pepper's request that the alleged murder weapon be subjected to ballistics tests was granted. The results were inconclusive.

Some say a trial for Ray will never solve the actual crime, that William Pepper would not be allowed to present any evidence of a conspiracy in his defense of Ray. Indeed, the truth may never come out, at least not before 2029, when FBI and CIA documents relating to the assassinations of both Dr. King and John F. Kennedy, which were locked away by the House committee, are released.

In an ironic twist of fate, on March 27, 1997, Martin Luther King Jr.'s youngest son, Dexter King, sat down and talked to James Earl Ray face-to-face in the Tennessee prison where he is incarcerated. King asked Ray directly: "Did you shoot my father?" Ray, who was critically ill with liver disease, replied, "No, no I did not." After a strained but cordial conversation before television news cameras, King solemnly assured Ray, "This is a burden my family has carried for a long time. We are going to do everything in our power to make sure that justice will prevail. We will do everything in our power to bring what has occurred in the darkness into the light."

JUNE 5, 1968

ROBERT F. KENNEDY (1925–1968)
U.S. SENATOR FROM NEW YORK AND CANDIDATE FOR THE DEMOCRATIC NOMINATION IN THE 1968 PRESIDENTIAL ELECTION

Robert Francis Kennedy was born November 10, 1925, the seventh child and third son of Joseph and Rose Kennedy. Robert's political career was overshadowed by that of his older brother John for most of his life. He had followed in his brothers' footsteps, attending Harvard University, but interrupted his studies to serve in the U.S. Navy during World War II, then returned to the university and graduated in 1948. After receiving a law degree from the University of Virginia Law School in 1951, Robert began his political career in Massachusetts by managing his brother John's successful campaign for the U.S. Senate. Robert Kennedy achieved national prominence in 1953, when he served as assistant counsel to the Senate Permanent Subcommittee on Investigations, which was headed by Joseph R. McCarthy. In 1957, he became chief counsel to the Senate select committee conducting investigations into labor racketeering. This was the beginning of a long-standing feud with Teamsters Union head James R. Hoffa. When John Kennedy began his campaign for U.S. president in 1970, Robert Kennedy resigned his Senate committee position to run his brother's campaign. Upon JFK's election to the presidency, he appointed Robert to the cabinet post of attorney general. In that position, which he held from 1961 to 1964, Robert tackled many of the day's tough issues, including the Vietnam War, urban decay, racism, the Middle East, and unemployment. But the issues of human rights and organized crime were predominant. After President Kennedy's assassination in 1963, Robert Kennedy resigned his cabinet post to run for the U.S. Senate. As a senator representing New York, he actively promoted civil rights legislation and frequently opposed the Johnson administration's conduct of the war in Vietnam.

Robert Kennedy embarked on his own presidential campaign in the spring of 1968, seeking the Democratic nomination.

ASSASSIN: Sirhan Bishara Sirhan was a Palestinian born in Jordan on March 19, 1944. After the territory where the Sirhan family lived was occupied by Israel, they spent nine years as starving refugees before emigrating to the United States when Sirhan was thirteen years old. Living with his family in Pasadena, California, Sirhan attended local elementary, junior high and high schools, presenting no disciplinary problems to his teachers or his parents. He attended Pasadena City College but dropped out to get a job when his sister became ill and later died. Sirhan was considered a good worker in various jobs, and his mother would later say he got involved with strange companions several months before Robert Kennedy's assassination. Although he had always seemed stable, his style of living changed, and he began keeping uncharacteristically late hours.

HISTORY: When President Lyndon Johnson made the surprising announcement that he would not run for reelection in 1968, the Democratic presidential ticket was up for grabs. Robert Kennedy set out to defeat the other Democratic contenders; his strongest competitors were Vice-President Hubert Humphrey and Senator Eugene McCarthy. During his rigorous campaign, Kennedy, as a young (he was forty-two), bright, talented, and handsome representative of the vision of his slain brother, drew massive crowds of young voters who treated him like a pop star. Despite death threats and a disappointing defeat in the Oregon primary, Kennedy pushed forward through an exhausting schedule to the coveted California primary of June 4, 1968. Although he showed every sign of winning California, Kennedy's campaign targeted not only young idealist voters but minority voters as well. After whirlwind stops in San Francisco, San Diego, and Los Angeles, his statewide campaign ended with a drive through the downtrodden area of south-central Los Angeles.

EVENT: On the evening of June 5, 1968, as the California votes began to slowly come in, it became apparent that Kennedy had secured that state's 174 delegates with a 3 percent lead over McCarthy. Kennedy rested in a fifth-floor suite of Los Angeles's Ambassador Hotel, while downstairs in the Embassy Room a celebration of his victory in the pivotal California presidential primary had already started.

Although this win did not ensure Kennedy the Democratic nomination, he was positively buoyant as he went downstairs and took the stage to thank his supporters. Surrounded by his unofficial bodyguards—Los Angeles Rams lineman Roosevelt Grier, former Olympic decathlon champion Rafer Johnson, and Hispanic activist Cesar Chavez—Kennedy thanked his constituents. A loud cheer arose when he thanked Cesar Chavez. Then Kennedy thanked his staff, volunteers, and voters everywhere. He enthusiastically declared, "On to Chicago!" (the site of the upcoming Democratic convention) as his closing remark, then left the stage to go to the Colonial Room, which served as that evening's pressroom. In order to avoid large crowds waiting outside, Kennedy, his wife, Ethel, and his entourage—Grier, Johnson, author George Plimpton, and newscaster Roger Mudd—went through the kitchen pantry, accompanied by a local armed security guard named Thane Eugene Cesar. Carl Uecker, the Ambassador Hotel's maître d', led the way, firmly grasping Kennedy's hand, releasing it only for the Senator to shake hands with Juan Romer and Jesus Perez, two hotel employees, then quickly regrasping it as they continued through the narrow passageway.

Suddenly Sirhan B. Sirhan, a small, wiry man, his eyes glazed, stepped out of the crowd in the kitchen toward the senator. Kennedy and Uecker were facing north, and Sirhan was facing south as he raised a small, .22-caliber 8-shot Iver Johnson pistol, firing it once, then a second time at the senator. Kennedy threw up his right arm as more shots were heard. Witnesses saw the young, dark-complected man half-crouching three to six feet in front of Kennedy, firing a pistol with two hands. Uecker lunged for Sirhan and slammed the hand holding the gun against a steam table to his left, as other hands reached in from every direction, grabbing portions of Sirhan's clothing and flesh. Grier and Johnson tackled Sirhan, slamming him to the floor. Someone screamed, "Rafer, get the gun! *Get the fucking gun!*"

"I put my hand under the hammer so the gun wouldn't go off, then I wrenched it away from Sirhan," Grier would later recall. "I don't remember his size. All I know is he seemed to have a lot of strength." But some accounts say Sirhan emptied his gun into the crowd.

Sobs, screams, and echoes of "*Nooooo*" were heard throughout the hotel as Kennedy lay mortally wounded on the kitchen floor. Juan Romero moved in close to the senator and slipped a rosary into his hand, as Kennedy motioned him closer. "Is everyone all right?" Kennedy whispered. He had been hit by three bullets: Two entered within inches of each other near one armpit, the third entered the right side of his head behind his right ear.

After the scene was secured and an assessment began to be taken of the area, it was learned that Kennedy was not the only one shot. Also struck by bullets were Elizabeth Evan, Ira Goldstein, William Weisel, and Paul Schrade. Three other bullets were later recovered: two from the counter divider of the pantry doors at the entrance, and one from the frame of the door at the back of the stage.

Senator Kennedy was rushed by ambulance to nearby Central Receiving Hospital. On the way, the senator suffered cardiac arrest, and he reached the hospital breathless, pulseless, and lifeless. Although it was obvious that the bullet that had entered Kennedy's head created a fatal wound, the doctors hoped a miracle would occur. One of the attending physicians, Dr. Victor Basiluskas, and his assistants gave Kennedy closed cardiac massage, then placed him in a heart-lung machine before they administered oxygen, inserted a tube into his mouth to facilitate breathing, and injected adrenaline into the muscles. Nothing happened, but they waited until, miraculously, after ten or twelve minutes, there was a feeble breath and Kennedy's heart began to beat.

On an impulse, Dr. Basiluskas handed Kennedy's wife, Ethel, a stethoscope. She smiled tentatively as she stood beside her husband, holding the stethoscope against his chest, then asked Dr. Basiluskas, "Will he live?" His reply was "At this minute he's doing all right. Let's hope." The doctor then turned to an associate, Dr. Albert C. Holt, and told him that a neurosurgeon and a chest surgeon were waiting at Good Samaritan Hospital. A few minutes later, Senator Kennedy was in another ambulance being rushed to a hospital which was equipped with the most advanced technology in Los Angeles for dealing with the terrible wounds he had suffered.

Unconscious and on life support, Kennedy lingered for twenty-five hours, until his heart stopped at 1:44 the next morning. At 3 A.M., when Robert Kennedy's death was announced to the crowds waiting outside Good Samaritan Hospital, a mute grief took hold. Banners that read PRAY FOR BOBBY were lowered, and among a group of stricken young faces was a nun in tears, holding a rosary.

After Los Angeles County coroner Thomas Noguchi completed the most meticulous autopsy he had ever performed, Robert Kennedy's body was flown to New York City. A funeral service was conducted at St. Patrick's Cathedral, then thousands of people solemnly lined the tracks in the blazing sun and waited for the train carrying his body to the nation's capital. The bell of the funeral train rang incessantly as the twenty-two cars, the last of which transported Robert Kennedy's coffin covered by an American flag, carried an array of dignitaries on a journey of mixed memories. When the funeral train entered Baltimore, it was greeted by a silent mass of people, mostly black, who had waited for hours, and who sang "The Battle Hymn of the Republic" as it passed by. In Washington, D.C., there was a somber graveside service, with former astronaut John Glenn, a close friend, holding the U.S. flag. Millions watched these heart-wrenching events live on television, an emotional reminder of another Kennedy funeral less than five years earlier. Robert Kennedy was buried near his brother at Arlington National Cemetery.

PUNISHMENT: Immediately after Kennedy was shot, police whisked the battered assailant away from the scene. Sirhan refused to give his name, and police searching him found car keys in his pocket but no identification. Some reports say it was not until the next day, when his shocked brother saw Sirhan's face on television and telephoned police, that they learned his identity. Other reports say police discovered that the .22-caliber Iver Johnson pistol in Sirhan's possession was registered to a man named Munir Sirhan, of 696 East Howard Street in Pasadena, Sirhan's brother. A special investigative task force, called Special Unit Senator, was formed by the Los Angeles Police Department (LAPD). While awaiting trial, Sirhan joked with his police guards but spoke somberly of the sorry state of society and the violence that permeated it, saying he found the acts of the Boston Strangler to be simply terrible. Still, Sirhan allegedly told police that he had committed this terrible crime for his Arab brothers and arrogantly said Kennedy got what was coming to him. Sirhan's deep-seated hatred of Kennedy apparently came from the senator's well-known support for Israel and the Jewish people. His act of violence had made Sirhan a hero in parts of the Middle East, and in the streets of Arab cities were posters proclaiming "SIRHAN BISHARA SIRHAN, A COMMANDO, NOT AN ASSASSIN." So-called commando sources said that in shooting Kennedy, Sirhan had acted on behalf of all dispossessed Palestinians by striking out at a supporter of Israel.

On April 17, 1969, after a fifteen-week trial, during which he openly confessed to the assassination and exhibited unrestrained pride for his deed, Sirhan was condemned to death for murdering Robert F. Kennedy. He escaped the gas chamber when his sentence was reduced to life in prison by a 1972 Supreme Court ruling that abolished capital punishment as unconstitutional. Sirhan is currently in prison and actively seeking parole, which has always been denied.

AFTERMATH: As reports that more than eight shots had been fired that night started surfacing, other evidence added substantial doubt to the government's case against Sirhan as a lone assassin. Some witnesses insisted Sirhan had not gotten closer to Kennedy than two or three feet, but the autopsy showed there were powder burns around the fatal wound, indicating a weapon had been placed very close to the victim. In his medical report, Noguchi listed Kennedy's cause of death as a "gunshot wound of right mastoid, penetrating brain." Noguchi's professional opinion was that the bullet that killed Kennedy was fired from a position "very, very close" to the senator; he estimated that the muzzle of the gun was only "two or three inches from the edge of the right ear" when it was fired. Maître d' Carl Uecker, who was a perfectly placed eyewitness, disagreed, insisting even years later, "I told the authorities that Sirhan never got close enough for a point-blank shot. Never!"

Although a number of explanations were offered, ranging from mistaken eyewitness testimony to the possibility that Kennedy's body had been twisted by the impact of the shots and thrown against Sirhan's gun, other questions cast doubt on the LAPD's theory that Sirhan was the only shooter. Some reports said that a total of ten bullets were recovered from Kennedy, the other victims, and the scene, while Sirhan's .22 pistol could fire only eight shots without being reloaded. Since from the time of his first shot until he was tackled to the floor, Sirhan had no opportunity to reload his weapon, many thought it was apparent that another gun had to have been fired that night. Authorities explained that bullets ricocheting around the room created more bullet tracks than eight bullets would normally allow.

Some conspiracy speculators said the alleged second gunman was the private security guard, Thane Eugene Cèsar, who was standing directly behind Kennedy at the time of the shooting and, according to witnesses, drew his gun and fired it. When it was revealed that Cesar's service revolver was a .38-caliber weapon, some theorized that he could have carried a .22-caliber weapon in his sock, drawn and fired it, then passed it off to a confederate. Later, Cesar admitted that he drew his gun as soon as Sirhan began firing and that his gun might have discharged, but he denied that he could have shot Kennedy.

In another development, immediately after Kennedy was shot, a Youth for Kennedy worker named Sandy Serrano appeared on television breathlessly telling a reporter something she had seen. Serrano had been out on the terrace "for some air" as the senator spoke to the crowd inside the ballroom when suddenly, "a girl in a white polka-dot dress ran out of the hotel, shouting, 'We shot him.'" It was later reported that Sirhan was seen with a woman wearing a polka-dot dress in the pantry area of the hotel just before the assassination, and that this woman left before Kennedy entered through the pantry doors. Another witness also told police that he had seen the girl in the white polka-dot dress run out of the hotel, saying she was accompanied by a "dark-complected" man. In time, the LAPD produced a woman by the name of Cathy Fulmer, but Serrano could not identify her as the one she had seen. Several days after Sirhan was convicted, Fulmer was found dead in a motel room.

Many accused the LAPD of not conducting a thorough investigation. They did not test-fire Sirhan's gun to determine positively whether the bullet recovered from Kennedy or the bullet recovered from bystander William Weisel actually came from Sirhan's pistol. Supposedly, DeWayne Wolfer, head of the LAPD crime lab at the time of the investigation, had refused to test-fire Sirhan's gun. This report caused Marshall Houts, editor of *Trauma* magazine, an in-house organ of the field of criminologists, to send a letter to Evelle J. Younger, attorney general of the state of California, to express his "deep academic and professional concern over Wolfer's horrendous blunders." It was also reported that the gun tagged as evidence in Kennedy's assassination had the serial number H18602, while the serial number of Sirhan's gun was H53725, although the police supposedly admitted at the time of the trial that the guns had been reversed and Sirhan's had disappeared.

Since Kennedy's assassination, numerous books, documentaries, and movies have outlined various conspiracy theories. Many attempt to prove that the Mafia was responsible. The premise is that organized crime arranged the assassination of President Kennedy in order to stop Attorney General Robert Kennedy's campaign against them. They then assassinated Robert Kennedy to prevent him from becoming president. The problem with this theory is that, despite considerable effort, it has not been possible to convincingly link Sirhan to organized-crime figures. Other alleged conspirators include J. Edgar Hoover, the Teamsters, Jimmy Hoffa, the CIA, pro-Castro supporters, the Shah of Iran, Richard Nixon backers, Southern racist groups, and hard-line Cold Warriors. Although some conspiracy theorists insist Sirhan was not interested in

Arab affairs, library records show he checked out many books on the Middle East. Investigations found that his personal discussions indicated fierce hatred of Jews and Israel, leading to the assumption that since Kennedy supported the shipment of more bombers to Israel, Sirhan saw a Robert Kennedy presidency as the end of hope for Palestinian Arabs.

Coroner Noguchi's autopsy report, which contradicted almost every witness at the scene, was used in an attempt to overthrow Sirhan's conviction. In 1970, attorney Godfrey Isaac represented Sirhan in a judicial review of his conviction, the basis for which was summed up in an affidavit of William W. Harper, an investigator hired by Isaac. Harper, a consulting criminalist for the Pasadena, California, police department and a former naval intelligence officer, reviewed the available evidence in the case, including Noguchi's autopsy report, and concluded that two different firing positions were used during the shooting and that two weapons had unquestionably been fired. A comparison of a bullet removed from the abdomen of Weisel and a bullet that lodged in Kennedy's neck (which had entered near the armpit), showed no common class characteristics: The rifling marks were sharply different. This hard evidence convinced Harper that it was impossible for those two bullets to have been fired from the same weapon. Further, Harper unequivocally stated that Kennedy was shot from a firing position entirely different from where Sirhan was shooting. Several other criminologists, including Drs. Herbert Leon MacDonell, Vincent P. Guinn, and Lowell Bradford, agreed in theory with the conclusions of Harper's study.

Sirhan claimed that although he had taken the gun into the hotel kitchen, he had no memory of what happened after that. Although Sirhan's lawyer could not deny that Sirhan had fired at the senator, he alleged that the *fatal* bullet was triggered from another gun. While Sirhan's conviction was upheld, scientific evidence of soot, divergent bullet angles in Kennedy's body, and eyewitness accounts differing from the conclusions of the LAPD investigation all seem to indicate that there may have been a second gunman.

1970s

GEORGE WALLACE (1919–)

GOVERNOR OF ALABAMA AND
CANDIDATE FOR THE DEMOCRATIC NOMINATION
IN THE 1972 PRESIDENTIAL ELECTION

George Corley Wallace was born on August 25, 1919, in Clio, Alabama. He held various state jobs before being elected governor for the first time in 1963. That year he was propelled into national prominence as a segregationist when he defied a court order that permitted black students to enroll at the University of Alabama. (He later complied with the order.) In time, Wallace moderated his staunch anti-integrationist views, gained support from both blacks and whites in his home state, and served as governor for four terms: 1963–67, 1971–79, and 1983–87. Wallace ran for president of the United States in 1968 on the American Independent Party ticket and sought the Democratic nomination in 1972. He retired from politics in 1987.

WOULD-BE ASSASSIN: Arthur Herman Bremer was born on August 21, 1950, the fourth of five children, and grew up in a working-class neighborhood in Milwaukee, Wisconsin. His mother, who had been raised in an orphanage, mistrusted the world and often lashed out at her children and husband, a passive truck driver who drank to escape his troubles. The Bremer children were well known to Milwaukee social workers, who described their family as dysfunctional. Arthur Bremer, as a husky, five-foot-seven-inch teenager, had a good high school attendance record and average intelligence, then went on to technical school to study photography. Although he seemed to be a normal young man, he had no friends and was avoided by girls, who thought he was strange, angry, and erratic. By age twenty-one, Bremer was living alone in his own rented apartment and working part-time as a busboy at the Milwaukee Athletic Club and as a janitor at an elementary school. There he attracted the attention of a fifteen-year-old girl who served as a school monitor. They dated briefly, but she became disturbed by his interest in pornography, his prying questions, and his strange behavior in public. One time, at a rock concert, he kissed an unknown girl and applauded and yelled at all the wrong moments. When she decided Bremer was "childish" and "weird" and dumped him in January of 1972, it became a turning point in his life. He shaved his head, bought a .38-caliber revolver, and began keeping a diary, which became a record of his violent thoughts and attempts to manifest them. Soon Bremer quit his job and, according to his diary, devised plans to assassinate a politician.

HISTORY: Bremer was arrested for the first time in his life on November 18, 1971. While he sat in the 1967 Rambler he had purchased for $800 two months earlier, a police officer approached because he was parked in a NO PARKING zone. He saw ammunition on the seat next to Bremer and questioned him about the boxes of bullets. Bremer showed the officer the .38 revolver he had purchased in January. Originally charged with carrying a concealed weapon, Bremer was able to get the charges reduced to disorderly conduct, but the police department confiscated his gun. Undeterred, Bremer went out and bought two new guns: another .38 revolver and a 9-millimeter, 14-shot, semiautomatic Browning pistol.

On March 1, 1972, Bremer attended an organizational meeting for presidential candidate George Wallace at the Pfister Hotel in Milwaukee.

On March 23, he showed up at a Wallace rally and a twenty-five-dollar-per-plate benefit dinner at the Downtowner. Bremer attended a rally for Hubert Humphrey on April 3, and the next day he was at a Wallace victory party in the ballroom of the Holiday Inn Midtown.

Then Bremer took his political campaign stops out of state. In April he traveled to Canada, stayed in the pricey Lord Elgin Hotel in Ottawa, and made half a dozen attempts to get close to Nixon during a state visit. The president's tight security discouraged Bremer, who wrote in his diary: "My fuse about bernt. There's gona be an explosion soon. I had it. I want something to happen. I sopposed to be dead a week & a day ago. Or at least in a few hours. F————-ten-of-1,000s of people & tens-of-millions of $. I'd just like to take some of them with me & Nixy."

On April 7 and 8, Bremer stayed at the exclusive Waldorf-Astoria Hotel in New York, where Hubert Humphrey was also staying. From April 15 through 18 Bremer stayed at the Sheraton Motor Inn in New Carrollton, Maryland. On May 10, he was at a Wallace Rally in Cadillac, Michigan, where he sat beside an unidentified, neatly dressed, forty-year-old man. Bremer was next seen at a Wallace rally in Landover, Maryland, and one in Kalamazoo, Michigan, where he stayed at the Reid Hotel on May 12 and 13. Time and again, Bremer's photograph was taken with George Wallace on his campaign through Michigan and Maryland.

Bremer considered going after Democratic presidential candidate George McGovern but finally confided to his diary, "I've decided Wallace will have the honor." George Wallace, as governor of Alabama and a long-shot presidential candidate running primarily on a law-and-order platform, must have seemed more accessible to Bremer, who didn't know that after Robert Kennedy's assassination four years earlier, presidential candidates had been given Secret Service protection.

EVENT: On the warm and humid afternoon of May 15, 1972, George Wallace delivered a campaign speech to a crowd assembled in the parking lot adjacent to a Laurel, Maryland, shopping center. Wallace, who was concerned about his personal safety and possible assassination attempts against him, usually spoke from behind a bulletproof podium and wore a bulletproof vest, but this afternoon, because of the weather, he decided not to wear the vest. When Wallace's speech went well, and he was not heckled as he had recently been in Wheaton, Maryland, he decided to step out from behind the bulletproof podium and move around among the people, shaking hands. Standing nearby was Arthur Bremer, wearing Wallace buttons, and red, white, and blue clothing. Bremer caught the candidate's attention by shouting several times, "Hey, George! Hey, George! Over here!" He pushed close to Wallace, managing to squeeze through the ring of bodyguards. As Wallace approached the area of the enthusiastic young man, Bremer suddenly opened fire, hitting Wallace repeatedly. Almost immediately, Bremer was grabbed, but he emptied his weapon during a struggle. Three other people were hit by Bremer's bullets: Captain E. C. Dothard of the Alabama State Highway Patrol, Wallace's personal security officer, sustained a severe chest wound but survived; Secret Service agent Nicholas Zorvas received a serious throat injury; and Dora Thompson, a young volunteer campaign worker, was wounded in the knee.

In the Equitable Trust Bank across the parking lot, Wallace's wife Cornelia heard the shots and rushed to the side of her husband, who was lying on the hot pavement. A medical team quickly arrived, taking Wallace to Holy Cross Hospital in nearby Silver Springs, where he was placed under the care of Dr. Joseph Schanno. Schanno found that Wallace had been shot at least four times. Two bullets were recovered during immediate emergency surgery, which was able to control hemorrhaging and repair damage to Wallace's intestines and intestinal ligaments. His chest cavity was perforated by a bullet, and a bullet was lodged near his spinal column. Although Wallace survived the shooting, he was paralyzed from the waist down.

PUNISHMENT: Arthur Bremer was roughly taken away from the scene of the shooting by state and local police officials. Police searched Bremer's Milwaukee apartment and found substantial evidence that the would-be assassin had been in a murderous state of mind. In Bremer's three messy rooms were boxes of bullets, a booklet entitled *101 Things to Do in Jail*, and a newspaper article about the difficulty of providing protection for politicians. Bremer's decrepit 1967 Rambler Rebel contained binoculars, a radio that could listen in on police frequencies, a Browning 9-millimeter semiautomatic pistol, and two books about Sirhan Sirhan, Senator Robert Kennedy's assassin.

Arthur Bremer never explained his motive for shooting George Wallace, and at his trial, defense attorneys argued that he was insane and therefore not culpable. The jury didn't agree, finding Bremer guilty of assault with intent to murder. Before his sentencing, the judge asked Bremer if he wanted to make a statement. "Looking back on my life," he said, "I would have liked it if society had protected me." Bremer was sentenced to sixty-three years in prison.

In 1979, Maryland State Penitentiary warden George Collins described Bremer as a loner and said, "Bremer does not give interviews. In fact, he won't even see his mother. She came in all the way from Milwaukee at Christmas, and he talked to her for about five minutes and went on back down inside. He just doesn't want to be bothered."

AFTERMATH: In addition to not being able to walk again, George Wallace could not continue his presidential campaign, despite impressive primary wins in Michigan and, after the shooting, in Maryland, Tennessee, North Carolina, and Florida. Although he had been campaigning to win the Democratic nomination at the time of the assassination attempt, it was no secret that he intended to run for president of the United States as an American Independent if he was not nominated by the Democrats.

After being shot, Wallace changed his anti-integrationist position and later was elected governor of Alabama again, this time with the overwhelming support of Alabama blacks.

CONSPIRACY THEORIES: When evidence of Bremer's activities before he shot Wallace was presented during his trial, conspiracy theorists—perhaps suspicious of any political assassination attempt in light of the events of the sixties—believed there were too many unanswered questions.

During the eighteen weeks that Bremer stalked the political candidates on their campaign trails, he ran up bills totaling $5,000 and was able to pay them despite earning only $1,611 during 1971 and 1972. How did the unemployed part-time janitor's assistant and busboy come up with that kind of money? Many felt it was obvious that Bremer had resources other than his own. It was established that his parents did not give him any of the money he used during his travels or spent for the guns, ammunition, clothes, and records that were found in his apartment after his arrest. At that time, Bremer claimed to be worth about three hundred dollars.

Other questions arose about his activities. Although Bremer was described time and again as a loner by people who knew him and in a *Life* magazine article, other sources said he was constantly in the company of several individuals just prior to the assassination attempt. One of those individuals was identified as Dennis Cassini, but before Cassini could be questioned by officials, he was found dead of a heroin overdose, his body locked in the trunk of his automobile. Milwaukee officials reported this incident to the FBI, but no attempt was made by federal authorities, then under the direction of L. Patrick Gray, to investigate the matter further.

Bremer was also seen in the waiting room of the Chesapeake and Ohio Ferry in Ludington, Michigan, with an older, heavy-set gentleman with a "New Joisey" brogue. Reportedly, Roger Gordon, a former member of a government intelligence agency called the Secret Army Organization (SAO), identified Bremer's ferry contact as Anthony Ulasewicz, a White House operative who would become well known in the Watergate hearings, then leave the United States.

It was also reported that within an hour after Bremer shot Wallace, Charles W. Colson ordered E. Howard Hunt (also players in the Watergate scandal) to break into Bremer's apartment and plant Black Panther party newspapers and Angela Davis literature. The Colson assignment was allegedly carried out by an employee of a small news service. Later, in testimony before the Senate committee investigating Watergate, Hunt said that Colson had hinted that Hunt might want to "review the contents of Bremer's apartment." Further, it was reported that Colson was acting on direct orders from Richard Nixon, but Colson denied making any such suggestion.

When George Wallace was interviewed by Barbara Walters of the *Today* show in reference to the break-in at Bremer's apartment, the governor said, "So I just wondered, if that were the case, how did anyone know where he lived within an hour after I was shot?"

The break-in development led conspiracy theorists to say that knowledge of the suspect's identity and the location of his apartment so soon after the shooting could also indicate prior knowledge of the incident. Perhaps Bremer was not the loner he was made out to be, but was in collusion with some other party or parties in his attempt to assassinate George Wallace.

Many wonder if the assassination attempt on Wallace was engineered to eliminate him from the 1972 presidential race, in which he was certain to run as a third-party candidate. Wallace, who had nearly caused Richard Nixon to lose the 1968 presidential election, was more popular than ever in 1972, when his political message had become mainstream: law and order, hostility toward welfare, middle-class tax breaks, and reliance on "common folks" instead of Washington bureaucrats to return the country to moral values. A week before the election, when voters were asked how they would vote if Wallace was on the ballot, the results were Nixon 44 percent, McGovern 41 percent, and Wallace 15 percent. If that had actually happened, deciding the election would have gone to the House of Representatives, where Wallace supposedly was very influential. But with Wallace out of the running, virtually all his votes went to President Nixon.

MARCH 15, 1975

KING FAISAL (1905–1975)
KING OF SAUDI ARABIA FROM 1964 TO 1975

The illustrious career of Faisal Ibn Abdul Aziz greatly enriched his country diplomatically as well as financially. As the fourth son of King Saud, Faisal played a visible role within his country from an early age. He was given his first public assignment at age fourteen, when he was sent to Britain by his father as head of a delegation to congratulate the Allies on their victory in World War I. By age twenty-two, he had served as a courageous participant in the military reconquest of Arab territories lost during the war and had become viceroy of the province of Hejaz, where Mecca is located. In 1945, Faisal was Saudi Arabia's representative when it became a member of the United Nations. Although his brother King Saud was Arabia's official ruler until 1964, when he abdicated because of his declining health, Faisal served as its effective ruler from 1958. Faisal used all his influence and dedicated billions of dollars to the Arab alliance in the 1967 war against Israel. He fought against the atheistic intrusion of democratic and socialistic ideas during his reign, while promoting oil production and economic development. The great wealth amassed by his country during this time mostly benefited the more than three thousand members of the pampered Saud ruling family and did nothing to help the common people.

Despite all of King Faisal's wealth, success, and acclaim, in the end, philosophical and religious differences within his own family resulted in his murder.

ASSASSIN: Prince Faisal Musad Abdel Aziza, a nephew of King Faisal.

HISTORY: Prince Musad, the exiled brother of King Faisal, had two sons, Prince Khalid and Prince Faisal. In 1966, Prince Khalid learned that his uncle, King Faisal, planned to establish a new television station which would broadcast the human image. The Saudi royal family had always accepted the fundamentalist Wahhabi sect's strict interpretation of the Koran, which specifically banned projection of the human image, and Khalid was determined to stop this blasphemous abomination in his homeland. He gathered together a group of armed extremists and, as they stormed the television station, Prince Khalid was killed by King Faisal's police.

At the same time, Khalid's brother, eighteen-year-old Prince Faisal, was living the life of a wealthy playboy while getting an education in the United States. He first attended San Francisco State University, then moved to Boulder in 1969 and attended the University of Colorado. There, at age twenty-one, he was arrested for selling LSD but spent little time in jail. He was released after confessing to the crime and moved back to California, where he attended the University of California at Berkeley. By that time, Prince Faisal had become Westernized; he wore his hair long, dressed in Western-style clothing, and openly associated with militant Arab students who believed that King Faisal, as absolute monarch, was keeping Saudi Arabia from becoming a twentieth-century world power with his antiquated style of rule. The prince returned to his homeland inspired by these beliefs and determined to see that some changes were made.

EVENT: At 9:50 A.M., March 25, 1975, a celebration was being held to honor the 1,405th birthday of the Prophet Mohammed. A visiting delegation from Kuwait formed a reception line inside King Faisal's spectacular palace in Riyadh, the Saudi capital, and were greeted, one by one, by the sixty-nine-year-old monarch. Also in the reception line was the twenty-seven-year-old Arabian Prince Faisal, his long hair and Western-style clothing hidden underneath a flowing headdress and traditional white robe. As he approached, King Faisal immediately recognized his nephew and lowered his imperial head so that his nephew could kiss the tip of the king's nose, according to custom.

Instead of honoring his uncle, the prince reached inside his robe, pulled out a pistol, and shot King Faisal in the face three times. The first shot went through the king's brain and killed him instantly. Palace guards grabbed the prince and took him away as he shouted, "Now my brother is avenged!"

PUNISHMENT: At first Prince Faisal was declared deranged. He was to be locked away for life, because no member of the royal family had ever been executed—the usual punishment for murder. If the king's murder had been considered an act of vengeance within the royal family, the prince probably would not have been put to death. But investigators discovered that the young prince had been outspoken in his view that his uncle was standing in the way of the development of his country. Only by killing the king, Prince Faisal had said, could the path of progress be opened up by making room for more liberal and Westernized heirs to take power. Since politics was viewed to be Prince Faisal's motive for assassinating his uncle, his punishment was invoked according to the Koran's injunction "A soul for a soul." As ruler of the sandy medieval kingdom that guards Mecca, King Faisal was above all the chief defender of Islam, and his murder was considered an attack upon the entire faith.

In late June, an Islamic religious court declared Prince Faisal guilty and condemned him to be publicly beheaded for the murder of his uncle, King Faisal. As the prince was brought before the public in front of the Great Mosque of Riyadh, faithful Islamic scholars looked on, shaking their heads knowingly. Obviously the prince's actions were the product of too much travel and foreign influence. If he had not been sent to America—just two years after slavery was abolished in Saudi Arabia—he would not have gotten a heretic-tainted education, he would not have smoked marijuana and sold LSD, and he would not have conspired with exiled Arab militants, or assassinated his uncle.

A crowd gathered in the public square to watch as Prince Faisal was forced down onto his knees in the dirty sand and prodded upright with a sharp stick. An enormous golden-hilted sword was held ready, then, with one swift stroke, the young prince was beheaded. A sharpened stake was ready. His head was stuck atop it, and it was displayed for all the people to see before he was buried in wastelands nearby.

AFTERMATH: King Faisal was succeeded by his brother Khalid. During his eleven-year reign, until 1982, King Khalid maintained the relatively moderate policies of King Faisal, especially within the Organization of Petroleum Exporting Countries (OPEC).

 SEPTEMBER 5, 1975

GERALD R. FORD (1913–)
THIRTY-EIGHTH PRESIDENT OF THE UNITED STATES, FROM 1974 TO 1977

Gerald Ford became president when Richard Nixon resigned during the Watergate scandal. Ford was the first vice president in U.S. history to assume the presidency because the chief executive had resigned. He was also the first person to become president without being elected to either the office of vice president or president. In 1973, when Spiro T. Agnew was forced to resign his position as vice president, President Nixon appointed Gerald Ford to replace him. Until that time, Ford had served for twenty-five years in the Congress, the last nine of them as Republican minority leader. During Ford's term as president, there were two notable attempts to assassinate him, one on September 5, 1975, and another on September 22, 1975.

ATTEMPT OF SEPTEMBER 5, 1975
WOULD-BE ASSASSIN: Lynette Alice "Squeaky" Fromme, a twenty-six-year-old member of cult leader Charles Manson's so-called "murder family," was the first woman to directly try to kill a U.S. president. Fromme became a public figure in 1969, as a fringe member of the Manson family, when she shaved her head, carved a cross on her forehead and appeared in the courtroom with three other similarly transfigured Manson followers

at his trial for the vicious Beverly Hills murder of actress Sharon Tate and six others.

By 1975, Fromme had a long FBI record, as did all the suspected Manson family members. She had been arrested several times on charges ranging from drug possession to murder, but was convicted only once. In 1971 she received a ninety-day jail sentence, along with three other "family members," for trying to keep a witness from testifying in the Tate murder trial by doctoring a hamburger with the hallucinogenic drug LSD. Fromme had been one of Manson's most vocal out-of-court defenders during his trial, and a spokeswoman for those who were left of the group afterward. When Manson was transferred to San Quentin prison, Fromme made veiled threats against the judge's children and blamed political leaders for Manson's conviction.

EVENT: On the morning of September 5, 1975, Lynette Fromme, wearing a long robe, stood among the large group of well-wishers lining the route that President Gerald Ford was to take from his Sacramento hotel to the state capitol, where he was scheduled to speak against crime. When Ford strolled past, Fromme stepped up not more than two feet from him and pointed a Colt .45-automatic pistol at his stomach, saying "This country is in a mess. This man is not your president." As Fromme squeezed the trigger, Larry Buendorf, an alert and courageous Secret Service agent, jumped between Ford and Fromme, grabbed the gun and put the webbing between his thumb and forefinger on the gun to block the hammer. "It didn't go off, fellas, it didn't go off," Fromme chirped as agents knocked her down and handcuffed her. "Can you believe it? It didn't go off." As Fromme was shoved against a nearby tree, she shouted over and over, "He is not a public servant! He is not a public servant!"

Although President Ford was not shot, eyewitnesses said his face drained of color during the incident. The Secret Service agent's hand was cut when he seized the gun, apparently by the cocked hammer.

PUNISHMENT: At her trial, Fromme explained, "I just wanted to get some attention for Charlie and the girls." On December 17, 1975, when she was found guilty and sentenced to life in prison, Fromme threw herself on the courtroom floor and screamed, "You animals!"

AFTERMATH: On December 23, 1987, thirty-nine-year-old Lynette Fromme managed to escape from the Federal Correctional Institution for Women at Alderson, West Virginia. Her escape triggered a nationwide alert by law enforcement officials, as well as sensational media coverage saying she could be a threat to former President Ford. Fromme was captured some forty hours later as she walked along a country road only two miles from the prison on Christmas Day.

ATTEMPT OF SEPTEMBER 22, 1975

WOULD-BE ASSASSIN: Sara Jane Moore, known as Sally to friends and family, was a forty-five-year-old suburban matron whose private life has been described as "deprived." She was married five times (twice to the same man) and had four children, three of whom she allowed her parents in West Virginia to adopt. In 1975, Moore was living in San Francisco's Mission District, where working-class families mingled uncomfortably with young radicals. Although Moore had worked as a bookkeeper the year before, supporting her nine-year-old son, she suddenly left that job to work for a food-giveaway program set up in response to demands made by the Symbionese Liberation Army, a left-wing militant group who had kidnapped publishing heiress Patty Hearst. Moore told anyone who would listen that God had spoken directly to her, telling her to feed the needy with the Hearst family's goods. When Moore was fired from that job, she went to the FBI, informing agents that she had contacts with underground radicals, and would be an ideal undercover agent and informant. Allegedly, the FBI believed her and put Moore on its list of informers; Moore was acting as an informant for both the FBI and local police, and she ingratiated herself with the leftists she spied on. Although Moore thought she was accepted by both sides, in time she began to believe the leftists got wise to her FBI activities. Fearing for her life, she asked to be taken into protective custody, but when the FBI said no, she felt betrayed by everyone. With her feelings of isolation doubled, Moore saw news reports about Lynette Fromme's attempted assassination of the president and was inspired. Still, Moore supposedly returned to her role as an informer. She had a contact with the local police and was also doing some work for the Federal Bureau of Alcohol, Tobacco and Firearms.

On Sunday afternoon, September 21, 1975, the day President Ford was starting a San Francisco Bay Area visit, the police had reason to check on Moore and see if she had a weapon. They found her carrying an unloaded .44 revolver in her purse, and in her home they found two boxes of ammunition. Moore was arrested for carrying a concealed weapon, a misdemeanor under state law. Her gun was taken, and the police notified the Secret Service. Although an agent interrogated Moore later that day, apparently the fact that she was an informer for the police and a federal agency caused the Secret Service to let her go. When later questioned about releasing Moore after she was detained, police said that even though it had been less than three weeks since Fromme's attempt to shoot Ford, the Secret Service felt Moore "was not of sufficient protection interest to warrant surveillance."

On Monday, September 22, Moore dropped off her son at school, then drove to Danville, where she paid $145 for a .38-caliber Smith & Wesson pistol. She loaded the gun with bullets while she drove back into town across the San Francisco–Oakland Bay Bridge. Then Moore went to the St. Francis Hotel.

EVENT: At 3:29 P.M., when President Ford walked out of the St. Francis and stopped to wave at a crowd of about three thousand people who had gathered to catch a glimpse of him, Sara Jane Moore was waiting forty feet away. She raised the gun to a firing position and took aim at Ford, but as she fired, thirty-three-year-old Oliver Sipple, a former marine and an alert bystander, spotted Moore and grabbed her arm, deflecting the shot. The bullet missed Ford, ricocheted off a wall, and wounded a nearby cabdriver, who suffered a minor groin injury.

President Ford was hustled into a waiting limousine and immediately taken to San Francisco International Airport to board Air Force One and return to Washington, D.C.

PUNISHMENT: As Moore was taken to jail, handcuffed and bleeding, she told a reporter, "There comes a point when the only way you can make a statement is to pick up a gun." In custody, Moore said if the president had been any later coming out of the hotel, she would have had to leave "to pick up my boy" at school. Showing no remorse for her actions, she also said, "If I had had my .44 I would have caught him."

As in the case of Lynette Fromme, no assassination conspiracy was discovered, and Sara Jane Moore's actions were attributed to an attempt to solve a personal dilemma and relieve a sense of rejection with a startling political act.

Moore pleaded guilty to attempted murder and was sentenced to life in prison. She was sent to the Federal Correctional Institution for Women at Alderson, West Virginia, the same place as Fromme.

AFTERMATH: In 1980, Sara Jane Moore told reporters that her assassination attempt was a "valid political tool" and that her current ambition was to devote herself to writing and speaking.

NOVEMBER 27, 1975

ROSS McWHIRTER (1925–1975)
COEDITOR OF *THE GUINNESS BOOK*
OF WORLD RECORDS

Born to Scottish parents in Great Britain on August 12, 1925, Ross and his twin brother Norris were always fascinated by facts and read scores of newspapers every week. They were inseparable until World War II, when Norris was assigned to a minesweeper in the Pacific, while Ross served in the Mediterranean. After the war, they formed McWhirter Twins and did research for encyclopedias, periodicals, and other publications. In 1955, they were approached by an employee of Sir Hugh Beaver, managing director of the Guinness brewery, who asked if they would compile a book of records that could be used to settle pub disputes. The first edition of *The Guinness Book of Records* ("World" was later added to the title) was published that year. By the 1960s, when a new edition was published every year, the book had become popular in the United States, and by 1994 it reached worldwide sales of 74 million copies in twenty-nine languages.

Obtaining fascinating information was not Ross McWhirter's only interest. He considered himself a libertarian who "liked to see the laws kept," and while monitoring events in his native country, he initiated nine court cases (only one was related to himself personally) between 1954 and 1973, winning all but one. He also was a vocal opponent of the violent tactics of the Irish Republican Army (IRA), founding an organization called Self Help. Its goals were to have the death penalty reinstated for terrorists and to require all Irish Republic nationals living in England to register and carry identity cards.

Convinced that the British government was not doing enough to bring to justice the IRA terrorist bombers plaguing London, Ross McWhirter published a pamphlet entitled *How to Stop the Bombers*. He offered a fifty-thousand-pound reward for information leading to the capture of members of an IRA death squad believed to be responsible for eight car bombings that resulted in the deaths of eight civilians. Telling reporters he might be writing his own obituary soon, McWhirter said, "I live . . . in constant fear of my life. I know the IRA have got me on their death list."

ASSASSINS: Irish Republican Army terrorists. The declared policy of the decades-old armed-force wing of the Irish Republican movement is to force the withdrawal of the British from Northern Ireland and create a united Ireland even against the wishes of the Protestant majority in the north. In the late 1960s, the almost defunct IRA was given a new lease on life when the largely Roman Catholic civil rights campaign in Northern Ireland flared into open warfare, with Protestant hard-liners trying to stage pogroms against Catholics in Belfast and Londonderry. By 1970, there was a falling-out among various factions of the IRA, which led to a division of forces and philosophies: the Marxist-inclined "Official" IRA and the traditionalist "Provisional" IRA, the much larger of the two groups. The PIRA, which did not like the socialist policies of the OIRA, kept itself separate and embarked on campaigns to carry out the IRA's original mandate by means of violent bombings and shooting campaigns against the British and the Protestants.

HISTORY: The chance murder of Gordon Hamilton Fairley, on October 23, 1975, moved McWhirter to start the reward-for-capture campaign, which he called "Beat the Bombers," against the IRA. Fairley, a researcher of world repute who was a cancer specialist in charge of tumor research at Long's St. Bartholomew's Hospital, was the unintended victim of a car-bomb explosion as he walked through his neighborhood. The device had been planted in the vehicle of the actual target, Fairley's neighbor, Hugh Fraser, a Conservative member of Parliament, who was outspoken against terrorism. At the time of the explosion, Caroline Kennedy, the daughter of the assassinated U.S. president John F. Kennedy, was a Fraser houseguest. The blast occurred just as Fraser and Kennedy were about to leave the house to enter the car. Fraser's neighbor, Gordon Hamilton Fairley, was killed.

EVENT: On November 27, 1975, two gunmen hid in the garden of Ross McWhirter's home in Village Lane, England. When McWhirter's wife came home and approached the front door, McWhirter opened the door to greet her, leaving himself silhouetted against the light. At that moment, the assassins opened fire, shooting McWhirter in the head and elsewhere in his body. The assassins' aim was good; McWhirter's wife was not shot.

Ross McWhirter was rushed to the hospital, where he died.

PUNISHMENT: On December 6, four members of the IRA gang that authorities believed was responsible for McWhirter's assassination were chased to a London flat in Balcombe Street. There, they took hostages and held police at bay during a six-day siege, but they were finally apprehended. The four men, all in their twenties, were identified as Martin O'Connell, Harry Duggan, Edward Butler, and Hugh Doherty. They were convicted of murdering nine people, including Fairley, and wounding two hundred others in their bombing and shooting campaign, and sentenced to life in prison.

AFTERMATH: In June of 1980, information provided by the four terrorists led police to Ireland, where they arrested Brian Paschal Keenan, a.k.a. "Z," who was regarded as the mastermind of the IRA's London bombing campaign. Keenan was convicted of lesser charges of conspiring to cause explosives to endanger life and plotting to possess firearms. He was sentenced to serve eighteen years in prison.

After Ross McWhirter's death, his brother Norris continued his successful career as editor of *The Guinness Book of World Records* until 1986, when he gave up the position of editor but stayed on as an editorial adviser.

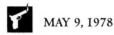 MAY 9, 1978

ALDO MORO (1916–1978)
ITALIAN STATESMAN AND CHRISTIAN DEMOCRAT; PRIME MINISTER FROM 1963 TO 1968, AND 1974 TO 1976

Born in Maglie, the son of a teacher, Aldo Moro was educated at the University of Bari, where he became active in the Catholic University Federation. After earning his Ph.D. in law in 1940, Moro taught criminal law at the university, becoming a professor at the age of twenty-four. He helped to establish a Christian Democrat Party (CDP) in Apulia toward the end of World War II, and was elected to the constituent assembly as a member of the CDP in 1946. In 1948, he was appointed undersecretary of state for foreign affairs. He became minister of justice in 1955 and minister of education in 1957. Two years later he became political secretary of the CDP, then succeeded Amintore Fanfani as prime minister in 1963. That year he assembled a left-of-center coalition of Christian Democrats, Socialists, Social Democrats, and Republicans. In 1976, he laid the groundwork for parliamentary cooperation between the Christian Democrats and the Communists. As one of Italy's leading politicians, Aldo Moro was expected to be named the next president of Italy.

ASSASSINS: Members of the urban guerrilla group the Red Brigade (Brigate Rosse), one of the largest European left-wing groups to grow out of the failure of the New Left in the late 1960s. Some say the Red Brigade also had roots in the old established Communist party of Italy. Believed to have had contacts with most of the main European and Middle Eastern terrorist groups, the Red Brigade specialized in kidnapping and murdering Italian judges, politicians, and businessmen. Its operations began in 1974 under the intellectual leadership of one of the most dangerous European terrorist organizers, Renato Curcio, and his wife, Margherita Cagol (who was killed in a shooting in 1975). When Curcio was arrested in January 1976, the Red Brigade tried to force the Italian government to release him by mounting a campaign of murder and intimidation, but after a lengthy and highly publicized trial, in 1978 Curcio was sentenced to life in prison, along with a number of his colleagues.

EVENT: On March 16, 1978, Aldo Moro was being driven through Rome under heavy escort when he was ambushed by a squad of eleven Red Brigade terrorists wearing stolen Alitalia airline uniforms. The terrorists had prepared the ambush site the day before, slashing all four tires of a florist's pickup truck usually parked at the intersection during business hours, so that it would not be in that location the next day. They drove out of a side street, blocked Moro's oncoming convoy, and opened fire with automatic weapons. During the attack, four of Moro's bodyguards were killed and another was mortally wounded. When the attack had ended, the terrorists had kidnapped the sixty-one-year-old former prime minister.

Italian authorities learned that the terrorists were using Moro as a bargaining chip when they received telephone messages demanding the release of the fourteen Red Brigade leaders who were among the defendants in a mass trial of terrorists being conducted in Turin. Instead of complying with the terrorists' demands, a total of fifteen thousand police and six thousand troops were deployed in a manhunt centering on Rome. They were not successful. Moro's kidnappers then released photographs of Moro being held captive and announced that he would be tried by their own "people's court."

During the nearly two months Moro was held, he was subjected to continual psychological harassment by his captors, who prompted him to write letters pleading for his life and, later, urging the government to accede to the terrorists' demands because he was afraid he might betray state secrets under torture. On April 4, a letter from Moro was sent to newspapers. In it, he called on Premier Guilio Andreotti and other Christian Democratic leaders to take quick action, saying he felt "a little abandoned by all of you." At the time the letter was delivered, Andreotti was announcing in parliament that he would continue taking a hard-line position against any negotiations with the kidnappers. It was obvious that the kidnappers were trying to produce chaos and friction within the ruling coalition, and hoping Moro's distraught family and friends would increase pressure on the government.

The manhunt by authorities was complicated by numerous telephone calls falsely announcing Moro's execution. Still not getting what they wanted, on April 18 the terrorists issued a letter with a photograph proving Moro was still alive by having him pose with a newspaper dated the day before. The letter said that the government had forty-eight hours to release its Red Brigade prisoners or Moro would die. Despite divided opinions about what they should do, government officials refused to strike a deal.

On May 5, the terrorists sent another message, this time saying they were carrying out Moro's execution because of the government's refusal to negotiate. On May 7, Aldo Moro sent a farewell letter to his wife, saying, "They have told me they are going to kill me in a little while."

Despite all the terrorists' threats, the public was shocked when it learned that on May 9 Aldo Moro's body was found in a car parked a short distance between the Christian Democratic and Communist parties' headquarters. Moro had been shot eleven times.

PUNISHMENT: On June 5 and 6, eight members of the Red Brigade were charged with kidnapping and murdering Aldo Moro. The Italian police investigation was assisted by two members of the British Army's Special Air Service (SAS). Later in the year, police raids in Milan uncovered documentary evidence of Moro's captivity and "trial" before the Red Brigade's "people's court." Also found were papers in which Moro supposedly described corruption inside the Italian government, but because they were obviously written under duress, their publication had little political effect.

In January of 1983, almost five years after Aldo Moro's assassination, thirty-two Red Brigade terrorists were convicted and sentenced to life imprisonment. Among them were Moro's accused executioner, thirty-three-year-old Prospero Gallinari, and nine women. The defendants had been betrayed by some of their comrades, who were given lesser sentences in exchange for their cooperation. One of those sentenced to life was Laura Braghetti, who had been named as Moro's keeper during his captivity. She screamed at Antonio Savasta, an informer-terrorist confined in a separate cage, "You bastard, you would even sell your mother!"

AFTERMATH: Aldo Moro's kidnapping and assassination provoked a political crisis in Italy, prompting the resignation of the interior minister. The July 8 election of socialist Sandro Martini, eighty-one years old, as president assured continued cooperation between Italy's Communists and the Roman Catholic Christian Democrats.

As political chaos persisted in Italy, a split occurred between members of the Red Brigade; many thought they should have freed Moro on the grounds that returning him unharmed would have added to the embarrassment of the ruling political parties. Additionally, a dissident faction of the terrorist group criticized the leadership for focusing on attacking eminent individuals instead of trying to broaden support for radical social change.

Later, a document was smuggled out of the prison where many of the Red Brigade terrorists were confined. Printed by the newspaper La Republica, with the headline, THE ARMED STRUGGLE IS OVER, the document said, "The phase of revolutionary struggle which started in the early 1970s . . . is substantially finished." It also said that the armed struggle was "short-circuited" and advised comrades to "seek new means of revolution."

Although many believed that members of the terrorist group had recognized that assassination was of limited value in bringing down the establishment, by 1982 it was estimated that the Red Brigade had killed fifty people, kidnapped another fifty, and cost the Italian state around $90 million in damages.

AUGUST 27, 1979

LOUIS MOUNTBATTEN (1900–1979)
MEMBER OF THE BRITISH ROYAL FAMILY, STATESMAN, AND ADMIRAL

Louis Mountbatten, earl of Burma, was born on June 25, 1900, at Frogmore House, on the grounds of Windsor Castle. He was the son of Prince Louis of Battenberg (who took the name Mountbatten during World War I) and Princess Victoria of Hess-Darmstadt, a granddaughter of Queen Victoria, making Mountbatten a second cousin of George VI and an uncle of Prince Philip. At the age of thirteen, Louis entered the Royal Navy as a cadet. He would go on to have an illustrious naval career and was continually promoted because of his bravery and courage, until finally he reached the rank of admiral. In 1922 he married Edwina Ashley, an heiress whose grandfather, Sir Ernest Cassel, had been financial adviser to Edward VII. The couple had two daughters. During World War II, Mountbatten was a prominent British naval leader; he was appointed governor-general of India in 1947. In that position he made what was perhaps the only mistaken judgment of his career when he negotiated the partition of the subcontinent into the two independent nations of India and Pakistan. This resulted in an explosively confrontational structure between Pakistan's Muslims and India's Hindus. Still, he served as governor-general of India in 1947 and 1948, before retiring to his native England. Beginning in 1953, he served as a personal aide-de-camp to Queen Elizabeth.

ASSASSINS: Irish Republican Army terrorists.

HISTORY: Lord Mountbatten spent one month each summer at Classiebawn, his turreted stone castle in Mullaghmore, County Sligo, Ireland. The castle was located only twelve miles from Northern Ireland, in an area well known as a refuge for Provos (members of the Provisional

IRA) who were fleeing across the border. Despite that, and the fact that
the IRA reinstituted its campaign of terrorism against Britain in 1969,
Lord Mountbatten refused the maximum security protection offered to
him by the queen. Eventually, he also asked the Sligo police to withdraw
the discreet watch they kept on his castle, saying it was a waste of public
funds. "What would they want with an old man like me?" he asked.

EVENT: At 11:30 A.M. on August 27, 1979, seventy-nine-year-old Lord
Mountbatten and several members of the British royal family set out
from Classiebawn for their ritual fishing holiday in Donegal Bay, aboard
Mountbatten's unimposing yacht, *Shadow V.* As they sailed into the bay
to inspect lobster pots Mountbatten had set that week, about a few hundred yards from the coast, people on the beach suddenly heard a tremendous roar. The *Shadow V* had been blown apart, its passengers hurled
into the water. Some accounts say a radio fuse bomb had been planted in
the craft's engine room. Others say the bomb was hidden in a lobster pot.
Either way, the radio signal that exploded the bomb came from a clifftop
overlooking the bay.

Stunned fishermen arrived at the scene within minutes and began
pulling bodies and survivors from the oil and bloodstained water. Lord
Mountbatten's fourteen-year-old grandson, Nicholas Knatchbull, and
fifteen-year-old Paul Maxwell, an Ulster boat boy, were floating facedown in the water, dead. Although Lord Mountbatten was still alive, his
legs had been nearly torn off. The fishermen dragged him into one of
their boats, where he died within minutes.

Four other people aboard the vessel were badly injured: Lady
Brabourne, Mountbatten's daughter, and her husband, Lord Brabourne;
Timothy Knatchbull, Nicholas's twin brother; and the Dowager Lady
Brabourne, the mother of Mountbatten's son-in-law. By the time the
fishermen got the victims to the wharf at Mullaghmore, two Belfast doc-
tors who were on holiday in the area had set up a makeshift aid station.
Ambulances soon arrived and took the wounded to Sligo General
Hospital, where doctors worked through the night to save the Dowager
Lady Brabourne. She died the next morning.

The bodies of Lord Mountbatten, his grandson Nicholas Knatchbull, and the Dowager Lady Brabourne were flown to Broadlands, Mountbatten's Hampshire estate. There they would lie in state until Mountbatten's state funeral. The funeral, which he had planned in specific detail to be a happy event, was held in Westminster Abby.

PUNISHMENT: Within hours of the Mountbatten killing, an alert Irish police officer stopped a car for a routine check and became suspicious when the driver and a passenger seemed extremely nervous. Francis McGirl, the driver, who was a twenty-four-year-old farmer, and his passenger, Thomas McMahon, who was a member of the Provos, were taken into custody on suspicion of being members of the IRA. Eventually McGirl was acquitted, but there was substantial forensic evidence against McMahon. Traces of nitroglycerin were found on his clothing; sand on his boots was identified as coming from the slipway at Mullaghmore, where Mountbatten's boat had been berthed; and flakes of green paint on his boots matched that of the hull of the *Shadow V*. McMahon was convicted of Mountbatten's assassination and sentenced to life in prison with no appeal.

AFTERMATH: Queen Elizabeth, who deeply loved Lord Mountbatten, was immediately notified of the murders; she and other members of the British royal family were devastated, especially Prince Charles, who had an exceedingly close relationship with his uncle.

On the day Lord Mountbatten was assassinated, there were numerous bombings in a multiple assault planned by a faction of the IRA. At Warrenpoint, just inside the Ulster border, a bomb planted in a hay wagon was detonated as a three-ton army truck came near. The truck was thrown across the road by the blast, killing six British paratroopers inside. Another bomb exploded in a nearby gatehouse, killing British colonel David Blair, eleven of his men, and wounding several others. When the stunned soldiers opened fire on two British tourists who had innocently stopped by to see what had happened; one was killed, and the other was wounded.

The next day a bomb exploded near a bandstand at the Grand Palace in Brussels, where the British military band was scheduled to play in celebration of the Belgian capital's millennium. Four band members and twelve spectators were injured by the blast.

Within days the Provos released a statement saying, "The IRA claim responsibility for the execution of Lord Mountbatten. . . . This operation is one of the discriminate ways we can bring to the attention of the English people the continuing occupation of our country." They also declared that the British army had acknowledged that it could not defeat the IRA, "yet it continues with the oppression of our people and the torture of our comrades in H Block"—a reference to the group of prison cells where IRA members were being held. And "for this we will tear out their sentimental imperialist hearts."

Further investigation indicated the reason why Provos had selected Mountbatten as a target for their assassination team, which included McMahon. They wanted to one-up a rival splinter group, the Irish National Liberation Army (INLA), which had assassinated British Tory member of Parliament Airey Neave the previous March. Neave's assassination had gotten the INLA considerable publicity and, for the first time, recognition outside the Republic of Ireland. Mountbatten was assassinated because of terrorist rivalries.

 OCTOBER 26, 1979

PARK CHUNG HEE (1917–1979)
PRESIDENT OF SOUTH KOREA FROM 1963 TO 1979

In 1960, the dictatorial regime of Syngman Rhee, the first president of the Republic of Korea (a.k.a. South Korea), was brought down by student-led protests. A democratic regime that followed did not last long, with General Park Chung Hee seizing power in 1961. Because Park's U.S.

supporters insisted on a civilian government, he staged elections but essentially named himself president. He declared martial law in 1972 and forced the adoption of a new constitution, continuing his rule under his terms: All opposition to his government was outlawed, and under his emergency decrees, suspected critics could be arrested without warrants and imprisoned without trial.

President Park's government spared no effort in suppressing dissent by students, religious activists, intellectuals, and workers. Government agents openly followed dissenters, secretly examined their tax records, and watched for signs of disloyalty. Church meetings of suspected dissidents were monitored. And Park established a computerized ID-card system for all citizens.

While Park justified such extreme measures by pointing to a constant threat of communist takeover from the north, the Korean Central Intelligence Agency (KCIA) maintained an estimated thirty thousand domestic agents as well as foreign operations, which guaranteed there would be no opposition to Park's military rule. The KCIA spied on Koreans living abroad and bought influence in the United States and Japan. Although the United States officially deplored Park's constant violations of human rights, American policy makers recognized that his rigid rule was necessary to provide cheap labor for the United States and other foreign corporations and continued to prop up Park's regime militarily and economically. But during 1976 and 1977, the Park government and more than one hundred U.S. congressmen were embarrassed when U.S. news reports exposed illegal activities carried out by Park Tong Sun, a Korean businessman based in Washington, D.C. A popular host of social gatherings in the U.S. capital, Park Tong Sun had made campaign contributions and provided favors to at least 115 members of Congress, chiefly Democrats, while he maintained close ties with leading Republicans. His illegal lobbying is said to have resulted in the passage of controversial military-assistance legislation.

Under Park's rule, South Korea had one of the world's fastest-growing economies, but his regime was dependent, both militarily and economically, on external support. Important backing came from anti-communist right-wing evangelical Protestant organizations, such as the Reverend Sun Myung Moon's Genri Undo sect. The U.S.-based Campus Crusade for Christ staged "Expo '74," an evangelical student congress, in South Korea, drawing several hundred thousand believers. Still, South Korea's economy was controlled by the United States and Japan, with the assistance of the International Monetary Fund, and the United States actually had operational control of the military.

While Park's increasing authoritarianism made his country politically unstable, he tried to reinforce his position with the help of the KCIA. But South Korea's dissatisfied military leaders would prove to be stronger, forcing Park to dismiss the KCIA director in 1973. That same year, the KCIA kidnapped Kim Dae Jung, Park's 1971 presidential opponent, while Kim was in Japan, and smuggled him back into South Korea. Later in 1973, large student demonstrations and a national petition containing hundreds of thousands of signatures called for democracy. In response, Park's regime arrested hundreds of students, journalists, churchmen, and others.

Although the United States may have been unhappy with Park's despotism and probably could have replaced him, it had no desirable alternative.

ASSASSINS: The Korean Central Intelligence Agency (KCIA), masterminded by its director, Kim Jae Kyu.

An attempt to assassinate Park in August of 1974 was generally attributed to North Korean intelligence, but Park's assassination in 1979 was the work of his own intelligence force.

ATTEMPT: On August 15, 1974, President Park Chung Hee was delivering a Liberation Day address to some fifteen hundred people at the National Theater in Seoul when an assailant charged down the center aisle firing a pistol. Standing behind a bulletproof podium that deflected some of the shots, Park was not injured, but Park's wife, Yook Young

Soo, who was sitting on the stage behind her husband, was struck in the head by one of the bullets. A seventeen-year-old girl who was participating in the program was killed by another stray bullet.

The would-be assassin was wounded by return fire from security guards and captured. When the turmoil subsided, while Madame Park was being rushed to the hospital, President Park finished his speech before going to check on his wife, who died six hours after being shot.

The assassin was identified as Mun Se Kwang, a twenty-two-year-old Korean who had been living in Osaka, Japan, and entered South Korea on a false Japanese passport. Mun was a member of the Korean Youth League, a Japan-based anti-Park organization. In October, during his trial, Mun said he had attempted to assassinate Park on orders given to him by two North Korean agents operating in Japan. Further, he said one of the agents, whom he had met while aboard a North Korean cargo ship in Osaka, told him Park's assassination was personally ordered by North Korean president Kim Il Sung. Mun was convicted of murdering Madame Park and was executed on December 10, 1974.

EVENT: On October 4, 1979, South Korean opposition leader King Young Sam was ousted from the National Assembly, and three days later all seventy members of the Assembly had resigned in protest.

KCIA chief Kim Jae Kyu invited President Park Chung Hee to have dinner with him on the night of October 16, 1979, at KCIA headquarters, a two-story annex near the presidential Blue House compound in Seoul. Sitting at a table filled with food in the KCIA dining room, Park and five of his aides, including his chief bodyguard, Cha Chi Chol, were discussing intelligence matters when a violent argument broke out between Kim and Cha over student riots that had occurred in Pusan. Kim, who was afraid he might be dismissed from his post, accused Cha of causing him to lose his standing with President Park.

When things had calmed down, Kim reportedly walked out of the dining room and told two of his men: "I am going to finish them off today, so when you hear gunshots in the dining room, you fellows finish off the security agents outside." Grabbing a pistol, Kim returned to the dining room, then went out again to make sure his men were ready to carry out his plan. He returned once more to the dining room and, according to the testimony of two hostesses who were serving the meal, Kim referred to Cha as "an insect," pulled out his pistol, and opened fire. Cha, who was unarmed and only slightly wounded, escaped into a nearby bathroom. Kim shot President Park in the chest, went to find Cha, who was hiding behind some furniture, shot him in the stomach, then went back and shot Park in the head. Both Park and Cha were dead.

When Kim's men heard the gunshots, which were their signal, they split into two teams. One shot and killed three security guards waiting inside the nearby kitchen while the other team shot and killed a deputy presidential security chief and a security guard in another room.

PUNISHMENT: Initially, authorities in Seoul released a statement saying President Park and his aides had been killed "accidentally," but one of Kim's aides quickly confessed to the assassination. Although some say Kim assassinated Park as part of a military coup and that he planned to establish martial law, one Korean authority insisted Kim had taken his drastic measures only because "he was afraid of losing his job."

On May 24, 1980, Kim Jae Kyu and four members of the KCIA were hanged for the murders of Park and his associates. Park's chief of staff, Kim Kae Won, had also been sentenced to death for taking part in the assassination plot, but his sentence was commuted to life imprisonment.

AFTERMATH: Chaos set in while some of Kim's followers attempted to carry out a coup, which did not fully develop when the army would not give its support. During that time, U.S. military troops in South Korea were put on full alert, with warnings given to the North Korean government that it should not attempt to exploit the situation.

Premier Choi Kyu Hah became president of South Korea and released imprisoned dissidents.

1980s

 SEPTEMBER 17, 1980

ANASTASIO SOMOZA DEBAYLE (1925–1980)
NICARAGUAN SOLDIER AND POLITICIAN, WHO HELD THE OFFICE OF PRESIDENT IN 1967–72 AND 1974–79

As dictator of his country, Anastasio Somoza Debayle, a U.S.-educated West Point graduate, ran one of Latin America's most corrupt and brutal regimes until his overthrow in 1979 by Sandinista guerrillas. He then fled into exile in the United States and Paraguay.

The Central American country of Nicaragua has a constitution that calls for its government to be run by elected officials—a president and a bicameral legislature—as is the government of the United States. But beginning in 1934, the Somoza family ruled in near-dictatorial fashion for more than forty years. During those years, the family developed wide business interests and amassed a huge personal fortune, estimated to be worth as much as $150 million.

In 1912 the United States established military bases in Nicaragua at the request of the government, in order to oppose a guerrilla group led by Augusto Cesar Sandino. U.S. troops remained until 1933, when they were withdrawn after setting up and training a national guard commanded by General Anastasio Somoza. Although Sandino was assassinated in 1934, reputedly on Somoza's orders, some of his followers continued their guerrilla activities, becoming known as the Sandinista National Liberation Front, or the Sandinistas.

General Anastasio Somoza was elected president in 1936 and held the position until his assassination in 1956, when his son Luis became president. When Luis passed along the position to his brother Anastasio in 1967, the family dictatorship continued but with a much harsher regime than before. In 1972, because Anastasio was constitutionally unable to succeed himself, he vacated the presidency but handed the government over to a three-man junta while a constituent assembly drafted a new constitution that would enable him to be reelected in 1974. In the meantime, a catastrophic earthquake on Christmas Eve of 1972 destroyed Managua, killing some ten thousand people and injuring another fifteen thousand, giving Somoza an excuse to publicly take back control of his country. The National Emergency Committee was formed, with Somoza as its chairman. He was accused of substantially increasing the family fortune during that time by raising prices of family-controlled vital commodities, such as building materials and food, while the country was in a state of disaster, prompting one Nicaraguan official to say the country was being run as a "kleptocracy."

Somoza was officially reelected president in 1974, but his family remained dogged by the memory of Cesar Augusto Sandino, the assassinated Nicaraguan rebel who had become a martyr and a source of inspiration for the guerrilla group who took his name.

ASSASSINS: The Sandinista regime was accused of complicity in Somoza's assassination, but Paraguayan police blamed the Ejercito Revolucionario del Pueblo (ERP), an Argentine left-wing terrorist group that was set up in July 1970 as the military arm of the Trotskyist Partido Revolucionario de los Trabajadores (PRT), an affiliate of the Fourth International. The ERP was responsible for a long string of assassinations in Argentina—among its victims were policemen, army officers, and moderate trade-union leaders. In 1972 the ERP kidnapped and then killed Oberdan Sallustro, Fiat's general manager in Argentina, and in 1976 it killed the chief of police of Buenos Aires.

HISTORY: While the Somoza family, backed by Nicaragua's top industrialists and merchants, had almost total control of the country, there
was a long history of both direct and indirect U.S. intervention in
Nicaraguan affairs. The United States supplied Nicaragua with considerable military assistance, and used the country as the Central American
jumping-off point for the CIA-sponsored Bay of Pigs invasion of Cuba.
At the same time, U.S. political and economic interests were apparently
able to overlook the years of repression Nicaraguan citizens suffered
during the Somoza regime.

In 1962, after a period of relative inactivity, the Sandinistas set out
to overthrow the Somozas. During a bloody revolution, Anastasio
Somoza's power waned as U.S. support of his government decreased.
After Pedro Joaquin Chamorro, an outspoken opponent of the Somoza
dynasty, who was editor of his family-owned *La Prensa* newspaper, was
brutally assassinated in Managua on January 10, 1978, obviously on the
orders of Somoza, the United States finally accused Somoza of massive
human rights violations.

Chamorro's assassination also united diverse elements in Nicaragua.
On the night of January 10, some fifty thousand people escorted his coffin from the hospital to his home; the next morning, some thirty thousand mourners showed up to pay their respects. That night, the capital
was rocked by tens of thousands of rioting protesters who set fire to
buildings and automobiles, looted stores, and stoned police. Soldiers and
firemen were called in to control the chaos. Although the Somoza government condemned Chamorro's murder, pledging to spare no efforts to
find his killers, no one believed it. Business and labor leaders called a
general strike, demanding a real investigation, and demands were made
for Somoza's resignation.

In 1979, as his government crumbled, Somoza finally resigned and
fled to Miami, taking with him a personal fortune estimated to be
around $100 million. Still, Somoza could not escape his past. Constantly
faced with recriminations, and afraid his opponents would come after

him, Somoza fled Miami, going first to the Bahamas, then to Paraguay, a police state where he believed he would be protected.

EVENT: On September 17, 1980, fifty-four-year-old Anastasio Somoza Debayle was riding in his Mercedes with his bodyguard and a financial adviser through the center of Asunción, Paraguay, when he was cut down by a rain of bazooka and submachine-gun fire. Somoza, his driver, and his financial adviser were all killed, and every member of the assassination squad escaped.

Somoza's body was flown to the United States and buried in the Cuban quarter of Miami.

AFTERMATH: On October 1, 1980, the Paraguayan government broke off diplomatic relations with Nicaragua, accusing the Sandinistas of responsibility for Somoza's assassination. The Paraguayan police, however, blamed the ERP.

When Somoza resigned and fled Nicaragua in 1979, the Sandinistas established a provisional junta of national reconstruction led by Daniel Ortega Saavedra. The junta published a guarantee of civil rights, and an appointed council of state until a national election could be held and a new constitution approved. After the election of President Ronald Reagan, relations between the United States and Nicaragua quickly deteriorated. Economic assistance to Nicaragua was cut off, and the United States claimed the Sandinista government was supporting attempts to overthrow the government in El Salvador. The Reagan administration threw its support behind the counterrevolutionary forces of the Contras, despite the fact that they were known to have executed prisoners, killed civilians, and engaged in forced conscription. The Contras received generous financial support from the U.S. government and kept up their campaign against the Sandinistas, until promised elections were finally held in 1990. Violeta Barrios de Chamorro, widow of the slain newspaper editor, was elected on a U.S.-backed National Opposition Union (UNO) ticket. The Bush administration spent $9 million on her election campaign. Although the Sandinistas were officially no longer in power, they remained a persistent force behind the scenes in Nicaragua.

 MARCH 30, 1981

RONALD WILSON REAGAN (1911–)
FORTIETH PRESIDENT OF THE UNITED STATES
FROM 1981 TO 1989

Ronald Reagan was born in the small Illinois town of Tampico to poor parents but created a life of success that any parent would be proud to see. He had his first taste of politics in college, where he led a successful student strike against curriculum cutbacks. After college, Reagan became a well-known actor. He served as president of the Screen Actor's Guild from 1947 to 1952, and as his entertainment career began to decline, he entered politics. In 1966 he was elected governor of California; in 1968 and again in 1976, he sought the Republican nomination for president, losing both times. Undeterred, he worked hard for the nomination in 1980, and at age seventy-nine he became the oldest man ever elected to the office of president of the United States.

WOULD-BE ASSASSIN: John W. Hinckley, Jr., the son of an affluent Evergreen, Colorado, oil executive, grew up in Dallas before moving with his family to Colorado in 1974. Hinckley was an on-again, off-again student of Texas Tech University but never graduated. He made frequent trips across the country, apparently taking no steps to embark on a career. In 1978 he joined the National Socialist Party of America, generally referred to as the Nazi Party of America, but the party would not renew Hinckley's membership the next year. A party official would later say of Hinckley, "He kept talking about going out and shooting people and blowing things up. When a guy comes to us advocating that, we make the assumption that he is either a nut or a federal agent trying to entrap us. Either way, we don't want them."

After John Hinckley Jr. saw actress Jodie Foster play a twelve-year-old prostitute in the 1976 film *Taxi Driver,* he became an obsessed fan. In the film, actor Robert DeNiro plays an obsessed gunman who plans to assassinate a presidential candidate, a character inspired by Arthur Bremer, the man who shot Governor George Wallace in 1972. Hinckley wrote fan letters to Jodie Foster and received the standard autographed picture in return. He then followed her to Yale University, where she was a student in September 1980, and left notes at her dormitory, phoned her, and stalked her at a distance. Foster ignored him. On December 8, 1980, Hinckley's fragile hold on reality suffered a crucial shock when John Lennon, his idol, was gunned down in New York by a stalking fan. Early in March of 1981, Hinckley received another jolt: On one of his visits with his oil-wealthy parents near Denver, his father, who had been disappointed by his son's lack of motivation, told him he was on his own. More than ever, Hinckley wanted to get the attention of Jodie Foster.

EVENT: On March 29, 1981, Hinckley checked into a hotel in Washington, D.C., taking with him two .22-caliber pistols and the same type of .38 used to kill John Lennon. The next morning he loaded bullets into one of the .22s and wrote a note to Foster, put the note in his suitcase, and left his room.

Hinckley crouched down among a crowd of people waiting for President Reagan to emerge from the Washington Hilton after giving a speech. Television news cameras were broadcasting their usual coverage of the president's comings and goings as Reagan stepped out of the hotel, smiled, and waved at the small crowd while approaching his limousine. Suddenly, Hinckley fired four to six shots from a .22-caliber revolver, a weapon often referred to as a Saturday-night special. According to a reporter at the scene, Reagan "just sort of stood there, then the smile just sort of washed off his face." The president froze for a moment at the door of his limousine until a Secret Service agent brusquely pushed him inside the vehicle, and it immediately drove away.

Security officers swarmed over Hinckley, who was standing near the reporters at the scene. One Secret Service agent held a submachine gun poised upright in one hand and issued orders amid the chaos, while three seriously wounded victims were still lying on the sidewalk. Timothy J. McCarthy, a thirty-one-year-old Secret Service agent, was shot in the right side; the bullet damaged his liver. Thomas Delahanty, a forty-five-year-old District of Columbia police officer, had a bullet lodged in his neck. James S. Brady, the president's press secretary, was the most seriously wounded; a bullet had struck him above the left eye and lodged in the right side of his brain above the ear.

As the president's limousine headed back to the White House, he complained of a pain in his side, which he believed was a simple injury caused by being shoved into the vehicle. Secret Service agents immediately drove him to George Washington University Hospital, about twelve blocks from the hotel. As Reagan walked into the hospital, his knees buckled.

Initial reports were that the president was not shot, and even Reagan himself did not realize he had been hit until he reached the emergency room. There it was discovered that he had been hit by a bullet that ricocheted off his limousine's fender. The bullet entered under his left armpit, pierced his chest, bounced off his seventh rib and was lodged in the left lower lobe of his lung. As a decision was made to operate, an official report was released at 3:18 P.M. that the president was wounded. During the following three hours, as Reagan underwent a two-hour operation performed by Drs. Benjamin Aaron and Joseph Giordano, Vice-President George Bush rushed back to Washington from a speaking engagement in Texas.

At 7:30 P.M. Dr. Dennis O'Leary, the university's dean of clinical affairs, appeared at a press briefing to tell the waiting nation that President Reagan had "sailed through" the operation and was in stable condition. O'Leary described the operation as "a relatively simple procedure": an incision of about six inches was made, the bullet was removed, and the incision was closed. He said the bullet had forced a partial collapse of Reagan's left lung, and the lung had been reinflated as part of the operating procedure. The president was described as an "excellent physical specimen," and his prognosis was "excellent." O'Leary reassured the public that Reagan was "alert and should be able to make decisions by tomorrow" but that there was an estimated recovery period of two-and-a-half to three months.

Lyn Nofzinger, Reagan's political director, soon reported that the president had kept his sense of humor during the ordeal. When Nancy Reagan arrived in the emergency room, Reagan said, "Nancy, honey, I forgot to duck" (a quote from boxer Jack Dempsey to his wife after he lost to Gene Tunney). As his top aides gathered at the hospital, Reagan asked them, "Who's minding the store?" And in the operating room, he said to doctors, "Please tell me you're Republicans." Although he was unable to speak in the recovery room afterward because of tubes inserted in his body, Reagan wrote a note saying, "All in all, I'd rather be in Philadelphia" (actor W.C. Fields's suggestion for his own epitaph).

It was decided that the president would not be told until the next day of the serious wounds of the others. McCarthy and Delahanty were doing well, but James Brady was another story. By that time, the bullet lodged in Brady's brain had been removed during a four-and-a-half-hour operation, but damaged sections of his brain, including the right frontal lobe, also had to be removed. Although doctors said his progress was "extraordinary," his prognosis remained "guarded." Tears appeared in the president's eyes when he was told.

INVESTIGATION AND PUNISHMENT: Hinckley was indicted for the shooting in August of 1981. Soon afterward, the FBI was satisfied that Hinckley had acted alone, but CIA director William Casey was not convinced. He launched an intensive investigation into the possibility that the Russian KGB could have been involved with Hinckley. Only after CIA experts had thoroughly looked into that theory and found it not to be true was Casey finally convinced.

During other investigations, it was discovered that on October 9, 1980, Hinckley had been in Nashville, Tennessee, when President Jimmy Carter was there. After airport X-ray equipment revealed that Hinckley had three handguns and ammunition in his carry-on bag, he was arrested. His weapons were confiscated, and Hinckley was fined $62.50, but federal authorities did not place Hinckley under security surveillance. Four days after he left Tennessee, Hinckley turned up in Dallas, where he bought two .22-caliber handguns in a pawnshop. One of those weapons was used in the Reagan shooting.

Hinckley had apparently flown from Denver to Los Angeles on March 25, 1981. The following day, he had taken a Greyhound bus for Washington, D.C., arriving there on March 29, the day before his attack. The investigation showed that Hinckley had been infatuated with movie star Jodie Foster, and that he had written a number of letters to her. An unmailed letter he had written, dated March 30, 1981, 12:45 P.M. (just one hour and forty-five minutes before he shot the president), was found in his Washington hotel room. It read: "Dear Jodie, There is a definite possibility that I will be killed in my attempt to get Reagan. It is for this very reason that I am writing to you now. . . ." Hinckley went on to say that he loved her and that "although we talked on the phone a couple of times, I never had the nerve to simply approach you and introduce myself. . . . Jodie, I would abandon this idea of getting Reagan in a second if I could only win your heart and live out the rest of my life with you, whether it be in total obscurity or whatever. I will admit to you that the reason I'm going ahead with this attempt now is because I just cannot wait any longer to impress you. I've got to do something now to make you understand in no uncertain terms that I am doing all this for your sake. By sacrificing my freedom and possibly my life, I hope to change your mind about me."

In May of 1982, Hinckley went on trial, with psychiatrists convincingly testifying that the young man had gradually lost the ability to distinguish between reality and fantasy. The country was shocked when, based on his insanity defense, a jury found Hinckley not guilty. He was committed for an indefinite period of time to St. Elizabeth's Hospital, a mental institution in Washington, D.C.

While Hinckley remained in hospital confinement, it was revealed in January 1987 by the Secret Service that despite its strong objections, he had been allowed to leave the hospital the previous December for a twelve-hour visit with his family in a facility in Reston, Virginia. Hinckley had been escorted to the reunion by hospital personnel. The following year, St. Elizabeth's Hospital proposed allowing Hinckley to have a one-day, unescorted Easter visit with his family in McLean, Virginia, but when it was disclosed that Hinckley had been corresponding with convicted serial killer Ted Bundy while Bundy was awaiting execution in a Florida prison, the hospital withdrew its request to the court.

In September of 1996, Hinckley claimed he had recovered his sanity and asked a federal judge to grant him monthly passes to spend days alone with his parents outside St. Elizabeth's. Although Hinckley's attorney claimed he was no longer a danger to himself or others, he was not asking that Hinckley be released from the institution.

AFTERMATH: All those injured in Hinckley's assassination attempt on Reagan recovered, although James Brady, severely wounded, was hospitalized for months and never regained full control of his body. While he remains in a wheelchair most of the time, he is able to walk short distances. During the following years Brady and his wife, Sarah, became active campaigners for gun-control laws, something President Reagan had long opposed and continued to oppose even after the attempt on his life. The Bradys's efforts were successful in November of 1993 when Congress passed and President Clinton signed the Brady Handgun Violence Protection Act, commonly called the Brady Bill. The law, which went into effect in March of 1994, imposed a five-day waiting period for the purchase of a handgun and requires local law-enforcement authorities to do background checks on all prospective handgun buyers. The law specifies that convicted felons, minors, substance abusers, and illegal immigrants will be ineligible to purchase guns, and the bill authorized

$200 million per year of federal funding to help states develop a computerized system for the background checks.

A book written by *Washington Post* reporter Bob Woodward was published in 1987 and immediately caused an uproar. In *Veil: The Secret Ways of the CIA 1981–87,* Woodward disclosed that President Reagan had come closer to death after Hinckley's assassination attempt than officials admitted and that his recovery was much more difficult. Reagan's supposedly quick, almost miraculous recovery had been largely an act, and after the smiling and waving, he would walk "with the hesitant steps of an old man. He was pale and disoriented." Woodward said Reagan often needed an inhalator and could concentrate for only a few minutes at a time and "remain attentive only an hour or so a day."

Further, Woodward said William Casey was especially obsessed with the president's safety after the assassination attempt, which caused the CIA and the White House to overreact to an unconfirmed intelligence report that hit squads had been dispatched by Libyan leader Muammar al-Qaddafi to kill Reagan. Some of the hit-squad stories were eventually traced to Manucher Ghorbanifar, an arms merchant with links to Israeli and Iranian intelligence, who later played a major role in U.S.-Iran arms sales.

 MAY 13, 1981

JOHN PAUL II (1920–)
POPE OF THE CATHOLIC CHURCH SINCE 1978, AND THE FIRST NON-ITALIAN TO ASSUME THAT POSITION SINCE 1522

Pope John Paul II was born Karol Wojtyla near Krakow, Poland. He was conscripted at the beginning of World War II for forced labor by the Germans, working in quarries and a chemical factory. In 1942 his study for the priesthood began illegally in Krakow. When the war ended, he taught ethics and theology at universities in Lublin and Krakow before becoming archbishop of Krakow in 1964. He was made a cardinal in 1967 and elected pope upon the death of John Paul I.

WOULD-BE ASSASSIN: Mehmet Ali Agca was from the shantytown of Yesiltepe, a suburb of Malatya, in Turkey. In 1966, when Agca was seven, his alcoholic father died, leaving a wife and three children in poverty. As the eldest child, Agca earned money for his family by selling spring water at the local railway terminal. During Agca's youth, Turkey was a violent place to live, with the extreme right and extreme left battling savagely for political dominance. In 1975, while Agca was attending the Malatya's Teachers Training High School, it was taken over by a right-wing anti-West group called the National Action Party. Soon he became associated with militant young members of the Grey Wolves, a branch of an organization called Turkish Idealists, which was affiliated with the National Action Party.

Although Agca's new companions were often arrested, his own record remained spotless until June 25, 1979. By then a student at Istanbul University, Agca was arrested for the murder of Abdi Ipekci, the outspoken editor of the leftist newspaper *Milliyet*, who had been shot to death in Istanbul on February 1, 1979. Almost five months had passed before an anonymous caller told Istanbul police that they would find "Ali," Ipekci's murderer, at the Marmara, a right-wing student coffeehouse. Mehmet Ali Agca confessed to the murder and insisted that he had acted alone, despite eyewitness testimony to the contrary. He was incarcerated at the Kartal Maltepe maximum security prison. But one month into his sentence, Agca put on an army uniform that had been smuggled in to him, coolly walked past prison guards, and disappeared into the night. He left behind a letter for *Milliyet*, calling Pope John Paul II "the Crusader Commander" and saying the pope's impending visit to Turkey was a Western imperialist plan to erode the unity of "the brotherly Islamic countries." While Agca swore he would kill John Paul if he came to Turkey, the pope's visit proceeded as planned, and Agca never appeared. He may have been busy elsewhere. A month after Agca's escape from prison, the Grey Wolf informant believed to have fingered Agca for the Ipekci murder was tortured and killed in Istanbul.

During 1980, Agca reportedly wandered aimlessly from Turkey to Iran, back through Turkey, on to Bulgaria for a few months, then to Yugoslavia. By autumn he was in West Germany, where he was suspected by police of the November 25 murder of a former Turkish Idealist in Kempten. A month later, Agca was in Italy, apparently making preparations for the spring day when he would go to St. Peter's Square.

EVENT: On the afternoon of May 13, 1981, more than ten thousand people packed St. Peter's Square in Rome, straining for positions at the wooden barricades protecting a narrow pathway around the perimeter of the square. Pope John Paul II stood in the back of a white Jeeplike vehicle as it slowly drove along the path. Over and over again the vehicle stopped so that the thin, wry pope from Poland could bless those nearest him. The spiritual leader of nearly 600 million Roman Catholics reached down and touched the outstretched fingers as they came in his direction.

At around 5:15 P.M., as the pope's vehicle paused near the Vatican's Great Bronze Door, he reached down to the sea of waving hands, unaware that one of them held a semiautomatic pistol. Two rapid shots cracked through the air; one grazed the pope's right arm and left hand, the other struck him in the abdomen. Spectators watched in horror as the Holy Father raised one shaking hand to his face, then collapsed. His white garments were smeared with blood.

As the young assailant, tightly holding a nine-millimeter Browning pistol, turned to escape, Suor Letizia, a robust young nun standing several yards behind him, was already in pursuit. Mehmet Ali Agca tripped on the cobblestones and dropped his weapon, and Suor Letizia grabbed him. "Why did you do it?" she shouted into the gunman's thin, dark face. "Not me, not me!" he cried, but she and others securely held Agca until police arrived.

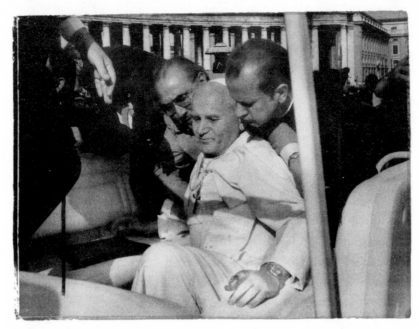

Pope John Paul II

Pope John Paul II was badly wounded, but emergency surgery was immediately performed, saving his life.

PUNISHMENT: Although authorities quickly learned the identity and background of the pope's attacker, twenty-three-year-old Agca remained something of an enigma. While some observers considered him a lone religious fanatic, based on the contents of the *Milliyet* letter he had left behind in prison, others believed the cool young Turk was more political. One official who questioned Agca said, "He is a terrorist with a capital *T*; cold, lucid, and certainly well trained to shoot." Police suspected Turkey's National Action Party was involved, but they could not link it to the shooting. Agca insisted he had acted alone and would say little more. He was asked about reports that another man was seen fleeing St. Peter's Square on the day of the shooting, but Agca would say nothing. He also refused to say how he had financed his travels around Europe.

In July of 1981, Mehmet Ali Agca was convicted of attempted murder of the pope and sentenced to life imprisonment.

AFTERMATH: After spending ten months in an Italian jail, Agca finally began to talk. He said Bulgarian officials had offered him $1.25 million to kill the pope, and naturally, he accepted their offer. Members of Bulgaria's secret police, the Darzhavna Sigurnost (DA), had already been implicated in terrorist attacks and at least one murder, and were considered players in illegal arms and drug trafficking. Although the Italian government was reluctant to take action, Agca's account was full of convincing details, so it decided to move. In November of 1982, officers arrested Bulgarian airline official Sergei Ivanov Antonov and issued warrants for embassy cashier Teodorov Ayvazov and Guelio Vassiliev Kolev, secretary of the embassy's military attaché. Although Ayvazov and Kolev had already left the country, eventually they were arrested, along with four other Turks.

On July 8, 1983, as Agca was being moved from police headquarters, he threw questioning reporters an irresistible morsel, saying offhandedly, "In the attack against the pope, even the KGB took part." The accusation made sense to people who believed the Soviets wanted to silence the pope's vocal support of the Solidarity labor movement in communist Poland, but no Russians were ever arrested.

In June of 1985, the Italian government put the three Bulgarians and four Turks on trial, charging them with conspiracy to assassinate the pope. Of the three Bulgarians charged, only Antonov was present for trial because the other two, who had avoided arrest by quickly leaving the country, went to Sofia, where they were safe from extradition. Agca, who was the prosecution's main witness, quickly made a mockery of the trial when, on the first day, he announced: "I am Jesus Christ. In the name of the omnipotent God, I announce the end of the world. No one, neither the Americans nor the Soviets, will be saved. There will be destruction." Depending almost entirely on the reliability of Agca's testimony, the prosecutor said confidently, "When he starts speaking of facts, he is very believable." Then Agca altered his testimony, saying there were even more conspirators: members of a secret Italian Masonic lodge and the Italian secret service. After a trial of more than nine months, all of the defendants were acquitted for lack of evidence. Mehmet Ali Agca remained the only person locked up in a high-security prison in Ancona, Italy, his contact with other inmates limited, for the attempt to assassinate Pope John Paul II.

 OCTOBER 6, 1981

MOHAMMED ANWAR AL SADAT (1918–1981)
EGYPTIAN STATESMAN AND PRESIDENT FROM 1970 TO 1981

Anwar Sadat was a charismatic leader, who was awarded the Nobel Peace Prize jointly with Israel's Menachem Begin in 1978 for their courage in trying to bring about peace in the Middle East.

The son of a hospital clerk, Anwar Sadat was born in a small village in the Nile Delta. As a young man, he attended the Cairo Military Academy, graduating in 1938. During World War II Sadat was imprisoned by the British on charges that he was a spy for Germany, but he quickly escaped from a Cairo prison and remained a fugitive until the war ended. Dedicated to the overthrow of the British-dominated Egyptian monarchy, Sadat was arrested again in 1945, charged with participating in a failed attempt to assassinate Egypt's prime minister, Nahas Pasha. He escaped from prison once more and in 1950 resurfaced as a member of Colonel Gamal Nasser's Free Officers Movement. After King Farouk was deposed by Nasser's successful Neguib coup in 1952, Sadat was appointed to various important positions in the new republic's government headed by Nasser. Sadat was minister of state (1955–56) when Nasser tried to nationalize the Suez Canal, causing an international crisis. Sadat was vice-chairman (1957–60) and chairman (1960–68) of the National Assembly, then became vice president of the republic (1964–66, 1969–70). During Sadat's vice presidency, Egypt allowed Palestinian guerrillas to use Cairo as a jumping-off point for attacks in Israel, resulting in the Six-Day War, with Egypt suffering a major defeat. Although Nasser resigned immediately after the Six-Day War, there were massive demonstrations throughout the country, and he took up his position again within twenty-four hours. Nasser's regime then attempted to strengthen its relationship with the United States and kept the Palestinians under control.

When Nasser died of a heart attack on September 28, 1970, Sadat became acting president and was formally elected to the office in October of that year. Determined not to be overshadowed by his predecessor, Sadat introduced measures to decentralize Egypt's political structure and diversify the economy. Altering Nasser's foreign policy, Sadat expelled Soviet technicians and advisers in 1972, and in 1976 he annulled Egypt's 1971 treaty of friendship with the Soviet Union. While he courted the United States for support, he also launched the costly Arab-Israeli Yom Kippur War of 1973, after which, under pressure from the United States, Sadat began to work for peace in the Middle East. He created an international sensation by flying to Jerusalem in 1977, despite condemnation from other Arab countries, to initiate peace negotiations. When Sadat's efforts on behalf of his country, combined with those of Menachem Begin of Israel resulted in the Israeli-Egyptian Peace Treaty of 1979, the two men were awarded the Nobel Peace Prize.

ASSASSINS: Anwar Sadat's assassination was plotted by an *'anqud* (cell) of Muslim fundamentalist extremists led by Abdel Salem Farag, a twenty-eight-year-old electrical engineer and author of a religious book called *The Absent Prayer.* Farag's privately printed book influenced Khaled El Sambouli, who was already hostile toward Sadat's policies. Sambouli's brother, Mohammed, had been arrested in September 1981 for anti-Sadat activities, particularly his alleged participation in a Muslim fundamentalist attack on Islam's holiest shrine, the Grand Mosque of Mecca, in November of 1979.

Colonel Abboud Zumr, the military leader of the *'anqud* that planned Sadat's assassination, had spoken out against the idea, but he was overruled by Farag, El Sambouli, and the other members. They believed Sadat's death would spark a fundamentalist uprising that would rid the country of pro-Western Egyptians and those who had struck deals with Israel. The group decided the attack would be led by Khaled El Sambouli, an Egyptian army lieutenant who managed to replace members of his military unit with three Muslim extremists: Abdul Salam, Ataya Reheil, and Abbas Mohammed, one of the Egyptian army's best marksmen.

HISTORY: By 1978 Sadat had eliminated the nastiest and most repressive practices of Nasser's regime and enjoyed the support of most Egyptians, including the military and the Arab Socialist Union, his nation's only legal political party. But his political opponents claimed Sadat's regime was stocked with opportunists and profiteers who were taking advantage of his liberal economic measures. In fact, there was a widening gap between the rich and the poor, with living conditions becoming worse for most, and Sadat's support among the masses showing the strain. Egypt was an overpopulated, impoverished land where over 90 percent of the people struggled to survive on a per capita income of $200 a year. Tens of thousands of squatters lived in so-called "cities of the dead," mausoleums of Islamic cemeteries on the fringes of Cairo, while there was a conspicuous wealthy class in Cairo, who vacationed at Alexandria, the "Pearl of the Mediterranean," with its forty miles of beach and seafood restaurants.

To bolster his regime, Sadat suppressed political opposition from the left, including supporters of the late president, Gamal Nasser, and from the Muslim fundamentalist right. Sadat was immensely popular at times, maintaining his power by raising expectations of a higher standard of living for the masses. Although Egypt had an open door for foreign investment, most Egyptians did not benefit from their country's rapid growth of international economic activity. And after the Camp David accords in 1978, other Arab governments cut off their official aid programs to Egypt, making the United States an important economic, as well as military, ally. Because Sadat was considered one of the foremost powers in the Middle East and a valuable part of the peace process, the United States wanted to ensure his safety. Nearly $25 million went toward Sadat's security. The U.S. Secret Service began training Egyptian security men in 1974. President Nixon supplied Sadat with a $2 million Sikorsky CH-53E armored helicopter, and President Jimmy Carter provided AWACS (Airborne Warning and Control System) protection against Libyan fighters.

As part of the Israeli-Egyptian Peace Treaty, Sadat had gained more land for Arabs from Israel by negotiation than Arabs had been able to win by force. Still, Arab nationalists all over the Middle East considered Sadat a traitor. While he was being honored with the Nobel Peace Prize, concerns for Sadat's safety increased. Despite all the money that had gone into insuring his safety, the greatest threat of all came from within his own country, from men who had been arrested during Nasser's regime. One of Sadat's first acts after becoming president had been to grant amnesty and freedom to dissident extremists, including members of a fanatic Islamic organization called Al Taqfir wal Hijra, the most dedicated and ruthless of terrorist organizations. It was reported to have four thousand well-armed members in Egypt and ten thousand members elsewhere, walking time bombs waiting to go off.

Sadat was well aware of the dangerous elements within his own country but was reluctant to purge them for fear such actions would antagonize human rights advocates, particularly the U.S. government. In 1981, the fundamentalists became more brazen. Death threats forced Sadat to cancel a stopover in Vienna after his summer visit to the United States. In August, Egyptian intelligence uncovered a plot to assassinate Sadat and his wife, Jihan, in their Alexandria summer palace. Finally, Egyptian vice-president Hosni Mubarak and interior minister Nabawi Ismail warned Sadat that a coup attempt was being planned and advised him that a purge could no longer be avoided. Reluctantly agreeing in September, Sadat ordered security forces to arrest sixteen hundred dissenters, including government officials and cell leaders. At the same time he insisted the military, which he trusted implicitly, remain untouched.

EVENT: On October 6, 1981, Anwar Sadat prepared for a daylong celebration of the eighth anniversary of the beginning of the Yom Kippur War. Always the distinguished diplomat, Sadat wanted to make an impressive appearance and refused to wear his bulletproof undervest that day because it would spoil the line of his new, London-tailored uniform. Dressed in his gold-braided blue field marshal's uniform crossed with a green sash and numerous medals, Sadat rode in his black Cadillac limousine with the top open, surrounded by eight bodyguards. Their first stop was in Heliopolis, at the grave of Gamal Nasser, where Sadat prayed at the gravesite, then returned to the limousine. Joined along the way by Vice-President Mubarak and defense minister General Abdel Halim Abu Ghazala, they stopped to place a wreath on the pyramid-shaped Tomb of the Unknown Soldier, then drove to Nasr City to view a military parade.

The reviewing stand held a thousand guests, including military advisers, diplomats, ambassadors, and journalists. They watched as President Sadat took his seat in the center of the first row of the elevated stands, which were separated from the review field by a five-foot-high concrete wall. Sitting above Sadat in a glass enclosure at the top of the massive brick and concrete stand were his wife and grandchildren, who would be viewing their first military parade. The event began with readings from the Koran, then Defense Minister Abu Ghazala stood to deliver a long speech praising the Egyptian military and its commander in chief. It was 11:30 A.M. when the first military units began to pass by.

Mortars fired miniature parachutes with tiny portraits of Sadat and the Egyptian flag, fireworks exploded overhead, followed by screaming jets in tight formations. Sadat watched the camel corps glide by and viewed stunt-flying jets through his binoculars. Around 12:30, a contingent

Anwar Sadat

of seventy-two Soviet-made Zil-151 camouflaged flatbed trucks, each towing a field gun, moved closer to the reviewing stand. Riding on one of the trucks, in the passenger seat beside his regular driver, was First Lieutenant Khaled Ahamed El Sambouli. In the back of the truck were three soldiers he had selected from another army unit three days earlier, telling parade officials his regular three-man gun crew had fallen ill and were given a leave of absence. Because the Zil-151s were not particularly impressive to look at as they passed by, drama was added by a group of F-4 Phantom and Mirage trainer fighter jets swooping low over the spectators, painting red, orange, green, and gray smoke in the sky.

As everyone watched the jets, El Sambouli pulled a hand grenade out from under his tunic and ordered the driver to stop their Zil-151 directly opposite President Sadat. When the startled driver hesitated, El Sambouli reached over and pulled the truck's hand brake. He then jumped out of the truck and approached the reviewing stand. Sadat and Mubarak thought the lieutenant wanted to pay his respects and rose to greet him. But instead of saluting, El Sambouli pulled the pin of his hand grenade and lobbed it directly at President Sadat. At that instant, the three soldiers on the Zil-151 stood up on the back of the truck and opened fire toward the reviewing stand with their AK-47 assault rifles. When the grenade he had thrown landed at the feet of Abu Ghazala and did not explode, El Sambouli reached into his pocket, withdrew another grenade, pulled the pin, and threw it. This grenade struck major general Abdrab Nabi Hafez directly in the face but didn't explode either. El Sambouli was ready with a third grenade, which he threw. When it exploded at the front of the reviewing stand, he ran back to the truck and grabbed a submachine gun. His three men jumped down from the truck and ran along with him toward the stands, firing steadily as they went. They encountered no resistance whatsoever from the score of security guards protecting President Sadat and the other Egyptian officials and international diplomats in the stands as the bullets began to hit their targets.

While hundreds of dignitaries and journalists overturned chairs in their rush to escape the onslaught, the gunmen concentrated their assault on the front rows. Firing ceaselessly, two charged directly at the podium, one to the left and one to the right, as they emptied the clips in their weapons into the dais from both sides.

Sadat was struck many times before those around him rushed toward him, forced him to the floor, and shielded him with their bodies and with overturned chairs. Forty-five seconds after the attack began, Sadat's personal bodyguards finally reacted. Just as the assailants' guns were emptied and they ran toward the truck, the bodyguards chased after them, firing as they went. One assassin was killed; the other three were wounded and captured.

President Sadat was lying in the reviewing stand, bleeding profusely from his mouth. Ten others were killed or fatally wounded, and twenty-eight were injured, including Vice-President Mubarak and Abu Ghazala, who quickly took charge of the situation. He ordered the young, red-bereted soldiers who were entering the reviewing stand to help the wounded tangled up among overturned chairs. He radioed a nearby military facility to immediately send a helicopter, and when it arrived three minutes later, Anwar Sadat's wife, Jihan, had just managed to push her way past the security guards and reach her mortally wounded husband. Sadat was strapped to a stretcher, and Jihan followed along as he was loaded into the helicopter.

Vice-President Hosni Mubarak, who suffered only a cut hand, was driven in a presidential Volvo to Maadi military hospital, where Sadat had been taken. In a fourth-floor operating room of the heart and chest surgery unit, a team of eleven doctors saw that Sadat had bullet wounds to his neck, chest, legs, arms, and face, and he had no pulse or reflexes. The doctors worked furiously to save him. They removed clotted blood from his larynx, inserted an air tube into his throat, administered artificial respiration, and gave him massive blood transfusions. They opened the left side of his chest and inserted a tube to remove air and blood that would prevent his lungs from functioning. They tried open chest massage and electric shock to stimulate his heart to start beating. It would not.

Anwar Sadat was already clinically dead when he reached the hospital, but the official time of death was reported as 2:40 P.M., two hours after he had been wounded by five bullets and several pieces of shrapnel.

Sadat's body was flown by helicopter from the hospital's mosque to a sports stadium in Nasr City. From there it was carried on a horse-drawn caisson the final eight hundred yards to the same reviewing stand where the assault occurred. His family, sitting in the same row where he had been shot, received dignitaries from around the world: Israel's Menachem Begin, French president François Mitterrand, England's Prince Charles. Although President Ronald Reagan did not attend because he was still recovering from the attempt on his own life, the United States sent a huge delegation, including former presidents Carter, Ford, and Nixon, defense secretary Casper Weinberger, U.N. ambassador Jeane Kirkpatrick, and Henry Kissinger. Sadat was buried in a grave beside the Tomb of the Unknown Soldier.

PUNISHMENT: More than eight hundred people were arrested in subsequent investigations, but only two dozen were indicted for murder and conspiracy. Authorities determined that Lieutenant Khaled El Sambouli, who led the attackers, was also the ringleader; he and four others were sentenced to death. Seventeen others received prison sentences ranging from five years to life at hard labor. Two defendants were acquitted. In April of 1982, El Sambouli, Abdul Salam, Abbas Mohammed, and Ataya Reheil were executed along with fellow conspirator Abdel Salem Farag.

AFTERMATH: Anwar Sadat was succeeded by his vice president, Hosni Mubarak. Realizing there was a coup in the making, Mubarak ordered security forces to purge his country and the Egyptian army of Islamic militants. Among the 356 members of Al Taqfir wal Hijra who were arrested was Sheik Omar Abdul Rahman, who would later be released and settle in the United States, where he was implicated in the 1993 bombing of the New York World Trade Center. The investigation of Sadat's assassination led Mubarak to believe the conspirators intended not only to eliminate Sadat but to replace his entire political structure with a Muslim religious government, as in Iran. But the popular revolt the religious extremists had hoped to ignite by assassinating Sadat did not happen. Although crowds of fundamentalist Muslims in Libya danced in the streets, waving flags and shouting approval, in Egypt there was enforced calm: In addition to a forty-day mourning period, the government declared a one-year state of emergency, prohibiting public gatherings and marches. Even during Sadat's funeral, as two thousand people assembled only to honor their slain leader, police fired shots into the air to disperse the crowd.

Mubarak's stern security measures and a subsequent public trial of the accused assassins not only foiled the *jihad*, the Islamic fundamentalists' holy war, it also strengthened Egypt's ties with the West.

 AUGUST 21, 1983

BENIGNO (NINOY) AQUINO JR. (1932–1983)
POLITICAL OPPONENT OF PHILIPPINE PRESIDENT FERDINAND MARCOS

Benigno Aquino rose swiftly through the political ranks of his province, then his country, becoming the youngest mayor, the youngest governor, and the youngest senator in Philippine history.

Aquino was born on November 27, 1932, into a prominent family in the province of Tarlac. After working as a journalist, he entered politics and was elected mayor of Concepción at age twenty-two. In 1959, he was elected vice-governor of Tarlac Province, and governor two years later. In 1966, the Liberal party chose Aquino to be its secretary-general, and the next year he was elected to the Senate. In 1955, Aquino had married Maria Corazon Conjuangco, the daughter of a prominent landowning family. She had been educated in the United States, where she obtained a bachelor-of-arts degree before returning to her country and marrying Aquino while he was still a political journalist. Many believe Corazon's wealth and connections helped Benigno launch his political career and propel him at a young age into a position of responsibility. As a senator, forty-year-old Benigno Aquino was distinctive and popular, and many believed that when Ferdinand Marcos's term of office as president expired, Aquino would succeed him.

ASSASSIN: Rolando Galman, a young Filipino airport worker, was initially blamed for Aquino's murder, but after an extensive investigation, the government was forced to admit that Galman was not the assassin. Investigators eventually uncovered a conspiracy that implicated President Marcos in Aquino's assassination.

HISTORY: By 1972, when Philippine president Ferdinand E. Marcos faced losing his position because his term of office was ending and he

Benigno Aquino

UPI / CORBIS-BETTMANN

could not constitutionally succeed himself, everyone believed Benigno Aquino was his obvious successor. But Marcos and his wife, Imelda, evidently didn't want to lose the rewards of his powerful position, so an alternate plan was executed. On September 23, 1972, Marcos declared martial law, naming himself supreme commander, intending to stay in control of his country perhaps for the rest of his life. One of Marcos's first dictatorial acts was to purge his political rivals. Benigno Aquino, at the top of Marcos's list, was arrested and charged with murder, rape, illegal possession of firearms, and subversion. Although Aquino was convicted on all counts and given a death sentence in 1977, Marcos put off having him executed. During the several years that Aquino was held in prison, he developed a heart condition that required expert medical attention. Reportedly, in response to international protests against Aquino's imprisonment, the Carter administration persuaded Marcos to commute Aquino's death sentence in 1980 and allow him to go to the United States for medical treatment. After being released, Aquino and his family went to Boston, where he underwent open-heart surgery. During the next three years, while Aquino pursued research fellowships at Harvard University and MIT, conditions became worse in the Philippines.

The Carter administration, which endorsed preserving human rights in the Philippines, was replaced by the Reagan administration, which was more interested in containing communism. While Marcos maintained a friendly relationship with Washington, he also repressed the civil rights of his people and accumulated a vast fortune that was supposed to go to the welfare of his country and its citizens. Marcos's advancing age, a diagnosed kidney ailment, and lupus erythematosus caused him to reconsider his political options. Martial law was lifted in 1981—perhaps in response to a visit from then Vice-President George Bush—and although Marcos was reelected president, the election was widely believed to be fraudulent. Plans were being made for Imelda to succeed her husband when he became too ill to continue in office.

Although the Marcoses never expected the Aquinos to return to the Philippines, reports about widespread oppression, corruption, and discontent in their home country were disturbing to the Aquinos. With the political left gathering strength and a parliamentary election coming up, the Aquinos felt Benigno had to be in the Philippines and take the lead if the moderates were to have any hope of gaining control of the country. In 1983, when Aquino openly discussed his plans to return to Manila, Imelda Marcos went to New York to talk him out of it. The Philippine consulate in New York refused to issue passports to Aquino and his family, but Aquino could not be dissuaded. He declared that his rights as a Philippine citizen entitled him to return to his homeland. Marcos restated the charges he had previously brought against Aquino, adding that he could not guarantee Aquino's safety if he returned. Although Aquino's friends in the Philippines urged him not to make the trip, he told them, "I'm committed to return. If fate falls that I should be killed, so be it."

EVENT: When Benigno Aquino announced that he would be flying home to Manila aboard Japan Air Lines, the Philippine government said it would revoke JAL's landing rights on any flight that carried undocumented passengers. So Aquino decided to take a circuitous route home. On August 14, 1983, accompanied by his family, a corps of supporters, and journalists, Aquino flew to China. He spent a week wandering through several Asian capitals; then, on August 21, using the name "Bonifacio," a nineteenth-century Filipino martyr, he boarded China Airlines Flight 811 in Taiwan, with a female reporter posing as his companion. To ensure his departure, other members of his party pretended not to know Aquino until they were airborne. Still, in Manila, everyone seemed to know the exact time that Benigno Aquino would arrive home. The city was decorated with yellow ribbons, and more than twenty thousand supporters, including his seventy-five-year-old mother, Aurora, tried to enter the airport to greet him. But government security forces had cordoned off the airport to keep Aquino's supporters away from any area of the airport where they could see his plane landing. The military cleared the airport lobby and locked the doors shut, then took control of AVESCOM, the aviation security command, and waited with a regiment of soldiers armed with M-16s on the tarmac. General Fabian Ver, armed forces chief of staff, had publicly stated that he would send Aquino "back on the same plane he arrived on."

Aboard the China Airlines Boeing 767, Aquino strolled to the washroom and put on a bulletproof vest under his white safari suit. "My chances of surviving this trip are 10 percent," he told a *Newsweek* reporter aboard the flight. As the plane landed and taxied toward gate number eight, then slowed to a stop, Benigno Aquino sat calmly in his economy-class seat. Three armed security men, one from the Philippine Constabulary and two from AVESCOM, boarded the front of the plane, walked past Aquino's seat and, when he stood up, surrounded him. They turned him toward the back of the plane, where the exit door had been opened and a steel staircase was positioned outside. Aquino's entourage tried to press close to him, but the security guards shoved them away while a triangle of three guards moved Aquino toward the rear exit. Waiting outside, at the top of the metal staircase, were more uniformed men, who closed in, surrounding Aquino. Journalists rushed to the plane's windows to see what was happening as guards shut the back door. Journalists then rushed to the door, intending to open it, but were pushed back by two security guards.

Suddenly a barrage of gunfire broke out. A television cameraman moved toward a window, his camera ready to film what was going on outside the airplane, but security guards slammed him against the bulkhead, preventing him from getting to a window. Some people who did manage to reach first-class windows saw Aquino laying facedown on the tarmac, blood spurting from a huge hole in the back of his head. Lying near him, also facedown, was a man wearing an airport mechanic's blue coveralls. Standing over Aquino were three AVESCOM men, still shooting into Aquino's body. The guards who had led Aquino out of the plane were not in sight, while swarms of AVESCOM troopers crisscrossed the scene, firing their rifles into the air. Finally, two AVESCOM troopers picked up Aquino's body, threw it into an AVESCOM van parked near the steel staircase, and drove away.

AFTERMATH: The body of Benigno Aquino was put on display in an open, glass-covered coffin at the Aquino's suburban Manila home. For three days, as some thirty thousand mourners filed past, they could see that although Aquino had been embalmed, no effort had been made to disguise his face, which was horribly disfigured by the bullet wound. Then, during a ten-hour journey from the Quezon City church of Santo Domingo to the Manila Memorial Park cemetery, over a million people accompanied Aquino's funeral cortege, shouting, "Democracy, freedom, revolution."

Authorities initially blamed Aquino's assassination on a lone gunman named Rolando Galman, the man also lying facedown on the tarmac, who had immediately been shot dead by security forces. But an investigation suggested that there had been a high-level conspiracy within the corrupt and demoralized Philippine army. Eventually, fifteen senior army officers, including chief of staff General Fabian Ver, were arrested and tried for Aquino's murder, but all were acquitted in December of 1985.

In the meantime, Corazon Aquino, who had not previously assumed a public role, became the symbol of moral opposition to Marcos's corrupt regime. She addressed large protest rallies during this period of political turmoil in the Philippines, and, as former Marcos supporters defected, Corazon announced that she would run against Ferdinand Marcos for the presidency of the Philippines. During their bitter election battle, the Marcos regime was accused of trying to rig the electoral process, and the Philippine military threw its support behind Corazon Aquino. When Marcos was declared the winner in February of 1986, independent observers charged his regime with widespread fraud. Faced with the desertion of his allies and mounting public disorder, Marcos was deposed on February 25, 1986, and fled, along with his wife and his cousin, General Fabian Ver, to the United States. Corazon Aquino was elevated to the presidency of the Philippines and vowed that her husband's assassins would be brought to justice. While Ferdinand and Imelda Marcos were living in exile in Hawaii (where he died on September 18, 1989), Corazon Aquino's new regime launched a campaign to locate and recover an estimated $3 billion that the Marcoses had salted away throughout the Western world.

The acquittal of those previously charged in the conspiracy to assassinate Benigno Aquino was overturned by the Philippine Supreme Court, and a new trial was ordered. General Luther Custodio and fifteen other defendants were found guilty on September 28, 1990, and sentenced to life imprisonment.

OCTOBER 31, 1984

INDIRA PRIYADARSHINI GANDHI
(1917–1984)
PRIME MINISTER OF INDIA FROM 1966 TO 1977,
AND FROM 1980 TO 1984

Indira Gandhi was regarded as a strong-willed matriarch who dominated her country's affairs both nationally and internationally for nearly eighteen years.

Indira was born in Allahabad, India, the daughter of Jawaharlal Nehru. After being educated at the University of Bengal and at Somerville College, Oxford, she followed in her father's footsteps and entered politics, joining the All-India Congress Party in 1938 at age twenty-one. In 1942, Indira married Feroze Gandhi, a man not related to Mahatma Gandhi. When India achieved independence in 1947 and Indira's father became prime minister, she served as his political hostess, often traveling with him abroad. Her father completely depended on the affectionate assistance of his only child, who had moved back into his house with her two sons, Rajiv and Sanjay. During that time, Indira gained insight into Indian politics, leading to her election as president of the Congress party in 1959. When Prime Minister Nehru died in 1964, Indira Gandhi became minister of information and broadcasting in the government of Lal Bahadur Shastri, her father's successor. After Shastri died in 1966, Indira Gandhi was elected leader of India's Congress party and prime minister.

Gandhi first demonstrated her strength as leader of her nation when she intervened decisively in the Pakistani civil war beginning in 1971. By the time the Bengalis of East Pakistan, with the support of India, achieved independence and their own nation of Bangladesh in 1972, Gandhi was praised for her handling of the situation both in India and abroad. She pursued a policy of nonalignment in international affairs, and in 1974 saw her country emerge as a nuclear power with the explosion of a nuclear device in northern India's Rajasthan Desert. Still, widespread political unrest, exacerbated by droughts in 1972 and 1974, and a struggling economy posed a continual threat to her rule. Gandhi perceived this unrest as a threat to national security and instituted a state of emergency in June of 1975. Political opponents were imprisoned, the press was censored, civil liberties were restricted, and measures were introduced to control population growth (by sterilization) and to clear slum dwellings in Delhi, leading to widespread civil unrest. Gandhi's youngest son, Sanjay, assumed a prominent role in these activities. Faced with the unpopularity of her emergency measures, Indira Gandhi called a general election in 1977 and was defeated by Morarji Desai, who was head of the Janata party. But Desai's new government proved to be indecisive, and in the next general election, in 1979, Gandhi was returned to power. That same year, her politically promising son Sanjay was killed in a plane crash. Indira Gandhi's second term of office was plagued by religious disturbances: Some three thousand people died in ethnic clashes in Assam between 1982 and 1984, and extremist Sikhs of the Punjab, who were demanding autonomy, initiated terrorist activities.

Indira Gandhi believed, as her father had, that India could function as a nonreligious democracy, a belief that was not shared by the Sikhs of India's Punjab state, whose lives and faith were tightly bound. Wearing distinctive turbans and beards and following a religion that is a kind of hybrid of Hinduism and Islam, the Sikhs suffered greatly in the 1947 partition, when their homeland of West Pakistan was taken away from them. Known for their incorruptibility and ferocious courage, they acquired enormous influence in India; even though they composed only about 2 percent of the population, they made up about 15 percent of the Indian army and were similarly well represented in government ranks. When Indira Gandhi returned to power in 1980, the president of her party was Zail Singh (Singh, meaning lion, is a name all Sikh men use), and police officer Beant Singh became a member of the inner circle of her residential guard.

ASSASSINS: Beant Singh was born in 1950 in the Punjab village of Maloya, near Chandigarh, and was only sixteen when Indira Gandhi first came to power. He left his wife in Maloya to join the police in 1975 and then joined New Delhi's armed police in 1980. Beant Singh was chosen to be a member of the prime minister's trusted guards, the Special Security District, in 1982. A large, gregarious man, Beant Singh sometimes traveled with Indira Gandhi when she went abroad. Having the same rare blood type as Gandhi—type O negative—he was more than just a bodyguard; his blood could save her life. He was aided in the assassination by Satwant Singh, a Delhi police constable.

HISTORY: During her years in power, Indira Gandhi was fiercely dedicated to her concept of a united India, consistently placing other interests second to that primary goal. Opposition state governments were repeatedly suspended and force was used, as in the Sikh rebellion in the Punjab, whenever the Indian federation appeared to be threatened. But she also allied herself with a humble Sikh cleric named Janail Singh Bhindranwale, who was preaching in the Punjab. Encouraged by Gandhi's support, Bhindranwale had evolved radically, urging the creation of a Sikh nation that separatists called Khalistan. Gathering the zealous around him in 1982, he embarked on a violent campaign of terror, resulting in hundreds of deaths in Punjab. For his stronghold, he chose the Sikh's holiest of shrines, the Golden Temple at Amritsar, and fortified it against an inevitable siege. That siege came in June of 1984 while subinspector Beant Singh was on a month's leave in Maloya, but the Indian army's assault, called Operation Bluestar, on the Golden Temple went terribly wrong. Instead of encountering poorly armed civilians cowering behind the ornate temple walls, the army came up against a force of some five hundred highly trained, well-equipped Sikh warriors who held the battle's key vantage points and fields of fire and were prepared to die for their cause. During three days of heavy fighting more than one hundred soldiers were killed, including Bhindranwale, along with hundreds of militants and pilgrims inside the shrine. An estimated six hundred to one thousand people died in the siege.

Indira and Rajiv Gandhi

UPI / CORBIS-BETTMANN

Afterward, there was an angry backlash among India's Sikhs. Soldiers mutinied, and Sikhs demonstrated in the streets, and in one case Sikh cadets shot an Indian army brigadier. In July, a Sikh guard for a cabinet minister hijacked a domestic airliner to protest the Golden Temple raid. On a tour of the ravaged Golden Temple, President Zail Singh prayed for forgiveness of Indira Gandhi, but one Sikh leader living abroad said, "Mrs. Gandhi made a fatal mistake. Every man who thinks himself as a Sikh can never forget that she has signed her own death warrant."

Sikh bodyguards, including Beant Singh, assigned to protect the prime minister were reassigned to an outer cordon around her New Delhi compound, which served as both her office and her residence. When she learned of this, Mrs. Gandhi personally insisted that the Sikhs be restored to positions of trust, saying she would not be secular and single out one group. Despite intelligence warnings that it would be dangerous to keep Sikh guards close by, the prime minister felt that reinstating them would strengthen her image. Weeks before, she had said, "I've lived with danger all my life, and it makes no difference whether you die in bed or you die standing up." On October 30, she told a political gathering, "If I die today, every drop of my blood will invigorate the nation."

EVENT: Among the Sikh detachment, an assassination conspiracy was underway. In the New Delhi home of Beant Singh's uncle, Kehar Singh, the young guard secretly rendezvoused and decided what must be done. Satwant Singh, a brawny twenty-one-year-old constable who had joined the Delhi Armed Police in 1982, was brought in to help. On October 30, 1984, Beant Singh asked to change places with a colleague on the next day's duty roster, a routine substitution, so he could take up a position at the gate on the path that linked the prime minister's home and her office building. Satwant Singh, who was normally assigned to an outer-perimeter guard position, asked to be stationed near the same gate as well, saying he had a bad stomach and needed to be near a lavatory.

On October 31, 1984, Beant Singh and Satwant Singh were at their stations at 9:10 A.M. Beant Singh held a .38-caliber service revolver. Satwant Singh carried a Sten, a light submachine gun. Indira Gandhi, leading a procession of aides and bodyguards across the compound for a television interview with British actor Peter Ustinov on the far side of her office building, approached the guards from her residence. Recognizing Beant Singh, who had spent years at her side, she smiled and greeted the subinspector. He responded by shooting Gandhi three times in the abdomen. Indira Gandhi buckled as Satwant Singh emptied his thirty-round Sten-gun magazine in the direction of her and her bodyguards, who scattered for cover. "We have done what we wanted to," Beant Singh said, dropping his pistol and raising his arms. "Now you can do what you want to."

When Sonia Gandhi, the wife of Indira Gandhi's elder son, Rajiv, heard the gunshots, she ran from her upstairs quarters to her mother-in-law's side. Security guards and Indira Gandhi's assistant, R. K. Dhawan, carried her lifeless, blood-soaked body to her white limousine and placed it inside. Sonia cradled the prime minister's head in her lap as the limousine rushed to the All-India Institute of Medical Sciences hospital. There, Indira Gandhi, still showing no signs of life, was rushed to an eighth-floor operating room, where twelve doctors desperately tried to revive her. Not accepting that she was dead, doctors put her on life support, removed seven bullets from her body, and gave her several pints of blood. The official announcement of her death was made at 1:45 P.M., one hour before her son Rajiv, who was on an airplane returning from Calcutta, would arrive and be told his mother had been assassinated.

PUNISHMENT: Beant Singh and Satwant Singh were quickly taken away by a special commando unit assigned to guard the compound. Minutes later, inside the guardhouse, the commandos claimed, the two men attempted an escape. Beant Singh was shot to death, and Satwant Singh was wounded eight times. As Satwant Singh was recovering, he told doctors that he was a member of a conspiracy to kill both Indira Gandhi and her son Rajiv. Satwant Singh was later tried and convicted of murder, along with two of his coconspirators. In January of 1989, after exhausting all appeals, Satwant Singh was hanged, along with Beant Singh's uncle, Kehar Singh, a former government clerk.

AFTERMATH: Word of Indira Gandhi's assassination by Sikh hands spread across the subcontinent, causing rioting and fighting. During the following three days, some three thousand Sikhs were killed by mobs in eighty cities, more than two thousand of them in Delhi.

Indira Gandhi was succeeded as prime minister by her elder son, Rajiv Gandhi, who had become her close adviser after his brother's death in 1980. Rajiv Gandhi's position was confirmed with an overwhelming victory during a general election in December of 1984.

In March of 1989, a secret government report was released which indicated that a powerful Gandhi aide, Rajendra Kumar Dhawan, had been closely investigated for possible involvement in the plot to assassinate Indira Gandhi. Dhawan was ousted from his position by Prime

Minister Rajiv Gandhi, but after the investigation was completed, Dhawan was reinstated. After the report was officially released and Dhawan was cleared, Home Affairs Minister Buta Singh added mystery to the situation by claiming that investigators had uncovered a larger conspiracy in Indira Gandhi's assassination and legal actions would soon be taken. Observers concluded that those charges would implicate an unnamed foreign agency from Pakistan, which inspired and trained Sikh terrorists in an effort to destabilize India.

 FEBRUARY 28, 1986

SVEN OLOF PALME (1927–1986)
SWEDISH SOCIALIST-DEMOCRATIC POLITICIAN AND PRIME MINISTER FROM 1969 TO 1976 AND 1982 TO 1986

While he was prime minister, Olof Palme carried out constitutional reforms, turned the Riksdag into a single-chamber parliament, and stripped the monarch of power. He gained wide respect for supporting Third World countries.

Olof Palme was born into a wealthy Swedish family. He was educated in Sweden and in the United States, where he graduated from Kenyon College in Gambier, Ohio. He then spent several months hitchhiking around the United States. Back home in Sweden, Palme joined the socialist party in 1949, became secretary to the prime minister in 1954, led a socialist youth movement from 1955 to 1961, and in 1963 began working in various government positions. While serving as minister of education and religious affairs in 1968, Palme caused a stir by marching in a demonstration against U.S. involvement in Vietnam. A passionate democratic socialist and champion of Third World causes,

Palme also spoke out against the 1968 Soviet invasion of Czechoslovakia. Although he was an admirer of the United States, when forty-two-year-old Palme was sworn in as prime minister in 1969, U.S. president Richard Nixon, displeased with Palme's socialist views, refused to accept the credentials of the Swedish ambassador-designate for almost two years. When Palme's party, the Social Democrats, was defeated in 1976, displacing him from the position of prime minister, he became a member of the Brandt Commission, which studied problems of the Third World. The Social Democrats regained power in 1982, and Palme became prime minister again.

In 1982, the Swedish secret police begged Palme to enhance his personal security, but the prime minister mocked the tight security precautions taken to protect other world leaders and took pride in feeling he could walk the streets of Stockholm unguarded. He allowed only a small group of bodyguards and often dismissed them when staying close to home.

EVENT: On February 28, 1986, Prime Minister Olof Palme informed the Swedish Security Police that he would be spending a quiet evening at home and told them they were not needed. Later that day, Marten, one of the Palme's three sons, invited his father and mother to go with him to a movie. The Palmes left their home, took the subway to Stockholm's main thoroughfare, and met Marten and his girlfriend at the Stockholm Grand Cinema. The foursome waited in the ticket line with everyone else, but when they reached the cashier, they were told the showing of *The Brothers Mozart*, a new Swedish comedy, was sold out. Before they could leave, the cashier recognized the prime minister and gave him four tickets that were reserved but not claimed.

After the movie, Palme and his wife, Lisbet, said good-bye to their son and his girlfriend, then began walking back toward the subway. Six minutes later, at 11:21 P.M., as they reached the intersection of Tunnelgatan, Lisbet Palme walked momentarily ahead of her husband. Suddenly she heard a loud bang. She turned and saw a man in a dark coat with a cap pulled over his forehead, who had just shot her husband twice in the back. The assailant fired another time, grazing Lisbet Palme's fur coat, then he ran up Tunnelgatan and disappeared in a maze of nearby streets. Prime Minister Palme fell onto the pavement. A passing nurse attempted to resuscitate him, but Palme died at the scene within minutes of the attack.

AFTERMATH: Police initially showed an inclination toward inefficiency in pursuing Palme's assassin, perhaps because a political assassination had not occurred in Sweden for two hundred years—the last was in 1792, when King Gustav III was killed at a masquerade ball. It was 12:40 A.M. before officials stopped trains from leaving the nearby Central Station. An order to watch roads going out of the city was given ten minutes after that, and the country's airports were not shut down until 2:05 A.M. Instead of securing the scene and searching for physical evidence, police allowed mourners to cover the sidewalk with red roses, the symbol of Palme's Social Democratic party. Although two bullets were found, it was by ordinary citizens long after the shooting, not by police. After looking at the copper-cased lead-tipped bullets, investigators announced that they were unusual, maybe even handmade, but journalists were able to buy boxes of the same bullets at a store two blocks away from police headquarters.

There were reports that the West German Red Army Faction (RAF), a left-wing terrorist organization, claimed responsibility for killing Palme, but Swedish police thought the assassin may have been an individual with a grudge against the prime minister. Speculation focused on one of many refugee groups—Palestinian, Croatian, Chilean, Kurdish, Syrian, and Iranian—that had found shelter in Palme's liberal Sweden.

The assassination was a huge shock to the Swedish public, which had always regarded their nation as a rational society, largely immune from random violence seen elsewhere. The impact of the crime became even worse when the press referred to the official investigation as "a shambles." Newspaper ads appeared worldwide offering cash rewards of more than $8 million for information that could lead to Palme's assassin.

On March 12 police finally arrested a suspect. Ake Viktor Gunnarsson, a thirty-three-year-old schoolteacher who had heckled Palme at political rallies, was a follower of the European Workers' Party (EAP), a right-wing group founded by American fanatic Lyndon H. LaRouche. The EAP had been quoted as saying Palme was "the devil of devils," and the group had distributed bumper stickers saying, "A new Palme is born every day: wear a condom." But soon the case against Gunnarsson was discredited: Powder marks found on Gunnarsson's clothes did not match those found on Palme, and it was learned that one witness had been shown Gunnarsson's photograph before picking him out of a police lineup. Although Gunnarsson was released within a week of his arrest, he was rearrested in May, then released again.

The investigation was increased to a 140-man task force, with the focus shifted to foreign terrorist groups. One group of particular interest was the Kurdish Workers' Party (PKK), a Marxist organization campaigning for an independent Kurdistan, whose known assassins shot their victims in the back of the head. On January 20, 1987, thirteen Kurdish immigrants were arrested, and police charged three of them with being accessories in Palme's assassination. Some reports say officials theorized that the Kurdish extremists had been hired by Iran to kill Palme in retaliation for the prime minister stopping Swedish arms shipments to Iran. Other reports say the Kurds' motive was retaliation for the Swedish government's refusing to grant a residence visa to the PKK's leader. In either case, the Kurds were all released for lack of evidence. As a result, when Hans Holmer, Stockholm's chief of police, was removed as the key investigator, he resigned his job, insisting his successors were disorganized and not up to the task of solving this crime. He subsequently wrote a book spelling out his unproved case against the PKK.

On December 14, 1988, authorities arrested a suspect referred to as "the bayonet man." Despite Swedish press regulations dictating that anyone held by police or even brought to trial may not be identified in print, the foreign press quickly revealed that the new suspect was Gustav Christer Pettersson, a forty-one-year-old unemployed laborer. Reports showed that Pettersson had spent much of his adult life either in prison or undergoing compulsory psychiatric treatment, and that he had a history of drug and alcohol abuse. Of his sixty-three convictions, two were notable: In 1970 he had killed a youth with a bayonet and served three years in prison with mandatory psychiatric care under Sweden's liberal jail policies. In 1975, Pettersson was sentenced to fourteen months for assault with a bayonet. In 1977 he was falsely arrested for killing his father, and he was released. He was soon imprisoned again, that time getting five years for attempted murder. Once again, his weapon of choice was a bayonet.

When Pettersson went on trial for Palme's assassination on June 5, 1989, an opinion poll indicated that only 18 percent of the public believed he was guilty, and 42 percent thought he was innocent. He was tried before a panel of two judges and six jurors, called lay assessors, chosen along political party lines from a pool of 707 prospective jurors. Three of the jurors were Social Democrats, like Palme, and three were from the rival conservative parties. Prosecutors presented almost no forensic evidence. They offered no murder weapon and provided no clear motive. Although Mrs. Palme had not actually seen Pettersson shoot her husband, she identified him as the man she saw a few feet away from her dying husband an instant after the shooting. While she said she was certain "beyond any doubt," Pettersson denied he had committed the crime. When the verdict came in, all six lay assessors voted guilty, but the two judges found him not guilty, pointing out that Mrs. Palme did not have an opportunity to identify the defendant in a videotaped police lineup until December 14, 1988, almost two years after the crime. Still, Pettersson was sentenced to life in prison.

Swedish television aired a number of interviews with various legal experts as well as the general public immediately after the trial. The general consensus was that the verdict had not settled many key questions about whether Pettersson or some other individuals with political purposes had assassinated Palme. The original verdict was reversed in October of 1989 by an appeals court made up of four professional jurists and three lay assessors. Their verdict was 7–0 for reversal, with the court president saying: "Our present judgment is that the investigation into the case is insufficient for a conviction." Pettersson was released that same day. Police officials said the investigation would be renewed immediately.

1990s

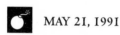 MAY 21, 1991

RAJIV GANDHI (1944–1991)
INDIAN POLITICIAN AND PRIME MINISTER
FROM 1984 UNTIL NOVEMBER OF 1989

As the elder son of Indira Gandhi and the grandson of Jawaharlal Nehru, Rajiv Gandhi was born into the Kashmiri Brahmin family that had governed India since 1947, except for four years. Instead of becoming involved in the family business of politics, Rajiv became a pilot with Indian Airlines. But after his brother Sanjay died in a place crash, Rajiv was elected to Sanjay's Amethi parliamentary seat in 1981. After his mother was assassinated, Rajiv Gandhi was elected prime minister by a record majority in December 1984. Despite his popularity, a scandal involving alleged kickbacks to senior officials in an arms deal with the Swedish munitions firm Bofors tarnished Rajiv's reputation and, following his party's defeat in the general election of November 1989, Gandhi was forced to resign as prime minister.

When Rajiv Gandhi began a campaign for reelection as prime minister in 1991, threats to his security were a serious concern. Besides the Sikhs of Punjab, other secular groups had organized in India. One group in particular, the Liberation Tigers, a budding revolutionary army drawn from the Hindu Tamil population of northwestern Sri Lanka, had been given tacit support by Indira Gandhi's government.

ASSASSINS: A group of conspirators who were members of the Liberation Tigers of Tamil Eelam (LTTE).

HISTORY: During the nineteenth century, the British had shipped thousands of Tamils across the twenty-six-mile-wide Palk Strait to work at the island's tea estates in the then English colony of Celon. But in 1947, as independence ignited the separatist aspirations of Indian Hindus, Sikhs, and Muslims, it also gave hope to Hindu Tamils of Sri Lanka, where almost 80 percent of the population is Buddhist Sinhalese. As the Tamils became an increasingly powerless minority, they campaigned to reestablish Eelam, the provincial capital of India's Tamil Nadu district on the northern section of the island, as their homeland. Indira Gandhi's government had not looked too closely at the training camps that sprang up in the Tamil Nadu district of southern India, or the traffic that moved continuously across the Palk Strait. By the early 1980s, even before Indira Gandhi was assassinated, the LTTE, a separatist movement, had started raiding Sri Lanka's northwestern settlements.

Rajiv Gandhi was less friendly toward the LTTE than his mother had been. Giving a speech in Madras in 1985 as the new prime minister, he said, "I will not allow Eelam." As Sri Lanka headed toward civil war, Rajiv Gandhi tried to intercede, helping to arrange a cease-fire between the Sri Lankan army and the LTTE in July of 1987. But the agreement was detested by LTTE supremo Villupillai Prabhakaran, who said it was really a call for his own troops to lay down their arms, and the truce collapsed. Prime Minister Rajiv Gandhi sent some sixty thousand troops, called the Indian Peace Keeping Force (IPKF) into Sri Lanka, intending to restore order and protect civilian interests in the north. Although there had been some five thousand guerrilla troops there in 1987, by 1988 fewer than fifteen hundred remained. Nevertheless, the stubbornly aggressive LTTE still managed to kill more than three thousand Indian "peacekeeping" soldiers during 1990.

When Rajiv Gandhi lost the 1989 election to Vishwanath Prataz Singh, his shield of protection by an impregnable Indian security force was dropped. In November of 1990, Rajiv campaigned, without the protection of heavy security, to become prime minister again in a May 1991 election. LTTE leader Prabhakaran, who considered Gandhi's sending in the army against his followers to be an unforgivable affront, summoned four of his lieutenants. Prabhakaran told the lieutenants that Gandhi's anti-Eelam sentiments were well known, and that the LTTE could not risk having him back in power. They must strike quickly, and they must do it on Tamil ground, in Madras.

The plan was set in motion. A thirty-three-year-old senior LTTE agent named Shivarasan would be the field commander of the scheme, while other LTTE members would find a safe house, acquire materials, and make a bomb. In Madras, a radical student was recruited, and his parents' house was used as the LTTE hideout. Two free-lance photographers, Ravi Shankaran and a man called Haribabu, were enlisted to photograph the actual assassination—an LTTE trademark—and an electronics expert was asked to design and build the bomb. When Shivarasan arrived in Madras during the first week of March, a satisfactory bomb had been prepared. It was composed of six grenades linked by silver wires and fastened to a denim girdle. Each grenade contained eighty grams of C4-RDX high explosives and 2,800 two-millimeter steel shards; the grenades were then encased in TNT. The bomb was powered by a single nine-volt battery with two toggle switches—one to control the bomb-armed circuit, the other to detonate the grenades. Finally, the bomb would have a human delivery system: one of Shivarasan's young female cousins named Dhanu; another cousin, named Subha, would be her backup.

EVENT: On May 19, 1991, the Congress party announced that Rajiv Gandhi would speak at a campaign rally near Madras on the afternoon of May 21. That day, Dhanu slipped into the grenade-packed denim girdle, then dressed in an orange salwar-kameez, the long shirt worn by men and women in urban India. The shapeless garment gave no hint that she was padded with explosives. The conspirators arrived by bus at the site of the rally, then took up their positions. Shivarasan stood near the dais. Haribabu, carrying a borrowed Pentax camera, and Dhanu, carrying a sandalwood garland, waited near the red carpet that Gandhi would follow to the platform. The candidate's motorcade arrived at about 10 P.M., and he slowly made his way through the throng of people. Dhanu waited tranquilly, with Shivarasan standing less than ten feet behind her. Haribabu focused on Dhanu through the Pentax viewfinder, clicking frame after frame to preserve this moment in LTTE history.

As Rajiv Gandhi approached her, Dhanu flipped the first toggle switch, tripping the bomb-armed circuit, then stepped forward, raising the garland toward Gandhi. An alert female constable nearby held out an arm to stop Dhanu from getting close to Gandhi, but he intervened. "Let everyone have a turn," he said, smiling. "Don't worry. Relax." He turned back to Dhanu, who placed the garland around Gandhi's neck, then knelt down as if to touch his feet. When Gandhi bowed slightly to lift her, Dhanu smiled at him briefly, then flipped the second switch.

Although only four of the six grenades detonated, they were more than enough. The bomb blast ripped Dhanu apart, sending her severed head tumbling through the air. The explosion pounded into Rajiv Gandhi, tearing away the left side of his face, crushing his skull, and excavating his abdomen and chest. The photographer, Haribabu, who had positioned himself too close to Dhanu, was killed, along with fifteen bystanders. Shivarasan was untouched and was on his way back to Madras within minutes of the assassination.

AFTERMATH: Although Haribabu did not survive the blast, the film in his borrowed Pentax did. Indian officials developed the thirty-five-millimeter roll of film and used the damning images of Gandhi's assassination to identify dozens of conspirators and Tamil sympathizers. While many were being rounded up, many others committed suicide to avoid arrest. Shivarasan, Subha, and five others managed to escape but were cornered three months later near the southern Indian city of Bangalore. Surrounded by commandos and police prepared for a shoot-out, the LTTE death squad took cyanide. They died on August 20, 1991, Rajiv Gandhi's forty-seventh birthday.

After Rajiv's assassination, his widow, Sonia Gandhi, was appointed by the Congress party as its candidate for prime minister, but she declined their offer to succeed her husband. With that, the Nehru dynasty, which had dominated the Congress party and Indian politics since partition, was essentially ended.

 APRIL 10, 1993

CHRIS HANI (1942–1993)
SECRETARY GENERAL OF THE SOUTH AFRICAN COMMUNIST PARTY AND PROMINENT ANTI-APARTHEID AFRICAN NATIONAL CONGRESS LEADER

At the time of his death Martin Thembisile "Chris" Hani was the second most popular black figure in South Africa, surpassed only by Nelson Mandela, president of the African National Congress (ANC). While Mandela was older and more moderate, Hani was idolized by many radical black youths who preferred his leadership.

Born in Colimvaba, Trenskei, on June 18, 1942, Chris Hani graduated from the predominately white Rhodes University with a degree in classics. In 1962, he joined the armed struggle against apartheid as a member of the ANC's military wing, Umkhonto we Sizwe (Spear of the Nation), but fled his country months later, after being sentenced to prison under the Suppression of Communism Act. While in exile, Hani joined the fight against white rule in Rhodesia (now Zimbabwe) and was imprisoned for two years in Botswana for weapons possession. After his release he moved to Lesotho, where he ran an Umkhonto network for seven years, whose guerrillas infiltrated South Africa and carried out bombings. In 1987 Hani became the Umkhonto chief of staff, and in 1991 he was named secretary general of the South African Communist Party (SACP). He survived two assassination attempts during his time in Lesotho.

Despite antiapartheid groups being legalized in 1990, Hani was initially reluctant to participate in power-sharing talks between South Africa's white-minority government and black political organizations because the state had demonized him as an agent of communist revolution. In time, though, he began to stress to his followers the importance negotiations could play in achieving majority rule. He even became the first black leader to call on the militant Pan-Africanist Congress to stop violent attacks on white civilians.

ASSASSIN: Janusz Walus, a white right-wing extremist who had emigrated from Poland to South Africa in 1981 and became a South African citizen.

HISTORY: Black South Africans began their long and bloody struggle against an oppressive apartheid government soon after South Africa gained independence from Great Britain. British Parliament initiated South Africa's independence by passing the Statute of Westminster in December of 1931. Its formal acceptance by South Africa came in 1934. The white minority of the independent South Africa immediately took control of the government and moved to limit the powers of nonwhites, creating designated areas, or homelands, where nonwhites were obligated to live. These efforts were formalized on May 26, 1948, when the conservative Afrikaner-dominated National party won parliamentary elections and gained control of the South African government. Under the direction of the party's new premier, Daniel F. Malan, steps were taken to implement South Africa's national policy of racial separation, called apartheid. On June 13, 1950, the Group Areas Act was enacted, which segregated communities, with the majority black population relegated to live in a minor percentage of the nation's land. On July 7, 1950, the Population Registrations Act was enacted; it required all South Africans to register their race with the government. Pass laws, which required blacks to carry passbooks so that their travel within the country could be regulated, were enacted in 1952. A Separate Amenities Act, which established separate public facilities for whites and nonwhites, was enacted in 1953.

By 1960, nonwhite political groups had organized underground movements against the country's apartheid policies. Among those fighting for the liberation of blacks and mixed-race South African citizens was the African National Congress. Although some of these organizations were militant, many staged peaceful demonstrations. One in particular took place in Sharpesville beginning March 21, but ended violently on April 5, when sixty-nine unarmed protesters were killed by police. The government responded by banning all opposition groups. In reaction, the African National Congress joined other opposition groups on June 26, adopting the Freedom Charter, which called for equal political rights for all races.

The racial conflicts in South Africa drew worldwide attention. The country's 23 million blacks could not even vote, while the 4.5 million whites controlled their government. On November 12, 1963, United Nations General Assembly president Abdelaziz Bouteflika, of Algeria, suspended South Africa from participating in assembly sessions for the remainder of that year. The following day, South Africa recalled its U.N. ambassador and froze its $1 million annual contribution to the organization. The white-minority government tried to take control at home on June 12, 1964, when Nelson Mandela, leader of the ANC, was convicted of sabotage and trying to overthrow the government, and was sentenced to life in prison. Civil unrest escalated, with 575 people being killed during eight months of demonstrations, including a student protest in the black township of Soweto on June 16, 1976. Some progress for blacks was made on October 16, 1976, when Transkei became the first homeland to be granted nominal independence; ten homelands would eventually make up about 13 percent of South African territory. One year later, Steven Biko, one of the nation's most influential black student leaders, reportedly died from a hunger strike while in police detention.

As a conciliatory attempt to calm internal strife, on November 2, 1983, white voters approved a new constitution that created separate chambers in the legislature for Asians and people of mixed race, but blacks still had no official voice. Riots and widespread strikes continued. On June 12, 1986, a national state of emergency was imposed, giving virtually unlimited powers to white-controlled security forces and imposing restrictions on the press. Although the government tried to show a positive intention toward black South Africans one month later by abolishing the laws requiring blacks to carry passbooks for identification, it was not enough to appease worldwide opposition to apartheid. On September 29, 1986, the U.S. Congress overrode President Ronald Reagan's veto and imposed strict economic sanctions against South Africa.

Finally, in response to internal unrest and external pressures, on September 14, 1989, reformist F. W. deKlerk of the National party was elected president. Although the government was still controlled by a white minority, deKlerk soon announced plans to scrap the Separate Amenities Act, which was subsequently repealed. In February of 1990, deKlerk lifted restrictions on thirty-three opposition groups, most of which had been banned for their antiapartheid activities, and ANC leader Nelson Mandela was released after serving twenty-seven years in prison. By October, the state of emergency was lifted in every part of South Africa. In January of 1991, black students entered previously all-white public schools. In June, the Land Acts of 1913 and 1936 were repealed, as were the Group Areas Act and the Population Registration Act, both of 1950. The United States responded to South Africa's progress against apartheid in July of 1991, when President George Bush lifted most U.S. economic sanctions against South Africa. In September, President deKlerk outlined his government's proposals for a new constitution that would give the black majority the right to vote for the first time. On December 20 and 21, 1991, when delegations from nineteen political groups met in Johannesburg for talks aimed at ending white-minority rule in South Africa, seventeen signed a declaration pledging they would work toward a nonracial democracy. On March 17, 1992, South African whites turned out in record numbers to vote for a referendum to negotiate an end to white-minority rule through talks with the black majority. DeKlerk's reform policies were overwhelmingly endorsed.

Still, in some regions of the country civil unrest continued. On June 17, 1992, more than forty blacks were killed in the South African township of Boipatong, prompting the ANC to withdraw from constitutional talks for four months. Mandela and the ANC urged the government to take steps to curb violence in the townships, which had already claimed fifteen hundred lives during 1992. Differences would finally be resolved in February of 1993 when the government and the ANC agreed on a transitional "government of national unity" and pledged to work as partners while the terms of the agreement were being presented to other political groups. The agreement called for white-minority rule to end by April of 1994, when there would be an election of a new four-hundred-seat assembly. South Africans of all races would be allowed to vote for the assembly members, who would serve as the parliament until around 1999, and part of their responsibility would be to write a new constitution. Any party that won at least 5 percent of the assembly seats would earn a position in the new cabinet, and a new president would be elected from the party that won the most votes in the 1994 election. At the end of this five-year transitional period, a new government would be elected under the terms of the new charter, with expectations that the country's black majority would finally rule South Africa.

After three days of vigorous debate among the moderate and radical wings of South Africa's National Executive Committee, the agreement was approved with a unanimous final vote. The five-year period of power sharing, they believed, would not only stabilize internal strife within the country but also provide an opportunity for the weakened economy to grow as the nation's business community and foreign investors became more confident of the future. Still, serious problems remained. Primarily, the roles of the army and the police had to be clarified, and the future status of the black homelands needed to be addressed. While moderates were comfortable with the length of the transition period, radicals wanted it shortened. Moderates cautioned that a short transition period might cause a backlash among white security forces, and pointed out that deKlerk's National party would, no doubt, be a minority after the 1994 election. Polls indicated that in a multiracial election, Nelson Mandela's ANC would win 50 to 60 percent of the vote, while deKlerk's National party would have only 20 to 30 percent. Hard-liners, including Marxist Harry Gwala and Communist Chris Hani, campaigned unsuccessfully for the agreement to be voted on by the entire rank-and-file membership of the congress.

EVENT: On April 10, 1993, fifty-year-old Chris Hani gave his body-guards the day off, then bought a newspaper at a supermarket near his home in the Dawn Park section of Baksburg, an interracial suburb of Johannesburg. He drove home, pulled into his driveway, and had just stepped out of his car when a white man approached and shot him four times. The gunman immediately drove off, but a white neighbor saw what had happened, took down the gunman's license-plate number, and called the police as Hani lay mortally wounded.

Ten days later, Hani's funeral service, which was held in an overflow-ing Soweto soccer stadium, was one of the biggest political events in South Africa since ANC president Mandela was freed from prison in 1990. Four million blacks stayed home from work that day in one of the country's biggest strikes. At Hani's funeral, Nelson Mandela was intro-duced as the country's next president, and delivered a eulogy that was intended to dissuade blacks from retaliating for Hani's assassination and to focus instead on the upcoming multiracial elections. "We want peace, but we are not pacifists," Mandela said. "We are all militants. We are all radicals." Also speaking at the funeral were ANC leader Tokyo Sexwale, Anglican archbishop Desmond Tutu, and Joe Slovo, chairman of the Communist party. Even Cuban president Fidel Castro sent a tribute to Hani to be read before the crowd. No government officials attended Hani's funeral.

Following the ceremony, Hani's body was laid to rest in a formerly whites-only cemetery in Boksburg, the interracial suburb of Johannesburg where Hani had lived. At the grave, as an honor guard from the ANC's military wing, Umkhonto we Sizwe, raised its rifles for a twenty-one-gun salute, some people in the crowd pulled out guns and also fired a final salute to their fallen leader. Nervous white property owners living across the street from the cemetery had accepted an offer of protection from members of the Afrikaner Resistance Movement (AWB), a neofascist paramilitary organization, who stood guard over their houses. But relative calm during the day's events was mostly credited to the ANC's 14,000 uniformed crowd marshals, who helped maintain discipline among the estimated eighty thousand mourners who attended Hani's funeral.

INVESTIGATION: Police apprehended Janusz Walus within hours of the shooting and found two guns in his car; a ballistic test would later identify one of them as the pistol that killed Hani. While searching Walus's apartment, police found a list of names and addresses of prominent politicians, including Hani. Although police immediately offered protection to each person on the apparent hit list, the ANC complained that months earlier, when ANC members had asked that Hani be protected, the police had turned down their request. On April 16, the *New Nation*, a Johannesburg daily newspaper, published nine names on the list found in Walus's apartment. In addition to Hani, other apparent targets were deKlerk, Nelson Mandela, Winnie Mandela, Joe Slovo, Foreign Minister Roelof (Pik) Botha, trade-union leader Jay Naidoo, Justice Richard Goldstone, who headed an independent commission investigating political violence, and Louis Skweyiya, the ANC's director for constitutional affairs.

Retha Harmse, Chris Hani's white neighbor who had witnessed his assassination and had given police the license-plate number of Walus's car, was placed under police guard on April 15 after she received death threats over the telephone. Nelson Mandela had paid tribute to Harmse at a rally on April 14, telling blacks to use her example "to build a new community."

While detectives from Great Britain and Germany were asked by the South African government to help in the police investigation, it was discovered that the murder weapon had been part of an arms cache stolen in April of 1990 from an air-force armory in Pretoria, the capital. The theft had been carried out by a far-right extremist group, Piet Rudolph, which was aligned with the AWB. On April 12, although AWB leader Eugene Terre'Blanche confirmed that Walus was a member of his movement, he insisted that Walus had acted alone, not on AWB orders. While Terre'Blanche condemned Hani's murder as "an atrocious deed," he also said it was "an assassination and not a kill in a real war," adding, "If it had been a proper battle I could have killed Mr. Hani myself." Many observers believed Terre'Blanche's claim that Walus had acted alone and that Hani's assassination apparently was not an act of racial animosity but Walus's means of striking out against communism. Walus had immigrated from Poland to South Africa in the early 1980s as part of a wave of Polish citizens escaping their country's communist regime.

Still, on April 17, Clive Derby-Lewis, a leading English-speaking politician in the Conservative party, a former member of Parliament, and a member of the President's Council, was arrested in connection with Hani's murder after police questioned Walus. Apparently the two men had met in 1985 when Derby-Lewis founded the Stallard Foundation, a pro-apartheid, anticommunist group that had recruited Eastern European immigrants, such as Walus. The Stallard Foundation reportedly had links to white-supremacist groups around the world. Five more whites were detained by police on April 21. Two were questioned, then released; the three who remained in police custody were Derby-Lewis's wife, Gaye, editor of the Conservative party's weekly newspaper *Die Patriot*; Arthur Kemp, a journalist for that publication; and Faan Venter, a Boksburg real-estate broker and AWB member.

PUNISHMENT: On October 4, 1993, thirty-eight-year-old Janusz Walus and fifty-seven-year-old Clive Derby-Lewis both pleaded not guilty to charges of murder, conspiracy to murder, and illegal possession of firearms. During their trial before Judge C. F. Eloff, neither man took the stand in his own defense. On October 14, Walus was convicted of shooting Chris Hani to death, and Derby-Lewis was found guilty of murder because he had supplied Walus with the gun used to kill Hani. The next day, both men were sentenced to death, although the death sentences could be reversed if the new postapartheid government dissolved the death penalty, which was suspended at that time.

During the trial, a third defendant, Derby-Lewis's fifty-four-year-old wife, Gaye, was charged with conspiring to kill Hani and with composing the alleged hit list of eight other antiapartheid advocates. Gaye Derby-Lewis admitted she had known of the list found in Walus's possession but claimed it was not a hit list. Rather, she explained, the list had been compiled by a right-wing journalist at her request as part of material to be used in articles she intended to write for the newspaper *Die Patriot,* and she insisted she did not know how Walus obtained the list. Although the judge was not convinced by her claims, he ruled that the defense had not supplied adequate evidence to prove she was involved with Hani's assassination.

In reaction to the verdicts, the ANC, which considered the trial a test of the equity of South Africa's postapartheid justice system, praised the police work which linked Clive Derby-Lewis to the gun used by Walus and applauded Retha Harmse, the prosecution's key witness, for testifying about seeing Walus shoot Hani. But the ANC also said it was "deeply disturbed" by Gaye Derby-Lewis's acquittal. In its statement released October 14, the ANC said, "Once again, white man's justice was meted out in a white man's court." They demanded that Gaye Derby-Lewis, an Australian-born former nun, be expelled from South Africa and accused the white-minority government of failing to initiate an inquiry into a wider conspiracy against antiapartheid leaders.

AFTERMATH: Nearly all of South Africa's political leaders expressed regret at Hani's death and urged their supporters to control their desire for revenge. ANC leaders and government officials appealed for calm, and both groups vowed that Hani's assassination would not derail negotiations on the transition to black majority rule.

Despite appeals for calm, several black townships erupted in violence. The ANC called for April 14 to be a national day of mourning for Hani and tried to channel the anger of blacks into strikes and peaceful demonstrations. Yet, protests that day turned out to be the most violent in years. As many as eight people were killed, hundreds were injured, and buildings were pillaged in most major cities. In Cape Town, some twenty thousand mourners went on a rampage downtown, a peace monitor was knifed, trains were derailed, and a prominent ANC official was assaulted. In Soweto, white police officers fired, allegedly without warning, on a peaceful demonstration outside a police station. Late that day, President deKlerk condemned the riots, saying, "What happened in South Africa today cannot be tolerated in a civilized country." And he announced that more security forces were being dispatched to bolster the twenty-three thousand troops already posted throughout the country.

On the day of Hani's funeral, when President deKlerk told Parliament in Cape Town that Hani's death "had plunged our country into crisis," the entire delegation of the liberal Democratic party walked out as a gesture of sympathy for Hani.

Despite the death of six blacks in violence related to the funeral, an anticipated repeat of the rioting that had wracked South African cities the previous week did not materialize. On April 19, the *Financial Times* noted that there had been twenty-eight politically motivated killings since Hani's death, a number well below the weekly average.

Chris Hani's death was felt most strongly by the South African Communist party, which didn't have a candidate of comparable stature to replace him. It also created problems for the African National Congress in its negotiations with the government because the South African Communist Party and the ANC were longtime allies who shared many of the same members, and Hani had been a member of the ANC's policymaking National Executive. Because of his revolutionary credentials, Hani was one of the few ANC elders capable of selling a power-sharing deal to disaffected black militants who worried that the ANC was conceding too much to whites. Without the approval of the volatile black militant segment of the population, a new government was given little chance of taking power without violence erupting again. Hani's death also deprived the ANC of one of its rising stars, a man who was considered a potential successor to Nelson Mandela as head of the organization, and possibly a future president of South Africa.

Still, many analysts were surprised when Hani's assassination appeared to strengthen the rapport between the ANC and the state, with both sides agreeing that power-sharing talks should be accelerated.

On July 2, 1993, a date was confirmed for South Africa's first universal suffrage elections, and on September 7, 1993, a multiracial council was formed to help oversee election preparations. In response, on October 8, 1993, the U.N. lifted most of the remaining economic sanctions against South Africa.

In October of 1993, it was announced that the Nobel Peace Prize—which carried a monetary award of 6.7 million Swedish kronor ($825,000)—was awarded jointly to fifty-seven-year-old F. W. deKlerk and seventy-five-year-old Nelson Mandela for their efforts in dismantling South Africa's system of apartheid and negotiating the country's ongoing transition to a nonracial democracy.

Between November 18 and 23, 1993, twenty-one of South Africa's black and white political parties approved a majority-rule constitution providing fundamental rights to blacks. Nelson Mandela and F. W. deKlerk officially launched their respective election campaigns at the end of January 1994. On April 10, 1994, one year to the day after Chris Hani was assassinated, at an ANC rally in Soweto, Mandela paid tribute to Hani, saying, "The best way we can honor his memory, the best monument, is to elect a democratic government and to build peace and security and a better life for our people."

South Africa's first universal-suffrage elections took place from April 26 to 29, 1994, with blacks being given their first opportunity to vote. During one historic moment on April 27, ANC leader Nelson Mandela was proudly photographed as he cast the first ballot of his lifetime. An estimated 22.7 million eligible voters participated in the four days of polling, most of them, like Mandela, taking advantage of their first chance to help decide the shape of their nation's government. Effectively dissolving the last remnants of apartheid, the elections marked the end of a decades-long struggle led by black organizations, including the ANC, that had sought liberation from three centuries of white-minority rule. Although the days leading up to the voting had been marred by bombings, allegedly orchestrated by white rightists, voters were undeterred by the violence. They began standing in line at some polling stations at 4 A.M. Many waited as long as twelve hours to cast their first ballots ever. President deKlerk declared a national holiday to allow voters extra time to cast their ballots. Still, despite voting hours being extended, another day of voting was added so that all who wished to participate would have their opportunity. Three hundred international observers monitored the elections to assure that they were free and fair.

At 12:01 A.M. on April 27, 1994, a new South African national flag was raised, replacing the one that had been introduced in 1928. As the country's new constitution and bill of rights took effect, the black homelands that had served as a symbol of apartheid for decades were dissolved, with nine new all-race provinces being established.

Nelson Mandela was the landslide victor in South Africa's first all-race elections. F. W. deKlerk offered his cooperation in the postelection government, and the new Parliament was set to meet the following week.

 MARCH 23, 1994

DONALDO COLOSIO (1950–1994)
PRESIDENTIAL CANDIDATE OF THE INSTITUTIONAL REVOLUTIONARY PARTY (PRI), WHICH HAS GOVERNED MEXICO SINCE 1929

Luis Donaldo Colosio Murrieta, the son of an accountant, was born on February 10, 1950, in Magdalena del Kino, in the Mexican state of Sonora, which borders Arizona. As a young man, Colosio took part in a four-month strike by university and high-school students in Mexico City in 1968, during which more than one hundred people died in clashes between demonstrators and police. Colosio would later play down his protest activities, saying they were emblems of the youthful idealism of the 1960s. Completing an economics degree at the Technological Institute of Higher Studies in Monterrey in 1972—the same year he enrolled as a PRI member—he went on to earn a master's degree in regional development and urban economics from the University of Pennsylvania. In 1979, Colosio, who was perceived as a technocrat, became secretariat of budget and planning on the staff of Carlos Salinas de Gortari. He was elected to a congressional seat representing Sonora in 1985, and in 1988 was elected a senator. By then Colosio was a member of the PRI's executive committee and managed Salinas's successful presidential campaign. Soon after being elected president in 1988, Salinas appointed Colosio head of the PRI; his three years in that position were marked by running battles with the labor movement. Colosio was named secretary of social development in 1992, a high-profile position from which he directed the government's domestic-welfare program, the National Solidarity Program. The stage was set for Salinas to announce in November 1993 that Colosio was his heir apparent as the PRI's presidential candidate in the 1994 elections. Accepting the nomination, Colosio characterized himself as the "candidate of the down-trodden" and pledged "major social reform" that would address the plight of the nation's poor.

ASSASSIN: Mario Aburto Martinez, a twenty-three-year-old industrial mechanic, originally from Zamora, Michoacán, who lived in Tijuana and considered himself a pacifist.

HISTORY: On New Year's Day 1994, the Zapatista National Liberation Army (EZLN), based in the southern state of Chiapas, took up arms against the government in an effort to secure improved living conditions for indigenous peasants. Although a cease-fire was called on January 12, and an uneasy truce followed, the rebels and their presumed leader, Subcomandante Marcos, had by then caught the public's imagination and vastly expanded their influence beyond their few thousand poorly armed fighters in Chiapas.

Luis Colosio's presidential campaign had been forced off the front pages while newspapers focused on events surrounding the Chiapas uprising. Even after the cease-fire, the news was filled with speculation about whether Manuel Camacho Solis, the government's Chiapas negotiator, would announce an independent challenge to Colosio's candidacy. Finally, on March 22, the forty-seven-year-old Camacho announced that he would not run for president, saying, "Between seeking a candidacy for the presidency and the contribution I can make to the peace process in Chiapas, I choose peace." Only after Camacho publicly set aside his presidential ambitions did Colosio's campaign again become a front page story. It was widely believed that he would win his bid for the presidency, extending the PRI's sixty-five years of continuous rule in Mexico. Colosio had served as director of Solidarity, Mexico's antipoverty program, and his political platform offered reforms that would serve the needs of all economic classes.

EVENT: On March 23, 1994, PRI presidential candidate Luis Colosio gave a speech before a crowd of some four thousand people in the poor Lomas Taurinas section of Tijuana. At about 5 P.M., following his speech, as the forty-four-year-old Colosio mingled with the crowd, Mario Aburto Martinez maneuvered himself into position among security guards, raised a gun above his head, then lowered it and shot Colosio in the head and abdomen at close range. As Aburto was grabbed by security guards, Colosio was rushed to Tijuana General Hospital, where he underwent emergency surgery but later died.

Colosio was the first Mexican presidential candidate to be assassinated since the 1928 shooting death of President-elect Alvaro Obregon. At noon on March 25, Luis Colosio was buried in his native Magdalena del Kino, in the state of Sonora.

AFTERMATH: Colosio's assassination further disrupted a nation already shaken by the New Year's Day uprising in Chiapas, and the prolonged street demonstrations and economic volatility that followed. Manuel Camacho Solis, the government's negotiator in Chiapas, called the shooting "an attempt against the peace and dignity of the country." Nobel Prize-winning writer Octavio Paz said, "Verbal violence and ideological violence of the kind that has been written and spoken since January are the antecedents of physical violence. That's exactly what we saw with the death of Colosio."

On March 24, President Salinas, hoping to amend expected financial shock waves set off by Colosio's assassination, ordered Mexico's stock market, banks, and currency-exchange institutions to close for one day. The country's economic uncertainty was compounded by its heavy dependence on foreign investors for capital inflows. U.S. president Bill Clinton telephoned Salinas to extend his condolences and reassure him that the United States was ready to take measures that would sustain Mexico's "fundamentally strong" economic and political institutions. Clinton also directed the U.S. Treasury Department and Federal Reserve Board to jointly set up a temporary facility to permit Mexico to draw on a credit line of $6 billion in order to help Mexico sustain its currency, the peso, if panic selling sent it plummeting. Public assurances by the Clinton administration seemed to help calm heavy selling of Mexican securities on the New York Stock Exchange, limiting the decline in share prices of U.S.-held Mexican stock.

Donaldo Colosio

REUTERS / CORBIS-BETTMANN

Also on March 24, an emergency meeting was held by Salinas and
other PRI leaders to discuss the possible candidates to succeed Colosio as
the ruling party's presidential nominee. Finding a replacement candidate
was complicated by a constitutional stipulation that cabinet ministers
and state governors had to resign their positions a minimum of six
months before running in a presidential election. This left a number of
otherwise potential candidates out of the running unless the law was
changed or the election was postponed. Five days later, the PRI selected
as their new candidate forty-two-year-old Ernesto Zedillo Ponce de
León, a U.S.-trained economist who was Colosio's campaign manager, a
former education minister, and a budget and planning minister in
Salinas's cabinet. At party headquarters in Mexico City, Zedillo gave a
twenty-minute acceptance speech, extolling the legacy of Colosio and
mentioning the slain nominee's name some thirty-five times.

Riding a wave of public sympathy in the aftermath of Colosio's assassination, Zedillo became the instant front-runner in the upcoming election, although many political analysts expected his campaign would lack much of the public appeal that Colosio had begun to summon on the eve of his shooting death. While Zedillo and the PRI presented themselves as the most dependable vehicle of progress and credibility amid the uncertainty that prevailed in the wake of Colosio's assassination, a stream of questions arose concerning the motive for and means of Colosio's killing and the government's determination and ability to uncover the facts.

CONSPIRACY THEORIES: The day Luis Colosio was shot, President Salinas sent Attorney General Diego Valades to Tijuana to open an investigation into the assassination. Although Valades said on March 24 that Mario Aburto Martinez had confessed to killing Colosio, various reports indicated that during his interrogations by Mexican officials, Aburto said he had not intended to kill Colosio, but "when I raised my weapon, somebody bumped into me or shoved me." Reportedly, Aburto said he had intended only to wound Colosio in order to call attention to issues of public concern and thereby "save the country from something that nobody wants." Among Aburto's concerns were the living conditions of peasants in the state of Chiapas. By March 28, when Mexican authorities announced the arrest of a second suspect, rumors were already circulating about a possible conspiracy. It was reported that while being questioned, Aburto told government investigators, "Nobody knew anything of this [plan to assassinate Colosio], only the persons with whom I was linked," but he did not further identify his associates. The next day Valades's office said it would bring charges against the second suspect, fifty-seven-year-old Tranquilino Sanchez Venegas, a part-time security guard, who had been detained by federal agents in Tijuana.

Hugo Morales, a spokesman for Attorney General Diego Valades, said that Sanchez had been hired by the PRI office in Tijuana on March 23, the day of the shooting, as part of a security contingent for Colosio at the campaign site where he was killed. A videotape of the shooting, taken by federal agents at the scene, suggested that Sanchez had cleared the way for Aburto to gain access to Colosio. The tape also showed that Sanchez had made no attempt to deflect the .38-caliber revolver Aburto was holding overhead in the seconds before the shooting. On March 29, the Mexico City–based newspaper *Reforma* reported that a sixteen-year-old girl who was a friend of Aburto said she had seen Aburto and Sanchez engaged in a conversation a few days before the assassination. There were also reports from the attorney general's office that the U.S. FBI had joined with Mexican officials to investigate possible ties between Aburto and unidentified groups in Los Angeles.

Miguel Montes Garcia, who had been named the government's special prosecutor, said on April 4, "several people [had] teamed up to carry out a concerted action" to assassinate Colosio, that four people had been arrested for conspiracy to help Aburto murder Colosio, and that another two men who had been identified as accomplices remained at large. Montes also said that a careful review of videotapes and photographs of the rally and follow-up interviews "unequivocally leads to the idea of a mutual and previous understanding" among the suspects, a number of whom were retired police officers who had served on Colosio's forty-five-member security unit at the rally. Because they had been recruited at PRI offices in Tijuana, some theorized that Colosio's killing was directed by elements from within his own party. Videotapes appeared to show that some of the suspects either cleared a path through the crowd for Aburto, or slowed Colosio's path or distracted the candidate's immediate security contingent so that Aburto could ultimately get a clear shot at Colosio's head and abdomen at point-blank range.

José Rodolfo Rivapalacio, a PRI official in Tijuana and a former state judicial policeman in Baja California who had helped to recruit security volunteers on the day of the shooting, was identified as the ringleader of Aburto's alleged supporting group. Former police officers Tranquilino Sanchez Venegas and Vicente Mayoral Valenzuela, as well as Rodolfo Mayoral Esquer, Mayoral's son, were all named as suspects who had been recruited into the conspiracy. On April 7 Aburto's attorney said his client did not know any of the four people the government suspected as being involved in the shooting of Colosio. Three days later, Judge Alejandro Sosa, presiding over the government's assassination probe, reduced the central charge against Aburto from premeditated murder to murder with malicious intent. But the government's case against the others quickly unraveled. Due to lack of evidence, Judge Sosa dismissed criminal-association charges against all of the accused. Although Sosa ordered Rivapalacio to be freed, he also ordered that Sanchez and the Mayorals remain in custody on charges of aiding and abetting Aburto. Two of the six suspects were never formally charged, and another suspect, Jorge Antonio Sanchez Ortega, a state security agent arrested by Tijuana police on suspicion of being a second gunman, was released after a gunpowder test to determine whether he had recently used a firearm proved inconclusive.

It was reported on May 12 that Aburto's father, Ruben Aburto Martinez Sr., insisted his son was innocent. In a telephone interview from Los Angeles he said that his son had attended a "political meeting" in Tijuana with PRI officials ten days before the shooting, and that the other suspects in the assassination had also been present at that meeting. Lawyers for the Aburto family said on May 23 that his mother, Maria Louisa Martinez de Aburto, two of his sisters, and three other relatives had illegally crossed the Mexican border into the United States seeking political asylum. They had told U.S. immigration officials that they would have faced physical danger if they remained in Mexico. On May 25, Peter Schey, a lawyer for the Aburto family, said in Los Angeles that six weeks earlier Aburto Sr. had told him that before the shooting his son had met with Sanchez Ortega, a security agent arrested at the assassination site but later released.

In an interview on April 27, Tijuana police chief José Federico Benitez Lopez said that he had been conducting an independent investigation into Colosio's assassination, but related files had recently been stolen from his office. The next day, Benitez and his bodyguard-driver, returning from the airport after investigating a bomb hoax, were ambushed and killed. Benitez, who tried to root out police corruption in his city, which was Mexico's main drug-trafficking base, had also raised questions about the government's version of Colosio's assassination, particularly the contention that only one gunman was involved. Some speculated that Benitez was murdered because he had uncovered information that could implicate others in Colosio's assassination. Although police detained eleven suspects for Benitez's murder, all were released the same day for lack of evidence. The situation was further complicated on June 1 when the governor of Baja California suspended the investigation into Benitez's death, saying the safety of state investigators could not be guaranteed.

Mexico's attorney general Diego Valades Rios was sharply criticized by the conservative National Action party (PAN) after he ordered the May 3 arrest of Sergio Ortiz Lara, the deputy attorney general of Baja California, a PAN-controlled state. Valades charged that Ortiz had provided police protection for drug traffickers in Tijuana. He also indicated that Ortiz was being investigated in regard to the murder of Tijuana police chief Benitez. While PAN officials dismissed the accusations as politically motivated, it was reported on May 11 that Eduardo Valle Espinoza, director of an antidrug unit in Valades's office, had charged in his May 1 letter of resignation that Mexico was a "narco-democracy" in which drug traffickers played a leading role in government decisions, and alleging that drug lords had probably been behind Colosio's assassination. Attorney General Valades suddenly resigned without prior notice, and on May 13, when President Salinas named Humberto Benitez Trevino to replace Valades, more questions were raised about Mexico's law-enforcement structure.

In early June of 1994, the investigation into Colosio's assassination, which was being conducted by Special Prosecutor Miguel Montes Garcia, was nearly complete, but the conduct and conclusions of the Montes probe were met with widespread public disbelief. The entire five-member commission appointed on April 20 by President Salinas to assist Montes in his independent investigation had resigned, reportedly saying it had not been granted the authority that would enable it to carry out its task. Rumors that the conspiracy to assassinate Colosio was headed up by drug lords, local political leaders, or PRI officials opposed to Colosio's reformist agenda seemed to have been ignored. Montes said Aburto had apparently acted alone and that there was insufficient evidence to support the government's earlier contention that an assassination plot had involved at least seven people. Still, in a statement issued on June 3, Montes said that although the available evidence strongly suggested one lone gunman, he would not yet drop charges against three other suspects, who would remain in prison, and that the search for evidence against them would continue. Then, in his closing report of the investigation, released on July 12, 1994, Montes said that Mario Aburto Martinez had unequivocally acted alone, and that Aburto's unclear state of mind was the singular factor in his actions. Montes's conclusions seemed not believable to most Mexicans in light of all the contradictory evidence that had surfaced during the investigation. Juan Velasquez, a prominent criminal lawyer hired by Colosio's widow to serve as her representative, dismissed Montes's report as "ridiculous—period."

In response to widespread controversy about Montes's conclusions, President Salinas announced two days later that a new commission would reexamine the government investigation. Salinas said, "I am giving precise instructions that the case remain open and that the investigation go deeper in order to determine if anyone influenced Mario Aburto to commit his crime." Olga Islas Magallanes de Gonzalez Mariscal, a law professor, was named to head a six-member commission of legal experts appointed by Salinas to review the findings of Special Prosecutor Miguel Montes Garcia.

PUNISHMENT: In October of 1994, Mario Aburto Martinez was sentenced to forty-two years in prison for shooting Colosio to death.

AFTERMATH: On February 25, 1995, under the direction of the newly sworn administration of President Ernesto Zedillo Ponce de León,

Mexican federal agents arrested an alleged second gunman, Othon Cortez Vazquez, in the March 1994 slaying of Luis Colosio. Zedillo had broken with tradition by appointing Antonio Lozano Gracia, a member of the National Action party (PAN) as attorney general. Lozano's investigation of Colosio's assassination determined that "irregularities," including manipulated evidence, had flawed the earlier findings. He said that a bullet found at the Tijuana campaign rally scene of the crime had been planted and that new tests showed that the two bullets that had fatally wounded Colosio could not have been fired by the same person. Also arrested that day and charged with perjury in connection with Colosio's assassination was Fernando de la Sota, who had headed up one of Colosio's security contingents and had hired Cortes to serve as a security aide at the campaign rally on the day Colosio was shot. Cortes, twenty-eight, had previously worked in Tijuana as an aide and driver for several prominent local PRI politicians, and he had worked on the 1989 gubernatorial campaign of Margarita Ortega Villa in Baja California, the state in which Tijuana was located.

While officials in charge of the investigation would not speculate about a motive for Colosio's assassination, only giving information about the arrested suspects, new questions were being asked about a possible conspiracy. The fact that Cortes had worked for Ortega fueled suspicions. Although Ortega, a gubernatorial candidate of the PRI, which had controlled the state since the party was founded in 1929, had purportedly won the 1989 election, the PAN challenged the results, claiming there had been widespread fraud. Luis Colosio, the PRI leader at the time, had overruled Ortega's victory and ordered that the PAN candidate be instated as governor. That ruling by Colosio allegedly caused bad feelings between federal and Baja PRI officials.

Authorities who arrested Cortes said they had three witnesses who had claimed to have seen Cortes shoot at Colosio and that other evidence against Cortes was recently uncovered by Pablo Chapa Benzanilla, the new special prosecutor. *El National,* the government-owned newspaper, reported on February 25 that on the day of Colosio's assassination, Cortes had assisted General Domiro Garcia Reyes, the government-appointed director of security for Colosio. Officials said that shortly after Colosio was shot, Cortes had been photographed riding in a car with Garcia. Two days later, it was reported that both Cortes and de la Sota had formerly served as agents in the Federal Security Directorate, a reputedly corrupt state-security network that was disbanded in the mid-1980s.

On August 7, 1996, Federal Judge Mario Pardo Rebolledo ruled that prosecutors had failed to prove Othon Cortes Vazquez was a second gunman in the 1994 murder of Luis Colosio. Although Pardo's ruling prompted calls for Attorney General Antonio Lozano Gracia's resignation, President Zedillo did not withdraw his support of Lozano, the only opposition party member of his cabinet. But on August 13, Zedillo did dismiss Pablo Chapa Bezanilla, a special prosecutor in the Colosio investigation.

At least two Tijuana officials who were murdered during 1996—José Arturo Ochoa Palacios, killed on April 17, and Jesus Romero Magana, killed on August 27—had been prosecutors in the investigation of Colosio's March 1994 death, keeping alive theories that there was a conspiracy in the assassination of Luis Donaldo Colosio Murrieta.

 JULY 3, 1995

HOSNI MUBARAK (1928–)
EGYPTIAN POLITICIAN AND PRESIDENT
BEGINNING IN 1981

Hosni Mubarak became vice president of Egypt in 1975, while Anwar Sadat was president, and succeeded him after Sadat's assassination. As president, Mubarak has mostly continued Sadat's moderate domestic and foreign policies, as well as his efforts to repress the growing Islamic fundamentalist movement. But in some ways Mubarak has taken a different approach, curtailing civil liberties by banning union and other unofficial gatherings, presenting a bill that would jail reporters convicted of defaming government officials, and jailing thousands of suspected Islamic activists without allowing them to be tried.

Born at Kafr El-Moseilha in the Nile Delta, Mubarak studied at the Egyptian military academy at Cairo, then joined the Egyptian air force in 1950. He became director-general of the Air Academy (1967–69), then Air Force chief of staff (1969–72), and was appointed head of the air force by Sadat in 1972. Highly praised for his direction of Egyptian air operations during the 1973 war with Israel, Mubarak was subsequently promoted to air marshal. In 1975 Mubarak was chosen as Sadat's vice president. He played an important role in the complex negotiations between the various Arab powers.

After becoming president following Sadat's assassination in 1981, Mubarak established closer links between Egypt and other Arab nations and distanced himself from Israel when that country invaded Lebanon in 1982. Taking a moderate political position, he cautioned fundamentalists within Egypt and improved his country's technological base. Mubarak earned the respect of foreign leaders and increased his popularity at home. In 1987 he was endorsed for a second six-year term as president. During the Gulf War of 1991, Mubarak risked division with other Arab powers by aligning Egypt against Saddam Hussein and his regime. Later that year, he played an instrumental role in arranging the Middle East peace conference of November 1991.

Through the years there have been numerous plots to assassinate President Mubarak, but only one attempt has been well publicized.

WOULD-BE ASSASSINS: Islamic extremists.

EVENT: On July 3, 1995, at around 8:15 A.M., a team of Islamic assassins had a lookout posted in a rented house overlooking the main airport of Addis Ababa, Ethiopia, where Hosni Mubarak was arriving to attend a summit meeting of the Organization of African Unity. Sources said later

Hosni Mubarak

UPI / CORBIS-BETTMANN

that the would-be assassins had obtained, from connections with Ethiopian officials, Mubarak's arrival time and the exact route he would travel from the airport. They watched through binoculars as Ethiopian president Meles Zenawi greeted Mubarak, and as their motorcade pulled out of the airport and onto a tree-lined boulevard leading to the Ethiopian capital. Mubarak's armored limousine was placed third in the four-car convoy. A signal was radioed to a hit squad waiting in three vehicles parked along a small side street as the motorcade, led by a silver Volvo sedan, slowly approached an intersection. When the motorcade came into sight, one of the assassins' vehicles pulled out onto the boulevard, blocking the road. Mubarak's vehicle was about seventy meters away when two or three gunmen jumped into the road and opened fire with AK-47 assault rifles, killing two policemen on duty along the route. The assassins' bullets repeatedly struck Mubarak's armored limousine, but none could penetrate it. As Mubarak's driver screeched to a halt and started to turn the vehicle around, two Ethiopian and several Egyptian security men opened fire with rifles and pistols, shooting two of the would-be assassins. The others quickly escaped.

The convoy immediately turned around, taking Mubarak back to the airport, where he boarded his jet and flew back to Cairo. Mubarak then made a series of public appearances to prove he was unhurt and seemingly unfazed by the attempt on his life, saying the attack was "nothing," that his car was armored and, "I was cool all the time." During a rally in Cairo to celebrate Mubarak's safe return, he placed responsibility for the assassination attempt on Muslim extremists from neighboring Sudan. He said he doubted that the government had planned the attempt, but that Islamic cleric Hassan al-Turabi, considered to be the power behind Sudanese president Lieutenant General Omar Hassan Ahmad al-Bashir, was more likely responsible. Al-Turabi appeared on Sudanese television saying, "We have no connection with this incident," and al-Bashir, who was in Addis Ababa for the summit, also denied any involvement in the attempt to assassinate Mubarak.

INVESTIGATION: Ethiopian police later discovered that during their escape the assailants had abandoned four vehicles filled with an assortment of weapons. One contained a trunkful of explosives and two rocket-propelled grenades that could have penetrated the most well-armored vehicle. Authorities also found large quantities of ammunition, Kalashnikovs, grenades, and rocket-propelled grenades in the apartment where the assassination team was hiding out. Mubarak's survival of this assault was credited to the quick response and accurate fire from security men who instantly killed some of the assailants, preventing them from collecting the more powerful weapons and using them. Within the week, Ethiopian radio announced that security forces had tracked down and killed three people suspected of the assassination attempt.

AFTERMATH: Reports of other attempts on Mubarak's life began to surface. The French publication *Issues* said that in the first three weeks of January, Islamic extremists had attempted to kill Mubarak three times, but Egyptian security foiled the attempts and concealed their occurrence. Western security sources said Islamic extremists planned to kill Murbarak during his three-day visit to Rome in November of 1994, but Italian authorities learned of the plot and warned Mubarak, who changed his schedule. A dozen men were later arrested by Italian police, whose investigation determined that there was an Islamic network based in Rome which was connected to the Islamic Jihad and other extremist groups.

Although sixty-seven-year-old Hosni Mubarak shrugged off the Ethiopian incident, many are concerned that since taking office he has not named a vice president and apparently has never chosen his successor. While intelligence sources believe attempts on Mubarak's life would be difficult to execute in his own country, where security is extremely tight, the closeness of the attempt in Ethiopia proved that he is still vulnerable.

 NOVEMBER 4, 1995

YITZHAK RABIN (1922–1995)
ISRAELI POLITICIAN WHO SERVED AS PRIME MINISTER FROM 1974 TO 1977 AND FROM 1992 TO 1995

During his illustrious military career, Yitzhak Rabin was a commanding force in Israel's expansion and dominance in the region. His successful peace-based political career earned him the Nobel Peace Prize in 1994.

Born on March 1, 1922, in Jerusalem to Russian-born parents Nehemiah and Rosa Rubitzov, Yitzhak Rabin graduated in 1940 from Kadoorie Agricultural School in Lower Galilee. He enlisted in the Palmah, an underground Labor Zionist commando unit in 1940, and participated in World War II allied forces raids into French Vichy-controlled Lebanon. As deputy commander of a Palmah operation in 1945, he helped to liberate two hundred illegal immigrants from the British Atlit detention camp south of Haifa. Rabin was appointed deputy commander of the Palmah, under Yigal Allon, in 1947. The next year he commanded the Harel Brigade in Operation Nahshon, which opened the road to besieged Jerusalem during Israel's War of Independence, and captured the Jerusalem neighborhoods of Sheikh Jarrah and Katamon. As operations chief on the southern front, Rabin oversaw the conquest of the Negev and Eilat. In 1948, a U.N.-supported British plan of partition was enacted, the Palestinian mandate was ended, and Israel was proclaimed an independent nation. That same year, Yitzhak Rabin married Leah Schlossberg. From 1950 on, Rabin's illustrious military career continued as he was progressively promoted to higher positions until, in 1967, he led Israeli forces in the Six-Day War that ended with a victorious Israel newly in control of East Jerusalem, the West Bank, the Gaza Strip, the Sinai Peninsula, and the Golan Heights. Rabin left the military in 1968 when he was appointed ambassador to the United States and moved to Washington, D.C. He returned to Israel in 1973, was elected to the Knesset as a member of the Labor party, then was appointed minister of labor by Prime Minister Golda Meir.

When Meir stepped down in the bitter aftermath of the 1973 Yom Kippur War, Rabin was selected by the Labor party as prime minister in 1974. In that position, he signed an interim peace agreement with Egypt in 1975, then authorized the heroic July 4, 1976, raid on Entebbe, Uganda, during which Israeli commandos rescued more than one hundred Jews from a plane hijacked by Palestinians. Rabin resigned as prime minister in 1977 during a convoluted scandal involving a so-called illegal U.S. bank account. After publishing his autobiography, *The Rabin Memoirs,* in 1979, he returned to government in 1984, serving six years as defense minister in Labor-Likud coalitions. The next year he presented a proposal to the government for Israel Defense Forces withdrawal from Lebanon and the creation of a security zone along Israel's northern bor-

Yitzhak Rabin

REUTERS / CORBIS-BETTMANN

der. In 1989 Rabin published his program for phased negotiations with the Palestinians. It was accepted by the government and formed the basis of the Madrid conference and the peace process that followed. He campaigned against Prime Minister Shimon Peres to regain his position, promising to intensify peace efforts. Rabin was elected prime minister for a second time in 1992. On September 13, 1993, he reluctantly shook the hand of PLO chairman Yasir Arafat at the White House, sealing their joint Declaration of Principles: the framework accord providing for the phased granting of autonomy to Palestinians of the West Bank and Gaza Strip. The Oslo I accord, granting self-rule to Palestinians of Gaza and Jericho, was signed in Cairo on May 4, 1994. Rabin joined Jordan's King Hussein in Washington on July 24 to sign a declaration ending the forty-six-year state of war between Israel and Jordan, with the formal Israel-Jordan peace treaty being signed October 26.

Rabin's efforts for peace were rewarded in 1994 when he was presented the Nobel Peace Prize along with his former enemy, PLO
Chairman Yasir Arafat, and his political rival, Israel's Shimon Peres. The
Oslo II agreement, expanding Palestinian self-rule in the West Bank, was
signed by Rabin and Arafat at the White House on September 28, 1995.

ASSASSIN: Yigal Amir, a twenty-five-year-old right-wing Jewish law student. Amir lived with his family in Neveh Amal, a poor neighborhood of
the coastal town of Herzliyah, just north of Tel Aviv. He contemptuously
opposed the Rabin government's peace policies and Jewish withdrawal
from the West Bank.

Yigal Amir was born on May 23, 1970, the second of eight children.
His parents, Shlomo and Geulah, were Yemenite immigrants. His soft-
spoken father earned a meager living as a scribe of religious documents,
and his mother, the dominant figure in their household, was a strictly
Orthodox, strong, confident woman, known in their neighborhood as a
sympathetic listener. She supplemented the family income by running
a successful kindergarten at home for neighborhood children. Yigal was
a quiet, unremarkable, self-sufficient child. He tended to be a loner,
choosing to study or pray instead of playing with other children in his
neighborhood. He attended an ultra-Orthodox school close to home
and regularly accompanied his father to the local Yemenite synagogue.
At age fourteen, Amir began taking the bus each day to Tel Aviv, where
he attended the Yishuv Hehadash yeshivah, an ultra-Orthodox high
school. Although most of its graduates go on to full-time religious
study, avoiding military service, Amir wanted to join a combat unit. He
found a five-year *hesder* program, which offered a combination of army
service and religious study. Amir alternated between service in the
Golani combat unit, which mostly patrolled in the Gaza Strip or the
tense Israeli security zone inside South Lebanon, and study of the Torah
in the idyllic rural environment of Kerem B'Yavneh yeshivah south of
Tel Aviv. A fit and strong young man with a deceptively wiry physique,
Amir was a dependable soldier who was trusted but not beloved by his

comrades. Unlike most soldiers, Amir was known for his readiness to volunteer for extra or arduous duty when others would try to avoid the additional work. While on duty in Gaza, he was highly regarded by his commanders for his "thoroughness" during house-to-house searches for suspected violent Palestinian activists.

Although many young Israelis take a year off to travel and see the world after their army service, when his *hesder* program was completed in 1992, Amir got a job for the summer with the somewhat shadowy Liaison Bureau, an office supervised by the prime minister's Office, that sends emissaries to the former Soviet Union, where they teach Hebrew and carry out other less-publicized missions. Amir was trained for his assignment, got his security clearances, and was sent to Riga for three months. When he returned, he enrolled at Bar-Ilan, a university outside Tel Aviv that has a reputation as a hotbed of right-wing political activism. Amir signed up for an exhausting program that combined law studies, some computer classes, and long hours in the university kolel—the campus yeshivah where about four hundred of the most dedicated Orthodox students spend any free time they had examining religious texts.

Yigal Amir had entered Bar-Ilan just weeks after the Rabin-Arafat handshake on the White House lawn, and although opinion polls showed that about two-thirds of Israelis supported Rabin's so-called "gamble for peace," Amir did not agree. Previously not outspoken about politics, Amir seemed suddenly changed. He became close friends with a small group of fellow students at the kolel, including one former activist named Avishai Raviv, and Amir became an active opponent of the Rabin government.

After a five-month romantic relationship was ended by Amir's girlfriend, his right-wing activism reportedly became frenzied. He helped organize student protests near Bar-Ilan, he organized campus hunger strikes, and when settlers devised ways to subvert Rabin's declared freeze on building in the West Bank, Amir went there to give them support. He helped establish the illegal settlement of Ma'aleh Yisrael, and in the summer of 1995 he joined the settlers of Efrat, near Bethlehem, during a passive-resistance protest against army evacuation from a symbolic new neighborhood on a barren hilltop at the settlement's edge. On the eve of the Knesset's neck-and-neck vote to confirm Oslo II, which would expand Palestinian control of the West Bank, Amir organized a demonstration of Bar-Ilan students outside the Ashkelon home of Knesset member Alex Goldfarb, who had defected from a right-wing party to support the Rabin coalition. When Oslo II was passed, only on the strength of Goldfarb's support, Amir, along with some eight hundred other army reservists, signed a statement declaring that they would refuse to participate in the West Bank pullout.

Finally Amir organized "solidarity Sabbaths" for like-minded students who would pile into buses and spend the weekend with the 450 isolated settlers in the heart of Hebron, or the thirty courageous families at Netzarim, to the north of the Gaza Strip. The most successful of those weekends began on Friday, September 19, 1995, the Sabbath between the Jewish New Year and the Day of Atonement. Avishai Raviv was among those who, along with Yigal Amir, had enthusiastically recruited students on the Bar-Ilan campus to spend the Sabbath in Hebron as a way of sending an unmistakable message of defiance to the government in addition to giving support to the settlers. More than five hundred people showed up and jammed eight buses. Among them was Yaron Kaner, a journalist who was writing an investigative article on Avishai Raviv's Eyal movement. Kaner wrote that the sheer mass of people was a triumph of solidarity, that "Yigal Amir and his look-alike older brother, Hagai," were among the group, and that Yigal Amir was clearly a main organizer.

The success of this weekend seemed only to make Yigal Amir more intent on seeing that the handing over of West Bank land was stopped. Reportedly, he, his brother Hagai, and their closest confidant, Dror Adoni, a friend from Yigal's army days who had also regularly attended the settler weekends, had been stalking Rabin and Peres with increasing intensity throughout 1995. Hagai had stolen a considerable amount of material from the army. Eric Schwartz, another of Yigal's friends from the Kerem B'Yavneh yeshivah and a commando in the Golani brigade, had allegedly gotten some more. Their cache of weapons, hand grenades, and explosives was stashed at the Amirs Herzliyah home, where Geulah Amir's kindergarten children innocently played each morning.

Killing Rabin and Peres was not the only idea of this small group of conspirators. They also earmarked some of the explosives for attacks on Arabs, particularly prisoners that were released during the peace process, Palestinian official Faisal Husseini, and even Yasir Arafat himself. Still, although they discussed attacking Palestinians with other Bar-Ilan students and a West Bank settler assigned to that project, Peres and especially Rabin were their main priorities.

To clear their way, Yigal Amir, Dror Adoni, and another Bar-Ilan student all reportedly sought rabbinic sanction for killing Rabin. But while Adoni later told investigators he found no rabbi willing to grant approval, Hagai Amir said one West Bank rabbi did tell Yigal and Adoni that Rabin deserved to die. And so the Amir brothers and Adoni debated the best ways to carry out the murder.

HISTORY: Downtown Jerusalem was filled with right-wing demonstrators on October 5, 1995, as the Knesset debated the Oslo II accord. Likud opposition leader Benjamin Netanyahu addressed the crowd, attacking Yitzhak Rabin for basing his coalition's Knesset majority on Arab Knesset members whose children did not serve in the army and on two right-wing legislators who had crossed over to back the prime minister. The crowd was further heated up as other secular right-wing Knesset members spoke out against Rabin's government and Oslo II. Among the demonstrators were Kahanist activists, reportedly including Avishai Raviv, head of a shady radical group called Eyal (a Hebrew acronym for Jewish Fighting Organization). Raviv, a friend of Yigal Amir, reportedly was an informant of the Shin Bet, Israel's secretive security agency. Tens of thousands of protesters marched from Zion Square to the Knesset, where hundreds of them hurled burning torches at policemen, trying to break through police lines and reach the plaza in front of the building. Stones were thrown at Housing Minister Binyamin Ben-Eliezer's car as he drove away from the building. Others located Rabin's empty car and smashed it.

After the Knesset approved Oslo II, peace activists decided a pro-peace rally would demonstrate the public's support of their side. The rally was planned for the night of Saturday, November 4, 1995. When the idea was proposed to Yitzhak Rabin early in October, he was pessimistic because of the series of increasingly vitriolic protests that had been organized by the Israeli right wing. For more than two years there had been demonstrations, some of them turning to riots, but during the previous few months the protests had become particularly menacing. At one rally, crude posters showing Rabin in Nazi uniform had been distributed; placards showing Rabin's face overlaid with the cross-hairs of a rifle sight were now commonly brandished; a West Bank settler had tried to run left-wing environment minister Yossi Sarid's car off the main Jerusalem–Tel Aviv highway; and Police Minister Moshe Shahal and army chief of staff Amnon Lipkin-Shahak had both narrowly escaped angry mobs at the scene of a Palestinian bus bombing. Rabin had always argued that right-wing demonstrations did more harm than good for the opposition cause. He tended to dismiss most expressions of incitement as being "not serious," even though he had been threatened by right-wing activists and Arabs had tried to kill him numerous times.

Rabin finally gave his tentative approval to the idea of a massive gathering in Tel Aviv on November 4, but the theme of the rally was expanded from pro-peace to include antiviolence. The prime minister decided there was a need to moderate the hysterical tone of political debate in Israel, and that would be the centerpiece of his speech for that evening. Still, Rabin's fears that no one would come to the rally put added pressure on the organizers, who knew that fifty thousand people were needed to fill the Kings of Israel Square where the event would be held. Generating publicity was difficult. The state television and radio stations gave it little coverage, and the commercial television channel did not do much more; billboards were scarce, and only the newspapers spread the word. In order to draw crowds, the rally organizers got the idea that stars were needed. Several popular Israeli musical performers turned down the promoters' invitation, apparently because they were afraid that their appearance at such a rally might offend right-wing fans. Despite their disappointments, the organizers worked on, and somehow, in the last few days, the crisis mood began to lift, perhaps in response to a change of attitude from Rabin himself.

Final preparations went smoothly for military withdrawal from Henin, the northernmost Palestinian city in the West Bank and the first to pass into Palestinian control under Oslo II. This gave Rabin renewed confidence in the viability of the Palestinian autonomy process. Construction was progressing on bypass roads that would enable Jewish settlers to reach their homes without entering Palestinian-controlled territory. But the most favorable nonevent was that no Islamic extremist suicide bombers had struck inside Israel for more than two months.

During an Israeli television interview program on October 30, Rabin was grilled by a panel of three top journalists. He seemed generally relaxed and upbeat, highlighting Israel's improved international image, proudly assessing the successes of the peace process, and genially playing down suggestions that he might be too old to contemplate another term in office. But he said, sadly, that he did anticipate more "unruly instigation, verbal violence, violence in the street." This concern was repeated in a French magazine interview with Rabin that week, but despite all the threats of political violence, he insisted, "I don't believe a Jew will kill a Jew."

Rabin learned that on October 26, Fathi Shkaki, the founder and head of the fanatical Islamic Jihad Palestinian terrorist group, had been assassinated outside a hotel in Malta by two men who subsequently disappeared without a trace. Israel did not even bother to deny responsibility for the killing, but it did brace itself for the worst. Attempts to blow up two school buses between settlements in the Gaza Strip on Thursday, November 2, failed; the only fatalities were the two suicide bombers themselves. Although Israel's military analysts soberly warned that the bombers would surely strike again, at least their initial efforts for revenge had been frustrated. Even the usual several dozen right-wing demonstrators outside Rabin's apartment building shouting, "Rabin is a traitor," and "Rabin, resign," did not dampen his optimistic mood on Friday night as the prime minister said good-bye to his veteran driver, Yehezkel Sharabi, who had the weekend off.

The next day, a little past 7:30 P.M., as Rabin's relief driver, Menahem Damti, drove Yitzhak and Leah Rabin into Tel Aviv, a warning came through from the security services that there was a very real threat that Islamic Jihad activists might use that night's rally to stage a suicide bombing or other attack to avenge the killing of their leader.

At home in Herzliyah, twenty-five-year-old Yigal Amir, normally busy with right-wing activities on the Sabbath, had given himself the weekend off. As he and his brother, Hagai, walked to synagogue, they discussed the chances of killing Rabin and escaping unharmed at that night's Tel Aviv pro-peace rally. Hagai later told police, "I supported the plan to kill Rabin, but I wasn't prepared to die in the process." In synagogue that evening, Yigal prayed that he would be granted the opportunity to assassinate the prime minister, and that his own life would be spared. Back at home in his room, he took out his pistol from among some of his treasured possessions: a book published in memory of Hebron killer Baruch Goldstein, and Frederick Forsyth's methodical assassination thriller *The Day of the Jackal.* Yigal had gotten a license for the gun two years earlier by falsely stating on his application form that he lived in the West Bank, because under Israel's gun-control regulations, a need for self-defense must be established. He carefully loaded the nine-millimeter Baretta, alternating hollowed-out dumdum bullets, which Hagai had prepared, with ordinary bullets.

Yigal tucked the loaded gun between his pants and his right thigh, left his house, took a bus into Tel Aviv, and walked to the Kings of Israel Square. After wandering around the stage area, Yigal decided it would be impossible to get a clear shot at Rabin from there. Looking around the area further, he found the poorly lit, improperly secured VIP parking lot at the left of the stage and down some stairs. He hung around in the shadows where at least twenty people without the necessary security tags were milling around. Yigal casually stood with his hands in his pockets, or sat on a large white knee-high concrete planter. One uniformed policeman who spotted Amir assumed he was a detective or a Shin Bet agent, like the other young plainclothesmen in the area. Small, slight, and curly-haired, wearing a plain blue shirt and beige trousers, obviously a Jew, not an Arab, Yigal Amir looked harmless. He had even put his black skullcap into his pocket, so no one would think he was a settler or a right-wing sympathizer as he waited for his victim.

EVENT: The Rabins arrived at the Kings of Israel Square around eight o'clock, and when Yitzhak was escorted to the front of the stage, all his fears that no one would come to the rally were put to rest. He looked out and saw a sheer mass of people, an estimated 250,000 or more, filling the square and spilling out into the side streets as far as he could see. When the crowd saw him and started shouting, "Rabin, Rabin, Rabin," he caught his breath in awe.

As the crowd quieted, Rabin began, "I want to thank each one of you who has come here to make a stand against violence and for peace." In his speech to the thousands of upturned, supportive faces, Rabin emotionally reminded them of the pressing need to confront the escalating undercurrent of violence. With passionate conviction, he reaffirmed his commitment to the peace process, saying it represented the only way to guarantee Israel's security into the future. He looked down at the diplomatic envoys from Egypt, Jordan, and Morocco sitting in the front-row seats, and expressed his delight to see the "representatives here of countries with which we live in peace." He praised the PLO as "a partner in peace among the Palestinians . . . which was an enemy and has now forsaken terrorism." But Rabin was also realistic about the likely obstacles on the road ahead. "There is no painless way forward for Israel, but the way of peace is preferable to the way of war," Rabin said. Speaking as a military man, as a minister of defense, Rabin said it was for the families of the soldiers of the Israel Defense Forces and for the sake of the children and grandchildren of Israel that his government was exhausting every tiny possibility to move ahead and reach a comprehensive peace. In closing, Rabin said the rally "must send a message to the Israeli public, to the Jews of the world, to the multitudes in the Arab lands, and to the world at large: that the nation of Israel wants peace, supports peace. And for this, I thank you."

The crowd's response was immediate and extraordinary, sweeping up the prime minister in a vast wave of cheering and applause. The crusty former general who never showed public displays of emotion, was so moved by the crowd's enthusiastic support that right up on the stage in full view of everyone, he embraced Foreign Minister Shimon Peres, a former political rival who had become his close friend during their pursuit of peace.

Vocalist Miri Aloni joined Rabin and Peres at center stage to sing the "Song for Peace," which had been denounced as defeatist when it first appeared in the late 1960s but had since become an anthem of the peace movement. Rabin reluctantly accepted a lyric sheet and standing to the singer's left, with Peres at her right, they joined in. Considered a shy man, especially uncomfortable about his singing abilities, Rabin valiantly struggled to follow the words. When the song was over, he precisely folded the lyric sheet into four and slipped it into his inside jacket pocket. Next, Aviv Geffen came on stage, dedicated his song "to all those people who won't be fortunate enough to see peace dawn," and performed "To Cry for You." When the song's last aching notes faded away, Geffen, who took public delight in obtaining a medical release from military service, walked with his arms outstretched toward the prime minister. Rabin hugged the waifish singer, telling him, "Your song was wonderful."

Because the rally was such a success, the organizers suggested Rabin and Peres walk down among the crowd. Tel Aviv's police chief at first objected, fearing for their security, but then consented. But in the end, when the national anthem, "Hatikvah" (The Hope), brought the rally to a formal conclusion, Rabin and Peres walked toward the back staircase to go down to the parking area where their drivers were waiting. Delayed a few moments as they spoke with Gidi Gov, a popular rock star turned talk-show host, and his wife and children, Rabin and Peres went down the first few stairs to the parking lot together and then stopped. Rabin turned back to say a few words of thanks to the rally organizers, saying it was one of the happiest days of his life, then exchanged final farewells. Peres and his bodyguards, who had gone ahead of Rabin to the parking lot, walked past Yigal Amir, standing half-hidden in the shadows to the left of the stairwell. Approaching Rabin's driver, who was waiting by the prime minister's car, Peres asked when Rabin was coming down. The driver told him they had said on the walkie-talkie that Rabin would be down any minute. At first Peres said he would wait a few seconds, then he said, "You know what, I'll go."

Back on the stage, Tel Aviv's police chief and one of the Shin Bet security chiefs, relieved that the Islamic radicals had not terrorized the rally, congratulated themselves on a difficult operation successfully completed. Rabin's group was at the top of the stairs again. He looked over to his right, where hundreds of people, mostly teenagers, were shouting, "Peace, peace," and "We're with you." The prime minister waved at them, then started down the stairs with four bodyguards around him and one more walking ahead of him. Leah Rabin was following behind at a slightly slower pace as her husband took the final few steps toward the open door of his car. When Rabin reached the car and prepared to climb in, Yigal Amir, who had been standing to the prime minister's left, no more than three paces away, darted up to Rabin's unprotected back, pulled his pistol out from inside his pants, aimed, and shot once, twice, three times, from point-blank range. Rabin's driver and some of the policemen nearby said Amir simultaneously yelled, "It's nothing. They're not real bullets. They're blanks. It's not real." Rabin half-turned toward his assailant, then fell forward, collapsing onto his left side. One of his bodyguards, who was bleeding from a shoulder wounded by the third bullet, forced Rabin into the Cadillac and jumped in after him. The driver scrambled behind the wheel and sped away with a squeal of burning rubber.

Back at the scene, Yigal Amir was forced to the ground, then marched against a wall by a group of police officers. One had his left arm firmly across Amir's throat. All around him, everyone looked dazed and panicked, but Amir seemed utterly unfazed.

Because of the shouts he had heard that the bullets were blanks, Rabin's driver was hoping the prime minister was unharmed. When they were out of the parking lot, he called out, "Prime Minister, are you hurt?" Rabin groaned, and murmured, "Yes, yes." "Where does it hurt you?" the driver asked. "In my back," Rabin groaned. "It's not so bad." Those were the last words he spoke before losing consciousness, his head slumped forward. While his bodyguard tried to provide some kind of first aid to the dying prime minister, his driver, contrary to standard procedure, had not been briefed on the best escape routes. He set off for nearby Ichilov Hospital but was forced by the huge crowds leaving the rally to avoid the most direct route, only seven hundred meters. His circuitous route covered about 1.7 kilometers, which, he said, took him ninety seconds. As he tried to make a final right turn toward the hospital, a police roadblock stopped the car. Rabin's driver frantically screamed out to a policeman to get in and help escort them through. As they pulled up, it was obvious that the hospital had not been alerted: Only one man was in sight, a security guard. The driver shouted at him to get a stretcher, quick, and when the hospital guard returned, he, the driver, and the bodyguard lifted Rabin out of the car and onto the stretcher and carried him into the building. Inside there were no medical staff to be seen. "The prime minister is hurt," Rabin's driver called out desperately. "Come and take care of him." Finally, the doctors came running.

Utter confusion reigned back at the square, where nobody was sure whether Rabin had been hit. While some policemen were saying that the bullets were blanks, one bent down in the parking lot and picked up the spent shells, insisting they were real. Despite her protests, Leah Rabin was quickly taken away to a Shin Bet security facility nearby, where Shimon Peres's car had also been rerouted according to routine emergency procedure. On the way, Leah frantically looked at the traffic behind her, asking why her husband's car was not in sight. "They told me, 'It's not real,'"

Leah said later. "Where's Yitzhak? If it's not real, where's Yitzhak?" Leah had asked. "We don't know," they said. "When we know, we'll tell you."

Meanwhile, Rabin's spokesperson, Aliza Goren, was frantically dialing every possible Rabin contact number on her cellular phone but getting no answer anywhere. Most of the people who had left the rally to the strains of dance music playing over loudspeakers were blissfully unaware that anything bad had happened.

In the hospital emergency room, Dr. Motti Gutman and his medical team inserted a tracheal tube, respirated Rabin, inserted a chest drain, and administered various drugs. When a weak pulse was restored for a brief period, Rabin was rushed to the operating room, but the pulse died away. Still, for fifty minutes, they massaged Rabin's heart, trying to get the pulse back, while simultaneously giving him twenty-two units of blood and other treatment. Dr. Yoram Kugler later said, "This time I looked at the operating table and saw the leader I had admired for so many years, and I thought, What will happen to the state, to the people of Israel if he dies?" But Professor Gabi Barabash, head of the hospital, said afterward that Rabin's heart had already pumped air rather than blood to the brain, causing brain damage. Although the medical team tried everything possible to resuscitate Rabin, he was actually dead within nine minutes of arriving at the hospital. Rabin's lungs had been penetrated by dumdum bullets adapted to inflict maximum injury.

When Leah Rabin and Shimon Peres finally arrived at Ichilov Hospital, a crowd was gathering outside as the news was spread over radio and television. Journalists from every local television and radio station fought to get the latest word on the prime minister's condition.

Gabi Barabash left the operating room at 11:10 P.M. and went to the room next door to see Leah Rabin and her family. Outside the hospital, rumors of Rabin's death were already circulating when Eitan Haber, Rabin's right-hand man, emerged holding a note he had hurriedly scribbled, and was swallowed up by the crowd of reporters. He tried for long moments to call for quiet, and for the pack of media to stop shoving. Finally, he barked out the words he had written on the paper in his hand:

"With horror, great sorrow, and deep grief, the government of Israel announces the death of prime minister and defense minister Yitzhak Rabin, murdered by an assassin."

INVESTIGATION: Yigal Amir, who had been taken away by the police for initial questioning, formally and indifferently acknowledged that he had pulled the trigger on the gun that killed Rabin. "I did it to save the state," he said. "He who endangers the Jewish people, his end is death. He deserved to die, and I did the job for the Jewish people." Amir also said that he had not expected to survive the assassination himself. "I came to the scene fully recognizing that I would have to give up my life for the success of the holy mission," he said. "I had made no escape plans."

Amir told his interrogators matter-of-factly that he could easily have shot Shimon Peres, as well. The only known filmed evidence of the assassination, shot from a low rooftop opposite the parking lot by an amateur cameraman named Ronni Dempler, shows clearly that Amir was right.

Although Hagai Amir and Dror Adoni, Yigal's army buddy, were implicated in the plot to kill Rabin, they consistently said they did not know in advance of Yigal's specific plan to kill Rabin at the rally on November 4. Yigal, who was happy to take solitary blame, walked into the room smiling broadly at various court hearings. Many Israelis were revolted by his body language in court: his openmouthed gum chewing and his cocksure smile. There were calls for him to be hidden behind a screen and out of the view of news cameras in court. Undaunted, Amir maintained the arrogant demeanor of a man certain he had done no wrong. He even requested a day's leave from his isolation cell, in jail near Beersheba, to attend the December wedding of one of his sisters. His request was denied.

Yigal Amir, who showed no hint of remorse or self-doubt, made a habit of using the minutes before court proceedings began to issue long monologues explaining his actions. During the hearings leading up to his indictment, he offered clear, simplistic justifications for the assassination: He questioned the government's legitimacy; he rejected the right of Arab

Israelis to vote because they did not serve in the military; he gave specific reasons why he believed Rabin had contemptuously abandoned Jewish settlers; and he called Arafat and the Palestinians unreformed terrorists. All of these were opinions commonly heard from right-wing factions in Israel, but Yigal Amir went even further. As he had done in debates with friends and fellow students, he invoked Jewish religious law to justify his assassination of Yitzhak Rabin, saying that "according to religious law, when a Jew gives up his land and his people to the enemy, one is obliged to kill him."

The question of which rabbi sanctioned the murder of Rabin was asked time and again in Amir's court proceedings, but he always answered, "I acted alone." Still, he had reportedly acknowledged to interrogators that he had received unequivocal rabbinical sanction for the killing.

PUNISHMENT: On March 27, 1996, a three-judge panel found twenty-five-year-old Yigal Amir guilty of the murder of Yitzhak Rabin and sentenced him to life in prison. The death penalty in Israel is reserved for Nazi war criminals. Amir, still unrepentant, responded by shouting, "The state of Israel is a monstrosity."

CONSPIRACY THEORIES: Despite the fact that Yigal Amir calmly and consistently assured everyone that he and he alone assassinated Yitzhak Rabin, conspiracy theories still surfaced, with two seeming at least plausible.

Tel Aviv University historian Michael Har-Segor initiated one theory: that a conspiracy extending deep into the Shin Bet was responsible for Rabin's assassination, with at least one of the prime minister's own bodyguards on that night being involved. That bodyguard was supposedly responsible for shouting that the bullets were blanks, not real. While Yigal Amir did the actual shooting, he was carefully selected because he had had a Shin Bet file since 1992, when he reportedly underwent a Shin Bet weapons and security training course before going to Latvia. Avishai Raviv was an integral part of the setup, by helping incite Amir at Bar-Ilan

and encouraging his anti-Rabin sentiments. As this theory goes, the traitorous bodyguard was executed by the Shin Bet after Amir shot Rabin.
Amir himself added fuel to this theory in one of his court appearances by
shouting at journalists, "Why don't you publish that they [the Shin Bet]
liquidated one of Rabin's bodyguards?" While the mysterious death and
secretive burial in the Yarkon military cemetery of an Israeli security
agent named Yoav Kuriel was reported by the Israeli media, both Israeli
officials and Kuriel's family denied that he had ever worked for the Shin
Bet or had any connection with Rabin. Kuriel's death was, instead, an
unrelated suicide. Further, the amateur videotape of Rabin's assassination shows no evidence that any of Rabin's bodyguards were involved.

The second theory, also involving the Shin Bet and Avishai Raviv,
was promoted by a small group of fringe right-wing activists, who claim
Raviv, and perhaps other intelligence sources, told Shin Bet agents about
Yigal Amir's assassination plans. Supposedly, Amir's inner circle was then
penetrated by agents who substituted blanks for the bullets in Amir's
gun. Amir, realizing the bullets had been switched, replaced them again.
After shooting Rabin, Amir hoped to avoid being shot himself by shouting that the bullets were blanks. This theory was further supported by
several facts: that Shin Bet agents around Rabin did not think the prime
minister had actually been hurt, that nobody called ahead to the hospital
where Rabin was being taken, and that Leah Rabin was told something
about a toy gun. Supposedly, as part of this plan, Raviv sent a beeper
message to several Israeli journalists immediately after Rabin was shot
and claimed responsibility on behalf of a right-wing extremist group,
saying, "We missed this time, but we won't next time." In the alleged Shin
Bet plot to entrap Amir for his extremist right-wing activities, Raviv
assumed Rabin was not harmed because Amir was being allowed to
shoot at him only with blanks.

SHAMGAR COMMISSION OF INQUIRY: A three-member state
commission of inquiry, headed by former Supreme Court chief justice
Meir Shamgar, was formed two weeks after Rabin's assassination to

investigate the breach of security that allowed Amir to shoot the prime minister. Shin Bet chiefs and agents, policemen, and eyewitnesses were all called in and questioned on the assumption that Rabin's assassination was the act of a lone gunman, Yigal Amir, who slipped through a split-second lapse in security. But the initial assessment that Amir had taken advantage of a one-in-a-million momentary security breakdown was gradually disproved by mounting evidence that there was a serious problem within the Israeli law-enforcement and security network. Security officials had not taken the recent series of assaults on the government by right-wing extremists as a serious warning, because they believed, as did Yitzhak Rabin himself, that a Jew would never kill a fellow Jew for political reasons.

In preparation for the rally, extensive briefings had been held for various units of the Shin Bet, the police, and other relevant parties who would carry out a highly complex security operation that night. One thousand security men from various agencies were deployed. All the windows were lit up in the thirteen-floor City Hall behind the stage in Kings of Israel Square, to prevent a Lee Harvey Oswald–type attack. Both Rabin and Peres were given extra bodyguards, and escape routes were planned in case of an emergency. Because of the previous week's assassination of Islamic Jihad leader Fathi Shkaki, the entire focus of security was on the possibility of a Palestinian fundamentalist attack either by snipers, bombers, or suicide bombers. No one considered the possibility of a Jewish assassin.

Still, many people at the rally that night described security as "a joke." Several VIPs on the stage with Rabin were disturbed by how easy it was for obviously unaccredited personnel to gain access to the area, which should have been highly restricted. An amateur photographer with a fake press pass had no problem getting past overworked security men at the side of the stage, where personal passes were being thrown back and forth. Security lapses were even worse in the parking area, where Yigal Amir's presence, though unaccountable, was dismissed as not important by two rookie policemen on duty in the lot that night.

Even plainclothes detectives deployed to the area were not concerned about Amir, because he was clearly Jewish. Yet amateur cameraman Ronnie Kempler, filming from above, immediately noticed that Amir looked suspicious—"like a potential murderer" he said later—and filmed many seconds of Amir that night. Besides Amir, eyewitnesses said at least twenty other people without the required security tags were in the area that was supposed to be "sterile."

Adding to the security problems that night was the fact that Rabin's Cadillac, parked and waiting for him at least an hour before his departure, was an obvious marker for an assassin. Although ten bodyguards were supposed to fan out around Rabin when he moved from the stage to his car, only five bodyguards were close to him as he came down the stairs into the parking lot. One was a few paces ahead and cleared his route to the car, one walked at Rabin's right, and two more were at his left, where Amir was waiting. The amateur video taken that night showed all four bodyguards looking ahead toward the car; none was scanning the surrounding area. The fifth bodyguard's job was to protect Rabin's back and watch the area behind him as they moved toward his car, but as they reached the bottom of the stairs, the prime minister reportedly asked him to find out why Leah was a few seconds behind them. Because that fifth bodyguard responded to Rabin's request, his attention was diverted, allowing Yigal Amir to rush in from the prime minister's left and shoot him at point-blank range. If Rabin had been wearing a bulletproof vest, it might have cushioned the impact of the shots, but Leah said later that security agents never suggested her husband wear one; besides, she said, even if they had, he would have resisted the idea.

After the fatal shots were fired, the incompetence continued. Confusion was compounded by the fact that somebody, perhaps Amir, shouted that the bullets were blanks. Leah Rabin stood in shock, unprotected for several seconds. While Rabin's driver, who had not been briefed on the best escape routes, sped toward the hospital via the only unblocked streets he could find, not one person in that mass of security had the presence of mind to call ahead and warn the hospital that the prime minister was being brought there. When Rabin's gray Cadillac finally pulled up at the hospital door, nobody was there to receive him, leaving everyone asking if Rabin's life would have been saved by more immediate medical attention. The Shamgar Commission called in Ichilov Hospital's director, Gabi Barabash, and asked him that question. Barabash paused, then chose his words carefully, "Even if he had arrived a couple minutes earlier, it is unlikely that he would have lived. But the fact that we managed to revive him," he said, "leaves that question open."

The day after Yigal Amir was sentenced to life in prison, the Shamgar Commission said that the Shin Bet, which has enjoyed a reputation as one of the world's finest intelligence agencies, had ignored warnings that Jewish extremists were planning an attempt on Prime Minister Rabin's life. This was a scandal for Carmi Gilon, who had been appointed head of the Shin Bet in early 1995, despite objections by several leading right-wing activists. (Gilon's master's thesis at Haifa University and much of his fieldwork in the Shin Bet had focused on countering right-wing extremism.) In the summer of 1995, Gilon had met with Prime Minister Rabin and opposition leader Benjamin Netanyahu, warning them that there was an urgent need to find a way to moderate the smoldering polit-ical climate before it sparked into real violence. At the same time, Gilon had taken an unprecedented step for the usually secretive Shin Bet: He had met with a group of leading journalists, telling them the same thing he had told Rabin and Netanyahu.

The Shamgar Commission's investigation into Rabin's assassination revealed that after Yigal Amir had discussed his plans to assassinate the prime minister with several of his university friends, one of those confi-dants contacted his former commander in the army's intelligence corps and told him about Amir's plans. The army officer reported the informa-tion to police, who passed it along to the Shin Bet. Reportedly, the prob-lem was that the informant, who was subsequently questioned by Jerusalem police, did not identify Amir by name, giving only enough information so that he could have easily been identified. The informant did say later, though, that if he had been pressed to reveal Amir's name, he would have done so.

Further, evidence surfaced that Amir's right-wing extremist friend Avishai Raviv was secretly employed by the Shin Bet through his Eyal group, which was funded by the Shin Bet in order to attract extremists and monitor their activities. Although Raviv consistently denied it, reportedly reliable information indicated that in the summer of 1995 Raviv was ordered by his Shin Bet controllers to compile a report for them on his campus colleague, Yigal Amir. While controversy remained regarding Raviv's knowledge of Amir's plans, there was no doubt that the Shin Bet knew Amir was a potential danger but failed to put that information together with the warnings that came through the Jerusalem police from the other informant.

It was reported in early December that the Shamgar Commission had rejected all the conspiracy theories circulating and based its deliberations on Kempler's amateur video of Rabin's assassination and the testimony of numerous witnesses. The commission concluded that Yitzhak Rabin's death was not the result of a sinister conspiracy but was caused by a complete collapse of security.

Although Shin Bet chief Carmi Gilon had offered to resign his position within days of the assassination, acting prime minister Shimon Peres urged him to stay on and help rebuild the agency's shattered morale. In a successful operation on January 5, 1996, the Shin Bet regained some of its stature. Yihiya Ayash, the elusive master bombmaker behind the Hamas suicide bus bombings of the past two years, was killed in his Gaza hideout when a booby-trapped mobile phone he was using exploded and blew off his head. Ayash had been at the top of the Shin Bet's wanted list for three years—before his assassination, Yitzhak Rabin had personally ordered that Ayash be captured or eliminated. With this success for the Shin Bet, Carmi Gilon, aware that the Shamgar Commission's findings would probably result in his dismissal, again submitted his letter of resignation to Shimon Peres on January 7. This time it was accepted.

THE FUNERAL: Within hours of Yitzhak Rabin's death, the astounding outpouring of grief elevated him into a national father figure, a guardian of security, the embodiment of peace. Thousands of Israelis flocked to Ichilov Hospital, where they lit memorial candles and sang bitter, tearful, plaintive renditions of the "Song for Peace." Tens of thousands who had gone home feeling uplifted from the rally that evening returned to the Kings of Israel Square, where they had stood earlier, when Rabin was alive and Israel was a different country. People gathered outside the Rabin home in Ramat Aviv and at his official residence in Jerusalem. Improvised banners mourned the loss of "Our dead father," "Our beloved Yitzhak." The television broadcast a marathon of grief and horror throughout the night to a country whose citizens were numbed by uncertainty and fear. On Sunday morning, a group of schoolchildren arrived outside Rabin's residence in Jerusalem, where the railings and the sidewalk were caked with the melted wax of thousands of memorial candles that, one by one, had been consumed by the flames of sorrow throughout the night. An eerie silence hung over Tel Aviv's trendy Sheinkin Street, where the usually vibrant café-society crowd solemnly read newspapers all with the same headlines: "RABIN ASSASSINATED."

At Bar-Ilan University somber students—some held signs reading, simply, WE CONDEMN—gathered for a memorial service and heard faculty members speak in disbelief that one of their own was responsible for Rabin's murder. During a press conference that followed, university president Shlomo Eckstein insisted, "We try to educate our students to love all Jews." He pointed out that Yoram Rubin, Rabin's bodyguard who was also shot, had been a Bar-Ilan student, and the doctor who tried to save Rabin's life had also attended the university.

In predominantly right-wing Jerusalem, the voices of opponents of Rabin's peace process could still be heard. Throughout the country, Israelis freely discussed their views of peace in their country and the giving away of their land. They argued with inflamed passion one moment, and the next, there was solemn silence in the tragic world where they lived.

At midday, as Rabin's coffin, accompanied by eight generals, was driven in an army truck the sixty kilometers from Tel Aviv to Jerusalem, traffic came to a stop along the route as people stood at attention. When the grim convoy passed under several bridges over the main Tel Aviv–Jerusalem highway, thousands of people crowded each bridge to catch a glimpse of their fallen peacemaker. Rabin's coffin arrived at the Knesset at 2 P.M. and was laid to rest on a raised bier in the broad forecourt of the parliament building draped in a blue-and-white Israeli flag. Leah Rabin, her children, and her grandchildren stood in tearful silence, then took seats at the side of the casket. Shimon Peres tenderly embraced Leah. The Supreme Court justices, chief rabbis, ambassadors, and other dignitaries paid their respects, and former military men turned Knesset members stood at attention to honor their fallen comrade.

Throughout the day and into the night an endless stream of ordinary Israelis carrying flowers, private messages, flags, and countless candles passed by Rabin's coffin. At four and five in the morning, it was still impossible to get within hundreds of meters of the Knesset because crowds of people were still arriving from all parts of the country to say their personal good-byes. Along the route up the hill to the Knesset, small, improvised memorials could be seen, with dozens of candles, some positioned to spell out "Why?" in Hebrew, or "Yitzhak." Photographs of Rabin were placed on rocks and surrounded by more candles.

On nearby Herzl, in the section of the national cemetery reserved for the country's most prominent figures, Rabin's final resting place had been dug, near the graves of former prime ministers Golda Meir and Levi Eshkol. Some of the Defense Ministry's memorial unit grave diggers had cried as they shoveled away the earth. "It's an appalling feeling, digging the prime minister's grave," said Ahron Hamamy. "But this is our job. We are doing this to give Rabin the last respects that he is due. Our hands are shaking. Our hearts are breaking."

As the sun rose on Monday morning, a massive ten thousand-strong contingent of Israeli security personnel prepared to protect the dozens of international leaders who had flown in for Yitzhak Rabin's funeral. Jordan's King Hussein—who had narrowly escaped death as he watched his grandfather die of an assassin's bullet on Jerusalem's Temple Mount forty-four years earlier—returned to the city where Rabin the soldier had taken control of Jordanian land, to mourn Rabin the peacemaker, who had become his ally and friend. Egypt's Hosni Mubarak—who had become president after Anwar Sadat was assassinated in 1981 and had himself escaped assassins' bullets weeks before—came to say good-bye.

Yasir Arafat was dining with the visiting Portuguese prime minister Mario Suares when Edward Abington, the American consul in Jerusalem and the State Department's "ambassador to the Palestinians," phoned to tell him that Rabin had been assassinated. Upon hearing the news, Arafat was sobbing so uncontrollably that he had to whisper to the consul, "Call me back in ten minutes." Desperately wanting to come for Rabin's funeral, Arafat spoke imploringly to Shimon Peres and to Leah Rabin, telling them that Yitzhak would have wanted him there. "We became real partners in the peace of the brave. Remember how he joked about me, after I made that long speech in Washington for Oslo II, he said he was beginning to wonder if maybe I was close to being Jewish?" Still, Arafat was too controversial, too divisive a figure when national healing and internal reconciliation was Israel's most pressing need, so security considerations were invoked; Arafat would not come.

Later in the week, on November 9, Arafat would make a secret late-night condolence call at the Rabin home, his first visit to Israel. His trip was carried out with the utmost secrecy and was announced to the press only after he had left Tel Aviv. Forgoing his usual military uniform and kaffiyeh, Arafat wore dark glasses, a long woolen overcoat, a hat, and a large dark scarf, making him unrecognizable. When he entered the Rabin apartment, Arafat removed his hat, kissed Leah and her daughter, Dalia, three times on the head; he kissed Leah's son, Yuval, three times on the head and twice on the cheeks; then he kissed each of Rabin's grandchildren, Noa and Jonathan, three times on the head. They all sat down in Yitzak Rabin's sitting room, surrounded by photographs of Rabin in uniform, a bust of him, and a certificate of the Nobel Peace Prize. In a calm, gentle voice, Arafat told Leah, "We lost a great man." He sat with the Rabin family, drinking tea and chatting with ease, even smiling, as he paid homage to his fallen peace partner. In a courteous, friendly manner, the PLO leader pledged to complete the work he and Yitzhak Rabin had begun together.

Yasir Arafat sent a delegation of senior officials to represent him at Rabin's funeral; he stayed at home in Gaza, where he was filmed respectfully watching the event on television.

A two-minute siren sounded at 2 P.M. Monday, calling for all of Israel to stand in silence to honor Yitzhak Rabin. There on the silent Jerusalem hillside near Rabin's grave in the bright, early winter sunlight, Leah Rabin stood with her family at her side and a family of nations around her. More than eighty countries were represented. Besides King Hussein, Hosni Mubarak, and Yasir Arafat's delegation, there were representatives from the Middle Eastern countries of Qatar, Oman, and Morocco. When Cyprus's president Alexis Galnos, who had met Rabin two years earlier, read in his newspaper that the Albanian president would be attending, he decided to change his plans and attend also. Royal figures from Britain's Prince Charles to Holland's Queen Beatrix were present, as well as heads of state and governments from Australia to Turkey. Estonia's outgoing president Lennart Meri came for the funeral, missing the swearing-in of his country's new government the next day. Eduard Shevardnadze, who had been reelected president of Georgia the day before, flew to Israel instead of attending his own celebrations.

Eleven speeches were given: heartfelt eulogies from Russian prime minister Viktor Chernomyrdin, from U.N. secretary general Boutros Boutros-Ghali, and from Spain's prime minister Felipe González, who was representing the European Union. Israeli president Eizer Weizman was among the speakers who gave fitting tributes to Rabin and his policies. Hosni Mubarak praised Rabin's vision of peace and described his death as "a severe blow to our noble cause." He argued that only by redoubling peace efforts could "those traitorous hands hostile toward our goal" be thwarted and Rabin's memory be properly honored.

King Hussein, who two nights earlier had frantically telephoned

Shimon Shamir, Israel's ambassador to Jordon, every ten minutes to get updates on Rabin's condition, set the emotional tone as he spoke, typically, from his heart. Hussein spoke as though Rabin was there with him, sighing, "I have never been used to standing, except with you next to me, speaking of peace, speaking about dreams and hopes for generations to come. . . ." In a firm yet quiet voice, King Hussein challenged all the people, both Arabs and Jews, who believed in coexistence to stand up and be counted, whatever the price. He said Rabin "lived as a soldier," and "died as a soldier for peace." Remembering his grandfather, who was gunned down at Jerusalem's Al-Aqsa Mosque, Hussein said he was another who paid the ultimate price for peace. He expressed his belief that it is the will of God that though many live, so must many inevitably die. But that those who leave something behind are fortunate. In closing, Hussein said, "And you are such a man, my friend."

Shimon Peres, whose colleagues had unanimously elected him acting prime minister on the night Rabin died, delivered a speech of sensitivity, grace, affection, and above all, respect for Rabin, who for years was his nemesis but had since become almost his second half. He recalled their last hours together at the Saturday-night rally and that he felt a special grace had descended on Rabin. That suddenly Rabin could breathe freely when he saw the sea of friends who had come to support his peace policies and to cheer him. Peres said Rabin had reached the summit and broken through the clouds to a place where he could view the new tomorrow that was his promise to the youth of Israel. "Yitzhak, youngest of Israel's generals. Yitzhak, the greatest trailblazer of peace," Peres said, "You did not leave us a will, but you left us a legacy . . ." Finally, he said that though the nation weeps for their loss, their tears are also tears of unity and resolve.

Those who had not already been brought to tears by the touching words of the illustrious speakers could not remain dry-eyed when Rabin's eighteen-year-old granddaughter, Noa Ben-Artzi, gave her tearful, heartrending eulogy. Speaking not of the peacemaker, not of the general and leader, Noa addressed Rabin, her grandfather. She said that although his death was a national tragedy, she did not know how to comfort an entire people or include them in her family's personal pain because an enormous void is left by his absence. Unable to hold back tears, she said, "Grandfather, you were, and still are, our hero. To the angels in heaven that are accompanying you now, I ask that they watch over you, that they guard you well. Because you deserve such a guard. We will love you, Grandpa, always."

U.S. president Bill Clinton, who considered Yitzhak Rabin a close friend, had flown to Israel on Air Force One along with his wife, former presidents Jimmy Carter and George Bush, and dozens of top officials and politicians from Capitol Hill. Wearing a black yarmulke over his gray hair, Clinton delivered a speech that showed a personal commitment to Rabin and to Israel. Mixing admiration and humor, Clinton spoke of Rabin's career, noting his preference for deeds rather than words. He recalled Rabin's opening line at the Oslo II ceremony on September 28: "First the good news. I am the last speaker." Clinton also stressed Rabin's understanding of symbolism, and as Rabin had done in Washington when he had urged his audience to take note of the presence on stage of peace partners who until recently were enemies, Clinton urged the viewing world to take stock of the notables gathered for Rabin's funeral. Seated before him to honor Yitzhak Rabin and for peace were the leaders from all over the Middle East and around the world. Clinton said that Rabin had brought everyone together again there, in word and deed, for peace. He called on all those present who love peace and all that loved Rabin, to carry on the struggle to which Rabin gave life and for which he gave his life. Speaking directly to the Israeli people, Clinton recalled his experiences of living through his country's shock and mourning over the assassinations of its pioneers for change. He urged the Israeli's not to lose their spirit in their hour of darkness because Rabin's spirit lives on. Clinton said that Rabin was a martyr for peace, but a victim of hate, and that people must learn to let go of the hatred of their enemies or else risk sowing the seeds of hatred among themselves. He concluded, "May our hearts find a measure of comfort, and our souls the eternal touch of hope." But as Clinton began to step away from the microphone, he paused for a last fond farewell. "*Shalom, haver,*" he half-whispered. "Peace, my friend."

Eitan Haber was an army private when he first met Yitzhak Rabin, his general, thirty-seven years earlier. Since then he had come to know him very well during years of working with Rabin and writing speeches for him. A few days after the murder, while he was emptying out Rabin's office drawers, Haber recalled how Rabin believed himself to be "absolutely" invincible. He never felt threatened by right-wing violence, but at the same time he had felt very much alone in the face of all the incitement. That last rally, Haber said, lifted Rabin to a personal high, and only some kind of genius director could conceive a finale like Rabin's. Tens of thousands of people had gathered to honor Rabin, sing with him and send him such warmth. At the end of the rally Rabin embraced Shimon Peres, left the stage, and then he was murdered.

At Rabin's funeral, Haber came to the microphone saying, "Yitzhak, this is the last speech." He lightened the mood a little, pointing out that Rabin had a thousand good qualities and a thousand advantages, that he was great, but his singing ability was not his strong point. Haber recalled that, at the rally, when the "Song for Peace" was over, Rabin neatly folded his lyric sheet and slipped it into his jacket pocket. He said that after the doctors and nurses in the hospital had cried, they handed him the folded sheet of paper which they found in Rabin's jacket pocket. In a bold and gut-wrenching gesture, Haber produced the page itself, protected in a clear plastic folder, its lines stained red with blood. He said he wanted to read some of the words from the paper, but it was difficult because Rabin's blood covered the printed words. "Your blood on the page of the 'Song for Peace.' This is the blood which ran out of your body in the final moments of your life, and onto the paper between the lines and the words." Then Eitan Haber read the lyrics of the song, Yitzhak Rabin's final song of peace.

Bibliography

Ali, Tariq. *An Indian Dynasty: The Story of the Nehru-Gandhi Families*. New York: G.P. Putnam, 1985.

The American Presidents. Danbury, Conn.: Grolier Incorporated, 1992.

Artzi-Pelossof, Noa Ben. *In the Name of Sorrow and Hope*. New York: Borzoi Book/Alfred A. Knopf, 1996.

Asimov, Isaac. *The Roman Republic*. Boston: Houghton Mifflin, 1966.

The Assassinations: Dallas and Beyond. New York: Vintage Books, 1976.

Ault, Warren O. *Europe in Modern Times*. Lexington, Mass.: Heath, 1946.

Bagdikian, Ben H., "The Assassin," *The Saturday Evening Post*, December 14, 1963, 22–29.

Belin, David W. *Final Disclosure: The Full Truth About the Assassination of President Kennedy*. New York: Scribner, 1988.

Bernier, Olivier. *Words of Fire, Deeds of Blood*. New York: Little, Brown, 1989.

Bishop, Jim. *The Day Lincoln Was Shot*. New York: Harper & Brothers, 1955.

Blakely, G. Robert, and Richard N. Billings. *The Plot to Kill the President: Organized Crime Assassinated JFK*. Alexandria, Va.: Times Books, 1981.

Bowder, Diana, ed. *Who Was Who in the Roman World*. New York: Washington Square Press, 1984.

Breslin, Jimmy, "A Death in Emergency Room No. One," *The Saturday Evening Post*, December 14, 1963, 30–31.

Briggs, Asa, ed. *20th-Century World Biography*. New York: Oxford University Press, 1993.

Buchanan, Thomas G. *Who Killed Kennedy?* New York: Putnam Sons, 1964.

Burner, David, Robert D. Marcus, and Thomas R. West. *A Giant's Strength, America in the 1960s.* New York: Holt, Rinehart and Winston, 1971.

The Cambridge Ancient History. New York: Cambridge University Press, 1970.

The Cambridge Medieval History. New York: Cambridge University Press, 1936.

Carlyle, Thomas. *The French Revolution.* New York: The Modern Library/Random House, 1934.

Carmichael, Joel. *An Illustrated History of Russia.* New York: Reynal & Company.

Carter, Dan T. *The Politics of Rage.* New York: Simon & Schuster, 1995.

Chua-Eoan, Howard. *Aquino.* New York: Chelsea House, 1988.

Clarke, James W. *American Assassins: The Darker Side of Politics.* Princeton University Press, 1982.

A Compact History of Mexico. Pedregal de Sta. Teresa, Mexico: El Colegio de Mexico, 1985.

Cone, James H. *Martin & Malcolm & America: A Dream or a Nightmare.* Mary Knoll, N.Y.: Orbis Books, 1991.

Cox, Jack. *Nicaragua Betrayed.* Boston: Western Islands, 1980.

Crimes and Punishment, vols. 8 & 12. London: BPC Publishing, Ltd., 1974.

Davis, John H. *Mafia Kingfish: Carlos Marcello and the Assassination of John F. Kennedy.* New York: New American Library, 1989.

———. *Mafia Dynasty.* New York: Harper Collins, 1993.

Davis, Lee. *Assassination: Twenty Assassinations That Changed History.* New York: Transedition Books/BDD Special Editions, 1993.

De Jonge, Alex. *The Life and Times of Grigorii Rasputin,* New York: Barnes & Noble/Putnam, 1982.

Diederich, Bernard. *Trujillo: The Death of the Goat.* New York: Little, Brown, 1978.

Donovan, Robert J. *The Assassins.* New York: Harper & Brothers, 1952.

Durant, Will. *The Story of Civilization* (10 volumes). New York: Simon & Schuster, 1939–1967.

Epstein, Edward Jay. *Inquest: The Warren Commission and the Establishment of Truth.* New York: Viking Press, 1966.

Ergang, Robert. *Europe Since Waterloo.* Lexington, Mass.: Heath, 1967.

Evans, Karl. *The Judas Factor: The Plot to Kill Malcolm X.* New York: Thunder's Mouth Press, 1992.

Ford, Franklin L. *Political Murder: From Tyrannicide to Terrorism.* Cambridge: Harvard University Press, 1985.

Friedly, Michael. *Malcolm X: The Assassination.* New York: Carroll & Graf/R. Gallen, 1992.

Gentry, Curt. *J. Edgar Hoover: The Man and His Secrets.* New York: Norton, 1991.

Gibbon, Edward. *The Rise and Fall of the Roman Empire.* New York: Penguin Books, 1977.

Gottschalk, Louis R. *Jean-Paul Marat: A Study in Radicalism.* Chicago: University of Chicago Press, 1967.

Grant, Michael. *Nero.* New York: American Heritage Press, 1970.

Green, Peter. *Alexander of Macedon. 356-323 B.C.* Berkeley, Calif.: University of California Press, 1991.

Groden, Robert J. *The Killing of a President.* New York: Viking/Penguin Books, 1993.

Gupte, Pranay. *Vengeance: India After the Assassination of Indira Gandhi.* New York: Norton, 1985.

Guzman, Martin Luis. *The Eagle and the Serpent.* Garden City, N.Y.: Dolphin Books, 1965.

Hair, William Ivy. *The Kingfish and His Realm: The Life and Times of Huey P. Long.* Baton Rouge, La.: Louisiana State University Books, 1991.

Hayes, Carlton J. H. *A Political and Social History of Modern Europe.* New York: Macmillan, 1926.

Haykal, Muhammad Hasanayn. *Autumn of Fury: The Assassination of Sadat.* New York: Random House, 1983.

A History of the Western World, Ancient Times to 1715. Lexington, Mass.: Heath, 1965.

Hough, Richard. *Mountbatten.* New York: Random House, 1981.

Jerusalem Report Staff, The. David Horovitz, ed. *Shalom, Friend: The Life and Legacy of Yitzhak Rabin.* New York: Newmarket Press, 1996.

Johnson, William Weber. *Heroic Mexico.* New York: Doubleday, 1968.

Jones, Penn. *Forgive My Grief.* Midlothian, Tex.: Penn Jones, 1966–1974.

Kaiser, Robert B. *R.F.K. Must Die!* New York: Dutton, 1970.

Kinser, Stephen. *Blood of Brothers: Life and War in Nicaragua.* New York: Putnam, 1991.

Kirkham, James F. *Assassination and Political Violence.* New York: Praeger, 1970.

Lane, Mark. *Code Name "Zorro": The Murder of Martin Luther King, Jr.* Englewood Cliffs, N.J.: Prentice-Hall, 1977.

Lasky, Victor. *JFK: The Man & the Myth.* New York: Macmillan, 1963.

Lentz III, Harris M. *Assassinations and Executions: An Encyclopedia of Political Violence 1865–1986.* Jefferson, N.C.: McFarland, 1988.

Lesberg, Sandy. *Assassination in Our Time.* London: Preebles Press International, 1976.

Life magazine editors, "Last Seconds of the Motorcade, *Life,* November 24, 1967, 87–95.

Lindop, Edmund. *Assassinations That Shook America.* New York: F. Watts, 1992.

MacDonald, Callum. *The Killing of SS Obergruppenführer Reinhard Heydrich.* New York: Free Press, 1989.

MacKinley, James. *Assassination in America.* New York: Harper & Row, 1977.

Manchester, William. *The Death of a President.* New York: Random House, 1967.

Marchetti, Victor, and John D. Marks. *The CIA and the Cult of Intelligence.* New York: Alfred A. Knopf, 1974.

Massie, Robert K. *Nicholas and Alexandra.* New York: Atheneum, 1967.

Mayo, Samuel H. *A History of Mexico.* Englewood Cliffs, N.J.: Prentice-Hall, 1978.

Melanson, Philip H. *The Murkin Conspiracy.* New York: Praeger, 1989.

———. *Spy Saga: Lee Harvey Oswald and U.S. Intelligence.* New York: Praeger Publishers, 1990.

Moorehead, Alan. *The Russian Revolution.* New York: Harper & Brothers, 1958.

Myers, Walter Dean. *Malcolm X: By Any Means Necessary.* New York: Scholastic, 1993.

Nash, Jay Robert. *Almanac of World Crime.* New York: Anchor Press/Doubleday, 1981.

The New Cambridge Modern History. New York: Cambridge University Press, 1957.

Noguchi, M. D., Thomas T., and Joseph DiMona. *Coroner.* New York: Pocket Books/Simon & Schuster, 1983.

Nossiter, Adam. *Of Long Memory: Mississippi and the Murder of Medgar Evers.* Reading, Mass.: Addison-Wesley, 1994.

Parkinson, Roger. *Zapata.* New York: Stein and Day, 1975.

Pastor, Robert A. *Condemned to Repetition: The United States and Nicaragua.* Princeton, N.J.: Princeton University Press, 1987.

Payne, Robert. *The Life and Death of Lenin.* New York: Simon & Schuster, 1964.

———. *The Life and Death of Mahatma Gandhi.* London: The Bodley Head, 1969.

Pepper, William. *Orders to Kill: The Truth Behind the Murder of Martin Luther King.* New York: Carroll & Graf, 1995.

Posner, Gerald. *Case Closed: Lee Harvey Oswald and the Assassination of JFK.* New York: Random House, 1993.

Ray, James Earl. *Who Killed Martin Luther King?* National Press Books, 1992.

The Record of Mankind. Lexington, Mass.: Heath, 1970.

Riasanovsky, Nicholas V. *A History of Russia.* New York: Oxford University Press, 1984.

Rosie, George. *The Directory of International Terrorism.* Edinburgh, U.K.: Mainstream Publishing Company, 1986.

Scheim, David E. *Contract on America: The Mafia Murder of President John F. Kennedy.* New York: Shapolsky, 1988.

Schellenberg, Walter. *Hitler's Secret Service.* San Diego, Calif.: Jove/HBJ, 1977.

Schevill, Ferdinand. *A History of Europe from the Reformation to the Present Day.* San Diego, Calif.: Harcourt, Brace, 1947.

Schlesinger, Jr., Arthur M. *Robert Kennedy and His Times, vols. 1 & 2.* Boston: Houghton Mifflin, 1978.

Shirer, William L. *The Rise and Fall of the Third Reich.* New York: Simon & Schuster, 1960.

Sifakis, Carl. *The Mafia Encyclopedia.* New York: Facts on File, 1987.

———. *Encyclopedia of Assassinations.* New York: Facts on File, 1991.

Summers, Anthony. *Conspiracy.* New York: McGraw-Hill, 1980.

Sykes, Sir Percy. *History of Persia.* New York: Macmillan, 1930.

Terraine, John. *The Life and Times of Lord Mountbatten.* New York: Holt, Rinehart & Winston, 1980.

Time-Life Books editors, *This Fabulous Century, vol. VII: 1960–1970.* Alexandria, Va.: Time-Life Books, 1970.

Toland, John. *The Last 100 Days.* New York: Random House, 1966.

Trager, James. *The People's Chronology.* New York: Holt, Rinehart & Winston, 1994.

Ulam, Adam B. *The Bolsheviks.* New York: Collier Books, 1976.

Vankin, Jonathan. *Conspiracies, Cover-Ups and Crimes: From JFK to the CIA Terrorist Connection.* New York: Paragon House, 1992.

Wallechinsky, David. *The People's Almanac Presents the 20th Century.* New York: Little, Brown, 1995.

Wallechinsky, David, and Irving Wallace. *The People's Almanac.* New York: Doubleday, 1975.

———. *The People's Almanac #2.* New York: William Morrow, 1978.

———. *The People's Almanac #3.* New York: Bantam Books, 1981.

The Way, The Living Bible. Wheaton, Ill.: Tyndale House Publishers, 1977.

Webster's New World Encyclopedia. Englewood Cliffs, N.J.: Prentice-Hall, 1993.

Wilson, Colin, and Donald Seaman. *Encyclopedia of Modern Murder 1962–1982.* London: Arthur Barker, 1983.

———. *A Criminal History of Mankind.* New York: Putnam, 1984.

Wyden, Peter. *Bay of Pigs: The Untold Story.* New York: Simon & Schuster, 1979.

X, Malcolm, with Alex Haley. *The Autobiography of Malcolm X.* New York: Grove Press, 1964.

Zinman, David. *The Day Huey Long Was Shot.* New York: Obolensky, 1963.

Other sources of information too numerous to list, yet invaluable, include: the Cable News Network, *Current History, Facts on File News Digest, Jerusalem Post, Los Angeles Times, Newsweek, The New York Times, Time,* and *U.S. News & World Report.*

A personal note of thanks to all reporters, throughout history, who have worked with diligence and integrity to provide the public with the truth based on facts. Without you, history would be only legend.

index